MIGRANT, REFUGEE, SMUGGLER, SAVIOUR

MIGRANT

REFUGEE

PETER TINTI AND TUESDAY REITANO

SMUGGLER

SAVIOUR

HURST & COMPANY, LONDON

This paperback edition published in 2018.

First published in the United Kingdom in 2016 by
C. Hurst & Co. (Publishers) Ltd.,
41 Great Russell Street, London, WC1B 3PL
© Peter Tinti and Tuesday Reitano, 2018
All rights reserved.
Printed in the United Kingdom by Bell & Bain Ltd, Glasgow

A Cataloguing-in-Publication data record for this book
is available from the British Library.

ISBN: 9781849049535

This book is printed using paper from registered sustainable
and managed sources.

www.hurstpublishers.com

CONTENTS

CONTENTS

ACKNOWLEDGEMENTS

It is a privilege to have had the opportunity to write this book. Not only does it provide a rare window into the workings of an illicit industry that is both difficult to research and understand, it shares the fragile hopes of hundreds of people during their personal quests for safety and a better future. To gain these insights which we share with you, we have the generosity, empathy, dedication and tolerance of so many people to thank. Our own efforts in transcribing this narrative pales in comparison to theirs.

We are deeply indebted to those dedicated researchers, journalists and translators in Lebanon, Libya, Niger, Egypt, Turkey, Greece, Germany, Italy, Sweden and across the Balkans, who sat down with us to speak to migrants about their experiences. A number of these people showed tremendous courage, using their connections to help us to speak to smugglers themselves about their work in this illicit industry. They include, but are not limited to, Juan Akkash, Muhammad H. Al-Kashef, Manu Abdo, Ibrahim Manzo Diallo, Angeliki Dimitriadi, Frederica Dolente, Nahla El-Nemr, Ombretta Ingrasci, Karl Lallerstedt, Maria Fausta Marino, Johannes Meerwald, Mark Micallef, Paola Monzini, Nour Nasr, Umberto Rondi, David Sarges, David Senarath, Nour Youssef and Tom Westcott. This book would not have been possible without them.

Secondly, we wholeheartedly thank colleagues, friends and donors who have supported, advised and inspired us along the way. Our research draws from many years of fieldwork, but it was thanks to funding from projects commissioned by the Organisation for Economic Cooperation and Development (OECD), the Institute for Security Studies (ISS), the Hanns Siedl Foundation (HSF) and our own organisa-

ACKNOWLEDGEMENTS

tion, the Global Initiative against Transnational Organised Crime, that allowed us to dig deep into this current phenomenon and get close to the ground on the migrant trail. Within these organisations, we must particularly express our gratitude to Anton du Plessis, Alessandra Fontana, Jessica Gerken, Wolf Krug, Ottilia Maunganidze, Iris Oustinoff, Adam Rodriquez and Mark Shaw.

We are grateful to Michael Dwyer and Jon de Peyer at Hurst Publishing for giving our ideas an intellectual home and a space in print, and for all their patient guidance along the way. Thanks to Sebastian Ballard and Sharon Wilson for their inspired work on the maps and graphics, and to our editor, Mary Starkey.

Peter Tinti: I would like to thank my co-author, Tuesday Reitano. This book is hers just as much as it is mine. I am in awe of your intellectual alacrity and so grateful for your professional support. I would also like to thank my parents, Aldo and Mary, and my sister, Mary, for quite literally everything. I could not have asked for a better family or a more loving home. Most importantly, I would like to thank my wife, Molly, for her love and patience. You are my inspiration and I am so lucky to have you as a life partner. Lastly, I would like to thank those who, for reasons I will never understand, took the time to speak with me as they embarked upon their impossible journeys. To those still wandering, may they find peace. To those who were lost along the way, may they rest in peace.

Tuesday Reitano: I would like to thank Peter, my co-author. It has been a fun collaboration, and his story-telling gifts are unparalleled. May this be the first book of many that you write. I'd also like to thank Mark Shaw, my mentor and friend, for the years of partnership, idea sharing, effort and inspiration. Much of what I am most proud of now is because of him. To my parents, Helen and Nigel, and my brother Edward, who are probably as surprised as I am that I would write a book, I am grateful for their lifelong love and investments. It has not been easy to carve the time to write a book around an intense full-time job with a hectic travel schedule, and those who lost out in the process were my friends and family. In particular, my infinitely patient, wise and tolerant husband, partner and best friend, Carlo, and my two amazing, loving and dynamic children, Giorgio and Valentina. There are not profound enough words with which to express my love and gratitude. They come last here, but they should come first.

SELECT ACRONYMS

AQIM   Al Qaeda in the Islamic Maghreb
ATT   Former Malian President Amadou Toumani Touré
CBP   Customs and Border Protection (USA)
CSDP   Common Security and Defence Policy (EU)
ECOWAS   Economic Community of West African States
EU   European Union
FDI   Foreign direct investment
FIU   Financial Intelligence Unit
GAMM   Global Approach to Migration and Mobility (EU)
HALCIA   French acronym for Niger's anti-corruption agency
IOM   International Organisation on Migration
MNJ   Niger Movement for Justice (French)
MNLA   National Movement for the Liberation of Azawad (French)
MSF   Médecins Sans Frontières/Doctors Without Borders
MUJAO   Movement for Unity and Jihad in West Africa
NCA   National Crime Agency (UK)
UN   United Nations
UNHCR   United Nations High Commissioner for Refugees
UNODC   United Nations Office on Drugs and Crime
UNTOC   United Nations Convention on Transnational Organised
            Crime

AUTHORS' NOTE

This book is an equal collaboration by two authors, Peter Tinti and Tuesday Reitano. Over the last several years we have both carried out research and reporting on migrant-smuggling networks on several different continents, in several different capacities, on behalf of several different organisations, and in several different contexts. This was truly a joint effort, and we are pleased to have the opportunity both to collaborate and to share our knowledge and experience, which we feel is stronger due to the combination of our diverse perspectives.

As with any collaborative effort, especially one that seeks to analyse a fast-changing phenomenon within the context of a new paradigm, the authors have made several editorial choices for the sake of clarity and transparency.

Portions of this book, for example, are written in the first-person singular in cases where one of the authors was present. For the sake of narrative coherence we decided not to devote space to clarifying which of the authors is present at a particular scene.

We decided to use the first person in certain chapters where it provides the reader with a sense of place and facilitates a more elegant narrative. From an editorial perspective, it reinforces the fact that this book is informed by on-the-ground reporting in addition to extensive secondary research. The authors would like to make clear, however, that 'I' is only used in cases where one of the authors was actually present. Some passages presented in the third person are also based on first-hand observation, but blended with secondary research or second-hand testimony. In these cases, rather than switch back and forth between first and third person, the text is presented in the third person, again, for the sake of clarity.

Which brings us to methodology and the subject matter at hand. This book is the product of several years of research, informed by fieldwork in over 20 countries and more than 400 interviews with government officials, experts, academics, migrants, interlocutors and, of course, migrant smugglers. Though the authors conducted the vast majority of the interviews that led to the final product, many interviews were conducted by colleagues who have been credited in the acknowledgements section. Other colleagues preferred to remain anonymous due to the sensitive nature of the subject. This book could not have been written without them.

Gathering information on illicit economies and organised crime poses its own challenges. For obvious reasons, those partaking in migrant smuggling and human trafficking have good reason to keep their activities hidden. This includes both migrants and refugees who are technically breaking the law in their quest to find safety and opportunity, as well as the migrant smugglers who enable them and traffickers who exploit them.

In order to obtain accurate information on migrant-smuggling networks, the authors used an array of research methods and reporting techniques. Some interviews were arranged on the condition of anonymity. Others took place in contexts in which the authors did not identify themselves as a journalist or researcher, and even posed as migrants seeking smuggler services. As a result, the authors have changed the names of certain individuals in cases where using their real names could complicate their asylum procedures or put them in danger, as well as in cases in which the individuals were unable or unwilling to respond to accusations lodged against them. In each of these cases we have placed an asterisk before their name the first time it appears in the text.

The goal of this book is to impart knowledge about the migrant-smuggling networks enabling the unprecedented flow of migrants and refugees into Europe, and to place their ascendency and development within the broader context of international peace and security.

We argue that the ways in which analysts, scholars, policymakers, governments and the general public thinks about these networks needs to be updated as it is triggering counter-productive responses, and we hope that this book plays a role in facilitating clearer thinking on the subject. We realise that some of the editorial decisions outlined above place the final product somewhere between a work of journalism and social science, but without technically being either. We are confident that these choices have enabled us to present information in a manner that is accurate, truthful and, most importantly, ethical.

Peter Tinti and *Tuesday Reitano*

INTRODUCTION

SMUGGLERS AND SAVIOURS

It is 8 a.m. and Ibrahim is chain-smoking in a clandestine flophouse with his new business partners of convenience, Adam, Ahmed, Barka and Sidi. All but Adam are in their mid-twenties. They sit on a cheap plastic mat that does little to soften the cracked concrete below it. As soon as one of them finishes a cigarette, another tosses the communal pack of American Legend in his direction. When one carton is kicked, a new one is taken from the stack in the corner and ripped open without hesitation. Breakfast on this morning appears to be sugar biscuits, nicotine and caffeine. The near-constant fidgeting suggests that some members of the crew might have something stronger coursing through their bloodstreams.

Ibrahim is not the leader of this impromptu team of entrepreneurs, he is just the most talkative, and the one who seems most interested in having people understand the extent to which his story is a modern parable of our times. He grew up in southern Libya, where he attended university in Kufra. After earning his degree in agricultural engineering he landed a job at a large-scale farm. He liked his life there, living comfortably off his salary and even saving enough to start a side business, a shop that sold canned goods, bottled drinks and groceries.

But on this stifling Thursday morning in April 2014, Ibrahim is in the darkest corner of a filthy room in a grubby ghetto of Agadez in Niger, 1,600 kilometres across the Sahara from Kufra, and a world away from the comforts of his previous life in Libya.

1

Ibrahim and his cohort are smugglers who specialise in the transport of a very specific commodity: humans. They move migrants who have come to Agadez from all over West Africa into southern Libya. From there these migrants, who are fleeing everything from war to political persecution to grinding poverty, will pay for the chance to be crammed onto an unseaworthy vessel that, purportedly, is destined for Europe. Some of them won't even make it to the coast. They might fall from the back of an overfilled truck and be left for dead in the Sahara, or they might be kidnapped and held for ransom by criminal gangs and Islamist militants. Others might be forced into unpaid labour, which for the women making the journey often means sexual exploitation.

Across the Sahara, 1,850 kilometres north of where Ibrahim operates, *Mansour watches a boat full of migrants launch out to sea from the confines of a half-built beachfront villa several kilometres outside the Libyan capital, Tripoli. Some of the people on board—Nigerians, Gambians, Senegalese, Malians and other nationals from West Africa—may have reached Libya courtesy of the services provided by Ibrahim and his colleagues. But the vast majority of those on Mansour's ship are from Eritrea and Somalia, which means that their trips to Libya were most probably facilitated by similar networks operating out of the Horn of Africa, which for decades have specialised in moving and extorting migrants throughout the region.

In 2013, when Mansour first got into the business of smuggling people, he was loading boats with Syrians who paid a premium for his services. Occasionally he would fill the remaining space on a ship with sub-Saharan Africans, padding his profit margin by packing those who paid less into the hold. Now, in 2015, with Syrians preferring alternate routes to Europe, Mansour's business is predicated on volume, and he loads any vessel he can get his hands on with as many Africans as he can find.

In Athens, 1,100 kilometres north-east of where Mansour watches his boat full of migrants disappear over the pre-dawn horizon, Tony waits for a bus. Only days before, Tony was in Latakia in Syria, with his wife and daughter. He paid a Syrian smuggler $500 to facilitate his passage through ISIS-controlled northern Syria and into Turkey. Once there, he meandered his way across Turkey to the coastal city of Izmir, where he paid $800 to a Syrian man who works for a Turkish smuggler to board an overcrowded dinghy. Under the cover of darkness, Tony and his fellow travellers managed to navigate the Aegean Sea courtesy of an unreliably cheap Chinese motor affixed to the back of their rubber contraption. They steered their boat towards a light in the distance, and, just before sunrise, they washed ashore on the Greek island of Kos.

Tony now waits in Athens alongside a hairless pre-teen from Syria who suffers from cancer. They both have dreams of reaching Sweden; but before they do they will board an unmarked bus leaving from a nondescript intersection in the heart of the city. If anyone asks the sketchy owner of the quasi-legitimate bus company, they are headed to the northern city of Thessaloniki. But everyone knows this bus is full exclusively of Syrians and is going directly to the village of Idomeni, on the Macedonian border. From there, Tony will try to join the unimpeded flow of migrants heading for Germany, but if Hungary decides to make good on its threats to build a wall and block anyone, including Syrians, from entering, Tony will seek out the services of another smuggler and enter into a succession of shadowy arrangements with men he has never met but has no choice to trust. 'Anywhere but Syria,' Tony says, in the broken English he learned from watching movies.

While Tony waits for his bus, *Ahmed, his wife and his two children are travelling in style. The owner of a chain of bookshops, Ahmed stubbornly maintained his life in Damascus even as the ongoing civil war was consuming every aspect of it. In the second year of the conflict Ahmed lost his summer home. First, it was commandeered by the army; then it was overrun by insurgent groups, who ransacked the place and sold off family heirlooms that stretched back generations. In the third year he sent his daughter to Beirut so she could continue her studies. Ahmed has barely seen her since Lebanon closed its borders with Syria. The next year, *Roula, Ahmed's wife, stopped leaving the house, paralysed by the fear of constant gunfire and explosions, and suffering from heart palpitations as she nervously waited for her two adolescent sons to arrive home from school each day.

Ahmed had clung to the business that his grandfather built. He had long hoped to pass it on to his children one day. But, as the war dragged on, it became increasingly difficult to maintain the fiction that things would ever return to normal, and so Ahmed did what he had promised himself he would never do. He unfolded a creased piece of paper he had kept in his wallet for several years, and called the number scribbled on it. A few hours later, the deal was done: $36,000—$10,000 each for him and Roula, $8,000 for each of the boys. His daughter would stay in Beirut and finish her studies, and perhaps join them later. The fake European passports and air tickets were ready in two weeks. They hope that Sweden, their final destination, will offer them peace, stability, the right to work, study, rebuild their lives as permanent residents.

Ahmed drives to Beirut and boards a plane with his family. Casting his eyes to the midnight sky, despite all he has lost, he offers thanks to the smugglers that made it all possible, the criminal heroes who allow him to start his life anew in Europe.

* * *

Ibrahim, Mansour, Tony and Ahmed are all active participants in the biggest mass migration Europe has seen since the Second World War in what has come to be known as the 'migrant crisis'.

There is a natural impulse—among scholars, journalists, politicians, activists and concerned citizens—to frame their stories within a broader human rights narrative. They remind us of the unfairness of the world and the injustice of global inequality. They remind us that people who live happy, fulfilling lives can suddenly find themselves facing a future more bleak, cruel and violent than they could have ever imagined. They remind us of the desperation with which people will risk what little they have for the chance of having something only marginally better.

But this book is not about the plight of refugees or the stories of those who yearn for a better life in Europe. Rather, it is about the smugglers, traffickers and networks of criminals that make their narratives possible.

These networks, tens of thousands of people strong, are facilitating an unprecedented surge of migration from Africa, the Middle East, Central Asia and South Asia into Europe. Although the drivers of the current 'crisis' are many—including but not limited to the concentric phenomena of conflict, climate change, global inequality, political persecution and globalisation—the actualisation of the crisis is enabled and actively encouraged by an increasingly professional set of criminal groups and opportunistic individuals that is generating profits in the billions.

INTRODUCTION: SMUGGLERS AND SAVIOURS

Some smugglers are revered by the people they transport, hailed as saviours due to their willingness to deliver men, women and children to safety and opportunity when no legal alternatives will offer them either. In a neoliberal world where the fates of individuals are couched in anodyne policy-speak, it is often the criminals who help the most desperate among us escape the inadequacy, hypocrisy and immorality that run through our current international system. It is certainly true that smugglers profit from the desperation of others, but it is also true that in many cases smugglers save lives, create possibilities and redress global inequalities.

Other smugglers carry out their activities without any regard for human rights, treating the lives of those they smuggle as disposable commodities in a broader quest to maximise profits. For all too many migrants and refugees, smugglers prove unable to deliver, exposing their clients to serious injury or even death. Even worse, some smugglers turn out to be traffickers, who, after luring unsuspecting clients with false promises of a better life, subject them to exploitation and abuse.

Meanwhile, efforts by European policymakers and their allies to stem the flow of migrants into Europe are pushing smuggling networks deeper underground and putting migrants more at risk, while at the same time doing little to address the root causes of mass migration. In lieu of safe, legal paths to seeking refuge and opportunity, new barriers are forcing migrants to pursue more dangerous journeys and seek the services of more established mafias and criminal organisations. These groups have developed expertise in trafficking drugs, weapons, stolen goods and people, and were uniquely qualified to add migrant smuggling to their business portfolios.

The result has been a manifold increase in human insecurity, not only in the Mediterranean and Aegean Sea crossings, which have received considerable attention in the international media, but also along the overland smuggling routes that cross the Sahara and the Central Asian Silk Road, penetrate deep into the Balkans, and continue into the grimiest corners of Europe's trendiest capitals.

What was once a loose network of freelancers and ad hoc facilitators has blossomed into professional, transnational organised criminal networks devoted to migrant smuggling. The size and scope of their operations is unprecedented. Shadowy new figures have emerged, existing crime syndicates have moved in, and a range of enterprising opportunists have come forward, together forming a dynamic, multi-level criminal industry that has shown an extraordinary ability to innovate and adapt.

Analysts have sought to explain the migrant crisis in Europe through traditional frameworks of push and pull factors, war, conflict and underdevelopment, but these explanations are no longer sufficient. What we are witnessing is not just the story of traditional migrant smuggling on a larger scale. Rather, we are witnessing a paradigm shift in which the unprecedented profits associated with migrant smuggling are altering long-standing political arrangements, transforming econo- mies and challenging security structures in ways that could potentially have a profound impact on global order.

Furthermore, the consolidation and codification of these networks also means that smuggling networks now seek to create contexts in which demand for their services will thrive. They have become a vector for global migration, quick to identify loopholes, exploit new areas of insecurity and target vulnerable populations whom they see as pro- spective clients. They no longer simply respond to demand for smug- gler services: they actively generate it.

This book is the culmination of over three years of research and reporting from the frontlines of the 'migrant crisis', everywhere from the borders of Syria, to remote Saharan outposts, to the shores of North Africa, to the beaches of Turkey and Greece, to seedy cafés in Europe. It aims to explain how these networks function, their evolution, the role they play for their clients, and what they mean for international peace and security in the future. It is neither a call to action nor a work of moral outrage (though both are in order). Rather, this book is an inves- tigation into one of the most important yet heretofore under-examined aspects of the unfolding migrant crisis: the smugglers.

To that end, we have divided the book into two main sections. The first section examines why demand for smuggler services has increased so dramatically in recent years; the nature of the migrant–smuggler relationship; the structure of the migrant smuggling industry; and the means by which smuggling networks operate. It posits that if we are to get beyond the facile and counterproductive narratives of villains and victims, we must start by examining smugglers dispassionately for what they are: service providers in an era of unprecedented demand.

INTRODUCTION: SMUGGLERS AND SAVIOURS

Armed with the frameworks established in Part 1, Part 2 will take readers to the key hubs where migrant-smuggling networks are operating in the context of the current crisis. In each of these locations we offer insights, through first-person observations and interviews with those directly involved, into the inner workings of migrant-smuggling operations and the ways in which local economies, political structures, military balances of power and criminal organisations are being transformed by the profits associated with migrant smuggling.

We conclude with some thoughts on what the future might hold, and what policies might succeed in combating smuggling networks and promote a constructive approach to migration. The stakes are incredibly high—for migrants, for refugees and for the rest of us.

PART 1

1

SMUGGLERS NEEDED

Every migrant journey begins with the decision to leave. In the case of the civil war in Syria, it doesn't matter whether that decision comes after years of deliberation or in the split second it takes to process the fact that the bullets in the distance are being fired in your direction. Getting out alive almost always requires a smuggler.

*Bilma, a Kurdish man in his early thirties, needed two smugglers in order to escape Syria: one to get him through hostile territory, and another to get him across the Turkish border. A tailor and musician from Aleppo, Bilma had run in Kurdish political circles for years. So, when the war started, his activist resume drew increased attention from Syrian intelligence officials. After two of his brothers were arrested and subsequently disappeared, Bilma realised he was living on borrowed time.

He tried to enter Europe legally by applying for a visa, but it was already the summer of 2014, and European embassies were operating under the assumption that anyone from Syria seeking a visa, regardless of whether it was for tourism, work or studies, was really an asylum seeker trying to bypass convoluted asylum processes.

A smuggler whom Bilma describes as a 'middleman' offered to get him a visa on the black market, but the price of roughly $5,000 was more than he could afford to pay. 'There was no other way,' Bilma explains. 'I asked my friends and they told me the only way was to hire a smuggler.'

For Bilma, the first order of business was to find someone who could move him out of Aleppo, past a string of government-controlled checkpoints. He found a smuggler who had access to a public-transport vehicle and had the requisite personal connections to bypass security screenings at each checkpoint. Each day fearing his inevitable abduction, Bilma had little choice but place his trust, and his money, in the hands of the smuggler.

True to his word, the smuggler greased the path through each government checkpoint, and when they reached roadblocks controlled by the Free Syrian Army and other anti-government militias, there the smuggler seemed to know the right people as well.

One's belief in a smuggler is only as strong as the last miracle he performs, however, and for people like Bilma, each checkpoint brought a new crisis of faith. At each nerve-racking stop, Bilma was convinced he would be taken captive, but he somehow reached Afrin, a town under the control of Kurdish forces, safely.

In Afrin, Bilma stayed in a house owned by his extended family until he found a smuggler who could take him across the Turkish border. He paid him $150, and in August the smuggler took him, along with other passengers, to the border by car. They crossed into Turkey early in the morning without any problems. 'I think the smuggler had a deal with the [Turkish] soldier who was in the watchtower,' Bilma explains. 'He saw us but he didn't try to stop us.'

Bilma lives in Athens. He worked in a restaurant for sub-standard wages and without papers until he was laid off. Now, he earns a living as a small cog in the industry that allowed him to reach Europe in the first place. He works on commission for a smuggling network based in Athens, within which he plays a small but crucial role in the transnational network of opportunists, criminals, entrepreneurs and humanitarians who move migrants across borders and around barriers. He trawls parks and restaurants where newly arrived Syrians and Iraqis congregate, and he puts them in touch with higher-level associates who can get them to their country of choice.

For those of us enjoying comfortable lives in stable pockets of the globe, meeting someone like Bilma can seem remarkable. But then you meet a few other people with similar stories. That handful becomes a dozen, then multiple dozens. And if you have the time, you can meet a hundred people just like Bilma after spending just a few weeks in Athens. That's when you realise there is almost nothing extraordinary about Bilma's escape from Syria, or his journey to Greece. With rare exceptions, everyone who escapes needs a smuggler. Without them, they could not have done it.

It goes without saying that those who leave Syria feel as though they had no choice. 'I was forced to leave my country. If I had stayed, who knows to where I would have disappeared to by now,' Bilma says. And like many of those interviewed in Greece, the worst part of their journey to Europe was not the maritime crossing on which Western observers fixate, nor was it dealing with shady and at times abusive smugglers in Turkey. Rather, the most terrifying part of their personal odyssey was getting out of Syria in the first place. 'There was fighting everywhere. Every checkpoint, the psychological pressure was very high,' Bilma laments.

One hesitates to call Bilma lucky, but the fact that he bears no physical scars from the war in Syria does make him relatively fortunate. For a friend of twenty-eight-year-old *Mohammed, who, like him, was an activist with a human rights organisation in the countryside outside Damascus, escaping Syria unscathed proved a bridge too far. Mohammed and his friend decided to flee Syria when an extremist militia took over the area and kidnapped members of his team. The organisation had previously been targeted by the Assad regime, so Mohammed had no choice but to leave. Both sides of the conflict considered Mohammed and his cohort enemies. 'I had to flee in order to save my life,' he says.

Mohammed couldn't take his own car or public transport for fear of being spotted by either the local militia or Assad's agents, so he and two fellow activists escaped on foot. 'We walked for three days in order to reach Darayya, in Damascus. For one day we were stuck in the middle of some battles [between the militia and the regime]. One of my friends was badly wounded. We had to carry him the rest of the way,' Mohammed explains. When Mohammed and his friends reached Darayya, they hired a smuggler to move them to Turkey in a van.

'We crossed more than ten regime checkpoints,' Mohammed says. 'When we left Damascus, we were stopped dozens of times by different militias, but they just checked our documents to be sure we were not soldiers, and let us pass.' When they reached Aleppo, their smuggler picked up two hitchhikers who were also trying to escape Syria. But at the first checkpoint after Aleppo, fighters from Jabhat al-Nusra, a militia affiliated with al-Qaeda, stopped the van and arrested the two hitchhikers upon identifying them. They let the rest of them continue.

When they reached the Turkish border, an ambulance took Mohammed's wounded friend to the hospital in Turkey, but the border guards would not allow Mohammed and his friend to go with him. An onlooker pulled them aside and offered to help them in exchange for $20. Their newfound smuggler agreed to speak with some soldiers he knew who would let them through. Not long afterwards, Mohammed and his friend were in Turkey contacting Syrian refugees on Facebook who could explain how to get to Greece.

Like Bilma, Mohammed says that the worst part of his journey to Europe was the escape from Syria. He describes the daily terror of being caught in the middle of gunfights, and wondering, at every checkpoint, if this would be the one where he was pulled out of the van and disappeared forever.

'Crossing the sea was just lovely compared to all of that,' says Mohammed, whose goal is to reach Germany, study human rights law, and continue his human rights activism from abroad. He is trying to convince his brothers to flee Syria as well. In fact, he says he would recommend it to anyone who has not yet been sucked into the conflict. 'I hate my homeland. Everybody is converting to extremism, joining militias and killing each other,' he says. 'If a person dies in the sea, at least they will be clean from blood.'

For people who have never been around violent conflicts, there is a tendency to think there are certain universal experiences that come with living in a war zone. But the truth is that while bombs and bullets do not discriminate, the implications of living in a country at war are anything but uniform. War affects everyone differently, and the after-shocks can reverberate for years, even across generations. Thus, while everyone fleeing chemical weapons, barrel bombs and the tyranny of young men with guns in Syria needs a smuggler who can navigate the military and political terrain, some need a smuggler to escape what war has done to their families.

*Fatima, for example, needed a smuggler who could transport an unaccompanied woman to Turkey, a proposition that required extensive connections because it meant traversing areas controlled by Jabhat al-Nusra and the self-proclaimed ISIS. Fatima's husband disappeared in August 2012. Six months later she received confirmation that he had been killed. She still doesn't know who killed him or why, but even knowing that wouldn't change the fact that Fatima found herself a twenty-seven-year-old widow, with a young child, in a country at war.

'I tried to continue my life in Latakia and take care of my child, but the explosions, the battles, and the disappearances of people didn't stop,' Fatima says. 'Many women were kidnapped and raped. The city's security was handed over to the government militias, constituted mainly by criminal gangs.'

Fatima says she didn't feel safe and she was worried about her son's future, but her situation was further complicated by the fact that her family was, according to her, 'too conservative' and didn't like the idea of a woman staying without a husband. They put her late husband's family in charge of her son and tried to find her a new husband. 'Even a few times my brother beat me because I rejected marriage,' she recounts.

Between the war, the fear of losing her son and the threat of abuse from what she calls 'a violent family', Fatima had no choice but to leave Syria, and it was the last remnants of her life before the war that allowed her to escape. 'I had a lot of gold gifts from my husband, which I sold, and I had also inherited money from him. I gathered everything and left.' Since Syrian law considered her late husband's family responsible for her son, Fatima could not obtain a passport and travel abroad with him unless she had his paternal grandfather's permission. She needed a smuggler who could move a woman, without documents or a husband, through jihadist territory and into Turkey.

Fatima went to her friend's house, from where her friend's husband had arranged a van to drive her to a village on the Turkish border. Her friend brought her a *niqab* to wear when she passed through areas controlled by extremist groups who required women to be fully covered in public. They crossed the first few regime-controlled checkpoints without incident, but at the last one she was pulled aside for questioning by Syrian authorities. They asked her why she wanted to cross into territory held by Islamic extremists, assuming that any woman who would do so alone must sympathise with their cause or, worse, be married to one of their enemies. They eventually let Fatima and her son pass, and when they entered territory controlled by Jabhat al-Nusra, Fatima immediately put on the *niqab*.

Fatima was heavily interrogated at the checkpoints under al-Nusra's control. The guards wanted to know why she was going to Turkey, and they harassed her for travelling alone without a man. 'I pretended that my husband was waiting for me there,' Fatima says. When they arrived at the Turkish border, a smuggler that her friend's husband had hired in advance was waiting for them. He drove them to the next border town and then they walked 200 metres to cross the border, where they reached a car that was parked at a farm. Fatima now sits at a café in Greece, planning her next move.

Like Fatima, *Rasha, a thirty-year old mother of two from the Syrian town of Hama, lost her husband to the war, but, as far as she knows, he is still alive. For many Syrians, leaving Syria is less about fleeing artillery than it is about escaping the psychological ruins of war. Rasha had passports for herself and her children, and she had money. What she needed was a smuggler who could move her out of the Hama countryside as quickly as possible.

Before the war Rasha was a philosophy lecturer at a local university. And when the war began she and her husband did not want to leave their families behind. But at the beginning of 2014 her husband's behaviour started to change. 'He started to become more religious. Slowly his ideas became fundamentalist,' Rasha explains. 'In July 2014 he disappeared, and after one month he called me asking me to join him in Raqqa, where he had joined ISIS.'

Rasha refused to join her husband in what had become the capital of the so-called ISIS, but in 2015 he came back to the countryside outside Hama. He started to threaten her and demanded that she and their daughters join him in Raqqa. In June 2015 ISIS captured a village near where Rasha was living with her daughters, and some relatives who lived in that village said that her husband was among the fighters who led the assault.

Rasha left for Turkey with her daughters immediately. She paid a man who said he could get the three of them to the Turkish border. Since they all already had passports, the real challenge was getting through check-points that were constantly changing hands. One day they would be under government control; the next, that of whatever militia had gained the upper hand. When they left the countryside they crossed six consecutive checkpoints controlled by the regime, but there were long delays because battles were taking place throughout the area. At the third checkpoint they had to wait more than eight hours because there had been a suicide attack. 'At least ten soldiers were killed and more than thirty civilians,' Rasha says. 'We could see how pieces of human bodies were falling from the sky after the explosion.'

With a long line of vehicles on each side of their van, Rasha's driver could not pull away from the checkpoint, so they decided to ditch the van and hide. After two hours of gunfire, the fighting finally subsided. According to Rasha, government forces rounded up and arrested lots of people in the area, allowing only women and children to continue their journeys. When they reached the Turkish border she and her daughters crossed into Turkey legally with their passports. Her brother, who was living in Istanbul at the time, sent a driver to find them. They hopped into the car and drove straight to sanctuary in Istanbul.

* * *

Similar stories can be told of any one of the hundreds of thousands of people who have used smugglers to escape the war in Syria. Yet not everyone who needs a smuggler to leave his own country is fleeing conflict. Sixteen-year-old Binyamin Abraham, for example, fled the tiny north-east African nation of Eritrea because it was the only way to avoid the indefinite military service and forced labour into which his father had been conscripted. As he told the *Wall Street Journal*, Binyamin waited until his mother and young siblings fell asleep before he slipped away; then he walked for nineteen hours, without food or water, until he crossed into neighbouring Ethiopia. 'I didn't tell my mother before I left, but I didn't have a choice,' Binyamin said, speaking from a refugee camp in the foothills of Ethiopia's Simien Mountains. 'I have to go to Europe so I can help my family.'[1]

Binyamin is one of thousands of people fleeing Eritrea every month, seeking refuge not from war but from Eritrea's authoritarian regime. Often dubbed the 'North Korea of Africa', Eritrea is not only one of the most underdeveloped countries in the world, ranking 182nd out of 187 countries in the UN's Human Development Report for 2014, it is also a closed society controlled by a highly militarised government. Its population of approximately 6 million people live in fear of harsh government reprisals for any kind of misdemeanour, and all citizens aged between eighteen and fifty are subject to forced labour under the guise of mandatory, open-ended military service which is justified by the 'emergency rule' the country has had in place for the last seventeen years, since the war with Ethiopia in 1998. If Eritrean citizens wish to travel abroad they must request permission from the government, which is rarely granted to those under fifty, and the government seeks to deter illegal migration through threats of violence—threats on which they regularly make good. The Eritrean military, for example, patrols the country's land borders with instructions to 'shoot to kill' anyone found attempting to leave, and Eritreans who do escape fear their families will be punished in their place.

Despite these government policies, conservative estimates suggest that 5,000 people flee Eritrea every month, and around 400,000 people—9 per cent of the Eritrean population—have already left. Eritreans have consistently been among the most common nationalities arriving in Europe to seek asylum, and the age of those fleeing becomes younger every year, as youth seek to avoid indefinite military service. Unsuccessful asylum seekers and other returnees from Eritrea, particularly those evading national service or deserting from the military, face torture, detention and disappearance once they are returned.[2]

With such high risks, many of those leaving Eritrea will use a smuggler to get them out of the country as safely as possible, and to traverse the difficult physical and political terrain that lies beyond its borders. Many, like Binyamin, go to refugee camps in neighbouring countries of Sudan or Ethiopia, or to one of the region's capitals, where they will either seek work as undocumented migrants or contact another smuggler who will help them with onward passage to North Africa, Europe or the Gulf.

For those in Eritrea, whether they are trying to escape poverty or political persecution, smugglers constitute a lifeline and, in many cases, the only hope of reaching safety. Yet at the same time Eritreans are among the most vulnerable of migrants, and those they hire as smugglers often turn out to be traffickers, who subject them to physical abuse, extortion and kidnapping for ransom. More Eritreans than any other nationality have drowned while making the Mediterranean crossing from Libya, a result of smugglers willing to put them on the most unseaworthy vessels. Even with these risks in mind, Eritreans, along with migrants from all over the world, many of whom are fully aware that their smugglers view them as little more than something from which to derive a profit, view threats of physical violence, rape and extortion as a tolerable trade-off given the interminable or perilous future that staying at home guarantees.[3]

And for countless others from Africa, Asia and the Americas, a smuggler represents a chance to avoid brutal and grinding poverty. Across the globe hundreds of millions of people are on the move, seeking a better life and a better future than the one they were awarded by the lottery of birth. According to the UN, globally, an additional 2.5 billion people will move to urban areas by 2050, and 94 per cent of those will come from the developing world.

A discrepancy between the globalisation of trade and the absence of free movement of labour has created a labour-market crisis: while industries and employers can move their businesses wherever in the world is most favourable, their employees do not have the same luxury. A growing number of people vote with their feet, abandoning their homes and moving to cities and countries with better opportunities for employment, education and health care. Unprecedented access to communication technologies, information and the development of extensive diaspora networks have created a sense of aspiration—to seek a new, better life for themselves and their families—a momentum that the borders of nation-states cannot contain.

We met *Emmanuel from Nigeria fresh off a migrant boat in southern Italy. He had not come from the turbulent Niger Delta region or from northern Nigeria, where an insurgency led by the group Boko Haram has killed thousands and displaced millions. Rather, twenty-one-year-old Emmanuel is from a small town in the relatively peaceful region of Edo State, in southern Nigeria.

A quiet, studious young man with serious eyes, Emmanuel dreamed of a brighter future than working on his family's small farm. He had completed secondary school, but there were no jobs for him in town, or in nearby Benin City. He could see that with each successive generation, working the land was increasingly unsustainable. The farm barely brought in enough to feed his parents and his four brothers and sisters.

Emmanuel hoped to marry and have a family of his own, but with neither the money to pay for a wedding nor the means to support himself, never mind a wife and children, he found himself stuck in limbo. With no job, no relationship, and what he perceived as no future, Emmanuel decided that he needed to look further afield, and Europe represented hope.

'When I was a child I thought to leave because I was looking for a better future, but I tried to help my family in the farm. I also saw the news on television about migrants and the system of welcoming them,' Emmanuel recounts, having only recently arrived in Italy. 'I saw lots of happy people and I decided to leave. Now I am safe, if I had stayed at home I would have died.'

Regardless of whether Emmanuel would have died literally or figuratively had he stayed in Nigeria, and despite the tribulations of his voyage, which included repeated beatings, as well as being cheated and imprisoned in Libya, Emmanuel is convinced that life in Italy will be better than the marginal existence he could eke out back home. And what's more, by travelling to Europe he has the potential to improve things for his family in Nigeria. 'My mother sold the farm to pay for me to come here,' he told us. 'But soon, I will be sending money home, and then I will bring my mother and my sisters and they will also have a better life.'

Emmanuel's journey, in other words, is a resilience plan endorsed and supported by his family. For him, migration is a development strategy in the face of inadequate local alternatives.

Global mobility, driven by conflict, bad governance and unequal development, has reached an unprecedented scale; one which has expanded beyond the architecture of our current international system and outpaced the international community's capacity to make the necessary changes to manage it. Despite the high aspirations presented by the multilateral system in frameworks such as the Agenda for Sustainable Development—a lofty vision of 17 goals and 169 targets that aims to address not just the fundamentals of poverty, inequality, health and education, but also unite global leaders to reduce traffic accidents, stop the consumption of illicit tobacco and shift the world to renewable energy sources—the reality on the ground falls far short on all of these measures, even the least ambitious among them.

The multilateral system, embodied by the UN and its universal principles and international conventions, is no longer fit to manage the realities of the contemporary world. It fails to resolve conflict or hold accountable the most flagrant violators of human rights and international law. Compounding these failures, the current system has proven incapable of meeting the humanitarian needs of victims of war, let alone providing for those most vulnerable.

Our outdated international system and our inability to reform it are further exacerbated by a hesitancy to confront the basic realities of our current world. Rather than reaffirm the ideals that led to the creation of bodies such as the UN, many of the most powerful actors in the international community have preferred to sidestep the responsibilities that would come with re-codifying these values.

Put more bluntly, our international system is broken and short of bold action, it will remain that way for the foreseeable future.

Options in Exile

For Rasha, Fatima, Bilma and millions of other Syrians who have sought refuge in neighbouring countries, the international system has failed them twice over. Despite the fact that even the most cynical interpretations of international law would consider them 'legitimate' refugees, millions of Syrians find themselves trapped in the same impossible situation that decades of underfunding and a lack of political will have foisted upon refugee populations throughout the globe: perennial, protracted displacement.

The average refugee will spend twenty years in exile before being able to return home, and many spend far longer than that: 450,000 Palestinians live in twelve refugee camps spread across the tiny country of Lebanon, whose domestic population is only 4 million, and some have lived in these camps for as many as sixty-five years; 350,000 Somalis live in the Dadaab refugee camp in Kenya, called the 'world's largest camp', some of whom are the third generation of their family to live there. The Zaatari refugee camp in Jordan is home to approximately 80,000 people, and between 50 and 80 children are born there every week. In these types of camps, which house a large portion of the world's 21 million total registered refugees, the present is unbearable and the future is bleak.

Refugees have traditionally found solutions to their plight via three different avenues. The first is by means of voluntary repatriation back to their country of origin, carried out on conditions of 'safety and dignity' and followed by 'sustainable reintegration' there.[4] With the end of the Cold War in the late 1980s, voluntary return to countries of origin became the solution of choice for the largest number of refugees at the time, to the extent that then UNHCR chief Sadako Ogata dubbed the 1990s 'the decade of repatriation'. Large-scale repatriation became possible for huge numbers of people, such as in Mozambique (1.7 million returns), Cambodia (365,000), Central America (150,000) and Namibia (45,000), and therefore became the default option as well as the preferred choice of the international community in addressing refugee situations.[5]

In the period after the Cold War, however, the nature of conflict has shifted. Whereas the Cold War brought inter-state conflicts and civil wars that, while terribly violent and destabilising, contained a modicum of coherence that came with the bipolar global order, conflict in the post-Cold War system has most commonly come in the form of protracted insurgencies, unending civil wars and chronic urban gang violence that lacks any of the ideological or political clarity that defined Cold War violence.

As a consequence, the conflicts and political violence that trigger some of the world's most acute refugee-producing situations have gone unresolved, making it impossible for refugees to repatriate on anything like the scale that took place in the 1990s. In fact, refugee repatriation figures are now at historically low levels, with minimal levels of return to countries of origin such as Afghanistan, the Democratic Republic of Congo, Myanmar, Somalia and Sudan, as well as the region of the Americas known as the Northern Triangle (El Salvador, Guatemala and Honduras), where perpetual gang wars have resulted in a surge of homicides and displacement. In 2014 fewer than 130,000 refugees were repatriated worldwide, the lowest figure for thirty years.[6]

At the same time, the past five years have witnessed a spate of new refugee emergencies, provoked by armed conflicts in countries such as the Central African Republic, Iraq, Nigeria, South Sudan, Syria, Ukraine and Yemen, none of which seem likely to be resolved in the immediate future.

Thus, while the number of refugees worldwide has increased, the policy options available to the international community have stagnated. With the possibility of repatriation unavailable in most of these contexts, only two other viable options exist within the formal asylum system. The first is local settlement and integration in the country of first asylum, which entails the progressive acquisition of rights, including, eventually, the right of citizenship. The second option is organised resettlement from the refugee's country of first asylum to a third country that has agreed to admit them and provide them with permanent residence rights and the opportunity to be naturalised.[7]

However, the option of local settlement and integration is not available to most of the world's refugees. Major refugee-hosting countries, including Kenya, Lebanon, Pakistan, Thailand and Turkey, have made it very clear that the large number of refugees admitted to their territory have no hope of remaining there indefinitely or acquiring citizenship. The options for third-country resettlement are even narrower: in 2015 around 100,000 refugees benefited from this solution, around 70 per cent of them being admitted to a single country: the USA.[8] As a result, the number of people throughout the world who have been displaced by armed conflict and persecution has jumped to around 60 million, the largest number since the end of the Second World War,[9] and the gap between needs and resources to deal with the vulnerable is widening. For 2016, the UNHCR has called for $6 billion in aid, but is unlikely to receive it. In the last ten years the Agency's escalating budgets have never been funded at more than 60 per cent.

The UN Special Rapporteur on the human rights of migrants, François Crépeau, has been quoted as saying, 'Migration is always a dignity-seeking journey',[10] but regrettably, it is rarely a successful quest. In reality, living as one of the global displaced is a humiliating experience that, by its very nature, strips people of their dignity. Approximately 50 per cent of the world's refugees are now living in camps, where restrictive regulations by host states and chronic funding shortages result in populations that rarely have access to quality education, health care or decent living accommodation. The other half of the worldwide refugee population have become part of the global urban underclass, existing at the fringes of society as they attempt to scrape together a living in informal or illicit economies throughout the globe.

The 1951 Refugee Convention, which has been ratified by 145 of the world's states, obligates all state parties to offer protection to a person fleeing a life-threatening situation, such as civil war or a natural disaster, or someone who:

> Owing to a well-founded fear of being persecuted for reasons of race, religion, nationality, membership of a particular social group or political opinion, is outside of the country of his nationality, and is unable to, or owing to such fear, is unwilling to avail himself of the protection of that country.[11]

States are obliged to offer protection to refugees, who, on paper, have the right to housing, education, assistance, freedom of movement and work. The longer a refugee stays in a given country, the greater their rights are meant to become, but the reality is that host governments almost always fall short of this promise.

Access to productive employment in particular tends to be highly limited. Despite the fact that safe and lawful employment is a fundamental human right and that the right to engage in wage-earning employment and self-employment are explicitly provided for in '1951', as it is known, refugees are rarely given formal permission to work, and are often restricted to specific sectors.

Where work permits are granted, a series of de facto barriers often prevents refugees from accessing genuine livelihood opportunities, including social or cultural opposition by host populations, strict encampment requirements by host governments or exorbitant permit fees that place legal employment out of reach.[12] As a consequence, refugees are unable to provide for themselves, unable to use or build their skills, unable to provide for their families, and, for younger refugees who grow up on the margins, unable to complete basic rites of passage. They are dependent on handouts of humanitarian aid and remain in limbo, hoping for some distant, unspecified better future.

As time passes these hopes of a future dissipate, often vanishing altogether. Familial and social tensions grow, resentment festers, and violence becomes all but inevitable. When this futureless present becomes intolerable, some move on, preferring to abandon their refugee 'privileges' in order to move elsewhere and become irregular migrants. They try to move to places they hope might offer something better, or, at the very least, a degree of independence and self-determination. They search for a shred of dignity.

It is an equally harsh fate for those displaced populations that have avoided refugee camps altogether. Living informally in the shadow economies of other societies, they populate an ever-growing global underclass. Whether we speak of the Somalis in Kenya, South Americans in the USA, Africans in Europe, the Rohingya in Thailand and Indonesia or countless other peoples and populations, these displaced groups live almost entirely without rights, without protections and without access to social services or the possibility of personal development. The displaced are almost universally resented, looked down upon and sometimes feared by the local populations alongside whom they are trying to survive.

Sitting with Syrian refugees in Lebanon in a cramped, graceless concrete room with unpainted walls, you start to realise the extent to which those who have managed to carve out a tenuous and uncertain existence suffer just as much as those lingering indefinitely in refugee camps. Their Beirut apartment-cum-cell is furnished with mattresses on the floor, a few belongings piled into the opposite corner, and an overwhelmed extension cord that stretches across the space, snaking out of the window until it reaches a sputtering petrol-powered generator outside.

These makeshift apartments are meant for individuals, small families at most, but they often house extended families of eight of more. A bed-sheet might hang as a curtain to section off one part of the room, a modest attempt to permit a mother-in-law to sleep in privacy, but the rest of the family sleeps and works in shifts.

The husbands and brothers who have not been taken by the war or already departed for the migrant trail pass the time outside on the steps, smoking cigarettes and wondering how much longer they can last in these conditions. Women cook pungent dishes of inadequate amounts of food, when they aren't struggling to bathe and clothe their children.

Living in the shadows makes life impossible, the women say. Everything is difficult: you don't eat well, you don't sleep well, and you don't do enough of either. People are tense, they argue. Everyone is always worried and everyone knows the next news is most likely to be bad news. The default setting of waiting for things to get worse takes its toll, gradually infecting everyone in the crammed apartment.

Sometimes there is violence: men fight; even good men become so stressed and desperate they hit the women or the children. Everyone is looking for money, for any kind of a job. Even the kids have to work or beg on the streets, something that would have been unthinkable only a few short years ago when they were all going to school in Syria. They are treated with hostility and suspicion by the host population—cheated, taken advantage of and abused. People start out compassionate, trying to be kind to children, not to shout, to be neighbourly and gracious and hospitable. But after a while there's nothing left to share and desperation sets in. Humanity gives way to survival instincts, and people begin to hate the way they are treated, and to hate themselves for the way they treat others.

As one woman told us, 'It feels like you are dying, slowly, yet every day you wake up again and work out how you are going to survive.'

If you live in these conditions long enough, the decision to leave is never a question of 'if,' but 'when'. And the risks you'll consider taking to escape the day-to-day oppression of having no future are limitless.

Seeking Asylum: Rights and Privileges

Europe's crisis has not been caused exclusively by the war in Syria, or the countless other conflicts, insurgencies and violent upheavals that are driving people towards Europe. Conflict is just one part of the narrative that is far wider than Europe, or even refugee populations. Europe's 'migrant crisis' is actually a symptom of something much larger: a global migration crisis.

In strict definitional terms, the word 'migrant' means anyone who has moved. You can be a migrant within your own country, having moved from a rural area to an urban hub. There are an estimated 232 million international migrants in the world, and more than 740 million internal migrants.[13]

More pejoratively, however, the term is used to describe those who have moved primarily for livelihood reasons, often labelled 'economic' migrants, regardless of whether they have crossed borders legally or illegally. But while the aspirational goal of seeking livelihoods regardless of borders may be universally justifiable on a moral basis, it is not a legal right that is equally applied. A sharp distinction is drawn between refugees and 'economic' migrants, and the rights, entitlements and privileges that are afforded to them vary widely.

SMUGGLERS NEEDED

Regardless of levels of poverty or absence of economic opportunity, there is no requirement placed on states by '1951' or any other international convention to admit or care for economic migrants, aside from guaranteeing their basic human rights. Legal economic migration is a matter of bilateral agreements between states, allowing them to select which categories of people they choose to admit. More often than not, those desired are the skilled or unskilled workers who can be reasonably expected to contribute to economic growth, or fill gaps in the labour market that are unmet by the domestic population. For most states, preferred migrants are those who will integrate well and will not pose a burden on the state's welfare benefits and resources. As a result, the market for legal migration rarely includes those who are most desperate to move.

Those most likely to move are rarely the poorest of the poor, particularly for international migration. Migrating, even illegally, costs money that the poorest seldom have. It is typically those from the developing world who see opportunities in richer neighbouring states or countries further afield who will seize an opportunity to move abroad. Defined as 'irregular' migrants, they may enter a country illegally, or overstay on a legal tourist, student or temporary work visa. Those entering illegally must attempt to do so undetected, or they must find grounds to seek asylum.

'Asylum seekers' are those persons who have applied for asylum under '1951', and they remain asylum seekers for as long as their applications and subsequent appeals against rejection of their applications, are pending. Establishing an asylum seeker's rights to refugee status is an extensive process that can take months or even years, particularly when the host country's system is overwhelmed by applicants (as most are). Thus, in the interim period while they wait, depending on the country of application, asylum seekers are either left to roam free in society with minimal protections or are warehoused in facilities that range from dormitories to prison-like detention centres (some of which are state-run, others are run by private, for-profit companies) or given stipends and government-provided housing.

Those whose asylum claims are accepted are granted official refugee status, and are entitled to the full packages of rights and benefits offered by the states processing their asylum claims. But these rights and benefits can differ quite significantly from country to country, even within Europe.

Since 2005, the EU's approach to migration has been governed by the Global Approach to Migration and Mobility (GAMM). As with all EU policy, the GAMM upholds international norms and standards, but the EU bloc offers no possibilities for asylum seekers to apply for asylum outside the EU. Thus, in order to begin the process, an individual wanting to seek protection within the EU must reach and cross EU borders illegally. This paradox, in which the EU at once guarantees asylum seekers the right to protection, while systematically trying to prevent them from reaching the EU in the first place, is at the heart of why refugees seek the services of migrant smugglers. If one wanted to create a system that was designed to enrich the migrant smuggling industry, it would be this one.

Even when migrants do reach Europe, the Dublin Regulation, the pillar of Europe's policy on asylum seekers, dictates that migrants must seek asylum in the first country where they are detected, and cannot do so elsewhere. As a result, the Dublin Regulation further incentivises asylum seekers to use migrant smugglers to arrive in their preferred destination country or to avoid detection within Europe's internal borders.

Despite having a common asylum policy, the EU does not have a common package of support for those who are granted refugee status. While nearly all countries in Europe provide around €200 in financial support per month to pay for food and housing, and offer varying degrees of integration support, such as language lessons, there are enormous discrepancies when it comes to other entitlements, such as access to citizenship, rights to work and ability to send for family members (known as family reunification). Sweden and Germany, for example, not only provide some of the most generous packages of support to refugees, they are also the only two countries in Europe that offer family reunification, making them the most coveted destinations for asylum seekers.

Yet because the Dublin Regulation dictates that asylum processing must happen at the first point that an asylum seeker is detected, the differences in benefits creates additional complications for a migrant hoping to resettle in a specific European country. Asylum seekers must either land in the country (perhaps by air) where they want to register or evade detection while transiting through states where they prefer not to settle, for fear of being registered and forced to claim asylum there.

For many migrants, arriving in Europe means the beginning of a new process of avoiding detection. They can try to reach their desired destination on their own, or they can seek out the services of a smuggler. For *Mohammed, a twenty-year-old from Damascus in Syria, the fear and vulnerability that came with trying to reach Germany from Greece by hiking through the Balkans made the decision to hire a smuggler all but inevitable.

'The walk to Serbia was not easy. You can't be seen on the road otherwise you risk arrest. I got arrested twice and sent back to Greece,' Mohammed explains. 'The third time, I managed to escape and get to Serbia. But it had already taken me twenty days. That's longer than average. We only had Red Bull and Snickers throughout the whole thing. No one had money or the energy to get real food,' Mohammed continued. 'I don't know where we were in Serbia, but it was near a water plant. We took a bus to Budapest and from there we met a smuggler who took us in a car to Germany. It was expensive, but safer.'

Those whose applications for asylum are denied become illegal migrants, and subject to voluntary or involuntary return to their home states. Returns—or deportations—are expensive; in 2014 the US budget for the removal of illegal immigrants was $229 million. Between 2000 and 2015 the European countries that comprise the Schengen zone are estimated to have spent an incredible €11.3 billion on deporting people they have determined unworthy of refugee status.[14] In practice, however, less than 40 per cent of those for whom return decisions are issued are ever deported. The majority disappear into Europe's underground economy, preferring to live in the shadows illegally, perpetually vulnerable to detection and arrest, than to return home.

All of these processes are further complicated by the fact that the traditional distinction between 'refugees' and 'economic migrants' no longer appears to be as clear-cut as has often been assumed by the UNHCR and other members of the international refugee-protection regime.[15]

As refugee camps have increasingly failed to deliver meaningful opportunities, or even meet the most basic needs of their inhabitants, 'qualified' refugees have increasingly challenged traditional conceptions of refugees versus migrants by defying rules and creating new realities, either moving from camps to cities or by taking up residence in an urban area immediately on arrival in their country of asylum.

In addition, chronic cyclical insecurity in certain regions, coupled with globalisation has undermined the common assumption that an individual or refugee household could live in only once place at a time, whether it is their 'country of origin', 'country of asylum' or their 'resettlement country'. Instead, people's understanding of domesticity and mobility have fundamentally changed. Far from living in and belonging to only one place, migrants and refugees are now able to find solutions for themselves and their families by establishing transnational lifestyles.

Many of those arriving in Europe in high numbers are people for whom mobility has become an increasingly commonplace, valid and essential way of life. Many Afghans, for example, move on a periodic basis between their own country and Pakistan, depending on the economic opportunities and security situation in those locations at any given time. They might also move in order to work in Iran or the Gulf States, where they can earn the money required to support family members in other locations or to finance their onward journey to other parts of the world.[16]

Similarly, for the peoples of the Sahel, a zone that stretches across the African continent just south of the Sahara desert, mobility is a resilience strategy against economic hardship, political instability and environmental degradation. Dramatic variations in rainfall, cyclical drought and repeated cycles of conflict have meant that the populations of the region are traditionally highly dispersed and mobile, moving north to the Maghreb countries of Algeria, Libya and Morocco for work; or across the Sinai to the Gulf, or south into the heart of sub-Saharan Africa.[17]

As the international community's conceptions of rights and classifications increasingly fail to meet the needs of the most vulnerable, migrants are taking matters of destiny and dignity into their own hands. The extent to which they are unwilling to wait for governments and international institutions to live up to their own ideals is evidenced not only in the growing levels of labour migration and informality, but in the robust ways in which Syrians and other refugee communities have challenged the many obstacles placed in their way as they move from untenable living situations in the Middle East by crossing the Aegean and Mediterranean Seas to reach European shores.

Needless to say, the visa restrictions and border controls established by the world's more prosperous states invariably require such journeys to be undertaken with the assistance of human smugglers, document forgers, corrupt officials and other members of the burgeoning illicit 'migration industry'.

Smuggler or Saviour?

Smugglers are often portrayed as exploitative, profit-driven criminals; the villains who prey on the most desperate among us. Yet, as this book will demonstrate, such facile depictions are not only incorrect, they are counterproductive. They reduce the complex narrative of human migration into simple dichotomies of good and evil, in turn fostering bad policies that put migrants at risk while at the same time empowering criminal organisations.

In many instances, those who are promoting these narratives are deliberately conflating human smuggling with the much less morally ambiguous activity of human trafficking, hoping to operationalise universal disapproval of human trafficking to gain support for policies that are really intended to stem unpalatable migrant and refugee flows.

The most intellectually honest and useful way to think about migrant smugglers is to consider them dispassionately as service providers. They are the supply to someone else's demand, and, as outlined in the previous section, demand has never been higher.

Though every migrant has different motives, and different smugglers have different business models, fundamentally, all migrant–smuggler relationships are ones in which the smuggler is assisting the migrant— albeit for profit and often with little regard for the well-being of the migrant—to bypass barriers.

A barrier can come in the form of a wall, a guarded border or dangerous territory where there is violent conflict, banditry or even kidnappers who seek to abuse and extort migrants. Sometimes these barriers are natural or geographic, a desert that is hard to cross or a sea that is difficult to navigate. In other instances they are purely political, manifesting themselves in the form of stringent visa regimes or discriminatory policies.

Additionally, barriers can be cultural, in which migrants physically stand out from the local population, or in which for reasons pertaining to gender, age or language the migrant feels unable to navigate a foreign culture without the help of a smuggler. And because there are so many different profiles of migrants and so many different types of barriers to overcome, there are a number of different smuggling models within the migrant-smuggling industry.

As will be explored in this book, smuggling service providers exist on a spectrum. At one end are individuals who see a one-off business opportunity and form ad hoc alliances with other criminal entrepreneurs in order to pool their skills and deliver smuggler services. At the opposite end are highly professional organised crime syndicates that specialise in moving everything from drugs, weapons, stolen goods and people over borders undetected.

The more challenging the barrier to overcome, the more professional, specialised and, arguably, criminal the smugglers will need to be in order to provide their services. In situations where borders are easy to cross, there are low barriers to entry into the smuggling market and the profile of the smuggler trends towards the criminal opportunist. Where barriers are greater, there are fewer actors with the requisite skills to deliver smuggling services, which means that the smuggling market will consist of fewer individuals, and most often those already involved in organised crime.

It is far easier, for example, to find someone who can navigate a forty-five-minute sea crossing from Turkey to the Greek islands than it is to find a crew that can travel 2,000 kilometres in open sea from the tip of Indonesia to a landing point in Australia. Anyone who can afford a rubber dinghy and a cheap motor can get in on the former. The latter requires considerable expertise.

The same economic principles apply to the prices people must pay for smuggler services. In circumstances where borders are relatively easy to cross and there is competition between smugglers, prices are lower than in cases where the barriers are high and only a few actors can provide the services needed.

A recent report commissioned by the EU estimated that all of the more than a million irregular migrants who entered the EU illegally in 2015 used the services of a smuggler at some point in their journey.[18]

SMUGGLERS NEEDED

For the many people of different nationalities coming to Europe, a smuggler may be required in order to escape from their home state; to transit through various countries undetected and unharmed; to traverse land or sea borders in order to reach the Schengen territories of Europe; to arrive at their preferred destination; or all of the above.

In other words, smugglers have offered millions of people opportunity, security and assistance. They exist because, in the absence of safe and legal ways of seeking refuge and opportunity, their services are highly coveted. Smugglers may then go on to try and expand their markets through active recruitment of prospective clients, or lies and false promises, but rarely do they create a market out of nothing.

Smugglers exist, first and foremost, because in the world we have created, where necessity demands movement but few legal options are available, they are essential.

2

SMUGGLERS INC.

While hiring a smuggler is essential, hiring the right smuggler is the difference between life and death. *Waseem, who fled Syria because he did not want to kill his own people, learned this lesson the hard way. Waseem's penchant for pacifism was unsustainable, considering his profession. When he started his compulsory military service in 2012, Waseem planned on completing his two years of regular service and returning home to his Christian community. But with the onset of the war, the government refused to let him return to civilian life.

Waseem did not need just any smuggler. He needed one who had the skills to either create fake documents or procure stolen ones. After arranging a deal with a smuggler who could provide him with an ID that belonged to someone else, Waseem defected from his military unit, knowing that were he to be caught, he would meet the same fate as others who had tried to escape. 'I would be court-martialled and executed,' Wassem explains. 'It happened to many other persons in my military unit.'

When Waseem met his smuggler on the highway outside Homs there were two other soldiers and some civilians also trying to escape. They had to pass four checkpoints manned by the military and intelligence operatives. At each of the checkpoints the driver asked Waseem to give him $20 so that he could pay his contacts.

After leaving Homs, as their van drew closer to the town of Idlib, they had to pass three checkpoints belonging to three different militias.

Waseem was surprised that they were able to do so without any problems. But when they arrived at a fourth checkpoint, controlled by Jabhat al-Nusra, the fighters overseeing the post asked them all to get out of the van. That's when Waseem realised that his driver was actually himself a member of Jabhat al-Nusra.

Waseem knew what happened to soldiers caught by the likes of Jabhat al-Nusra and ISIS. 'If he is Sunni they will try to make him join them. But if he belongs to any other religion, in many cases, they slaughter him and publish videos,' he explains. Because he is a Christian, Waseem assumed that his execution would end up on the internet, and he began preparing for the afterlife. Those prayers, it turned out, were premature.

'One of the people at the checkpoint recognised me. We were childhood friends and had studied at the same school. He hid the fact that I am Christian and put me back in the van,' Waseem recounts. 'But the other soldiers were taken away and I don't know what happened to them.'

Waseem finally made it to a border town called Bab-el-Hawa, which was then under the control of the Free Syrian Army. He didn't have any documents, but there were taxi drivers offering passage into Turkey, no documents necessary. Waseem's real problem was that he did not have enough money to pay the 200 Turkish lira they were charging, and more than five times what the journey was worth. He called a brother who was living in a Turkish town just on the other side of the border and passed the phone to one of the taxi drivers. His brother convinced the driver to accept payment on arrival. That night Waseem crossed the border at an official crossing, without any problems from the customs agent. The taxi drivers at that crossing, Waseem learned, were business partners of the customs officials.

A Transnational Crime

The formal definition of the smuggling of migrants comes from the United Nations Transnational Organised Crime Convention (UNTOC), which has been ratified by 141 states. In a dedicated protocol, it describes smuggling as 'the procurement, in order to obtain directly or indirectly, a financial or other material benefit of the illegal entry of a person into a State Party of which the person is not a national or a permanent resident'.[1] The essence, therefore, is that smuggling is seen as a crime against the state, not against a person. Smuggling, after all, is often a consensual agreement between the smuggler and the migrant. More often than not, a smuggler is providing a service and meeting a demand for illicit movement.

By contrast, while the terms are often used interchangeably, trafficking is a non-consensual relationship that involves the ongoing exploitation of another human being in forced labour or forced prostitution. It is defined as 'the recruitment, transportation, transfer, harbouring or receipt of persons, by means of the threat or use of force or other forms of coercion, abduction, or fraud or deception'.[2] Unlike with human smuggling, no movement is implied. You can be trafficked in your home country just as you can be trafficked overseas, as many people have been.

The fact that human smuggling is singled out for a protocol within the UNTOC emphasises that, for the purposes of international and national law, facilitating illegal migration is considered to be organised crime. Both UNTOC and the EU legislation that is modelled after it are careful, however, not to criminalise the migrant himself, even if he has migrated illegally—but to ensure that the criminal penalty is applied only to the one who derives financial or other material profit from the illegal crossing of borders. Under these definitions, however, a broad spectrum of acts would appear to warrant the moniker of organised crime, which in many of these cases is a title either too serious or entirely inappropriate for the crime being committed. Further still, there have been cases in which individuals are prosecuted for smuggling migrants, even though they did so without any perceptible benefit to themselves.

Take the case of *Rania, for example, a twenty-something Syrian acquaintance of mine who holds both Syrian and American nationality. Having grown up in the USA, and now living and working in Europe, she was keen to help her cousins escape the increasingly hellish situation in Syria. At first she explored legal options with a number of European states, but even with Rania offering to support her relatives financially, they were confounded by the Dublin Regulation, which stipulates that no claims for asylum could be considered unless on European soil, and even a legal visa to visit was out of the question. When aerial bombing began in their home town the urgency increased, and Rania's cousins began to think a bit more creatively.

In the end, they hatched a plan by which Rania's boyfriend *Alex flew into Beirut, where he met her cousin *Zeina—her mother's sister's eldest daughter and the most similar to her in appearance. A few days later, Zeina flew back with Alex into Vienna, where he and Rania lived together, and where her much-stamped passport passed through Austrian immigration with barely a glance from the authorities. After a night out drinking to recover her nerves and a tranquil morning taking in Viennese history via a horse-and-cart tour, Zeina gave the passport back to Alex and bought a €30 train ticket for Munich—no visa or passport required within Europe's Schengen zone. After four pleasant hours reading a French magazine on the train, she declared herself as an asylum seeker with the Bavarian authorities upon reaching Germany. Two years later, her refugee status granted, Zeina is learning German, living independently in a small apartment and volunteering with an NGO providing legal support to the newly arrived refugees. She is currently making arrangements to have the rest of her family join her in Germany.

Did Rania commit a crime? Technically yes, though given the circumstances, it is hard to view Rania and Zeina's experience as anything but a success story in which justice prevailed over the inadequacies of international bureaucratic obstacles. But similar circumstances have led to concerned citizens with broadly humanitarian motives being prosecuted for smuggling. The Danish authorities, for example, prosecuted 279 people between September 2015 and February 2016, for giving lifts to migrants as they crossed the country on the way to Sweden.[3]

In another case, a forty-nine-year-old British aid worker, former soldier and father of four was prosecuted by French courts for attempting to smuggle a four-year-old Afghan girl into the UK at the behest of her father, whose only wish was that the little girl join family already residing in Leeds.[4] Having been stopped at the border, the erstwhile smuggler is now facing a possible five-year prison sentence, and the four-year-old and her father are entering their second year as residents of the informal 'Jungle' camp in Calais. Being compassionately right, but legally wrong, brought no benefits to any of the parties involved, but friends of mine who are aid workers all over the region tell me that they are constantly begged to 'just take my child'. Many mothers and fathers see no end in sight, and no legal ways to ensure the rights and futures of their children.

Those that help them, and those that act for other humanitarian reasons, are probably the most innocent of law-breakers, rarely acting for financial or material gain. But you only have to move an increment up the sliding scale of criminality for scheming humanitarians to start looking more like criminal opportunists. What if Rania had been *Bjorn, a young Swedish engineering student who earned €1,000 'renting' his passport for two weeks via a university friend, who passed it to a Turkish network that was charging Syrians $10,000 for valid documents and a flight into Stockholm? Bjorn is certainly breaking the law, and he is making a profit, but should he be prosecuted for organised crime? Or what if Bjorn was in fact *Abokar, a naturalised Somali in Germany, who specialises in helping people from his community back home to reach safety by breaking the law? And what about Danny and John, British truck drivers who are turning a pretty penny picking up migrants in Rotterdam's port and offering them a place in the back of their lorry to the UK for €1,500 a pop? Moreover, what may start as 'trying to help' might turn into smuggling over time, particularly when demand is high and risks are increasing.

In the spectrum of the migrant-smuggling industry, there are many shades of grey: it is not only the person who facilitates the actual illicit crossing who is a smuggler. There are a myriad of people with direct and ancillary roles in facilitating the smuggling of migrants—there are those who offer accommodation to migrants knowing the crime they will commit, those who sell life jackets (both real and fake) knowing the risk that the migrants will take; there are the security guards who intimidate and coerce migrants onto boats or trucks; there are the money holders and launderers; the document 'borrowers' and counterfeiters. Which of these deserves to be labelled a smuggler and prosecuted for organised crime? Many of the characters you will meet in this book are migrants themselves, who, having run out of money after paying smugglers for their own passage and having no opportunities to work in Europe, replenish their funds by seeking employment in the very industry that helped them to move.

Furthermore, it is not as if the 'smuggling industry' is an established, homogeneous entity with a clearly defined structure. Instead, as we will see, it is a wide spectrum of actors; a loose network of associates and alliances that form, dissipate and re-form around specific routes, flows and opportunities. It draws upon the expertise of criminal specialists, counterfeiters and money launderers, for example, and thrives along established trafficking routes for other commodities, where paths of corruption have already been paved. There is significant overlap between groups smuggling migrants towards and into Europe in the present crisis and groups previously involved in drug trafficking, gun running and human trafficking for sexual and labour exploitation.

It is only recently, however, that human smuggling within and towards Europe alone has become profitable enough for the formation of the kind of criminal enterprises that would exist and endure over time. Between 2013 and 2016, the number of migrants and asylum seekers trying to penetrate into Europe increased by 1,500 per cent, quickly making it one of the largest illegal market opportunities in recent history.

The Business Model of Human Smuggling

*Adnan and *Nidal sit at an outdoor bar, passing the evening getting drunk on Efes, a Turkish Pilsner brewed in Izmir but consumed throughout Turkey. Both men, who hail from Aleppo, in northern Syria, say they lost everything to the war, including most of their families. Adnan says that over the course of several weeks his parents and siblings were killed by the indiscriminate use of barrel bombs issued by the Assad regime. Nidal says he lost his father and his sister to a blast that took place when ISIS rebels first moved in on the city, but he doesn't know who exactly is responsible for their deaths.

'Daesh … very bad,' says Adnan in broken English, referring to ISIS by its common name in Arabic. 'Cigarette … Cigarette …,' he says, waving a pack of Marlboro Reds. 'Cigarette … No!' he continues, widening his eyes and making a throat-slitting gesture with his thumb. 'Alcohol', he continues, this time raising his bottle of Efes; 'No!' he says, once again making the gesture to slit his throat.

Both men take turns recounting the horrors of being caught between the Assad regime and rebel groups. Their lives are filled with worry, the baseline of which is concentrated on the few remaining family members whom they left behind. But on this serene evening in early September 2015 their most pressing concern is the fact that they are running out of money.

SMUGGLERS INC.

Adnan and Nidal flew to Izmir from the Turkish city of Gaziantep. They used a smuggler who went by the alias of 'Ronaldo', in reference to the Portuguese football star who plays for the globally popular Spanish team Real Madrid. Ronaldo came with a good referral from a trusted friend who was already in Europe. After a string of phone calls and meetings they gave $1,500 each to an associate of Ronaldo, who gave them his phone number and told them to be ready to leave at 1 a.m. and to meet him at Hatuniye Park.

Realisation of their naivety washed over Adnan and Nidal as they waited for a man who would never arrive. They called their interlocutor dozens of times over the course of several days, and it was only when they were able to find one of the brokers with whom they had interacted days before, that they learned that the person who had taken their money had skipped town.

According to Adnan and Nidal, the person they had paid was a low-level recruiter within Ronaldo's smuggling network, not authorised to collect money on his behalf. 'They told us that he was also refugee,' Nidal explains. 'He has left for Greece with our money.'

The interlocutor told them that Ronaldo—concerned about protecting his own reputation—would offer them passage on a wooden boat with fewer passengers for only $500 each, a package for which he would usually charge as much as $3,000 per passenger.

With only $700 in cash between the two of them, Adnan and Nidal could not take him up on the offer, though they were still considering it. Over beers, they vacillate between trying to find a new smuggler altogether, or whether to trust the men who purportedly work under Ronaldo one more time.

It may be that continuing with Ronaldo means that they will secure passage on a safer boat to Greece at a discount price. Or it could be that they are throwing good money after bad, setting themselves up to be cheated out of $500 more. Either way, the decision will have to wait until they can arrange to have friends or family in Europe and the Middle East send money to Izmir.

Every day in Izmir there are thousands of Adnans and Nidals handing over hundreds, thousands, and sometimes tens of thousands of dollars to someone who they believe can help them get to Europe. The same goes for places such as Bodrum and Istanbul. As well as Beirut and

Amman. And Cairo and Alexandria. And Kabul and Herat. And Khartoum and Asmara. And Lahore and Islamabad. And Baghdad and Erbil. And Tehran and Ankara. And Agadez and Tripoli. And Dakar and Port Harcourt. And Accra and Douala. And Lesbos and Athens. And Sofia and Belgrade. And Vienna, Munich, Hamburg and Calais.

Taken together, the tens of millions of dollars that change hands daily in cities around the world comprise a multi-billion-dollar human-smuggling industry.

* * *

Human smuggling is quintessentially a business, albeit a criminal one, and should be understood as part of a market which provides a service to those wishing to cross borders illegally. As with all markets, there are many different types of business models being employed, from the sophisticated and professional 'firms' that function almost as a travel agent would in the legitimate economy, to the mass-market bargain-basement-style traders, to smaller players and 'mom and pop shops' that can only provide a limited range of services to a small number of clients. It is an industry that operates at multiple levels, regulated by supply and demand, and constrained only by the depths of a migrant's pocket. Furthermore, it is an industry in which all actors can make money, including the migrant himself.[5]

In 1997 academics John Salt and Jeremy Stein were the first to develop a model that treated migrant smuggling as international business.[6] In order to better understand how the business is organised, Salt and Stein's model examined the structure and operations inherent in every transnational migrant-smuggling network. They conceptualised human smuggling as a system with inputs (the migrants) and outputs (the act of inserting a migrant into some element of the labour market or society of the destination country).

These inputs were linked together by the business processes of the smugglers, who take on specific roles, such as planning the smuggling operations, gathering information, financing the movement, and carrying out a 'set of specific technical and operational tasks', including 'provision of adequate financing, transport, information, documentation and forged documents'.[7]

Salt and Stein divided the trafficking process into three stages: mobilisation and recruitment in origin countries; transportation from origin to destination countries; and insertion and integration into destination countries.

While Salt and Stein's model did not dictate any particular size of operation, applying equally well to both large- and small-scale smuggling operations, the key distinction that they did draw was between the level of organisation. That is, how larger trafficking organisations, marked by central planning and management structures, may encompass all aspects of the model while other, smaller, groups may operate in only part of the system.

Salt and Stein's initial work spawned a whole series of ethnographic studies examining smuggling situations in different parts of the world, which revolved around the notion of the 'migration industry' and its 'professionalisation'. In these analyses migrants are seen as commodities and those who aid them are called smugglers, portrayed as illegal entrepreneurs whose businesses are structured in a variety of ways, from highly hierarchical to loose and opportunistic networks. The nature of the business model that develops is highly context-specific, and can change depending on the environment in which they are working. As these case studies have shown, and the current migrant crisis has certainly reinforced, smuggling networks are highly adaptable, capable of evolving and learning from previous mistakes. They form and dissolve operational alliances quickly, and are capable of making fundamental shifts in their conceptual business paradigm.[8]

The way in which certain smuggling networks are organised differs from place to place, depending on the size of demand and the groups controlling the market, including the roles and policies employed by the state. The nature of the market may also change significantly over time. As the subsequent chapters will demonstrate, what may start out as a disorganised and loose, informal network of opportunists can consolidate and transform into an established and highly controlled market dominated by a small number of long-standing and professional service providers.

Functionally, however, the smuggling industry organises itself along a spectrum that is defined predominantly by the reach and the level of services that each individual 'firm' can offer.

On one end of the spectrum are the highly structured criminal organisations that can control the entire smuggling process from recruitment and transportation to insertion at the destination. They can provide the full set of services needed along a migration journey, which may include: the procurement of visas, forged documents and papers, safe houses and local transportation. They will maintain a direct relationship with corrupt officials who will smooth the way and guarantee safe passage. Some smugglers offer assistance with settling in a final destination, finding housing and jobs for their clients. To offer 'full-package' smuggling solutions, these smugglers need access to a range of services with various specialisations. It is in their interest to keep service providers at a distance from one another and to rotate them relatively frequently, which ensures that none takes over the business, despite the relatively high entry barriers to do so.[9]

For migrants, this 'full-package' solution is an expensive option, as such services often cost several thousand euros per person, dependent on the journey. A large portion of the fee is typically required in advance, paid to an intermediary who will hold it in escrow throughout the voyage, disbursing payouts in stages as each leg of the trip is completed.

Due to the nature of full-package services, only relatively large, sophisticated and well-established smuggling groups can offer such migration solutions. The complex coordination of a range of specialised services cannot be easily or reliably procured on an ad hoc basis. It also requires a degree of funding capital, as procuring the necessary services, arranging transport and paying bribes mean that the smuggler bears a significant financial risk up front.

As an example, let us take Ahmed, the Syrian refugee we introduced in the introduction of this book. He reached an agreement with his smuggler to transport him and his family from Beirut to Stockholm for $36,000. Once this contract was agreed, the money was deposited with a mutually agreed third party who held it until the journey was complete. If the journey had been unsuccessful, it would have been returned to Ahmed, or to another pre-agreed recipient. However, while this money sat untouched, the smuggler had to cover considerable expense to make the journey happen.

The smuggler needed to pay the supplier of the new fake passports, and the forger to ink in the visa stamps. He had to pay for drivers, a safe house and for plane tickets. Anyone who flies internationally will have to show their passport three times. That means in cases where the fraudulent or fake travel documents are not absolutely indistinguishable from real ones, up to three people will need bribing to get through the system and onto the plane, and another one upon arrival.

Before smugglers receive any money themselves, an estimated 50 per cent or more of the money paid as part of 'full-package' arrangements is dispersed around the network of people involved in making the scheme work. Thus Ahmed's smuggler stood to lose $18,000 in investments before he could hope to receive what remained of his $36,000 fee, even after the money holder had taken his cut.[10]

The number of groups able to offer such services is limited. In smaller cities it may be a single individual; in bigger hubs, where the potential migrant pool is larger, more consistent and with access to financial resources, a few smugglers of this nature might be available.

In fact, the offer of full-package smuggling services can be surprisingly brazen. Across the developing world, in almost all major cities you can find small offices that look like travel agents, replete with posters and signs, literally advertising the price of Schengen visas or migration to specific destinations in Europe, the Gulf or North America. In some cases genuine travel agents are used as fronts for full-package smuggling services—in Lebanon, for example, along the Damascus–Beirut highway, or the road that comes down from the Syrian border and Tripoli in the north,[11] you can see enormous billboards advertising 'Cruises to the Greek Islands: No Visa Required', 5 metres high, 15 metres wide.

Smugglers offering the full package also advertise on the internet and through social media. On a private Facebook page, 'Air Travel to Europe', a smuggler promised that he could take a family 'away from the sea and the dangers of travelling by it' and offered direct flights for €12,000 to Norway, Sweden and Finland or for €11,000 to Germany, the Netherlands, Belgium, Denmark, Austria and Switzerland. The smuggler promised that he could provide passports for all refugees except 'veiled women' or children under the age of eighteen.[12] On the Arabic-language Facebook group 'Group for Smuggling Routes by Land, Sea, and Air', a number of different users offered limited services such as 'tourist apartments in Istanbul' with 'daily' as well as 'monthly' discounts.[13]

The act of recruitment is very much a two-way street. It may be that an aspiring migrant seeks out a smuggler, but, particularly in key hubs or fertile recruitment grounds, smugglers may also offer their services quite actively in search of clients. Like all negotiations, the balance of power between the smuggler and the migrant is critically important to how favourable the final deal will be for either of them.

On their side of the negotiating table, migrants typically have only two main points of leverage with which to bargain with a potential smuggler. The first, of course, is the amount that they can pay; the second is their capacity to enhance or damage the smuggler's reputation. For both of these reasons, Syrian migrants have proven to have more bargaining power than perhaps any migrant group in history. As a middle-income country, not only did the average Syrian have a far higher disposable income than the typical migrant seeking a smuggler, but each individual Syrian had the benefit of bargaining knowing that there were 4 million displaced behind him—a rich client pool that any smuggler would be desperate to access. Information on smugglers' performance, successes and failures can be communicated quickly between migrants and their communities through social media and online message boards, and unfavourable reviews have been threatened to negotiate a better deal.

To secure a migrant as a client, smugglers use a number of points of negotiation, of which the two most important are trust and price, and typically in that order. A good reputation for reliability and success is critically important in the industry, and once established it is a highly influential marketing tool. Migrants in Afghanistan, for example, will almost never use a smuggler with no reputation, but once that reputation is established all the men from an entire village will move along the same route using the same smuggler, eschewing competitors even if they promise a better price.[14]

As building a reputation as a reliable and successful smuggler is important, given the sums of money involved, full-package smugglers often use testimonials or referrals from successful migrants to secure new clients. Many of the smugglers we spoke to in Turkey, for example, were quick, eager and proud to have us listen to WhatsApp recordings from grateful clients reporting on their safe arrivals.

Another aspect of gaining trust depends partially on how a smuggler behaves with prospective clients, and what bonds he can create with the migrant. Part of the role of the smuggler, as described in the previous chapter, is to assist migrants socially and culturally in a place where they feel at risk or alien. Offering familiarity is a powerful confidence builder. Some particularly client-orientated services offer helplines of support for migrants in different countries, or provide travel advice down to the smallest detail, from locations of hotels and banks to advice about clothing and food. Regarding the last of these, one smuggler posted some information regarding Belgrade and said that, in the words of an internet translation function, Serbia is 'even cheaper [than] Turkey in green fruit and canned stuff and junk food'.[15]

But comparatively few migrants can afford the full package. Most move by less luxurious and less secure services; negotiating their voyage from place to place, leg by leg, with a variety of operators who function as a loose network, passing migrants hand to hand. This 'pay-as-you-go' methodology has characterised the vast majority of the journeys to Europe.[16]

Rather than operating as a formal smuggling operation, these networks function as a relay-race, with local groups facilitating movement within a sub-region or immediately contiguous sub-regions passing migrants off to the next group. They thrive in geographical regions where movement is relatively free and where borders are porous and can be crossed without documentation. For these types of networks, their level of sophistication and criminality will be commensurate to the costs and complexity of smuggling along that route, the level of risk and the scale of demand from prospective migrants.

Despite this model's relatively ad hoc nature, it still requires some degree of skill on the part of smugglers. These networks are made up of actors with specialised, often highly localised knowledge and experience. They might be uniquely able to chart a specific terrain, for example, as in the case of nomadic tribes that facilitate smuggling across the Sahara. Or they might be able to handle and navigate boats at sea. In some cases they can bridge languages or cultures in two regions and can operate and transact in both environments, perhaps because they speak two or more local languages, or because they belong to a diaspora group that spans several countries. In many cases they have honed their skills over the course of decades of moving other commodities, both licit and illicit.

Unlike in the hierarchical models of smuggling services, these networks have no controlling figurehead. Instead, groups work along predominantly ethnic lines and, to the extent that they can be considered part of the same organisation, form loose networks of associates. While they may establish cooperative working relationships, these are usually transactional rather than collaborative enterprises. People playing different roles and functions in the network are mutually accepted, but they may disperse and re-form in different combinations with other actors depending on the transaction involved. This type of smuggling market is organised along the 'supermarket principle': high volume with relatively low costs, high turnover, mass movement and often a high failure rate at border crossings, which in some cases leads to repeated attempts by migrants to cross.

The stratification between those travelling on the full-package options, with air-travel arrangements, and those travelling on a leg-by-leg basis happens early in the smuggling process and is consistent across all aspects of the migrant–smuggler relationship. Research undertaken in Istanbul, a city that functions as a major smuggling hub and where all types of smuggling services and border crossings can be negotiated, showed clearly the 'price–performance' relationship for those travelling by land or by sea. For those who have arranged to enter Europe by air, smugglers regularly offer apartments to individual clients or their families. For those paying for less expensive overland and sea packages, smugglers consolidate their clients in groups of thirty to forty people in apartments and safe houses, who are usually then moved together, as a group, to the next location in their journey.[17]

The distinction between the bespoke high end and what is essentially the 'cattle-class' mass movement emphasises the economies of scale that the smugglers are seeking to exploit. To quote a particularly vivid description of such an enterprise in West Africa:

> The whole range of smuggling professionals, from transport touts and various part-timers at the lower level, to professional transporters and high-level brokers, exists to service (or exploit) the basic needs of migrants. Migrants are considered to be like cattle heading to new pastures, in the sense that they can be milked throughout the length of a journey; while some migrants may die along the way, the important thing for those who make money from them is to maintain the flow.[18]

More importantly, key players often coalesce at certain hubs of a migration journey, which may include major capitals, or at strategic nodes such as port cities, specific border crossing points or major areas of recruitment such as refugee camps. But those who actually transport or guide the migrants across can be hired, or essentially subcontracted, from a vast contact list of part-timers and specialists as needed. These individuals could be drawn from the local pool of opportunists or criminals, or just members of the local community. A driver who works on a contract basis for the United Nations High Commissioner for Refugees (UNHCR) might do exactly the same for a local smuggling network.

Furthermore, the more dynamic the smuggling market (i.e. the larger the flow of migrants transiting through), the more likely it is that members of the community will be drawn into enabling migrant smuggling or providing services to migrants. Therefore, unlike in hierarchical, full-package models, where a migrant will encounter and engage with people who are predominantly from the same ethnicity as the smuggler with whom he made his contract (which in turn is likely to have been a similar ethnicity to himself—i.e. Arab migrants will work predominantly with Arab smugglers; West Africans with West African smugglers, etc.), those using the pay-as-you-go model, in which each leg is negotiated separately, are far more likely to deal with local operators.

With this relatively fluid system of networks and subcontracting, the recruiters and managers of the smuggling networks have far less control over how their 'clients' are treated once they move beyond their control, and this can often sit at the heart of the abuse and brutality that migrants face on their journeys. In many of these models the interaction between migrant and smuggler does not rely on reputation and trust, as payments are made up front, and there is no damage done to the smuggler if the migrant fails to complete his journey. In a complex market with multiple low-level players competing and little regulation or control, there is little accountability to clients for the services provided, and the smugglers that we have spoken to largely absolve themselves of the hardships and crimes their clients may face during their journeys.[19]

The type of service and treatment that a migrant will receive is determined first and foremost by his available funds. To quote migration analyst Khalid Khoser:

> Firstly, smuggling is a business. Smugglers will deliver a service that suits the depth of your pocket. If you cannot afford to go to the USA, they will

take you to Australia. If you cannot afford to fly, which is the safest way of travelling, they will make it cheaper and will do a combination of flight and boat. This is a business. You are a customer and they will find a way to get your money. If you are poor, don't worry, they will find a way to make it work.[20]

The price is set by a combination of factors and prevailing microeconomic conditions. The most comprehensive attempt to assess the cost of migrant smuggling from a worldwide perspective was done in 2005 by Melanie Petros for the International Organisation on Migration (IOM). She found that there are five main determinants of the prices paid for smuggling: the distance travelled; the mode of transport; the number and characteristics of the people being moved; and the complexity of the service. The price increases when the services offered by smugglers exceeds simple transportation, but also includes the provision of forged documents, secure accommodation in certain cities, and advice on how to pass certain borders. In short, the price increases when the challenge of penetrating the border is higher, either because the migrant is at risk of detection, detention, physical attack (in a conflict zone, or in an area hostile to migrants, for example) or when the terrain itself is physically challenging (a desert or a sea).[21]

For the same reasons, prices can also fall. A migrant interviewed for an EU study reported that during a football championship more than 1,000 migrants were smuggled from Turkey to Greece for a significantly reduced price—€900 instead of the usual range of €2,000 or more, 'because the policemen were watching the game'.[22]

There is one dynamic at play in the migrant-smuggling industry, which we have already alluded to, which highlights the shortcomings of viewing migrant-smuggling networks purely as 'business models'. That is, it is important to acknowledge the extent to which a migrant's personal connections have an influence over his migration experience. Emma Herman has argued that migrant smuggling should be seen as a 'family business' because of the 'overriding significance for most migrants of existing networks of friends, relatives, and acquaintances when undertaking the journey'.[23]

Consequently as smuggling networks establish and entrench themselves over time, they largely end up organising themselves along ethnic or linguistic lines. In West African countries, where the levels of mobility are very high and there is a long history of smuggling all manner of licit and illicit goods, the recruiter might literally be part of the extended family, and is referred to as 'uncle' or 'auntie'. They are often well-known members of the community and everyone has their mobile phone number. Most sub-Saharan Africans would rarely, if ever, be more than one phone call away from a smuggler who could set them on a migration journey.

Successful migrants enable the journeys of future migrants. Some of this is purely logistical. Earlier migrants tell prospective migrants of opportunities, provide transportation and arrange initial accommodation and employment. Knowledge of and communication with earlier migrants is the most popular motivation for and means of organising a migrant journey—a dynamic that has been highlighted by a number of studies with migrants over time and in various locations.[24] Migrants are advised and encouraged to migrate by the diaspora in other places, who may fund trips for other family or community members. Over time a culture of migration establishes itself, and migration becomes a social norm or even a modern rite of passage in which staying at home is associated with failure and a lack of ambition.[25]

Despite often being the characteristic most highlighted, exploitation and abuse is by no means an intrinsic part of the smuggling industry. As Kyle and Scarcelli observed in their research that looked specifically at the triggers of violence in the smuggling industry, smugglers run along a spectrum, from those who are completely benign, almost altruistic, in providing their services on one end, to criminal groups and networks who engage in other forms of illicit trafficking and trade, including in drugs, arms, counterfeit goods or violent extortion.[26] In communities where migration has become part of the culture, smugglers can be revered and respected figures. They are the saints and saviours who bring opportunities when none others exist. There is a legendary story of a Chinese smuggler, the 'Mother of All Snakeheads', who helped to smuggle thousands of Chinese families into the United States. The 'coxers' of West Africa are traditional figures in society and also highly respected.[27] By most definitions Oskar Schindler, the infamous Nazi who saved 1,200 Jews during the Holocaust, would also be considered a smuggler.

One thing that should not be overlooked in any discussion about the migrant-smuggling industry, regardless of the form it takes, is the degree of agency and control that the migrant has over his journey. While it may be beneficial or politically expedient to portray the migrant as a victim and the smuggler as a cruel, exploitative controller, this is a largely disingenuous characterisation. Migrants the world over are entering voluntarily into transactional relationships with their smugglers, relationships that should benefit everyone involved. Whether it is for refugees seeking to escape war, or a migrant moving predominantly in search of livelihood opportunities, smuggling is fundamentally an economic process, and everyone in the industry profits.[28] It is a calculated, generational investment on the part of migrants, their families, the smugglers, and even the societies and economies of the countries they leave from, transit across, and go to.

For each migrant and his family, using a smuggler to move irregularly, even when they pay thousands of dollars for the privilege, is a decision that all evidence suggests will pay dividends over the medium to long term, outweighing the hardship they might endure in the short term. Migrants knowingly enter into relationships with smugglers that will lock them into quasi-indentured servitude for months or even years. In Nigeria, for example, smugglers often run an established business that blurs with human trafficking, where the cost of a migrant's passage to North Africa, Europe or the Gulf will be met in exchange for an agreed number of years of bonded labour, domestic service or prostitution for women. In his book on Nigerian organised crime, Stephen Ellis describes a three-decade-long arrangement in Edo State, where women knowingly subscribe to a bond of €50,000 so as to be taken to Italy as sex workers, an industry that employs 20,000 to 30,000 Nigerian women. Approximately 5,000 sexual encounters later, a woman's bond will be paid and the profits will allow her to remain in Italy, or return wealthy and able to establish her own business or brothel back home.[29] It may look like exploitation or abuse to our eyes, but for certain communities, Ellis points out, it is an accepted and unstigmatised livelihood choice for the women of that society.

The likely return on investment for migrating is borne out in the numbers, and in part explains why the governments of source countries have little incentive to stem the flow of migrants abroad. For many communities, remittances (money that migrants living and working abroad send home to support their families) are a lifeline. For 2015 the World Bank estimated that $440 billion was remitted, an amount estimated to increase to a total of $610 billion in 2016.[30] These figures are more than double the levels of overseas development assistance (ODA), a measure of support that has been in decline for a decade. While the literature on the level of development impact of remittances for nations as a whole is contested,[31] there is little doubt that for the immediate families of migrants, remittances can prove an important tool in boosting household incomes, investing in health and education services for other members of the family, and increasing opportunities for other members to move overseas at a later date.

Thus, in viewing human smuggling as a business, it must be accepted that the industry is demand driven. Smugglers may try to compete to attract new clientele and to increase demand through incentives or false promises, but fundamentally these are consensual relationships in which the migrant is a willing partner, and the nature of the smuggling industry shapes itself around the scale and purchasing power of its clients.

Following on from this, what is also important to understand—and this should be intuitive—is that the demand for smuggler services increases as the challenges to migration increase. Where there are low barriers for migrants to overcome, they have little need for smugglers. But where barriers are high, so too is the demand for smugglers, and, as we saw in the case of Waseem at the beginning of this chapter, picking the right smuggler is essential.

Similarly, there are far fewer players in a challenging market, and the price that they can command is high. The opportunists and ad hoc smugglers fall away, leaving only the most professional, expensive, and arguably the most criminal actors to remain. They are the criminals with the best networks of corruption, and they are proficient at delivering threats, carrying out extortion and executing violence.

3

STRUCTURE AND DESIGN

In the city of Mytilene, on the Greek island of Lesbos, Hafiz and three of his friends from Afghanistan take turns posing for the camera. They start out with a series of tightly cropped group 'selfies', then transition into individual poses in front of the harbour. The jubilant photo-shoot ends as a slow drizzle sets in. They take shelter at a café normally patronised by tourists and local university students, and use the free wireless internet to post pictures to Facebook and send messages back home.

Hafiz and his friends are ecstatic, not only because they made it to Greece, but because they have more than enough money to reach Sweden, their desired destination. Only six days earlier they were broke and adrift in north-eastern Iran. They didn't have enough money to make it to Europe, and they had collectively ruled out returning to Afghanistan as soon as they left Herat.

'God is great,' Hafiz tells me. 'We could not have done this without God.'

Hafiz and his cohort left Herat with enough cash on hand to make it to Europe. Their first step was to pay a smuggler $500 per person to sneak across the Afghan–Iranian border, and another smuggler $500 to travel through Iran. They spent three days travelling across Iran, spending two nights in safe houses along the way. They changed vehicles several times throughout the trip, with different sets of drivers and handlers taking over each time.

When they arrived outside the north-west city of Urmia, their Iranian smugglers held them at gunpoint and demanded $1,500 each. With little choice but to hand over the cash, the group found themselves lingering in north-western Iran illegally without enough money to make it to Europe.

'They are bad people,' Hafiz says of his Iranian smugglers. 'They know we suffer and they do not care.'

According to Hafiz, their group was able stay at an inexpensive guest house while they searched for a trader in the market who could facilitate a money transfer from Herat to Urmia. Since many of the merchants in Urmia had contacts in Afghanistan, they were able to eventually find someone with connections in Herat. They arranged to have their middle-class families, who were supporting and funding their migration to Europe, transfer $15,000 in total to be spread across the four of them. Within forty-eight hours of running aground outside Urmia, Hafiz and his companions had the funds necessary to continue their journey.

They found a Turkish smuggler of Kurdish ethnicity who spoke Farsi, who agreed to take them over the Turkish border, across the country and into Greece, with lodging and meals provided, for $2,000.

Hafiz says they had no choice but to trust the smuggler they found in Urmia. 'We don't want to go back to Afghanistan,' he says. 'There is too much war and there are no jobs for Hazara. We want to go to university.'

Once they crossed into Turkey they were put on a string of buses and vans, with groups of other migrants from Afghanistan. This time their handlers were visibly armed, and made sure the migrants knew they were. 'I was so scared the whole time, but I had no choice. I can't go back to Afghanistan,' Hafiz repeats.

Hafiz isn't sure whether the guns were to keep the migrants at bay or a precaution in case they ran into Turkish authorities, but he believes that the latter was unlikely to happen, as they did not encounter any police officers during their entire trip.

According to Hafiz, he and about twenty other Afghans spent a night sleeping on the Turkish coast. In the early morning, three vans carrying 'Arabs and Africans' arrived. Their smugglers marched them towards the coast, where a rubber dinghy was waiting for them.

Hafiz says that they were around fifty in total, but he doesn't know for sure. What he can confirm is that everyone who was assembled on that shoreline ended up on the inflatable vessel. Those who refused were forcibly pushed onto the boat; those who put up a fight faced the barrel of a gun.

That was yesterday. Now, from the dry confines of a café in Lesbos, Hafiz and his friends might just be the happiest people on this island. They say they have almost $7,000 between them to get to Sweden, which, as of September 2015, was more than enough to make it that far. But if it doesn't work out, just reaching Germany will suffice.

'We want to study and work', Hafiz says, before adding the after-thought, 'and we want to be safe.'

As Hafiz tells the story of how they went from penniless in Iran to flush with cash in Greece, it becomes clear that regardless of whether or not divine intervention was responsible for their change in fortune, their miracle was delivered through a range of smuggler services and a global informal financial infrastructure that, when taken together, combined to bring them to safety.

* * *

Policymakers, law enforcement officials and the media often use the term 'smuggler' in a manner that obfuscates the mechanics of relatively complex operations, which rely on a number of people performing different roles and accessing a range of specialised services that increase in complexity depending on the sophistication of the service being provided.

As in the last chapter, the descriptions of the various actors and roles in the smuggling industry draws from a decade of different ethnographic studies of the way that the enterprise of human smuggling has been organised in various places and has evolved over time in relation to developments in technology and innovations within the industry.[1] While there are obviously variations and differences in modalities depending on the individual locality and context, the goal of this chapter is to provide a generic explanation of the way these different roles tend to fit together to ensure that a migrant is successfully smuggled from one place to another. In doing so, this chapter provides a structural framework by which to understand Part 2 of this book, which examines specific smuggling markets in places that have contributed to Europe's migration crisis.

While everyone from law-enforcement officials to journalists dream of criminal kingpins—masterminds of nefarious transnational operations—the reality is that these types of actors are few and far between, and are, in many cases, mythical. In fact, the organisers of sophisticated or large-scale smuggling enterprises are more likely to be businessmen from the travel industry who plan holidays for tourists during the day, and design bespoke journeys for migrants once the front door is locked. The boat smugglers packing ships full of people in Egypt may deal in export and import as a day job, but manage the human cargo on the side. In order to carry out their illicit activities, they typically have a background in cross-border trade, which already requires them to employ, contract and coordinate a whole host of people, bringing all the crucial components together at the right time. More often than not, the organiser will also be the main financial backer who stands to gain and lose the most money in the business.

The roles and responsibilities in a smuggling enterprise can broadly be divided into two categories: logisticians and specialists. The logisticians are the main crew: guides, drivers and skippers; spotters and messengers; enforcers and heavies responsible for discipline and security. The specialists are less likely to be permanent members of the team, but are called for as needed and paid according to the services that they provide. They are the escrow holders, money launderers and financiers; the counterfeiters and fraudsters; the fixers and corrupters who are either part of or closely connected to the institutions of the state. The specialists will be based in a hub town or a capital city and sell their services to many different types of criminal industries, from drug trafficking to corporate white-collar crime.

By contrast, the logisticians are generally your average citizen, pulled from the ranks of the underemployed and attracted to payrolls bigger than they could make in the legitimate economy. These functions are filled by all manner of characters, of every background, level of education and income. Often they may be migrants themselves. Bigger smuggling groups may comprise large teams of hundreds of people across multiple countries. Localised outfits who work as a network may only maintain a small dedicated crew, instead building alliances with other local groups to coordinate their operations.

STRUCTURE AND DESIGN

In on the Ground Floor

At the bottom of the pyramid, below the logisticians and specialists who make up the core of the business, are the brokers and recruiters. They are the first members of a network a migrant will meet, and the most visible faces of the industry. They are those who recruit potential migrants, and who will have the most interaction with a migrant throughout his journey. If anyone is going to travel with the migrants, it is the people operating at this level. If anyone is going to get arrested for smuggling, it is the recruiters and brokers on the street. In most cases they will not even belong to the smuggling networks, but work freelance with loose associations to handlers or fixers, who are an established part of the smuggling networks.

The recruiters and brokers are the used-car salesmen, the ambulance chasers of the industry. You will find them in every location in which potential migrants might be found. They lurk at bus stations and around the types of cheap hostels where migrants stay. They circle around refugee camps and slums, peddling promises and assurances. They hustle hard to drum up business and lock in migrants to travel with them. Like all salesmen, they put pressure on those who express tentative interest, insisting that the 'time to go is now', or that 'this opportunity won't come again'. To differentiate themselves from the plentiful competition, they make (false) promises for safe, swift transit, and offer guarantees that they cannot make good on later down the line. They also offer all kinds of ancillary services and benefits, such as safe accommodation and help finding work to pay for the trip. To offset the costs of accommodating migrants, recruiters sometimes contract them out for labour—occasionally fairly, with the migrant getting a wage and the recruiter taking a cut, but often exploitatively, with the migrant getting nothing for their work.

The brokers are almost always the only part of the smuggling ring who will work directly with the migrant on a one-to-one basis, and they tend to work predominantly within their own nationality or along ethno-linguistic lines. The ability to communicate is important, because that is how they build trust and sell their services. Whereas the rest of the actors in the business may never know the migrant's name—unless they have to forge a document with it—the broker will wheel and deal, calling the migrants not only by name, but as family. Prospective clients will be 'brother' or 'cousin', and the names of mutual friends, shared places and history will be invoked, whether they exist or not.

To attract their clients, brokers may offer special deals and group discounts, especially when they are nearing their quota of migrants, which will buy them a place on the convoy or a space on the boat. As they near the twenty, thirty or fifty that they need, they will start offering price incentives—bulk rates or last-minute deals. In the relatively free-flowing smuggling markets on the Libyan and Turkish coasts, we heard from many migrants that there was a group discount offered by smugglers as a standard deal: if you bring three (or four, or six, depending on the place) friends, you travel for free.[2]

Once recruiters have managed to reach the critical number of migrants needed, they contact the transporters to arrange for the next leg of the journey. Effective recruiters and brokers will have formed durable partnerships with those above them in the migrant-smuggling hierarchy, and may well have detailed agreements on specific responsibilities and how profits are shared.

Migrants pay their fee in cash in full to the brokers, who use it to cover costs of accommodation and security, as well as to pay the transporters for the migrants' onward passage. The faster that recruiters can reach the needed critical number, the fewer running costs they have, and thus the greater their profits. Recruiters thus have every incentive to mobilise as many migrants as they can in the shortest time, hence the discounts. If a recruiter has been efficient, he can credibly realise up to half of the total fee paid by the migrant, with the rest going to other actors higher up the pyramid.

If a broker is arrested, killed, or just grows disenchanted and leaves the industry, there are hundreds, if not thousands, ready and able to take his place. Policies that target recruiters and brokers, therefore, are unlikely to have any impact on the smuggling market. They are completely disposable and totally replaceable.

The Logisticians

Logisticians are the centre of every successful smuggling operation.

The obvious first set of logisticians are those involved in transportation. Most of the smuggling rings will have a handful of people responsible for coordinating and procuring transport, be it buses, boats, cars, yachts, jet-skis or planes. And since transportation is one the largest financial outlays of the smuggling enterprise, it is an important job typically held by someone close to the organiser, if not the organiser himself.

Another person pivotal to the transportation team is he who recruits, coordinates and pays the myriad of drivers, skippers and crewmen. Even though the drivers are at the bottom of the pyramid, and perhaps have little information or strategic role to play in the smuggling operation as a whole, they are at the front line of the industry, taking on significant risks (of being arrested by law enforcement, or of being attacked by rival groups), and they are ultimately responsible for whether an individual journey will succeed or fail. In some cases they require specialised knowledge—the drivers charting the desert path across the Sahara must know how to drive in the desert and be familiar with the terrain; crewing a yacht or a boat requires someone with navigational and sailing skills. Therefore, these individuals are often recruited from the local communities through which the group is transiting. While an individual driver is a low-level operative in most smuggling operations, nonetheless each one needs to be reliable and trustworthy. Drivers are not only the carriers of the merchandise, they need to be relied upon to execute complex, time-sensitive and risky handover processes. For example, if it has been arranged that border-control guards will be busy for an agreed hour to allow a van full of refugees to be handed over from one group to another on the border between Hungary and Austria, then the driver needs to ensure that he gets to the right place at the right time, no matter what.

The tragic discovery of the decomposing bodies of seventy migrants in a truck in Austria in August 2015[3] demonstrates what happens when something goes wrong with the transporters. In an effort to meet the sudden surge in demand along the Balkan route that occurred during that period, a smuggling group went on a frantic recruitment drive, bringing on additional drivers and facilitators and using people who were untested. In this case, the driver proved the 'weak link' in a new smuggling gang led by a Bulgarian organised crime group seeking to meet the increased demand to cross the Balkans. The migrants were estimated to have survived only half way through the six-hour journey from Hungary to Austria in a refrigerated meat lorry. When the driver discovered that the people in the back had died of asphyxiation on the way, he left the vehicle and absconded back to Hungary. A group of that size would easily have been worth $100,000 to a smuggling network, not a prize any criminal would intentionally abandon or jeopardise, especially given the possibility for referrals to other migrants looking for similar services.[4]

Therefore, the person tasked with selecting drivers and skippers and ensuring that they are briefed is one of the most important actors in the entire enterprise. Again, he will be a trusted member of the inner circle, with a relatively large amount of information about how the various operations work. If this member of the team makes a mistake, the whole operation will lose a lot of money. If he turns over information to the police or to rival networks, the entire organisation might be compromised.

The next group of logisticians are the intelligence gatherers: the informers and the spotters who serve as the eyes and ears of the industry. The migrant crisis in Europe has highlighted how incredibly knowledgeable the smuggling industry has become, and how finely tuned it is to even the slightest changes in European policy. Some of the most sustained smuggling businesses historically—those in Mexico or China bringing migrants to the United States, for example—maintain a permanent core group of informers who are responsible for managing the flow of information throughout sophisticated international communication systems. At this level, the job of the informant is to systematically gather information on everything from immigration policies, to transit procedures, to new regulations, to changes in asylum systems, to the activities of law enforcement, to patterns of border enforcement. They search incessantly for loopholes and weak spots. The Swedes can't test the age of asylum seekers? Excellent, then every migrant is a minor, whether aged thirteen or thirty.[5]

The capacities of informants to gather and disseminate knowledge across a vast network of smugglers and associates has been greatly enhanced by modern communication technology. Not only can organisers easily run a network of informants in all destination and transit states, coordinating them by using WhatsApp, Telegram, Facebook messenger, or any of the other messaging programmes, they can use these same applications to share relevant information with higher-level operatives and logisticians along the route. Communication among migrants, between migrants and smugglers, and between everyone in the migrant smuggling network, is instantaneous.

Social media has become critically important to smuggling operations, as they allow for faster communication between the different actors, which has contributed to networks being able to operate more flexibly and to easily adapt to new circumstances. Did immigration officials just arrest a corrupt associate minutes before a group of migrants was due to be winked through? No problem. A lower-level spotter strategically recruited as cleaning staff at the airport can communicate that instantly and cryptically with a touch of a button. And who these days looks askance at someone fiddling with their phone in the corner of the room?

Finally, the last set of actors that fall into the category of logisticians is made up of the heavies, the enforcers and the security guards—an archetypal figure in all organised crime groups. Any criminal or illicit enterprise will need protection for its activities, and this is achieved in two ways, either through financial incentives (bribes) or through violence or the threat of violence.[6]

Security is used to ensure that smugglers are not harassed or prosecuted by the state or threatened by rival gangs. It is also employed to maintain loyalty and internal compliance within the group, as well as to keep suppliers, service providers and even clients in line. As with the other sets of logisticians, the security group will also need someone whose responsibility it is to procure weapons without falling foul of the law. In many places where smuggling is prevalent, arms and violence are already commonplace, and it is not hard to recruit young men who are prepared to wield a gun, a stick or even a wire clothes-hanger to beat, whip and threaten a migrant to keep them in line. Armed protection is needed to guard safe houses filled with migrants and to accompany convoys and intimidate opposition, whether it comes in the form of law enforcement or rival groups.

Some smuggling enterprises move with minimal violence; others, with excessive amounts. Kyle and Scarcelli argue that there are three factors that determine the levels of violence: firstly, the nature of the market for smuggling services within a country as it is shaped or created by state policies; secondly, the features of the individual smuggling organisations, including specific routes and strategies; and finally, how the contracts are set up between the smuggler and the migrant, how the fee will be paid, and the level of enforcement required to honour that contract.[7]

In short, what their analysis concludes, confirmed by our own case studies and observations within the context of the current crisis, is that where there is already a prevalence of violence, security will be required to protect the migrants as assets. In such cases market competition may turn violent, as it is has done in the stretch from Niger to Libya. Where the level of enforcement and controls are increased by the state, the vulnerability of migrants is exacerbated, and the likelihood that smugglers can exploit and enact violence on their migrants also increases.

Taken together, these different sub-groups form the logistical core of the smuggling industry. As discussed in the previous chapter, they can range from relatively benign small groups, the family-business style of smuggling, to vicious armed groups and criminal networks who have experience in cross-border trafficking.

Around this core can gather a range of people in the community who provide additional services, knowingly or unknowingly, to support the migrant industry: the hoteliers and landlords who allow smugglers to rent rooms to house an ever-revolving clientele; the local women who deliver food to safe houses to feed the migrants held inside; the shopkeepers selling life jackets, waterproof bags and sim cards to migrants before the boat, or bottles of water and dry clothes just after.

One linchpin of the industry, which sits ambiguously within the nexus of core logisticians and specialists, as well as on the periphery, are the corrupt and the corruptors. To varying degrees corruption facilitates all aspects of a smuggling operation. It can take place at relatively low levels in the form of a border guard paid to let people cross without documentation, or an immigration official who sells blank passports. But it can also happen at higher levels, such as security officials receiving a salary in exchange for intelligence or justice officials being paid to ensure that specific cases are dismissed.

Some of the more sophisticated smuggling groups have dedicated 'corruptors', members of the enterprise who have cultivated specific relationships that enable corrupt practices. They are often in a position of authority themselves, which blurs the lines between state and criminal enterprises. In some smuggling cases the corruptor may be the controller. In all likelihood, however, it is more often that numerous corruptors are needed to secure routes to a final destination. Even at the lowest levels, if the target is only a border guard or local policeman, the ability to corrupt is usually not as straightforward as just throwing money at people. It requires gentle, subtle relationship-building before an overture can be made, and is very much helped by local knowledge and local contacts, which is why it is rare for one person to have the connections and relationships sufficient to corrupt everyone along a transnational journey.

A smuggling operation does not begin until a pathway of corruption has been secured along the entire route—and in fact it is far more likely that routes are adapted according to where corrupt pathways exist, rather than the other way around. For example, a smuggling ring may not be able to offer services to all destinations in Europe if they do not have corruption networks in each destination. These networks take time to develop and must be constantly refreshed and revitalised. When a corrupt contact is detected or is deemed no longer reliable, the smugglers have moved on by the time authorities can take action.

The corrupt public officials themselves can play a key role in facilitating and supporting an environment conducive to the smuggling industry. Migrant smugglers often pay government officials to obtain travel documents for their customers. Immigration and law-enforcement officials in many countries have been caught accepting bribes to enable migrants to enter and exit countries illegally. Either individually or collectively, these officials protect and enable the industry by lending their position, status and privileges to smugglers.

But government and security officials are far from the only ones leveraging their status to make a buck in the smuggling industry. As the next section will demonstrate, wherever there is a core group of smugglers, there is a veritable cottage industry of those seeking to profit from the investments migrants are making in seeking a new life and a better future.

Moving Money

Human smuggling is a transnational crime, and accordingly it makes use of a global criminal infrastructure that underpins grey markets and black economies of all forms. Certain specialists operate by selling their services to whichever groups are prepared to pay for them. These fall in two main categories: the informal money dealers and the counterfeiters.

The billions of dollars in profits to be made from smuggling migrants are underpinned by a complex nexus of financiers, escrow holders, money launderers and their intermediaries, who have developed sophisticated schemes without which the migrant-smuggling economy could not exist at its current size and scope.

In a muddy backstreet near the main outdoor market in Conakry in Guinea, an ethnic Fulani shop-owner named Abdoulaye* claims he can have money hand-delivered to just about any location between Guinea and Sudan within seventy-two hours. It is a bold claim for a man who lives in a city where ATMs are scarce and withdrawals are limited to small amounts of cash. Yet Abdoulaye's ability to partake in near-frictionless finance has nothing to do with bank accounts. It is made possible by the sprawling network of ethnic Fulani business owners spread across a vast swath of African territory.

If Abdoulaye does not know someone in the place where you want to send money, he knows someone who knows someone, and that person probably knows someone who knows the right guy. The same system works in reverse, which is why Abdoulaye often receives calls from Fulani businessman abroad looking to facilitate money transfers back home to Guinea.

If you want to send money to New York, Atlanta or Marseille, Abdoulaye has contacts within the Fulani diaspora who can make it happen. All he asks is a 1 per cent cut, which is a no-brainer, considering the anywhere from 5 per cent to 20 per cent Western Union, MoneyGram or a formal banking institution would take for the same transfer. For other cities in North America or Europe, Abdoulaye says he has to charge a bit more, only because he will have to reach outside his usual networks. Using more interlocutors with whom he might not share the unspoken trust that comes with common nationality or ethnic kinship means assuming more risk. The 3 per cent he recently charged someone to have money sent to Montreal, however, is still a better deal than using formal banking institutions.

An ethnic Hausa trader named Musa*, based in N'Djamena in Chad, boasts of being able to get money anywhere there are Hausa speakers, which is to say he and his intermediaries can move money quickly to far-flung locations spread across thousands of miles. He gives an example of a cousin who lives in the Central African Republic who wanted to conduct $10,000 worth of business with someone in Tripoli in Libya. For reasons that are better left unsaid, formal banking institutions were not an option, and no one liked the idea of transporting $10,000 in cash through southern Libya.

Musa knows someone in Tripoli, with whom he does business four times a year, invoicing him for $12,000 each time. He told his cousin that his business acquaintance in Libya could hand deliver the $10,000 to complete the business transaction on his behalf, in exchange for a 2 per cent commission. The next time his cousin is in town, Musa says, his cousin will pay him $10,000 plus $200 for the 2 per cent fee. If his cousin does not hand over the cash, Musa can reach out to his cousin's father and sort it out through him.

Musa's business partner in Tripoli agreed to complete the transfer in exchange for a 1 per cent surcharge and the understanding that they would settle up the debt the next time they do business. When the next quarter arrived, Musa sent him the standard invoice for $12,000, but with an unwritten agreement that his business partner would only pay $1,900, since Musa technically owes him the $11,000 (the $10,000 he fronted, and $100 more as a fee for fronting the money). This is international finance, trans-Sahara style.

On Acharnon Street in Athens, Syrians, Afghans, Bangladeshis, Somalis, Iraqis, Pakistanis, Iranians, Eritreans and Ethiopians rub shoulders, shuttling back and forth under the neon din of shopfronts that advertise in Greek and whatever language correlates to the non-Greek patrons who comprise the bulk of their clientele. Almost all of these people are busy planning and executing their next move—one step closer to central Europe—and it is only natural that a street containing many of the businesses that cater to different subsets of non-Greeks is buzzing with new energy. Migrants from all over the world have descended upon it.

MIGRANT, REFUGEE, SMUGGLER, SAVIOUR

A cohort of young Iraqi men enter a brightly lit department store called Dubai Shopping Center wearing the dirty clothes they have been in for days, across three countries and two continents. When they walk out, they are sporting fresh threads and carrying an expanded assemblage of kit and supplies. A twenty-year-old among them named Aram continues a few blocks north to a business that advertises money exchange and transfer services. Aram came to Greece via Turkey, but, afraid that his Kurdish surname might elicit extra scrutiny from Turkish authorities, he chose to carry only enough cash to get himself to Greece. On this night in August 2015 Aram is picking up €3,000 that his father, who lives in south-eastern Turkey, sent to him.

When Aram enters the shop he looks up the ten-digit code, comprising numbers and letters, that his father sent him via text message. In the five minutes it takes for Aram to write down the code, for the shop-owner to confirm it in his notebook, and for both of them to count the stack of bills, €3,000 has travelled 1,360 kilometres.

Just as with Abdoulaye in Guinea and Musa in Chad, the process by which Aram's father sent the funds was simple and inexpensive. It wasn't Western Union, the service advertised on the shopfront, nor was it any sort of formal bank transfer. Rather, it was an informal financial transfer system used around the world, often called *hawala*.

* * *

Though there many forms of informal financial transfer systems, *hawala*, which is historically associated with South Asia and the Middle East, has become a catch-all term for the types of informal financial transfer systems that are ubiquitous around the globe. Though not all people engaging in these transactions will use the term, informal financial transfer systems predicated on *hawala* principles are responsible for moving tens of billions of dollars annually without ever touching the formal banking system.

Versions of *hawala* pre-date modern banking by centuries, and have cropped up in different parts of the world throughout history. There are written references to it in Islamic sources as long ago as the seventh century AD,[8] when it referred to the payment of a debt through the transfer of a claim. By the tenth century *hawala* had grown to include not just the transfer of debts but also of money.[9] One antecedent believed to have developed in eighth-century China was called 'flying money', in reference to the scheme's ability to 'move' money over long distances. Traders on the ancient Silk Road used the system as a means to protect themselves from theft and to avoid moving large amounts of hard currency through areas where the threat of banditry was ever present. Similar schemes have long existed or recently emerged in different parts of Asia, Africa and Europe, as well as North and South America, to facilitate everything from paying school fees to laundering drug money. It is estimated that some $400 billion is transferred annually using *hawala* every year.[10]

Today, the vast majority of people using *hawala* and its variants are members of expatriate communities in Europe, the Persian Gulf and North America, who prefer them to formal financial transfer systems for a variety of reasons, chief among them being that they are cheaper than any of their formal counterparts. Not only are *hawala* transfers less expensive, they are often faster than their formal alternatives. Because *hawala* is not beholden to formal business hours or the regulatory processes that slow down formal transfers, a *hawala* transaction can move money instantaneously. Both the efficacy and appeal of *hawala* are tethered to the fact that because the money involved does not actually move, and because the primary mechanism for mitigating risk is trust rather than written contracts, there is virtually no bureaucracy involved.

People who oversee *hawala* transactions, sometimes referred to as *hawaladar*s or *hawala* traders, earn their profits either through charging commission, usually a percentage of the amount being transferred, or through currency fluctuations and spreads in the exchange rate. Since almost all *hawaladar*s offer their services within the context of legitimate commercial enterprises—most notably travel agencies, transport companies, import/export businesses, gold and jewellery exchanges and shipping companies—carrying out the transactions requires little, if any, overhead costs. The same lack of overheads also enables *hawaladar*s to offer exchange rates that are more competitive than formal institutions, which have the added burden of factoring regulatory costs into their prices. In the past, all that was needed was a telephone or a fax machine to carry out a *hawala* transaction. These days, thanks to widespread internet access and near-universal access to mobile phones, even less equipment is required.

For customers, *hawala* is incredibly appealing not only because it is cheaper than its formal alternatives but also because it shifts liability for the transaction out of their hands, and into the remit of the *hawaladar*s. Once the sending customer makes his initial payment to a *hawaladar* and the person on the receiving end picks up his funds, the liability for the transfer is between *hawaladar*s, which means that they will have to settle the balance of accounts among themselves. As previously noted, no money actually moves or changes hands in *hawala* transactions. Rather, outstanding debts are simply recorded and settled through either a reverse transaction or another financial arrangement at a later date. In many instances these debts are essentially IOUs between businessmen, which are cancelled out through reciprocal IOUs. *Hawala* debts are also often settled in non-monetary ways, such as through an exchange of goods or tradable commodities.

One of the most common ways of settling debts between *hawala* traders who regularly do business, as outlined in the example with Musa above, is through discounting goods and masking the debt through over/under invoicing. Debt settlements can also be reached, however, through transactions that may not involve the same traders as the initial transaction. Other intermediaries may enter the arrangement, meaning that accounts are settled or spread across several different traders. *Hawaladar* debts or surpluses can be consolidated, sold and transferred, and they can exist at a wholesale level or be multi-faceted.

With no formal records beyond random documents on computers, notebooks and scraps of paper, *hawala* transactions are regulated not through contracts or promissory notes, but via the honour system, and the trust that makes *hawala* possible can stem from several sources. In some cases it may be the result of a long-standing business relationship. In others the trust might appeal to, and be regulated by, shared notions of ethnic, ideological, tribal or national loyalty. In many of the communities where *hawala* transactions are commonplace, concepts such as familial honour and shame can have a tremendous regulatory effect. These norms are often further reinforced by the fact that reputation is an invaluable commodity in the world of interpersonal, informal trade. In some cases, especially those in which *hawala* is being used to by crime syndicates to launder illicit profits, the threat of potential violence is an added incentive that keeps everyone honest.

Hawala and other types of informal financial transactions move billions of dollars around the globe each year, and their popularity is, first and foremost, a testament to the fact that not only are they cheaper and more efficient than their formal counterparts but that they are also perceived among their customers to be more reliable. Yet many of the qualities that explain why *hawala* and its variants are sought after as alternatives to legal banking institutions are what make it so appealing to criminals.

To start, *hawala* is anonymous. The names of clients are rarely recorded, as *hawaladars* almost always use alphanumerical codes or passwords to verify the identity of clients. Second, because transactions between *hawaladars* are predicated on trust and existing relationships rather than contracts, the lack of a paper trail makes it almost impossible to trace transactions after the fact. Furthermore, since most *hawaladars* offer their services within the context of operating other businesses, *hawala* systems are an ideal conduit for evading taxes, bypassing government regulations and laundering money through legal companies. There is no trace of *hawala* transactions within the formal systems of financial institutions. There are no bank records or deposit slips. This means that the usual methods for countering money laundering—financial regulation, Financial Intelligence Units (FIUs), suspicious transaction reports—are all but useless.[11] It is the perfect system for laundering finances related to crime.

Reduced to its simplest form, money laundering is a three-step process often referred to as 'placement, layering and integration'. At the placement stage, illicit cash or 'dirty' money is deposited within a legitimate bank or business. From there, the illicit funds are 'layered' via wire transfers to other bank accounts or businesses, often multiple times. This 'layering' allows illicit money to mix with legitimate funds and thus become disguised. Finally, during the 'integration' phase the funds are injected into the legitimate economy, often through investments or the purchase of goods. By the time money is sufficiently scrubbed, it is nearly impossible to trace its origins.

There is nothing new about individuals or businesses seeking to move money in ways that bypass regulations, nor is there anything novel about individuals or criminal networks using the formal economy to hide their ill-gotten gains and launder their profits. But the windfall profits that come with migrant smuggling, which now far exceed those to be made from drug trafficking, have injected unprecedented amounts of cash into networks that were previously operating in denominations of hundreds or thousands rather than tens of thousands and hundreds of thousands. As with every industry, the promise of unprecedented profits has not only accelerated the development and professionalisation of existing informal transfer networks, it has spurred new and innovative financial systems that empower both smugglers and migrants.

These informal financial networks have also formed the monetary scaffolding with which the current migration industry could be built. Without financial systems such as *hawala*, neither smugglers nor migrants would be able to carry out their activities. Not only do they allow the absorption of the billions of dollars earned in the smuggling economy, but *hawala* networks and other forms of informal financial transfer allow migrants to send and receive money at various points in their journeys. *Hawala* and its variants allow many migrant communities to mitigate and overcome the risks of banditry and extortion during their journeys, or to plan their advanced phases. It is also empowers high-level smugglers to carry out their activities.

The travel agents, money changers and international businesses that occupy the legal, quasi-legal, and fully illegal spaces that cater to migrant communities, enterprising businessmen and outright criminals have coalesced around migrants and refugees. It is a truism that organised crime networks chase profits wherever they are, and there is perhaps no stronger indication that there is money to be made from the smuggling of migrants than the fact that, within the structures of *hawala*, innovations that are dedicated to the specificities of the smuggling industry are taking place. One such example is the emergence of 'migrant escrow' schemes that allow for migrants to protect themselves against smugglers, and allow for smugglers to distinguish themselves and build a reputation.

In the barely remembered days before smartphones, a classic strategy was for the recruiter to take a photograph of the migrant and tear it in half. One half was kept by the broker in the migrant's home, the other was held by the migrant throughout his journey. The migrant would then send his half of the picture back to his family by post, indicating his safe arrival. At this point the smuggler would return to the family with his half of the picture to recoup the balance of the payment for his services. The contemporary equivalent is now achieved through technology. Just as Syrian cash and Syrians' ability to leverage resources in some ways encouraged a degree of professionalisation and formalisation of smuggling practices, so too has it spurned innovation in how to pay for these services.

We met *Fahad in Izmir, sitting at a street-side table at a café just off Street 1367. Fahad had not eaten in twenty-four hours and he wanted to order lunch, but, unsure of whether he would have to leave the café abruptly, he opted for a double espresso instead. With his phone on the table, next to his pack of cigarettes, he was waiting for someone to meet him.

A Syrian friend who was already starting his new life in Germany had told Fahad that 'Abu Jihad' could be trusted. Fahad wondered if someone with such a ridiculous name could actually be a smuggler, but it was already September 2015, and Fahad knew that boat crossings would be getting more dangerous as the calm summer waters became autumnal waves. So when he stepped off the bus in Izmir, after having flown from Beirut to Istanbul, Fahad called Abu Jihad.

As soon as his liquid energy arrived, Fahad's phone started vibrating.

'Are you at the restaurant?' asked a voice that clearly did not belong to the same person Fahad had spoken with before.

'Yes,' Fahad responded.

'I am on the other side of the street.'

Fahad looked across the street and met the eyes of a man wearing a blue baseball cap, speaking via a Bluetooth earpiece. Fahad gestured towards the empty seat at his table, but the man shook his head and motioned for Fahad to come over.

'Are you Abu Jihad?' Fahad asked as he approached. The man sniggered and handed him a piece of paper under the guise of a handshake.

'Call this number and say you want to go west for a vacation,' he said.

That was the extent of the interaction. Before Fahad could ask any questions, the man had already turned his back and started walking away.

Fahad called the number and was given the address of a money changer and travel agent just off Fevzi Paşa Boulevard. 'It was a real business,' Fahad says when he describes the place. 'Everything seemed normal, I could not believe it.' Before Fahad could even explain who he was or where he was trying to go, he was ushered to the back of the shop, where he was told by a man with an Iraqi accent how much he would have to pay to go to Greece.

'I must look like a refugee,' Fahad jokes. 'They knew exactly why I was there just by looking at me.'

The sum, $1,100, was in line with what others had told him he would have to pay. Fahad was okay with the price, but he wondered about how payment would work. He knew better than to pay everything up front without any guarantee that he would make it to Greece. His friends had told him that there were offices throughout Izmir that acted as brokers operating migrant escrow schemes.

'That's why we are here,' the man with the Iraqi accent told him. 'We don't work for Abu Jihad. We work with Abu Jihad. But we also work with you, too.'

Fahad realised that the Iraqi man was working not for Abu Jihad per se, but as an interlocutor for the Turkish money changer who was operating one of these offices. After a brief explanation of the process, Fahad handed over $1,100, $50 of which was non-refundable. In return, the Turkish broker gave him a printed piece of paper, replete with a letterhead that had Al Zain, the name of the broker's office, at the top. The paper outlined the name of the customer, the name of the smuggler, the number of people paid for, the price and currency in which it was paid, and the amount paid in advance. It also included an alphanumerical code, which would be used to order the release of funds, and the date and time of the transaction. The receipt even included a signature and a QR code (a type of barcode used for smart phones) to guarantee authenticity.

'They told me that Abu Jihad would not receive any money unless I sent a picture of this paper or texted them the code,' Fahad recounts. 'So long as I have this paper, Abu Jihad is obligated to take me to Greece,' he explains. Three days later Fahad eventually made it to Lesbos, where he was quick to find himself a café offering WiFi and send the code back. 'It was the first thing I did when I arrived in Lesbos,' he says over the phone to me a few days later. 'I am done with Abu Jihad.'

Forging a New Identity

'You want a degree from Harvard?' a cynical Lebanese Army colonel asked me during a training session I was leading on human smuggling, 'go to Baalbek—there they can make you any kind of document you want.'

In the business model of the smuggling industry, the counterfeiters and fraudsters procuring fake passports and other documents for migrants have become specialised and highly sought-after professionals. For migrants who can afford it, the right documentation can make all the difference, both in terms of safety and success. It allows you to fly in comfort straight to your choice of European city. It offers a way around land borders and shady smugglers. It is a swift and successful conclusion of a migration journey, whether you are entitled to it or not. A false document can literally be the ticket to a new life.

Frontex, the EU's border agency, sent document experts to Leros and other Greek islands to pick out fake passports. But even at the height of the crisis in 2015 there were only ten experts on the case, and identifying a fake that has been printed on real Syrian passport books with real equipment is very difficult.

At Istanbul's Atatürk Airport, which is the top departure point for those using fraudulent documents, the Turkish authorities managed to detect only 529 users in 2015. At arrival points they fared slightly better: 8,373 cases were detected of people trying to cross EU borders with false or stolen travel documents, including visas and residence permits, which is a drop in the total numbers detected in previous years, despite exponential increases in the number of illegal border crossings. In their own dry words:

> The results and observations collected during an exercise carried out under [the] Frontex umbrella highlighted a series of vulnerabilities in the travel document inspection process. This points to the risk of detections of document fraud to underestimate the actual number of persons entering the EU upon presentation of fraudulent travel documents.[12]

Beleaguered border officials, dealing with thousands of people crossing the borders, have a minute or less to detect a false document, a challenge made all the more difficult by the adroitness with which modern counterfeiters create documents. While border police have taken to asking test questions to challenge the migrant to prove his claimed nationality and weed out the imposters, the resilient smuggling industry have quickly found ways around this cursory obstacle. Videos have proliferated online showing people how to obtain Syrian passports and impersonate Syrians. Crib sheets are posted on noticeboards in hubs like Calais, for example, to help migrants understand what they can expect: What does your national flag look like? What is the name of the village next to yours? Can you describe the coins and notes in your country?

For European immigration officials, it is an almost impossible task to maintain rigorous checks. How are they to distinguish Lebanese Arabic from Syrian Arabic, or a dialect from the north from one from the south? If a migrant claims to be from a small town rather than one of the big cities, what hope does a German, Italian or Serbian border policeman have of verifying the response? Their knowledge is always going to be cursory compared to a well-prepared migrant who has done his homework. To investigate someone properly and challenge their version of events would take weeks, even months, of research. With the numbers of men, women and children arriving daily, that is an unrealistic expectation, even for the most basic of data such as age or nationality.

Consequently, the demand for false documentation is enormous, and the ever-responsive smuggling industry basically has three ways to meet this demand, with varying degrees of complexity and chances of success. The easiest is to procure a genuine passport that has been lost, stolen, purchased or rented. There are criminal networks that specialise in collecting and modifying documentation, and then selling them on for use in all kinds of nefarious enterprises.

In some parts of the world these documents are shockingly cheap and easy to procure. In the wake of the Malaysian airlines crash in 2014, for example, a British reporter found agencies in China charging less than €1,000 for a two-day service to doctor a lost or stolen passport with new details.[13] 'Up to several years ago … it was quite easy to swap a photo. You would take a genuine passport and then glue your own photo on the stamp and it would work,' said a spokeswoman for Frontex.[14] This has become more difficult as passport security features have become more sophisticated, but the networks of counterfeiters have also raised their game.

Increasingly common is the 'impostor method', which requires finding a 'look-alike' passport of someone who closely resembles you, and to do as my friend did with her cousin Rania, by taking the chance that overwhelmed border officials won't look too closely. Finding an impostor has proven particularly successful for sub-Saharan Africans boarding planes at Istanbul airport. Turkish officials have admittedly struggled to identify visual differences between people from certain parts of the world, and thus migrants have been smuggled in significant numbers travelling on the valid passports of relatives or friends.[15]

This strategy can be combined with the 'double check-in method' that reduces the number of times that the migrant has to be scrutinised carrying the fake.[16] *Nour, a Syrian woman we met in Athens, was hoping that the double check-in method would be successful for her. She was getting desperate, wanting to leave Greece with her young son and make it to Sweden before the country stopped taking refugees. After the trauma of the sea crossing from Turkey, she was determined to take the last leg of her journey by air.

When she arrived in Athens she had done a deal with an Iraqi smuggler, who promised to send her and her child to Sweden for €7,500, to be paid on arrival. They assumed she would be an easy client: women travelling alone by plane with kids tend to get less scrutiny; but instead Nour was rejected several times at airport immigration, using different passports. Fortunately, they did not arrest her, but confiscated the fake documents and asked her to leave the airport, literally telling her to 'try again'.

So back in Athens she found another deal, which she was just a few days away from trying: the double check-in. This time, she will check in to her flight with tickets to Ecuador, one of the few remaining countries where Syrians can travel without a visa. At the same time, a smuggler has agreed for another man to check in with his family who will lend her his wife's and son's passports. Then, once both have completed check-in and they are past immigration, they will meet in the departure zone of the airport. Nour will meet with the man, who will hand over the look-alike passports, with fake entry stamps and flight tickets to Stockholm. The last passport scan before boarding the plane is usually the most cursory, and then they are on their way.

The networks transacting in false documents have an inventory of literally thousands of genuine passports to choose from, with the cost being determined by the 'value' of the nationality being sold. The illicit trade watchdog Havoscope lists the average prices of some documentation on the black market.[17] It cites the average price of a stolen passport for sale as $3,500, but the range is quite significant: a Peruvian passport, of little utility for illegal emigrants, costs a mere $1,750. According to Havoscope, the highly sought-after documents for Sweden run to as much as $12,200, but for the UK or the USA our interviewees reported paying as much as $15–20,000 per document. Despite the desirability of Sweden as a destination, Swedish passports are somewhat cheaper because the Swedes allow their nationals to hold an unlimited number of extra passports, thereby making them easier to procure. The Swedish police report criminal networks threatening or pressuring people, particularly from African or Middle Eastern diaspora populations, to hand over their passports.[18]

Some people, however, hand their passports over willingly. In countries such as Thailand it is relatively easy for criminal organisations to buy passports from partygoers or backpackers who have run out of money and are looking to make some quick cash. A tourist can easily report their passport stolen, get a new passport and resume their travels after filling in a quick, one-page lost passport report which they then take to their embassy.[19]

The best and most expensive of fraudulent documents is a blank passport that has been bought or stolen from the issuing country by seasoned criminals. Of all forms of passport fraud this is the most watertight. While fake, doctored or look-alike passports will always carry a risk of detection, authentic blank passports when correctly filled out are almost impossible to detect.

Foreign consulates used to be a good source of passports or legitimate visas. All states have systems of 'honorary consuls', which are nationals of the domestic state that are appointed to provide consular services in remote locations, including issuing passports, visas or temporary travel documents in the case of an emergency. The bigger embassies may well also have a number of national staff working in the visa-processing divisions, or in security for the embassy, and these are prime targets for smugglers. Cases over the years have revealed that these consular staff are offered thousands of euros to sell a genuine passport, which can be used as a template for the counterfeiters, or sold on for three or four times the price to illicit travellers.

According to South African newspaper the *Sunday Independent*, British citizen and terror suspect Samantha Lewthwaite—known as the 'White Widow'—paid $1,800 for fake South African documents from corrupt officials in 2005.[20] A separate NBC News investigation in 2007 found Peruvian officials willing to take payments for custom-made documents, and a broker who boasted a twenty-five-year career in counterfeiting.[21] A useful second best is to issue legitimate visas which will allow someone to travel on their own national passport into Europe. Research in Senegal found that in the mid-2000s a visa for France could be acquired illegally for around €3,000, for Italy for approximately €4,000, and for Portugal for €5,000. UNODC research conducted in 2009 found that in Mali a corruptly acquired United States visa could be bought for full-package travellers for about €4,500.[22]

Virtually the only way to detect a person travelling on an authentic passport is if he makes an error filling it out or if the passport number turns up in a database of stolen documents.[23] Interpol's database of lost and stolen travel documents contains 40 million records from 167 countries,[24] and migrants travelling on the full-package solution may be required to return their fraudulent documents once they reach their destinations, so that these may be reused by other migrants.

In recent years, however, the number of safeguards to prevent the diversion of genuine passports has increased. A former consular officer from Italy that we spoke to explained the complex system of passport registration, multiple signatories, counts, recounts and secured transport that makes it infinitely more difficult to procure a blank passport from the European embassies. But in some cases these measures closed the stable door after the horse had already bolted. In one notorious case, criminals targeted Belgian passports, stealing hundreds of them from minimally secured local government offices due to their lax decentralised passport-issuing system. Between 1990 and 2002, when the system was overhauled, the Belgian police estimated that an astonishing 19,050 had been stolen in total.[25]

Criminal networks have also managed to bulk up their inventories of false passports by counterfeiting or stealing other types of identification documents and applying legally for passports. Birth certificates tend to be relatively easy to fake in most places, as applying for a first or duplicate rarely requires unique identifiers such as fingerprints, in-person visits, or even photos. They can also be provided by multiple authorities, such as hospitals, municipal authorities or even, in some countries, by churches. Once these foundational identification documents have been legitimately secured, then applying for a passport to accompany them is quite straightforward, and the criminal networks specialised in this area will do this systematically, using nationally published birth or death records which may not be fully synchronised with the records of national passport offices.

If real passports cannot be bought, stolen or otherwise fraudulently procured, the other option is for the smuggling networks to make them from scratch. While it is more complicated to pass off fake passports as genuine than it is to doctor real ones, manufacturing counterfeits is a huge and vibrant criminal economy. In 2009 British police found 1,800 allegedly forged passports, which they valued at $1.6 million, in a London flat.[26] While Lebanon is a regional hub for counterfeiting in the Middle East, Thailand is considered a major hub for the global counterfeit business.[27]

But in the current climate having a European passport is a luxury most migrants simply do not need. As recently as January 2016, for example, there was enormous demand for Syrian passports: the Balkan states were allowing only Syrians, Afghans and Iraqis to pass through their borders; and nearly every European state was offering expedited asylum processing for Syrian refugees, who enjoyed an acceptance rate of around 99 per cent. For the enterprising or desperate Palestinian or Lebanese, a fake Syrian passport could prove the ticket to a new life in Europe.

Having a Syrian passport is more than good enough, and there are numerous ways the criminals have found to secure them, including by taking them off the Syrians themselves. *The Guardian* profiled a Syrian migrant named Mohamed who became a victim of passport theft:

> When Mohamed paid an Afghan smuggler several hundred euros to drive him and his friends from Thessaloniki to the Greek–Macedonian border in July, he thought the money was all the smuggler would want. Instead, once on road the driver feigned a problem with the engine and persuaded the Syrians to leave the car on the pretext of avoiding detection by the police. 'And then he stole our passports,' said Mohamed.[28]

A reporter with the *Daily Mail* claimed to have paid $2,000 for a Syrian passport, ID card and driving licence, purchased in Turkey. And last year, a Vocativ reporter interviewed a black-market 'merchant' selling fake Syrian passports on the Turkish–Syrian border. His going rate for a new passport: $1,800. The reporter met the unnamed passport peddler in a Turkish café:

> [The merchant] slaps a stack of passports on the table and begins showing me the different types of alterations: new photographs and names, clean visa pages and expiry date changes. He says he sometimes even buys old passports from desperate Syrians who have already made it safely to Turkey.

Some of these passports are not even technically fakes. When rebels first took over the Syrian town of Azaz just across the border from government forces, they also 'liberated' a passport-printing office, giving a crew of brokers and smugglers access to all of the equipment necessary to make new passports, or to alter existing ones. How many they may have produced is impossible to determine, but the fact that 10,000 fake Syrian passports were seized in Bulgaria, just one of the countries on the migrant route, gives an idea of the potential scale of the counterfeit industry.[29] In February 2016 the Turkish police in a raid on the smuggling industry seized more than a thousand original passports belonging to 50 different countries, as well as 33 identity cards, driving licences, 200 fake boarding passes and 10 different types of immigration stamps for Istanbul's Atatürk and Sabiha Göken Airports.[30]

Around the same time, German officials were estimating that nearly one-third of migrants in Germany claiming to be Syrian were not in fact from Syria,[31] and the prevalence of fake passports drew the ire of people from the Syrian refugee community, who feared it would reduce their own chances of a genuine claim being taken seriously in Europe. One of the information-exchange sites between migrants has been calling on Syrians to expose people carrying fake passports to border authorities.[32]

Fundamentally, however, these efforts are a losing battle. All nationalities of migrants have an interest in the thriving black market in documentation. Just as Arabs from all over the Middle East are obtaining fake Syrian passports, Iranians are obtaining Afghan passports to help them hustle through Eastern Europe. Since large numbers of Afghans live and work in Iran, and many people on both sides of the border share common ethno-linguistic attributes, it is relatively easy for some

Iranians to pass the basic tests border guards employ to try and detect fake nationalities. While this is probably the first time in history that anyone has actually coveted an Afghan passport enough to want to buy a forgery, there is a long history of Afghans getting fake passports in Pakistan, as 'you can buy anything in Pakistan'.[33] Temporarily holding a fake Pakistani passport can ease the dangerous route for an Afghan migrant through Iran on his way towards Turkey to join the flow across to Greece, where he can then revert to his Afghan passport.

All this is to say that the smuggling industry rests on a vast and diverse criminal infrastructure, within which counterfeiters and money launderers scattered all over the world use their specialised skills to ensure that the global migrant-smuggling industry can continue to thrive. The scope, complexity and ingenuity of these informal systems places them far beyond the investigative capacity of even the most sophisticated of national law-enforcement agencies. With corruption paving the way, individual smuggling markets have blossomed as a result of the booming demand for human mobility.

While human smuggling has existed for decades—even centuries—never before have we had a perfect storm of conditions quite like this: unprecedented displacement facilitated by communication technology that allows networks and associations to be formed, transact and disperse without detection. The narrative of Europe's migration crisis, which we shall be telling from here forwards, rests on this foundation.

4

ROUTES

It is an absurd scenario, but these are absurd times. Two men from the tiny West African nation of the Gambia, bicycling in short-sleeved shirts over the Borisoglebsk–Storskog border between northern Russia and Norway at the end of September 2015 when temperatures were barely hovering above freezing.

Despite snow and polar temperatures plummeting to −30°C, for a brief time in the final months of 2015 this obscure little border post became a popular route for those seeking asylum in Europe. The first pair of refugees came in February, both Syrians. By mid-August 420 had sought asylum with the Norwegian border-control officials, and by November it was 500 a week, with a plethora of nationalities including Syrians, Iraqis, Palestinians, Afghans and the two Gambians all arriving. Irritated Norwegian officials looked accusingly at their Russian counterparts across the border. As one Norwegian policeman grumbled to me in October 2015, 'It didn't used to be so easy to escape the Soviet Union.' Before the route was once again closed down some six months later, 5,600 people had crossed the border from Russia to Norway.[1]

Because Russia bans foot traffic across the border with Norway, and Norway fines drivers who carry migrants across, those who attempt this journey have to do the final mile by bicycle. Migrants take a train or fly into Muransk in Russia. Upon arrival, smugglers wait with mini-vans, asking for between $400 and $1,000 to drive migrants the 220 kilometres north through Russia's bleak tundra to Nikel, a mining town and the last stop before the Norwegian border. There they spend $200 on cheap bicycles shipped in by local criminal groups, who customise them without brakes or lights as a cost-cutting measure, despite the fact that by this time of year the region is subsumed by almost twenty-four hours of continuous darkness. Our intrepid migrants must pedal the remaining mile.

While the region is famed for being an excellent place to view the aurora borealis—or northern lights—it is hard to imagine that the determined migrants have much chance to look skyward as they wobble on the ice and battle through snow to cross the border. The bikes are promptly confiscated by the Norwegian authorities for failing to meet the standards of the prosperous nation's cycle safety code, and they join the mountain of hundreds of multi-coloured two-wheelers piled up behind the border post, pending compacting and recycling. In the mean time, successful migrants can rejoice in having penetrated Europe's Schengen zone.[2]

This esoteric route across a border 400 kilometres north of the Arctic Circle, now informally dubbed the 'Arctic route', is one of a myriad of examples of the resilience and desperation behind people's desire to migrate, and the incredible creativity and innovation of those who profit from helping them realise that desire. It also demonstrates how quickly a successful route will replicate and proliferate. First movers experiment, and if they are successful their numbers are reinforced by those seeking to emulate them. Once the viability of the route has been confirmed, there is the surge of mass movement, as the networks of migrants and smugglers coalesce around the new opportunity.

Some migrants travel extraordinary, logic-defying, distances. Officials from the International Office on Migration (IOM) in West Africa told me that they have had Syrians arriving in Dakar who took a 9,000 kilometre detour through Ecuador, where Syrians do not require a visa. From Dakar they then joined the Saharan land route on the back of a pick-up towards Libya and the Mediterranean.

The melting pot city of Bangkok in Thailand has also become a hub for a growing number of Syrians. Immigration records show a doubling of legal entries by Syrians into the country, from 5,000 people annually before the conflict to more than 10,000 a year by 2015. The number of

Syrians entering the kingdom illegally is estimated to be proportionally equivalent, if not higher. Once in Bangkok, a city that has long been a hub for all kinds of clandestine activities, Syrians can procure fake documents and attempt the journey to Europe.

In February 2016 the *Bangkok Post* released a story about Mustafa, a Palestinian who fled the Syrian conflict in 2013. Aiming to reach Sweden in order to apply for political asylum, he met a fellow Palestinian, a smuggler from Syria who had successfully achieved refugee status in the UK. His compatriot sold him a fake passport for $4,700 and organised his trip to Thailand, promising the hapless Mustafa that Thailand had a bilateral agreement with the EU to help Syrian refugees, particularly Palestinians, and that there was therefore no risk of arrest or detention. Unfortunately for Mustafa, his smuggling agent was trafficking in dishonesty, and he was stopped in Bangkok airport for using a fake passport while trying to board his flight for Stockholm. He was arrested and sentenced to two years in jail.[3]

For the most part, however, these kinds of extraordinary journeys remain an anomaly. There are a number of principal routes to Europe upon which the majority of migrants travel, and they long pre-date the current crisis. These routes have often been used to move people, either voluntarily or involuntarily, for centuries, and frequently are the same routes used to trade and smuggle commodities and traffic all kinds of illicit goods, including drugs and arms. They are well-worn pathways of corruption and complicity controlled and facilitated by the communities who live along those routes.

What the Bangkok example illustrates very effectively, however, is that almost more important than the routes are the *hubs* of the global migration industry. The routes linking various hubs may quickly rise or fall in popularity, based upon a number of factors. Policies that raise or lower the obstacles in various places may displace one connecting route in favour of another. The construction of a wall or border post along one popular route will put pressure on a parallel option or destination, or might spur the creation of a new route.

Yet a number of locations have endured as smuggling hubs for decades, persisting and growing in importance over time. These hubs serve as nodes from where routes are developed and defined. They bring structure to the incalculable options and itineraries on offer, and connect migrants from diverse places of origin with a variety of smuggling service providers to fit their budgets and individual circumstances. The key hubs are often major cities or remote border towns that have long facilitated trade and connected entrepreneurs operating in both the licit and illicit economy.

In the first half of 2015, for example, an estimated 57,000 asylum seekers crossed into Hungary irregularly, trying to make their way from Greece towards Germany. In response, in September 2015, and at a cost of €72 million, the Hungarian government built a 4-metre tall, 175-kilometre-long fence along its border with Serbia. Blocked by the fence, migrants and refugees immediately began trying to enter Hungary through Croatia instead, and when construction of another 350-kilometre fence started in October 2015 along that border, the migrants began to use Slovenia as the route to the preferred destinations.[4] At every point, smuggling networks were ready to help migrants adjust to the new realities on the ground, offering new packages that could bypass emerging barriers.

Similarly, the success of Spain in closing down the maritime routes from Mauritania and Morocco to mainland Spain and the Canary Islands has certainly intensified the concentration of traffic through Libya and the other North African countries.

'Everyone wants to go through Libya,' said a Malian man named Amadou, who had been living illegally in Nouadhibou in Mauritania for eight years after his plan to reach Europe was effectively blocked. According to Amadou, who says he lives comfortably off the salary he earns working for an industrial fishing company, many of the West Africans living in Nouadhibou have since left Mauritania to loop back through West Africa and up to Libya. 'It's completely open. There is nothing stopping them,' he told me.

Increased law enforcement and surveillance at particular points will also have an effect. A 'crackdown' on smugglers in one hub, either in the form of an increase in the number of arrests or the harsher legal penalties against convicted smugglers, will always impact the market, but one can rarely predict how exactly that impact will manifest itself on the ground. The smuggling industry follows classic microeconomic theory of the supply and demand in the market: smugglers offer a service and price it according to the costs of delivering the actual service. Law-enforcement action may deter some of the more opportunistic and informal players in a smuggling trade, but such actions often have the effect of concentrating smuggling operations in fewer hands with the risk transferred to the migrant in the form of price hikes. As prices rise, fewer migrants may choose to travel that route, moving elsewhere.

Smuggling organisations systematically exploit discrepancies between different jurisdictions and legal systems, and they not only shift their modes of operation reactively, they are also proactive in seeking out new opportunities to move people, seeking to corrupt a border guard or airport immigration officer in order to move a few hundred people before the window closes or policies change. As explained earlier, smuggling networks use information systems to quickly find loopholes in border control and legislation, and rapidly recruit clients in order to exploit new opportunities.

While we tend to break down migrant transit into three basic categories—land, sea and air—in fact the permutations of travel and means of transport are almost endless. Migrants have been penetrating Europe from all possible directions, and on all possible means of transport: boats, planes, trains and motor vehicles, and all manner of sub-varieties within.

As merry revellers all over the world rang in the New Year on 31 December 2014, the Italian coastguard was battling cold and rough winter seas to rescue the 797 Syrian migrants from the *Blue Sky M*, a long-retired rust-bucket of a shipping vessel that was programmed to collide directly into the Puglia coastline at the southernmost tip of Italy. Two days later the same crew were out again, this time to intercept the 450 migrants on board the *Ezadeen*, a fifty-year-old decommissioned livestock ship.

An enterprising Turkish smuggler had bought the *Ezadeen* and packed it full of migrants, predominantly Syrians, who had paid between $5,000 and $8,000 per head. Both the *Ezadeen* and the *Blue Sky M* left from the quiet Turkish port town of Mersin and sailed for ten days and 1,600 kilometres along the Turkish and Greek coasts to southern Italy. As the ships neared Italy, the crew turned the boats sharply towards the coast, programmed the auto-pilot and left the ship and the migrants to their own devices.

These 'ghost ships' represented a new tactic for smugglers, with eleven such vessels taking the same route in the last quarter of 2014, accelerating the mounting panic among European policymakers about the growing scale of the crisis. While this tactic was quickly cracked down upon, it was just one front in the escalating crush to get to Europe. In sharp contrast, for a brief period smugglers were offering the 8-mile passage from Morocco across the Straits of Gibraltar to Terifa in Spain on the back of high-powered jet-skis. This practice was quickly suppressed by the Spanish police, with a small ring of fifteen smugglers arrested.[5]

Ayman, an attractive thirty-something Syrian man from Aleppo, reported to us that he paid smugglers €4,500, five or six times the normal price, to sail from Turkey to Greece in what he insisted must be a seaworthy boat. After twenty days of waiting in a smuggler's grim halfway-house apartment, he received a call from the smuggler saying, 'Come to the seaport in Marmaris and dress as clean as you can. You need to look as a somebody who will take a tour in a yacht.' Ayman consequently made the four-hour crossing on a tourist cruising yacht, captained by a Turk, with fifteen adults and six children on board as passengers. They were given beers to hold, and told to stand on deck and look happy, so as not to attract the attention of the coastguard. Although drinking alcohol is *haram*—forbidden—according to Islam, Ayman did not hesitate to look the part.

Because the smuggling industry is defined by innovation and flexibility, networks can easily adapt their methods according to the structure and specific challenges of the routes. Working from the major hubs, they forge cooperative arrangements with other groups to pass migrants between them and onto whichever group or organisation controls the next section of territory. The way any individual migrant ends up arriving in Europe thus becomes a product of a number of independent variables: the migrant's means, nationality, connections, aspirations, the people they meet along the way, changes in policies of states of transit and destination, and often, just the luck of the draw. But the two most salient factors that shape a migrant journey are by far the nationality of the migrant and the resources available to him.

One of the greatest challenges in describing, analysing and responding to the current crisis is that it brings together people from so many

Map 1: The principal migrant routes to Europe[6]

different countries and cultures, travelling over extraordinary distances, by so many different forms of transport and driven by different motivations, and with the desire to end up in different countries. Together, as these individual stories intertwine, echo and reinforce each other, they become part of the larger narrative of the crisis.

For this reason, our analysis in Part 2 is organised around these hubs and focuses on the ways in which different markets for smugglers are structured and populated. Nonetheless, to understand the migration crisis as whole, the trajectory of the main routes and their interconnections is necessary, and an overview of the principal routes and their evolution throughout the crisis is outlined here.

Working backwards from the borders of Europe there are two major gateways, both of which involve a sea crossing followed by onward movement after the migrants have reached Europe's shores. These two gateways, the first across the central Mediterranean and the second across the Aegean, have distinct characteristics, and different nationalities pass through them, facilitated by different actors operating with varying degrees of criminality.

Central Mediterranean Route

The 'Central Mediterranean' route was the first major gateway of the current migration crisis, with two principal launching points. The first is from Libya, where boats launch for Italy predominantly from the western coastal towns near Tripoli. The second major departure point along the central Mediterranean route is from Egypt, principally from Alexandria and its environs. Prior to the most recent crisis, Morocco and Mauritania constituted key launching points for boats headed towards Spain, and in the period between 1990 and 2004 an estimated 15–20,000 people were departing the African coast per month.[7] But a subsequent decade of intensive investment in cooperation and capacity building by Spain and national authorities in Mauritania and Morocco has largely closed down that route. There are additional launching points along minor routes across the Mediterranean, from Algeria, Tunisia and Morocco, but for a variety of reasons none of them has developed to the extent that Libya and Egypt have. This is not to say that new networks using these countries as launching points will not develop in the future.

For the central Mediterranean route, Libya has become the epicentre and serves a catchment area for the entire African continent. Approximately 170,000 people used this route in 2015 and 150,000 in 2014, with the top three nationalities being Eritreans, Nigerians and Somalians. In 2013 only 40,000 attempted to cross the Mediterranean from Libya, of whom approximately 9,000 were Syrian[8]—the only year that Syrians were to move through this route in any significant numbers.

Instead, this route has long been a focus of migrant journeys from Africa to Europe, due largely to its proximity to Italy. The sea crossing from Tripoli to Italy's most southern point, the island of Lampedusa, is a mere 160 nautical miles (296 kilometres)—a crossing that in fair weather can be done in less than a day. While this crisis sees the number of people launching from Libya in large numbers, its role as a gateway to Europe is not without precedent.

Libya has consistently felt the pressure of African aspirations to seek different life chances in Europe. In 2009 Italy famously struck a bargain with Libyan dictator Muammar Gaddafi to control the Libyan coastline, to return any migrants found in sea patrols, and to hold migrants in detention centres. Although the arrangement was of dubious legality under international law, and had human rights advocates in full protest, it was devastatingly effective. Within one year of the Rome–Tripoli Accord going into effect, illicit migration into Italy from Libya fell by 75 per cent. Just months prior to Gaddafi's downfall in 2011, the wily Libyan leader was reportedly pressuring the Italians into expanding to a €5 billion incentive package, threatening that, without his support, 'tomorrow Europe might no longer be European, and even black, as there are millions who want to come in'.[9]

After Gaddafi fell from power, however, the subsequent transitional government was too weak and mired in infighting to have any capacity to manage the coastline. The Libyan coastguard now has only three patrol boats and insufficient resources to keep them fuelled, rendering its maritime surveillance and rescue capacities non-existent.

The second departure point that has developed from the North African coast, along the central Mediterranean route, is through Egypt. At the outset of the war in Syria many Syrians sought refuge in Egypt, as they did not need visas to enter the country and Egypt's policies towards Syrians were considered relatively welcoming. Following the fall of the Morsi government in April 2013, however, attitudes to Syrian refugees began to change, and the new administration was much more hostile to the Syrian refugee population, prompting many Syrians to attempt to move towards Europe.

Boatloads of Syrians began to leave towards Italy, reinforced by a large pool of Africans already residing in the country. The logistics of launching from Egypt are not quite the same as those required for departure from Libya. Boats leaving from Egypt take at least a week to reach Italy. It is a longer trip and requires more coordination to be successful, and these requirements have had a significant impact on the development of the smuggling market in Egypt.

While the departures from Egypt have never garnered headlines in the way that Libya and Turkey have, they have allowed a steady stream of migrants to reach Europe from Egyptian shores. In 2014 the majority of people leaving from the north coast of Egypt to cross the Mediterranean were Syrian. By 2015 the majority of those leaving and attempting to leave from Egypt's north coast were Sudanese and a mix of other, sub-Saharan African nationalities, including Somalis, Eritreans and Ethiopians. These demographic shifts are further reflected in the nationalities of those caught trying to depart by boat and are in detention on the north coast.[10]

But before reaching the North African coast, sub-Saharan Africans must pass through a number of towns which serve as migrant-smuggling hubs. Sebha is a major smuggling hub in southern Libya, located in the east of the country. The area around Sebha is notable for its farms, with a large percentage of the population being migrant workers, predominantly from West Africa. As a consequence there is a well-established route that passes between Sebha and Agadez, a small city deep in Niger's northern desert, which has become arguably the most important hub for trans-Saharan migration. A reported 3,000 people a week, from all over sub-Saharan Africa, have been congregating there waiting for a place on convoys that leave Monday every week, heading north into Libya.[11] The dust rises like a cloud as over a hundred four-wheel-drive vehicles leave the outskirts, each carrying between twenty-five and thirty-five migrants, perched precariously on the back of the trucks, clinging onto wooden poles fixed to prevent their falling off.

Agadez sits at the edge of a fifteen-country bloc called the Economic Community of West African States (ECOWAS), which permits freedom of movement to citizens of all member states. The region's topography, economy and history have ingrained mobility as a survival strategy, and its population sees freedom of movement as both a political and cultural right. The ability to migrate benefits the citizens and states of West Africa, and the remittances migrants send home are a major driver of the economies in the region, and a potent resilience mechanism for the families and communities within them.[12]

From East Africa the biggest hub is Ethiopia, and in particular its capital city, Addis Ababa. Ethiopia acts as the primary crossroads for migration out of the Horn of Africa—not only for Eritreans, but also for Ethiopians and Somalis. Of all of the networks that have flourished in the current crisis, the smugglers operating in the Horn of Africa were already the most professional, organised and profitable, thanks to the consistent flow of economic migrants, refugees and asylum seekers fleeing the repressive regime in Eritrea and conflict in Somalia. Numerous criminal networks are involved in recruiting and facilitating the smuggling of illegal migrants out of the Horn of Africa, both by land and by air, and there is a significant overlap with human trafficking through the plentiful number of labour-migration schemes available in Addis Ababa, Kenya and in the Horn more generally. In 2013 a survey by the Regional Mixed Migration Secretariat (RMMS) estimated that there were 1,000 illegal and unregistered 'agents' or 'brokers' and 406 registered private employment agencies at work in Addis Ababa alone.[13]

These form only one part of the numerous interlinking networks operating across the Horn of Africa to help potential migrants reach their destination countries, and this criminal infrastructure was very well placed to recalibrate itself around the incoming Syrian flow now heading for Europe.

From the Horn of Africa, the dominant overland route to Europe is through Sudan into Libya, or through Sudan and Egypt. Migrants and refugees from Eritrea travel south out of the country or from the large refugee camps to border crossings at Humera and Metemma, often via Gondar or Bahar Dahr. From Somalia, migrants cross into Ethiopia over the Tug Wajaale border crossing between Somaliland and Ethiopia, where smugglers reportedly entice their clients by offering free travel to Sudan, where they would be expected to make their first payment. Ethiopian police investigations have determined an integrated network that straddles both Sudan and Ethiopia.[14]

Eastern Sudan has long been notorious as a zone for various types of smuggling and trafficking. The two principal routes pass through the Kassala and Gederef areas, where smugglers take advantage of large, poorly controlled refugee camps to avoid government interference. From here the routes bifurcate, with some migrants turning north towards Egypt and the Sinai. Others continue their journey westward,

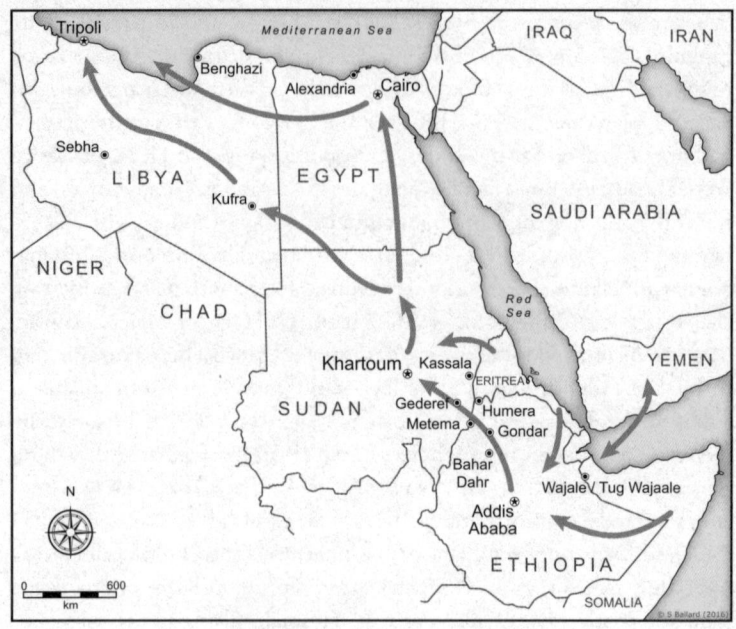

Map 2: Horn of Africa routes

towards Khartoum and its environs.[15] From Khartoum, the Sudanese capital, migrants find smugglers who will take them westwards to Kufra in southern Libya, where they may go further west to join the routes passing through Sebha, or northwards to the eastern cities of Libya's coast. In 2004, the governor of Kufra claimed that between 10,000 and 12,000 people pass through Kufra every month on their way north; a subsequent 2013 report estimated that the flow was in the region of 1–3,000 migrants per month.[16]

Migrants from Ethiopia and other countries in the Horn also travel southwards to East and South Africa, crossing into Kenya, Tanzania and even as far as South Africa. A long-standing route of importance has traditionally been to the Gulf countries, but this has now largely closed down. In 2013 stricter border controls in Israel and the Gulf states have led many to change their destination to Europe. Saudi Arabia has built a 1,800-kilometre fence along its border with Yemen, and has deported thousands of undocumented migrant workers. As a result, although many East Africans still make their way to Yemen, numbers have dropped significantly, to 58,000 in September 2013. Israel has also built a wall along its border, effectively halting migration flows. Only 36 irregular migrants crossed into Israel in the first nine months of 2013. In early 2015, Saudi Arabia announced that it would no longer tolerate irregular migrants, leading to the expulsion of tens of thousands of Ethiopians from the country. Prior to this decision, in the seven years preceding 2013, an estimated 500,000 people (mainly Ethiopians and Somalis) from the Horn of Africa were thought to have crossed the Red Sea and the Gulf of Aden. With the escalation of the conflict in Yemen this route has become increasingly difficult to monitor, although anecdotal evidence points to a slowdown in traffic due to the Yemeni conflict. Nonetheless, the UNHCR continues to document large numbers of Ethiopians and Somalis being smuggled on boats from the Somaliland and Puntland coasts. Between July and September 2015 almost 5,000 people were registered as arriving on the Arabian coast this way, although the true figure may be much higher. Small numbers of migrants and refugees also continue to travel from Ethiopia to Djibouti and onwards by sea to Yemen.[17]

Although these border closings have substantially impeded migratory flows eastward, they have failed to curb the desperation with which African migrants search for better opportunities, thus concentrating migration flows with even greater intensity towards Europe.

Aegean Route through Turkey

Vastly exceeding Libya in numbers, Turkey emerged as the other major gateway to Europe, serving as a portal by land, sea and air. Playing a pivotal role in the migration system of the Mediterranean basin for decades, Turkey has served as a funnel bringing migrants from Central Asia and the Middle East—mainly from Afghanistan, Bangladesh, Iraq, Iran, Palestine and India—as well as from the Horn of Africa to Europe.[18] Many of the routes used today have been there for decades, used not only by migrant smugglers but also by traffickers of various types of illicit substances, including drugs such as heroin.

Istanbul is the single most significant departure point for air traffic to Europe, representing roughly 6.5 per cent of total air traffic into the

EU globally. This number has been growing steadily since 2010. In parallel to the growth of legitimate air traffic, partially driven by Turkish Airlines' expansion into new routes in Africa and the Middle East, Atäturk Airport is also an important hub for irregular migrants travelling by air to several EU member states.[19]

This new development, coupled with Turkey's free-visa regime with Syria until late 2015, made it the key departure point of the European migrant crisis for those travelling by air. Yet it was Turkey's emergence as an easy and effective launching point for sea crossings into Europe that places it at the centre of the current migrant crisis. A confluence of geo-political factors led to a surge in migrant departures from Turkey and into Europe. For starters, conditions for the over 2 million refugees in Turkey became increasingly unsustainable. Increased gains by the Islamic State and its affiliates, Russian airstrikes in Syria and a ramping up of Turkish hostilities towards the Kurds on the shared border with Syria also led to an influx of movement through Turkey and into Europe. With networks emerging to facilitate the flow of Syrians from Turkey into Europe, Iraqis, Afghans, Pakistanis and other nationalities joined the migrant flow, further cementing Turkey as the migrant gateway to Europe. These events, combined with the August 2015 decision by German chancellor Angela Merkel to waive the Dublin Regulation, thus removing one of the key deterrents of trying to enter Europe via Greece, meant that the number of migrants using the Aegean crossing would come to dwarf those arriving via Libya and Egypt.

The numbers, and their exponential expansion, are extraordinary. Fewer than 12,000 people crossed the Aegean from Turkey to Greece in 2013. In 2014 this number rose to over 50,000, only to explode to an astonishing 885,000 in 2015. Of these 2015 arrivals, 500,000 claimed to have come from Syria, 210,000 from Afghanistan and 90,000 from Iraq. To put these numbers into perspective, no more than 170,000 have ever used the central Mediterranean route in a single year.[20]

Crossing from Turkey into Greece includes a short sea crossing from the Turkish coast to one of the Greek islands in close proximity to Turkey. After registering in Greece, migrants would take a ferry to the Greek mainland. Upon arriving in Athens or Thessaloniki, they then began a long, overland trek through Macedonia, sometimes Bulgaria, from where they continued through a string of Balkan and Eastern European countries until they reached Western Europe.

Although the Aegean crossing is a relatively easy journey compared to the Mediterranean route, the land portion is long, physically demanding and dangerous, factors that previously served as a deterrent to many migrants considering this route.[21] Not only are there several brutal and predatory organised crime groups operating at key borders and hubs along the route, but Eastern European governments, particularly their police forces, are relatively hostile to migrants. Similarly, the risk of being registered under the Dublin Regulation in a country that offered few, if any, refugee privileges made trying to reach Western Europe a risky gambit.

Following Chancellor Merkel's announcement of the de facto suspension of the Dublin Regulation, reaching Western Europe from Greece became a feasible proposition. Suddenly the short sea crossing from a beach on the Turkish coast to one of the Greek islands visible from the shore, a crossing that could take less than an hour in good weather conditions, was by far the easiest and safest route into Europe.

Nearly 50,000 migrants landed in July 2015, with 100,000 more arriving in August. 90 per cent of these arrivals took place on just four Greek islands. Out of nowhere, coastal communities and local merchants on both sides of the Aegean re-oriented themselves to serve the thousands of migrants appearing on their shores. With near careless abandon, migrants were put to sea in cheap dinghies manufactured in China and shipped over on special delivery. Life jackets, both real and fake, were available in every seafront shop. Hundreds died every month—686 in August; 268 in September, 432 in October, 106 in November and so on[22]—as boats overturned and the combined rescue facilities of the Turkish and Greek coastguards, supplemented by ad hoc crews of NGOs, struggled to deal with the innumerable boats leaving every night in the dark.

In 2015, a total of 750,000 people were recorded as having travelled along the route through the Balkans, mainly skirting Hungary and Croatia's borders with Serbia. Most of the migrants then left the Schengen zone to travel through Macedonia and then Serbia, where the Syrians, Afghans and Iraqis were joined by migrants from the western Balkans (mostly from Kosovo and Albania). At first they moved rela-

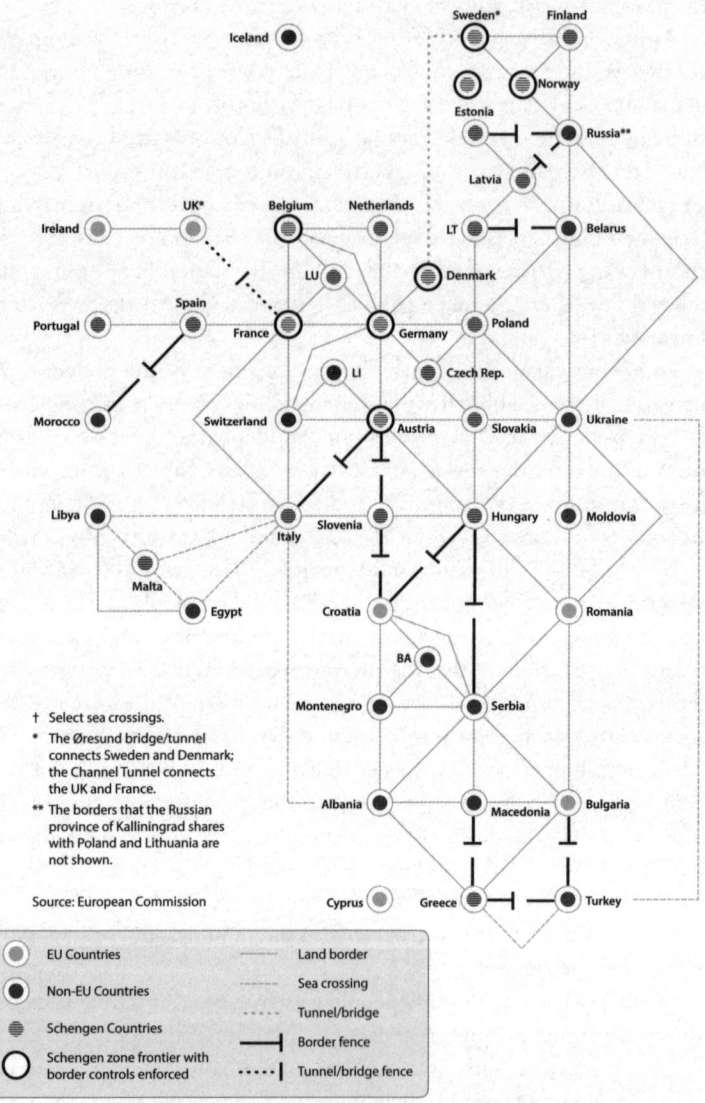

† Select sea crossings.

* The Øresund bridge/tunnel connects Sweden and Denmark; the Channel Tunnel connects the UK and France.

** The borders that the Russian province of Kalliningrad shares with Poland and Lithuania are not shown.

Source: European Commission

EU Countries		Land border
Non-EU Countries		Sea crossing
Schengen Countries		Tunnel/bridge
Schengen zone frontier with border controls enforced		Border fence
		Tunnel/bridge fence

Map 3: The border controls of Europe[23]

tively freely, walking en masse, using public transport where allowed, and in some cases even by dedicated trains and buses provided by countries determined to remain transit states.

With little need for a smuggler, a kind of 'do-it-yourself' migration through the Balkans, guided by advice on social media forums and by other migrants making the journey, became the dominant migration model. After Hungary constructed a temporary obstacle along its border with Serbia and border controls in Serbia were tightened in September 2015, however, demand for smuggler services spiked.

As this mass of migrants began to fan out across Europe, the Schengen zone all but collapsed, and temporary border controls were imposed, reinforced by the construction of new fences. In perhaps one of the most unlikely of cases, Austria proposed building a fence on its border with Italy, prompting violent demonstrations and heated diplomatic exchanges.[24]

The massive and uncontrolled surge of people resulted in a rapid and punitive response by the EU member states, which once again changed the environment for both migrants and smugglers. In February 2016 a NATO mission was deployed in the Aegean, with warship patrols intended to disrupt the sea-smuggling operations.[25] This mission was complemented by a highly controversial €6 billion agreement between the EU and Turkey whose sole function was 'to break the business model of the smugglers and to offer migrants an alternative to putting their lives at risk'.[26] The agreement included enhanced law-enforcement action, patrols along both coasts, and an arrangement by which any asylum seeker who reached Greece from Turkey could be sent back there, in exchange for an equal number of resettlement places in Europe for those who had processed their asylum claims through the proper channels in Turkey.

With migrants no longer able to move freely from Greece, a series of squalid camps sprang up along the Greek border with Hungary, providing fertile ground for smugglers to recruit those who had previously hoped they could walk through unfettered. As this book is being finalised the newly enlivened Turkish smuggling industry is inventing and developing alternative routes into Europe for the hundreds of thousands of migrants pooled in Turkey who hope to start life anew in Europe, or somewhere else that will take them.

PART 2

5

LIBYA

OUT OF AFRICA

*Esther came to Libya with dreams of living in Spain. Back in Lagos, Nigeria, she worked in a bank, a job she landed thanks to her degree in accounting. As a single, gainfully employed woman in her twenties, Esther had no problem saving money. But like any ambitious twenty-something she wanted more, and wondered what her life might be like if she lived elsewhere. One day she befriended a woman who said she had a supermarket in Spain and could arrange for Esther to live and work abroad. Without telling her family, Esther decided to take a leap of faith. Spain, she thought, could offer her something new.

Esther and her newfound friend left Lagos together and travelled on public transport through northern Nigeria and into southern Niger until they reached Agadez, from where they hired smugglers to transport them through the desert. She knew crossing the Sahara was a risky proposition and expected harsh conditions, but Esther was completely unprepared for the months of physical and mental abuse that awaited her.

The violence, Esther explains, started at the very first checkpoint outside Agadez. 'I was badly beaten in Niger at a checkpoint by security men because I refused to pay the bribe,' Esther recalls, now sitting in an outdoor café in the Libyan capital, Tripoli. 'They made me lie down on the ground and beat me twice with a belt on my back and twice on my hands with a stick.'

Her smugglers had only paid a portion of the required bribes, passing the remainder of the fees to their customers. According to Esther, women who refused to pay bribes were threatened with rape, and even those who did pay bribes were just as vulnerable. 'Many women get raped, sometimes even if they pay, they still get raped. The men take you into the desert and there is nothing you can do because they have guns.'

Despite being on the receiving end of their depravity, Esther displays a remarkable capacity for empathising with the Nigérien soldiers who abused her. 'They are government employees but they are stuck in the desert and are very poor,' Esther explains. 'Maybe they do not get paid their wages. I don't know. They seemed desperate … It is terrible there.'

When her truck arrived in Sebha in southern Libya, after eight days travelling through the desert with almost no food, very little water, and having endured physical abuse several times over, Esther assumed that the worst was behind her. But she quickly learned that her Nigerian friend in Lagos was part of a human-trafficking ring specialising in luring Nigerian women to Europe and forcing them to 'buy' back their own freedom by working as prostitutes in Libya. Esther tried to escape immediately, but she was caught and subsequently tortured. 'They caught me and beat the hell out of me,' Esther explains. 'They told me I had to work as a prostitute to pay my way out. I was held for almost three months.'

Esther says the prostitution ring was overseen by Libyans and Nigerians with houses in Sebha and Marzuq, where women lived like prisoners and were forced to have sex with 'filthy people, bad people' for the equivalent of $7. Eventually, Esther's handlers allowed her to call her mother and ask her to send money. They demanded $2,500 but in the end they accepted $1,600 as the price of Esther's freedom. 'They put the phone onto speaker phone and beat me so she could hear me being beaten,' Esther recalls. 'It is an evil world.'

Now in Tripoli, Esther says she thinks often of the women who are still being held prisoner. 'It is terrible for them. Many women get pregnant, too.' And despite all the hardship she has endured, or perhaps because of it, Esther is determined to reach Europe, where she hopes she can continue her career as an accountant and go to school for more qualifications.

Esther is not sure where she wants to end up. She lists Canada as one possible destination, but it is not clear whether she knows that

Canada is not in Europe. Either way, she knows a Nigerian man in Germany who might be able to come and get her once she lands in Italy. But first she needs to get on a boat, a project for which she is already making arrangements. She knows that the typical price these days is roughly $1,000, and thinks she can get a reduced price of between $550 and $600 by avoiding the middlemen in Tripoli and negotiating directly with the boat owners in nearby Zuwarah. Meanwhile, her mother is making preparations to send her money. 'When the money comes, I will leave', she says, but only when 'the waters are good and the time is right.'

Esther is only one of the over 500,000 sub-Saharan African migrants in Libya, many of whom arrived with hopes of reaching Europe when the 'waters are good and the time is right'. Though sub-Saharan Africans had been coming to Libya in search of employment for decades, often with the tacit encouragement of the Gaddafi regime, the aftermath of the 2011 revolution in Libya replaced forty years of authoritarianism with state fragmentation and, eventually, state collapse. Violent clashes between a mosaic of competing militias over political and economic control left the country in anarchy and, without a functioning government or state institutions, new criminal economies became an important source of income for those seeking to enrich themselves and empower their military and political networks. For irregular migrants, prior to the fall of Gaddafi, trying to reach Europe from Libya was a challenge thanks to geo-politics. With Gaddafi gone, it was only a challenge of geography.

Criminal Economies in Libya and the Greater Sahara

In losing Gaddafi, who regularly warned European leaders that he was the only thing preventing Europe from becoming 'black', Europe lost its most reliable border guard. Though he often used the rhetoric of an expert extortionist, preying on Europe's worst xenophobic tendencies, Gaddafi was not wrong when he warned that a power vacuum in Tripoli would mean tens of thousands of Africans trying to reach Europe from Libyan shores.

The dictator's four-decade rule in Libya was characterised by his unparalleled ability to use control over the licit and illicit economy as a means of ensuring support from a highly fragmented tribal society with deep suspicions of the central state. Gaddafi had managed to personalise the Libyan state, and he deliberately kept political institutions weak in order to 'draw closer to the [true] people, and to eliminate the distorting buffer of bureaucracy between government and people'.[2] In the first chapter of his manifesto, *The Green Book*, Gaddafi himself wrote that states are oppressive and dominating, as they require the surrendering of 'personal sovereignty', a concept to which he gave a great deal of emphasis.

Governance under Gaddafi meant the allocation of control over resources amongst a series of tribes, sects and interest groups. The state broadly centralised control over oil resources, which, from the 1950s onwards, were the most significant economic driver, with the wealth being distributed back to the population in the form of a panoply of subsidies. Libyans benefited from subsidies on all basic commodities, as well as allowances for marriage (including the wedding itself), children, housing and fuel. But for other industries and economies, Gaddafi allocated the right to participate in certain sectors and engage in trade, and the right to tax it, to certain actors in exchange for political support and relatively little taxation or interference from the central state. Ever the pragmatist, Gaddafi applied this principle both to the legitimate and illicit economies. To quote the man himself, from an address to a local revolutionary committee in 1988:

> You may think that black markets are negative. On the contrary. As far as we are concerned, as revolutionaries they show that people spontaneously take a decision and without government make something which they need: they establish a black market because they need it … What are black markets? They are people's markets.[3]

The result was a series of controlled criminal markets gifted to tribal elites and regulated by the permissiveness of Gaddafi himself. In the same way, access to government positions meant the ability to tax and control trafficking and trade within that territory through a system of bribes and payoffs.[4]

As Chapter 3 on Agadez and the Greater Sahel will emphasise, licit and illicit trade in the greater Sahara (encompassing the Maghreb and North African countries, as well as the Sahara–Sahel) is not a concept that can be understood from the perspectives of one single nation, or even within traditional conceptions of Western-style nation-states. Rather, these are a vast web of political and economic systems that stretch across the entire region. While different ethnic groups have different patterns of settlement, transhumance (livestock grazing) and nomadism, the harsh nature of the topography means that many peoples in the region use a degree of mobility in order to sustain themselves.

One such example in Libya is the people who comprise the Zuwaya tribe, who are spread across the heartland of southern Libya around Kufra. Historically, the Zuwaya move annually between the northern coastal strip of semi-desert and the oases of the central Sahara. They harvest cash crops along the coast and graze their livestock there seasonally. Afterwards, they move south in time for the date harvest, feeding their animals on fodder-dates and forage crops until it is time to move north again. Each year some portion of the tribe leaves their families on a wider economic pilgrimage, going southwards into sub-Saharan Africa, staying away for years, moving between the markets of the Sahel to exploit differences in prices between different markets and to buy camels with the proceeds. Through each territory they pass, they are likely to pay some sort of tax, tithe or bribe to a range of state and non-state actors, which may include local officials, the police, a relevant warlord or a militia. Traditionally, when they had acquired enough camels and other goods, they would move back north to sell half their camels and trade for goods that would be brought back to Kufra or sold along the route. Over time, the camels have been almost completely replaced by trucks and four-wheel drives, but the migration patterns predicated on trade remain.

While these types of trans-Saharan connections have been sustained over centuries by Islamic law and social capital maintained through clan-based affiliations, at the same time, shared legal traditions and familial bonds were not always sufficient to secure the safe passage of goods given the thousands of kilometres involved. Each clan and community, therefore, developed a capacity for 'protection offered by specialists of violence' within their ranks,[5] and this function has endured in various forms for centuries, continuing through the colonial period and to the present day.[6]

Protection, like everything else of value in the Sahel and Sahara, became a commodity that could be bought and sold.[7] And in the case of Libya, Gaddafi sponsored and controlled the protection trade, as he did with many other forms of economic activity, by outsourcing state security and military functions to specific militias and tribes, rather than creating and investing in an effective national army or police.

For centuries, both people and commodities across the Sahara and Sahel have been connected in a web of trade interdependencies.[8] Over

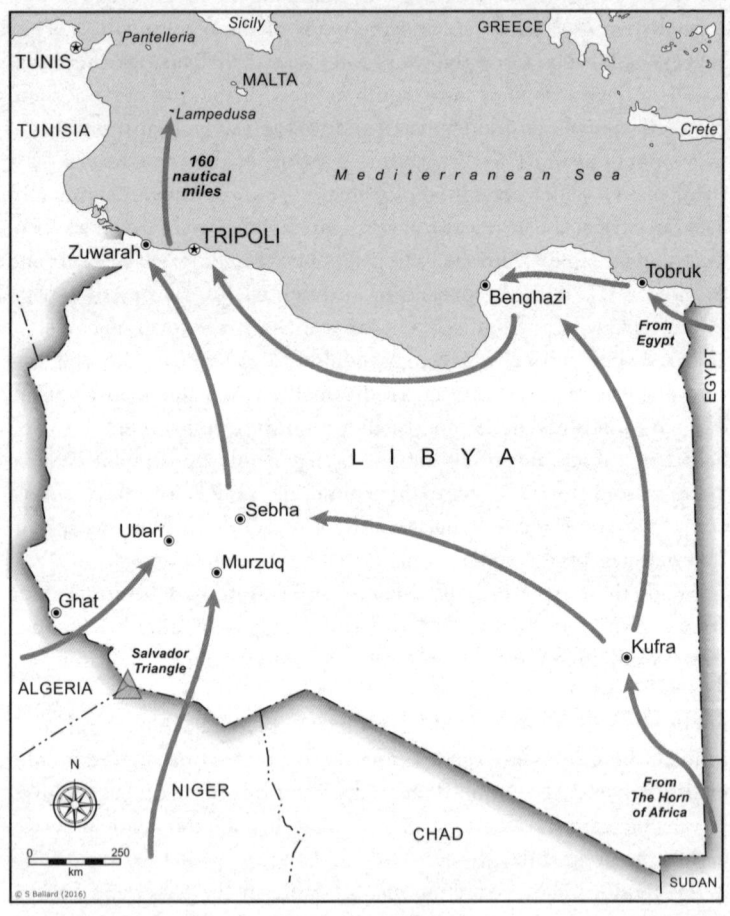

Map 4: Map of Libya

the past twenty years, however, a number of definitive shifts have served to strengthen these interdependencies in ways that increased the importance of the illicit economy. Firstly, a growing reliance on hydrocarbons in key North African states—namely Algeria and Libya—meant that other forms of trade and industry shrank as extensive subsidies were used to plug the lacunae of sustainable livelihoods. The existence of these subsidies also gave rise to a flourishing smuggling economy of subsidised goods from North Africa into neighbouring states where they could be sold for considerable profit.

The second shift came in the form of post-war containerisation and a greater global focus on transporting goods by sea. Since 2009 over 90 per cent of worldwide cargo is moved by sea, with 70 per cent as containerised cargo.[9] As the focus of the global movement of goods turned to the sea, the old Saharan land routes, long challenged by the emergence of more efficient sea routes, further contracted to barely subsistence levels, meaning that communities that had previously flourished due to their strategic locations along key trading hubs that linked sub-Saharan Africa to the Mediterranean now relied on port cities for even the most basic commodities.

The result is that the greater Sahara shifted from being a region of transit between markets to an outwardly focused region of global trade. The internal trade that once fuelled the economies on the edges of the Sahel–Sahara shrank significantly. North African and West African economies have concentrated themselves around a system of increasingly well-developed ports and, for the most part, become characterised by a heavy reliance on the import of goods and export of oil. While there are some exceptions to this, the cities and towns of the Sahara, once known as places of global commerce and scholarship, had little collateral to leverage in this new economic order, with one large exception: illicit trafficking.[10]

After Gaddafi's fall in 2011, his controlled system of favoured contractors in the licit and illicit economy was replaced by a factionalised free-for-all. During his four-decade rule the master manipulator had played his hand so skilfully that there were no obvious immediate successors or dominant ethnic elites. Instead, different groups and their armed protectors jockeyed for control over resources, transport infrastructure, trafficking routes and political influence, evenly matched and therefore unable to win the critical mass of control to stabilise and govern the place.

In the face of growing social unrest, Gaddafi had raised the level of subsidies to an astonishing €11.5 billion per year in food and fuel alone in an attempt to buy order—levels that subsequent transitional regimes have been unable to draw down.[11] The increase in subsidies emboldened the smuggling networks that moved these subsidised goods between Libya and its neighbours, further entrenching the trafficking culture just as the state was breaking down. Vehicles of varying size now traverse the desert with a combination of food-stuffs, cigarettes, hashish and sometimes cocaine, always protected by the omnipresent AK-47 or heavier weaponry. The licit and the illicit economy sit side by side, centred around tribes and communities that are dispersed across the Sahara and consider themselves independent, ungoverned, and, as is crucially important to their identities, 'per-sonally sovereign'.

In a 2014 report on illicit trafficking in Libya, Mark Shaw and Fiona Mangan identified four main illicit markets in Libya post-Gaddafi: basic smuggling of licit goods, weapons, migrants and drugs. They analyse these markets according to a natural hierarchy organised by financial return and strategic importance. At the very centre of the hierarchy is the illegal movement of people.[12] This placement is significant not only because the long-standing human-smuggling trade is interlinked with illicit trade and trafficking of numerous other commodities but because it is enabled by ethnic networks from across the region. Migrant smug-gling, and the subsequent victimisation of the migrants through forced labour and extortion, has proven a durable and consistent source of income for the tribes engaged in cross-border trading, with the risks and penalties (where they exist) being much less harsh than those for drug trafficking and other more stigmatised activities. Migrant smug-gling has thus been a reliable income source and important pillar of the Saharan economy in Libya and beyond.

Despite being an important and ubiquitous mainstay across the Sahara, human smuggling was largely an ancillary to other forms of smuggling, rarely an end in itself. For smugglers, moving migrants was a way of supplementing income on the return leg of a journey: a truck carrying subsidised fuel from Algeria into Mali might come back with

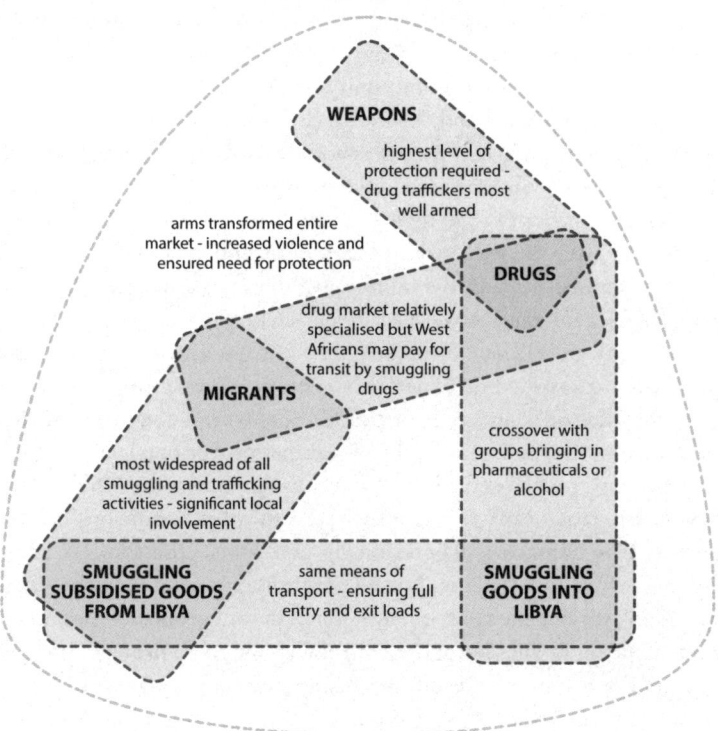

Figure 1: Migrants at the centre of the hierarchy of trafficked commodities in Libya[13]

a couple of West Africans keen to work in the hydrocarbon economies of North Africa.

With each migrant paying a few hundred dollars or less for a journey across the desert and around tricky borders, these meandering and opportunistic arrangements served all parties well. Migration was a positive economic opportunity for those able to afford the journey, and transporters and traffickers were able to increase their profits at no additional cost. Furthermore, the activity was barely considered criminal and stopping it was far from a priority for the states from which the migrants came, transited or settled. In fact, the revenues generated from taxing or collecting rents from the migrant-smuggling trade made for a steady contribution to the local economies of transit hubs and border towns across the Sahara.

For the international community, particularly Europe, migrant smuggling in the Sahel and Sahara barely registered as an issue worth time and resources to better understand, let alone stop. Though several European and North American countries were monitoring drug routes and terrorist groups in the region, and actively engaged in countering them, migration did not warrant the same attention because even with Libya in complete chaos, the numbers of migrants attempting to leave North Africa for Europe were relatively small.[14]

Germany, the UK and other northern European states consequently had little background or experience with the issue of migrant smuggling in Africa. As an agent of the UK Crown Prosecution Service explained to me, in the hierarchy of transnational crimes, illicit migration was never high on the list. It was considered a Home Office affair, and investigative capacity was dedicated to more pernicious crimes such as drug trafficking, cybercrime, or even human trafficking. Furtive migrants sneaking through borders and disappearing into the illicit economy was of little consequence, as northern European states relied on the Dublin Regulation and the littoral countries to protect Europe's external frontiers. As a result, many European policymakers trying to understand and respond to the quickly evolving migration crisis and the networks that were enabling it were starting from scratch.

Gaddafi, it turned out, was right. His absence would translate to thousands of migrants trying to reach Europe from Libyan shores. What he could not have known, however, was that an uprising in Syria, thousands of miles away from the chaos in Tripoli, would set in motion a chain of events that would transform the business of migrant smuggling throughout much of Africa.

Syrian Dollars on Libyan Shores

During the Libyan revolution and its aftermath, the migrant smuggling economy in Libya became increasingly commoditised. In Libya's major cities, migrants held in detention centres managed by revolutionary brigades were contracted out as informal work gangs, receiving no compensation but garnering revenue for those who controlled them.

Rounding up and imprisoning black African migrants for rented labour was only one business model; another, which has become popular among various militia groups, was to extort money from their families to purchase their release. And while it is the nomadic and semi-nomadic groups such as the Tuareg and Toubou that were primarily responsible for smuggling migrants across Libya's southern border, it was powerful, institutionalised groups established under the Gaddafi regime that controlled the Libyan trade to and from the coast.

At the top of these networks are many of the same actors to whom Gaddafi had granted informal smuggling licences and thus the ability to control alcohol, cigarette and especially fuel smuggling. Accordingly, these networks are well established and carry out tightly controlled operations, smuggling a variety of different illegal goods, which left them well placed to exploit the booming migrant-smuggling trade. Although these previously existing smuggling hierarchies were eager to take advantage of the power vacuum to put migrants out to sea, the majority of sub-Saharan migrants were unable to afford the costs of paying for smuggler services. It was only after Syrians began arriving in Libya in large numbers, seeking passage to Europe, that these networks truly began to flourish, and prices began to fall.

As early as 2012, thousands of Syrians began to arrive in Libya, travelling either by plane from Lebanon and Turkey or overland from Egypt. Syrian refugees had a far higher disposable income than their sub-Saharan counterparts, many of whom came to Libya to find work, in the hope of later funding onward journeys. Syrians, however, sought above all else passage Europe, and thus were ready to spend as much of their savings as was required.

Disparate and opportunistic smuggling networks quickly began to coalesce around Syrian demand for smuggling services and Syrian purchasing power. When Syrians first started departing Libyan shores in 2012, their smugglers were sending them on relatively seaworthy vessels procured from local traders and fishermen. Because these boats were valuable, costing upwards of $100,000, and because the cost of losing a ship to the Italian coastguard had to be incorporated into the cost of doing business, sending ships was only economically feasible if the revenues generated were a minimum of several hundred thousand dollars per launch. Though Syrians, with their ability to pay premium prices, were highly coveted as customers, they were not always leaving the Libyan coast in the numbers needed to make a departure economically viable from the smugglers' perspective.

Having built the requisite infrastructure on Syrian demand for their services, smuggling networks began to actively draw from the pools of sub-Saharan Africans living in Libya, offering them reduced rates to make the crossing, and thereby using their vast numbers to augment profit margins. Migrant-smuggling markets on the Libyan coast consolidated, therefore, around a model driven by economies of scale.

Between 2012 and 2013 Syrians reported paying an average of $2,000 to launch from Libya, while sub-Saharan Africans were paying as little as $800 to $1,000 for passage on the same ships. During this same period, the average boat arriving in Italy carried a minimum of 300 people, with numbers regularly reaching as high as 1,000. But with this price disparity came very different treatment. Syrians travelled on deck, whereas Africans were often locked in the hold. Syrians received life jackets and other provisions; Africans did not.

As we explained in Part 1, though there is no single business model or corporate structure that defines the migrant-smuggling industry, smuggling networks now operating along the Libyan coast tend to be organised along a layered pyramid structure, with high-level coordinators at the top of the pyramid, who remain far removed from the recruiters at the bottom. The coordinators rarely, if ever, have contact with migrants. Their role is to finance operations, ensure access to departure sites, bribe authorities on a grand scale, manage the military and political connections necessary to execute their activities, and generally create or maintain an environment conducive to carrying out their operations.

Managers one level below the coordinators make sure that there are safe houses in place and a steady supply of boats, and oversee the labour force needed to carry out day-to-day operations. Beneath the managers are people with an array of roles and responsibilities. Actors at this level might be those who house the migrants, literally operating farms and sites where migrants are held and consolidated, sometimes in the hundreds or thousands, or those charged with providing security, prepping launch sites and arranging transport from safe houses. Other responsibilities include collecting money from the recruiters and brokers below them in the pyramid, loading migrants onto the boats, and ensuring that someone is able to operate each vessel and is properly instructed what to do if approached by the authorities.

Finally, at the bottom of the pyramid is a vast, multi-ethnic network of 'samsars' (brokers) and recruiters, as well as the lower-level Libyan smugglers who coordinate with them. Though brokers and recruiters are at the bottom of the migrant-smuggling pyramid, they are by far the most visible. They are the people with whom migrants have the greatest contact, and are almost always those to whom migrants are referring when they talk later about 'their smuggler'. To that end, migrants' perceptions of their experiences, whether positive or negative, are shaped considerably by their interactions with their brokers, despite the fact that brokers are the most interchangeable and least specialised part of the entire industry.

Brokers might only serve one function, but it is an absolutely crucial one. They bring together groups of 50–100 migrants at a time, collecting money and negotiating the terms of their journeys. They recruit along ethnic and linguistic lines, operating in the main cities, towns and transit hubs within Libya and further into sub-Saharan Africa where migrants gather. They market themselves through a variety of methods, cajoling and even coercing migrants into selecting them as their smuggler. The strategies they use to differentiate themselves from the competition will depend very much on the individual and the context in which he or she operates. Some manipulate the prices, offering discounts or incentives, such as 'bring three friends and you'll travel for free'.

Other brokers establish relationships with recruiters operating earlier in the route, offering a cut of their profits for each successful referral. Since brokers are almost always the same nationality or ethnicity as the migrants they seek to recruit, they often try to build trust with the migrants, taking advantage of the fact that they speak local dialects, share a culture, come from the same villages or communities, and might even share familial connections or have friends in common. More often than not, these brokers are migrants themselves, having made the same journey as those they seek to recruit, and are often working within the migrant-smuggling industry as a means of funding their own future journeys. At bus stations and regular drop-off points in key hubs such as Sebha, Kufra, Ubari and Ghat, brokers circle like vultures, descending on new arrivals as soon as they disembark, and offering their services to those who might not speak the language or understand the culture of the places in which they have just arrived.

In order to make themselves valuable to those above them in the smuggling pyramid, brokers have to recruit groups of at least twenty-five, but more likely fifty or more migrants who have paid and are ready to board a boat. Of the entire migrant-smuggling chain, the sea crossing is by far the most expensive in terms of operating costs, and the most lucrative in terms of revenue and profits. As a result, it is the segment of the industry that is controlled almost exclusively by Libyans. Yet in order for those at the highest levels to ensure that their investments in boats, bribes and political capital are sufficiently hidden from scrutiny, these high-level smugglers are completely removed from the brokers and migrants themselves.

On the ground, it is the managers and their underlings who coordinate pre-departures, juggling multiple colours of cheap yet indestructible Nokia mobile phones, communicating with a web of brokers to see who has rounded up sufficient numbers to justify a departure: thirty Eritreans; fifty from Mali and Burkina; twenty-five from Somalia; forty from Nigeria. At this point the managers will coordinate with the high-level smugglers above them in the pyramid to finalise the details of the departure, specifying the date, time and location, and begin to allocate places in boats that are on standby, often clustering groups by nationality or language to make logistics easier.[15]

In the hours leading up to the night of the departure—and it is almost always night, to avoid the risk of being seen by the police or a rival smuggling gang—a fleet of minibuses will spend the day collecting migrants from prearranged way stations, halfway houses and hostels where they have been told to congregate or were gathered by their brokers, sometimes several days before the planned departure. As one Libyan smuggler explained to *The Guardian*, 'They gather in a specific place. Transport takes them from that location in a safe house. All their phones get collected. They bring no luggage. They're fed and watered and given access to toilets until the time to embark.'[16]

As night falls the buses depart from these locations and converge upon a quiet part of Libya's 1,770-kilometre shoreline, the longest coastline of any African country bordering the Mediterranean. These launch points are often privately owned beachfronts where rubber dinghies will be waiting to take the migrants out to sea.

The beaches of Khoms, Garaboli and Sabratha, all on the north-west coast, are popular places for smugglers to launch boats, but the majority of boats depart from an area near a small port city in the west of Libya called Zuwarah, sandwiched between the border with Tunisia and Libya's capital, Tripoli.

Zuwarah's emergence as a launching pad to Europe is due in part to geography. Located a mere 160 nautical miles from the Italian island of Lampedusa, Zuwarah is one of the closest possible launching points to Italian territory. But as with everything related to the migrant smuggling trade, politics is also part of the explanation.

A small city known for its beautiful beaches and abundant seafood, Zuwarah is a place where Tripoli's elite go to relax. More importantly, however, it holds a special place in Libya's political history. It was in Zuwarah, after all, that Gaddafi first proclaimed the Libyan 'cultural revolution' in 1973.

Zuwarah is dominated by the Amazigh Berber peoples, the largest of Libya's ethnic minority groups, who are commonly estimated to represent between 10–15 per cent of Libya's population. The Amazigh are concentrated along the western coast, but also deep into the southern oasis towns of Ubari, Ujula and Uweinat. They trace their roots in North Africa to before the Arab invasions of the seventh century, and speak their own language, Tamazight, which is derived from ancient Phoenician.

The Amazigh were marginalised by Gaddafi, who saw their cultural pride as an impediment to his vision of an Arab republic. He outlawed the teaching of Tamazight in schools, the publication of books in Tamazight, and the speaking of Tamazight in public. He even prevented children from being registered with traditional Tamazight names.

In the aftermath of the revolution, the high hopes amongst the Amazigh that they would be permitted greater freedoms and political inclusion in a post-Gaddafi Libya gave way to bitter disappointment. Not only were they systematically excluded from each successive transitional authority formed, but they were also denied a requested veto power in the constitution-drafting process. They sought influence over 'cultural components', such as the name and identity of the Libyan state, the flag, anthem and language rights. Their priority was to prevent post-Gaddafi Libya from consolidating its identity as an Arab state, and to leave space for inclusion of other national identities. In the aftermath of this failed lobbying effort the Amazigh have been conscientious objectors, boycotting elections and the process of drafting the constitution altogether.

Shut out of formal political and economic opportunities, the Amazigh asserted themselves in one of the largest and most lucrative of Libya's criminal economies: migrant smuggling. One way to view their involvement in the trade, therefore, is to consider it not just an act of economic opportunism, but of political survival. In the swirling maelstrom of Libya's militia-driven politics, the ability to secure resources is a critical component of ensuring future relevance. The profits of the smuggling trade have not only enriched the entire Zuwarah community and the Amazigh, they have afforded them a consistent point of leverage with the fractured Libyan government and the international community. As a result, rise of the migrant-smuggling trade in Libya is inextricably linked to the Amazigh struggle,[17] and for that reason the boats that leave from Zuwarah's shores are unhindered by the local police, authorities or competing militia groups prevalent on other parts of the shoreline. This peace through collusion appeals to migrants as well, who consider Zuwarah a preferred destination and launch point because of its relative security and lack of violence.

In order to transport migrants into international waters from the Libyan coast, a journey of just 12 nautical miles (22 kilometres), smuggling networks usually arrange for migrants to take two separate boats. From the shoreline they wade out to into the dark, cold sea to climb onto small dinghies in groups of twenty to thirty, which will then ferry them a few kilometres offshore where larger boats—often wooden fishing trawlers—are waiting for them.

Transferring people from one boat to another in the middle of the open sea is a delicate balancing act. To start with, people on both vessels have to remain evenly distributed while the whole operation takes place, or else the dingy might capsize.

'We give them direct instructions not to move too much', one of Libya's boat smugglers told *The Guardian*, 'if you have to move, we tell them to just stand up and sit down—don't go from side to side. If two or three start to do that, others want to do the same. That creates chaos that causes it to capsize.'[18] Many of the migrant deaths in the earlier years of the sea crossings are believed to have taken place during this phase of transferring ships.

The wooden fishing trawlers that receive migrants from the smaller boats—bought, borrowed or stolen from Libyan, Egyptian or Tunisian fishermen—can hold several hundred people. Thus, the process of transferring hundreds of migrants into a single ship can take several hours, with dinghies or smaller ships making multiple trips back and forth from the trawler to the shore. Over the course of research for this book, some migrants reported in interviews that they waited on boats out at sea for several days, with loading taking place over the course of two or three nights before they departed for Europe. But these examples appear to be exceptions rather than the norm.

After loading the migrants onto the main vessel, with the Africans often pushed down into the hold and the Syrians or higher-paying passengers on deck, the ship is ready to set sail towards Italy. Because large fishing boats need a crew with the skills necessary to navigate the Mediterranean, these larger vessels had crewmembers on board. In some cases the crew would consist of people hired by the smuggling networks who could pose as migrants upon arrival or if caught by European authorities. In other instances the crew might consist of migrants who were offered free passage in exchange for navigating the boat, thus allowing smugglers to get back into the dinghies and disappear into the darkness and toward the shore.

Mare Nostrum Changes the Game

From early 2012 Libya grew as a smuggling hub and launching point into Europe, with departures from the Libyan coastline steadily increasing and untold numbers dying at sea. But it was not until after a shipwreck in October 2013, in which 300 migrants died, that the crisis garnered widespread international media attention and European governments felt compelled to act.

Shortly thereafter, the Italian navy launched Mare Nostrum, a search-and-rescue operation that also, in theory, was designed to combat migrant smuggling. The operation turned out to be an important and necessary contribution to mitigating the huge humanitarian consequences of the migrant-smuggling trade, saving thousands of lives at sea.

119

But Mare Nostrum also significantly altered some of the core assumptions under which smugglers operated. With Italian ships now patrolling the sea, migrant smugglers no longer needed to plan for long sea crossings that reached Italian waters, and they changed their operations accordingly. From November 2013 until the end of October 2014, Mare Nostrum effectively shrank the distance over which smuggling networks had to transport migrants, from the 160 nautical miles needed to reach Italy to a mere 12 nautical miles needed to get beyond Libya's territorial waters and into the international waters traversed by merchant ships and patrolled by the Italian navy.

With smuggling networks incorporating Mare Nostrum into their business models, analysts immediately saw an increase in the rescue of boats without crews or enough fuel to make it to Italian waters. They also noticed that the boats being put out to sea were considerably less seaworthy than before. Fishing vessels manned by smugglers gave way to unpiloted rubber zodiacs or boats that otherwise would have long since been sent to the scrap yard.[19] Migrants who left Libya after Mare Nostrum confirmed the emergence of a new business model in which both the migrants and the boats that carried them were completely disposable. Several reported being put onto large rubber dinghies, a migrant at the helm and another primed with a GPS device and a mobile phone or satellite phone pre-programmed with the number of the Italian navy. Smugglers would point them out to sea, tell them to sail straight for four or five hours before making the call for rescue. At other times smugglers would accompany a dinghy for a while in a faster speedboat and then return back to shore to avoid being picked up.

'Mare Nostrum had an unexpected effect,' said the chief prosecutor of Catania, a province of southern Italy. 'The criminal organisations handling the migrant trafficking took advantage of the new opportunities and deliberately enhanced the danger of the situation in order to force the Italian navy to advance toward the African coast, lowering their costs and consequently the prices asked of the migrants'.[20] Demand surged still further as prices fell.

Not only did Mare Nostrum significantly alter existing smuggling networks, the substantially reduced operating costs eroded barriers to entry into the smuggling market, paving the way for new actors to emerge. With no government control and almost no criminal consolidation over the market, smuggling networks began to proliferate.

While established networks and families dominated the trade along the coast, the chaotic political situation opened some space for smaller groups of opportunists to facilitate smuggling on an ad hoc basis. A Libya-based journalist I interviewed in late 2015 noted how post-Gaddafi Libya became 'awash with people who not only had the opportunity but also the means, via access to weapons, to be able to operate a smuggling network'. As a result, in the first year after the revolution 'it was an extreme free-for-all where basically anyone could dip into this business and start sending boats'.

Citing budget constraints and dissatisfaction with the lack of burden sharing by the rest of Europe, Italy drew down Mare Nostrum in October 2014, and the operation was replaced by a stripped-down EU naval mission dubbed Triton. There were hopes at the time that, although a smaller mission meant that fewer lives would be saved at sea, the lack of a robust search-and-rescue mission might dissuade migrants from trying to cross. In theory, smugglers would have to start providing more seaworthy vessels and the number of newly emerged lower-level operators might be pushed back out of the market. But, after eleven months of unfettered profits, the smuggling industry had become firmly entrenched in Libya's political economy, with tentacles that stretched well beyond the coastline, across the Sahara, and deep into sub-Saharan Africa. Smugglers were no longer content with merely providing a service at the Libyan coast. In fact, they invested resources into creating demand.

With the 'back route' to Europe wide open, smuggling groups activated and invested in already established networks of facilitators and recruiters to take advantage of the unprecedented opportunity that came with anarchy in Libya. As the smuggling groups became richer and more active, the trade regularised and became more streamlined. The timeline between leaving one's village in a country such as Senegal or Benin and setting sail from the coast of Libya condensed from several weeks to as little as ten days. Migrants who had once developed migration plans predicated on living and working in several locations over the course of months, even years, until they could secure passage to Europe, suddenly expected to be calling their families from Italy within a few weeks of leaving home.

Thanks to the relative predictability of the journey, some families have even developed itineraries that include multiple trips across the desert before departing from Libya. *Demba, aged thirty-one, left his village outside the Senegalese capital, Dakar, with plans to work in Libya. Once he earned enough money, the plan went, he would return to Senegal and bring his parents and brother to back to Libya, at which point he would continue working until he could pay a smuggler to take them to Italy.

'It was a family decision to try to get a better life for us all,' Demba explains. 'My family sold everything we had, including our sheep, everything to get the money for me to get here.'

On the advice of some friends who knew people who had completed the journey to Europe, Demba took public transport from Senegal to Mali, and on to Niger until he reached the city of Agadez, from where he hired smugglers to take him to Libya. Despite seeing lots of dead bodies in the desert and witnessing people being abused by smugglers, Demba said that the trip is straightforward so long as you make smart decisions, hire the right middlemen, pay bribes to anyone who asks for one, and don't cause any trouble.

Having travelled to Libya twice, once alone and once with his family, Demba paid a Senegalese middleman approximately $3,000 for his parents to go to Italy on an inflatable boat. A few weeks later he paid $1,500 more for his brother to make the trip. That was two months ago, and Demba has not heard from any of them. He heard from a friend that his brother died at sea, and he assumes his parents met the same fate. His advice to anyone considering the trip is unequivocal. 'Do not make this journey. It is very risky and there is nothing here. Libya is not like it was before.'

The profits from the migrant-smuggling economy in Libya easily amount to hundreds of millions of dollars: one estimate suggests that Libyan smugglers earned between $225 and 323 million in 2014 alone.[21] Between countless bribes paid to armed groups and state security officials at checkpoints, rent paid to the owners of hundreds of safe houses, salaries doled out to armed guards and pilots of larger ships, commissions paid to brokers and recruiters, expenditures for boats, life jackets, fuel and satellite phones, and tribute paid to rent-seeking militias, mafias and government officials, the migrant-smuggling economy represents an industrial complex in and of itself. It stretches far beyond a simple smuggler–migrant relationship. And as various actors seek to continue generating revenue, migrant smuggling in Libya has become a far more violent industry, the consequences of which weigh most heavily on the migrants themselves.

In the post-Mare Nostrum environment, boats depart from Libya regardless of the weather or sea conditions, and the degree of violence used to manage the migrants on land has risen considerably. According to the accounts of migrants interviewed in Italy, arms are used not only to 'protect' them in the so-called 'safe houses', but also for loading them onto boats. A large number of the migrants that we interviewed in Italy, having recently completed their crossing, said they were forced to board unsafe boats against their will, as their smugglers threatened them with guns and clubs. They were sent to sea with no protection whatsoever. A statistical analysis that aligned fatalities to policies found conclusively that the EU's decision to replace Mare Nostrum with a more limited sea intervention, which did not put naval assets near the Libyan coast to provide search-and-rescue assistance, incontrovertibly led to a higher rate of mortality in the Mediterranean.[22]

Extortion and Abuse

Although reports and images of harrowing rescues at sea elicit the most media attention and force us to consider the unknowable number of lives lost to the Mediterranean crossing, there is arguably a much bigger tragedy taking place in Libyan towns and cities where human smuggling and human trafficking often intersect. The same infrastructure that facilitates migrant smuggling, it turns out, has been co-opted by human-trafficking networks that specialise in the exploitation, extortion and enslavement of sub-Saharan Africans in Libya.

Like Esther, who left for Libya at the encouragement of a woman who turned out to be working for a human-trafficking ring in Libya, *Abubakar left Nigeria at the suggestion of a new friend who had lived and worked in Libya for years and who said he could get him a job there. Abubakar had previously worked for a foreign-owned oil and gas company, but says the firm 'pulled out because of the political situation and corruption [in Nigeria]'. Unable to find a job and unwilling, in his words, 'to become a thief', he decided to take his new friend up on the offer. 'I did not tell my family I was going to make the trip to Europe because if I had, they would have tried to stop me,' Abubakar explains. 'Too many people die in the desert. Your family never wants you to go.'

When his funds ran dry, Abubakar called his mother back at his home village, and told her to sell his generator and other possessions in order to fund his onward journey. On receiving the proceeds he went with his friend to Agadez, where, upon reaching the desert outpost, he started to have doubts about his decision to go to Libya. His friend, however, encouraged him to continue and offered to lend him the money for the next part of his journey. He told Abubakar that he could pay him back in small instalments once he was working in Libya.

'I thought this man was my friend and was trying to help me,' Abubakar recalls. 'These people are so nice in Nigeria ... But when you reach Libya, they change completely and suddenly make big demands for money and treat you very badly.' In Abubakar's case, the bad treatment started once they reached Sebha. The city was ravaged with daily gunfights, and, as Abubakar puts it, 'big guns and bangs'. Abubakar's friend from Nigeria introduced him to some Libyan acquaintances, who promptly took his passport and told him he would have to pay $3,000 to get it back.

For eight months Abubakar was forced to work for a trafficking ring run by Nigerians and Libyans. 'The worst time for me was when I worked for three months in Qatrun as prisoner, basically, in a house of African prostitutes. They were also prisoners. I cleaned the place, washed their clothes, cooked for them and received [$5] per day,' Abubakar says.

When Ababukar had earned enough money to bargain for his passport, he found a Libyan official who helped him go to Tripoli by truck. Life in Tripoli was hard, so he decided to go to Benghazi, which turned out to be worse. 'It was crazy,' Abubakar says. 'I was arrested by Islamists. I was arrested and beaten by Libyans. I had guns held to my head. I thought I would die many times. And all the time, there is bombing and explosions.'

Abubakar paid a truck driver to take him back to Tripoli, where he now lives and is tentatively making plans to pay a smuggler to take him to Europe. 'I am scared of the crossing and I will do my best to get the best boat I can and do it as safely as possible,' Abubakar says, but he is ready to go if the situation in Tripoli further deteriorates. 'To get on the boat, you must be willing to die.'

Though he is not sure where he will go or what he will do in Europe, Abubakar says his only goal is to stay alive, work, and be able to send money home to his two children. He is confident that no matter where he ends up he will be treated better than in Libya, where he has been beaten by Libyan security personnel, militia members, Islamist gunmen, and his own countrymen who work for some of these groups. He says that Libyan thieves target people like him, stealing their money because they know black Africans have no legal recourse. He can't imagine that things could possibly be worse in Europe. In Libya, Abubakar says, 'they treat black people like animals'.

Perhaps no group has learned the extent of how precarious life in post-Gaddafi Libya is for sub-Saharan Africans more than Eritreans, Sudanese and Somalis, who are disproportionately targeted by both militias and Libyan government officials for detention, and human traffickers for extortion. Facilities run by both the de facto Libyan government and rival militias have been turned into holding centres, from where detainees are loaned and rented out as unpaid labour, including for sexual exploitation. Some of these facilities, often described as torture camps in which thousands of people are forced to live in squalid conditions, double as large-scale extortion operations. Those who can arrange for someone back home to pay a ransom can purchase their freedom. Those who cannot are at the mercy of their captors.

'When the guards don't like what someone does, they come in and shout and beat him with sticks,' a twenty-one-year-old Eritrean woman held at the Soroman migrant detention centre told Human Rights Watch, a research and advocacy NGO that issued a report documenting detainee abuses in Libya. 'When I arrived here, the guards put us [twenty-three women] in a room, told us to take off our clothes and then put their fingers inside our vaginas,' she recounted.

Other detainees described scenes in which people were hung upside-down and whipped with metal wiring, severely beaten if they did not obey orders, and tortured if they tried to escape. Libyan authorities told Human Rights Watch that they do not deport Eritrean and Somali nationals, due to the human rights abuses in Eritrea and ongoing conflict in Somalia. Yet for many, being neither deported from Libya nor released from prisons translates to indefinite detention with no end in sight.[23]

Despite all of the risks outlined above, migrants and asylum seekers from all over sub-Saharan and North Africa, as well as others from places as far afield as Syria and Bangladesh, come to Libya in search of economic opportunity and a path to Europe. Many make this journey fully aware of the risks involved, having concluded that the potential dangers and the possibility of death are worth it compared to the futures offered by the status quo at home. Others have been misled by smugglers and recruiters, or lack good information. In any event, smuggling networks in Libya, as with everywhere else, are first and foremost service providers. Having come together to provide the supply to migrant demand, however, they have in turn used their influence to shape and expand this demand for their services. This progression, in which unprecedented demand for smuggler services creates new political and security paradigms, first became clear in Libya, but it is taking place all over the globe as people seek refuge and opportunity in Europe.

6

EGYPT

THE NORTH COAST

As the migrant-smuggling market exploded in Libya, a parallel market for moving people quietly emerged in Egypt. With rare exceptions, boats leaving from Egypt are also destined for Italy, but migrant-smuggling networks operating out of Egypt's northern coast rely on a different business model from those in Libya. This is almost entirely due to the contrasting nature of the state: whereas the chaos and lack of government capacity in Libya has led to a smuggling free-for-all, marked by very high levels of violence, in the highly controlled state of Egypt, smuggling networks operate in the shadows, outside the purview of powerful Egyptian state security structures. Migrant smuggling operations on the coast the coast, therefore, can only be carried out by groups that have the ability to avoid detection, or that possess the requisite criminal connections to operate with the tacit endorsement of Egyptian security officials.

Though the voyage from Egypt to Italy is considerably longer than from Libya, leaving from Egypt's north coast is perceived to be less risky, partly because the chaos in Libya means that you might never make it to the boat, but also because Egyptian smugglers are generally believed to use safer boats. High death rates attract unwanted attention both from the domestic and international community, and Egyptian smugglers have done everything to avoid the spotlight.

*Rania, a twenty-four-year-old from a town outside Damascus, fled Syria with her twin sister when her father stopped allowing them to attend university. The fighting in the distance grew less distant by the day, and Rania's father decided that going to university was too dangerous. He paid for Rania and her sister to travel to Lebanon, from where Rania purchased a plane ticket to Cairo.

Rania chose Egypt for several reasons. She had a cousin living in Cairo who could help her adjust to Egyptian society, and the cost of living and education was less expensive than in Lebanon. Most importantly, Rania says, 'the Egyptian public loves Syrians more than the Lebanese do'.

At the time, Syrians did not need a visa to enter Egypt, which made it an appealing destination for hundreds of thousands of Syrians. The similarities between Syrian and Egyptian cultures, combined with the common language, were an added bonus. 'I felt like I was inside an Egyptian movie,' Rania thought when she first arrived, jarred by the dialect that she had seen in films but never heard in person.

Like almost all Syrians who come to Egypt, Rania saw the country as a place of refuge rather than a transit country. In fact, she began working with a local organisation that helps educate Syrian refugees about the dangers of trying to cross the sea to Europe. Although once horrified at the premise of risking one's life for uncertainty in Europe, Rania is now contemplating what she previously considered unthinkable. As she educates others about the risks of putting their fates in the hands of smugglers, she is considering doing just that. She knows that untold numbers of people have drowned in the Mediterranean, but she also knows lots of people who made it to Europe alive and who are thriving. Meanwhile, her situation in Egypt goes from bad to worse amidst aid cuts and a government that is increasingly hostile to Syrians.

The status of refugees and migrants in Egypt is a highly sensitive issue, in part because the government would prefer to maintain the fiction that migrants and refugees are integrating into Egyptian society. The UNHCR estimates that there are around 250,000 refugees and asylum seekers in Egypt, of whom about half are Syrian.[1] Refugees who register with the UNHCR in Egypt are given ID cards recognised by the Egyptian government. In theory, these cards allow them to establish residency and obtain various goods and services. On paper, refugees in Egypt have rights to access schools and the formal economy. In practice, these benefits are rarely realised. Syrian refugees, who tend to be better educated than their counterparts from Sudan, Eritrea, Somalia and Ethiopia, are considerably more likely to find employment. They also have comparatively better access to health care and education. Yet even for skilled migrants, including those who speak both Arabic and English, a mix of factors, including discrimination against certain ethnicities and nationalities, and cultural factors, such as attitudes towards women in the workplace, or beliefs that certain jobs are only appropriate for people of certain nationalities, conspire against them.

Although registered refugees receive aid from organisations such as the UNHCR, very few are able to rely on it as their sole means of survival. Most families supplement their modest stipends through some sort of income-generating activity, usually in the informal economy. As a result, those migrants who work in the informal economy are forced into the shadows, unprotected by labour laws and incredibly vulnerable to exploitation.

'I worked for nearly twelve hours a day as a secretary in a medical centre with a wage of 1,000 Egyptian Pounds [$127] while they assigned me more work to do that is not relevant to my job,' says Rania. 'One of the employees asked his colleague if I am Syrian, then he asked me for marriage but I refused.' When Rania was leaving the office, her jilted suitor offered her a chilling warning. 'You shouldn't act like this, lady, you are sold for only 500 EGP [$63.86] here,' he said.

Mohammed, a twenty-year-old Syrian who had been living in Cairo, decided to leave Egypt after his friend had been kidnapped. 'I couldn't take it any more. There is too much thuggery in Cairo, especially at Syrians,' he says. 'They know we are weak.' When his friend was kidnapped on the outskirts of Cairo, Mohammed went to the police, who, upon hearing his story, told him to 'figure it out himself'. Mohammed and a friend were able to make contact with the kidnappers, and negotiated his release for $450. A few days later, Mohammed says, the kidnappers tried again to kidnap all three of them. That is when he left Cairo and began contacting smugglers in Alexandria in hope of boarding a boat to Europe.

Yet even with the threat of being 'sold' or kidnapped looming over their heads, Rania and Mohammed are comparatively less vulnerable than most of their non-Syrian counterparts, many of whom live in Egypt illegally or under a quasi-legal status. Though it isn't prohibitively difficult for Sudanese to get visas for Egypt, for example, there are substantial Sudanese networks that specialise in smuggling Sudanese into Egypt without documentation. Some of these migrants are fleeing violent conflict in Sudan. Others have come in search of economic opportunities. Their vulnerability as irregular migrants, however, is further compounded by the fact that many of the networks that facilitate their transport overlap with human-trafficking networks that actively recruit sub-Saharan Africans into Egypt for exploitation.

Some of these networks in Cairo operate by offering 'fake employment' to foreign women, who, upon being invited for job interviews, find themselves kidnapped and incorporated into sex-trafficking rings. Other instances have been reported by human rights groups of foreign women being lured into one-off instances of gang rape through the guise of job interviews. More than one person working to assist victims of these types of crimes told me that Ethiopian and Eritrean women are particularly vulnerable to these crimes because they do not speak the language, and they have a 'physical profile' that is highly coveted by some Egyptian men, making them a target for sex traffickers. In the rare instances that women build up the courage to report these abuses to the authorities, the likelihood of any sort of prosecution, according to various aid groups, is close to zero.

In Cairo, experts told me that the Egyptian government's policies towards migrants and refugees were, on paper, 'pretty good'. One went so far as to characterise them as 'by far the best in the region'. Yet the actual status of a refugee or migrant in Egypt is one of extreme vulnerability, in large part due to Egypt's political transitions over the last five years. During the revolution that overthrew then Egyptian President Hosni Mubarak in 2011, many within migrant communities hoped that their place within Egyptian society would improve, and there was a sense that legitimate opportunities to migrate to Egypt might emerge. Since then, however, migrants have regularly been portrayed negatively for political gain. During his brief time in power, for example, Mohammed Morsi attempted to stir up nationalist support by demonising the presence of sub-Saharan Africans, particularly Sudanese and Ethiopians, in Egypt. For his part, current President

Abdel Fatteh el-Sisi has accused Iraqis and Syrians in Egypt of being pro-Muslim Brotherhood.

The Egyptian government is hesitant to publicly endorse programmes that specifically aid refugee and migrant populations for fear of upsetting Egyptian citizens, many of whom struggle to access basic goods and services themselves. Several analysts I spoke to in Egypt, from a range of nationalities and professional backgrounds, suggested a posture that amounts to a deliberate 'policy of not implementing a policy'. That is, the Egyptian government tacitly hopes that if refugees fail to attain decent livelihoods it will be an incentive for them to leave, or not come in the first place. Fears of foreigners 'taking jobs from Egyptians', which is a political issue as much as an economic one, preclude the Egyptian government from empowering migrant communities. The Egyptian government is similarly hesitant to support NGOs that are exclusively devoted to providing economic opportunities for migrants.

Internationally, foreign governments have few incentives, let alone the moral standing, to exert pressure on the Egyptian government to improve its policies towards refugees and irregular migrants. Most Western countries view Egypt as a vital security partner in an increasingly volatile Middle East and North Africa, and none of them wants to jeopardise first-order security imperatives for the sake of refugees, which most consider a second- or even third-tier issue.

The lack of a safety net for migrants, both as a result of deliberate domestic policies and lack of funding by the international community, means that the most vulnerable have no choice but to search elsewhere for a means of survival, and that elsewhere increasingly involves getting onto boats, either from Egypt or Libya, to make the treacherous journey to Europe.

One of the ironies, of course, is that by failing to provide adequate resources to international organisations trying to make life tenable for migrants in places like Egypt, Syrians such as Rania, who never wanted to go to Europe, feel compelled to try. Demand for smuggler services, in turn, has grown considerably.

For *Rami, a forty-four-year-old Palestinian who lived his entire life in Syria, the change in government attitudes and a reduction in support for refugee communities made the decision on whether to risk his life

131

crossing the sea an easy one. 'I came to Cairo and I just couldn't find a job. Everything was so expensive. People were friendly, even though they got less so after the overthrow of Morsi,' Rami says. Rather than stay in Egypt and 'eat' his life savings, Rami decided to look for a smuggler.

'A friend referred me to a smuggler and I paid him $3,000 upfront', Rami explains. 'We left from Alexandria. He made us walk 3 kilometres until he found the spot with the boats.'

The mind-set of both migrants and smugglers departing from Alexandria to Italy is completely different from those leaving the coasts of Libya or from Turkey. Where the latter think of voyages in terms of hours; the Egyptians plan for days. In Libya the goal of smugglers is simply to get migrants out to international waters, where they can be rescued by passing merchant ships, the EU and humanitarian rescue missions. Those missions do not, however, extend as far as the Egyptian coastline. Therefore, the smugglers using departure points from Egypt are more focused on making a long voyage all the way to Italian waters. Interviews conducted in Libya, Italy and Egypt suggest that Syrians, more than other migrant groups, are acutely aware of the fact that the maritime voyages from Egypt tend to be safer than from Libya.

According to Rami, before loading about fifty passengers onto a metal fishing vessel, the smugglers offered each passenger the chance to purchase a life jacket for $11. The smugglers also asked the passengers to hand over whatever local currency they had in their pockets, since 'they wouldn't be able to use it in Europe'. Food was supposed to be provided, but everyone knew, according to Rami, that there was no way to ensure that the smugglers would make good on their promises, and many people brought their own provisions. The smugglers did actually cook some rice and pass it around on the ship, but Rami, who had little appetite thanks to the sea, lived off of some dates and mineral water he had brought with him.

Rami says his smugglers, both on the beach and the five that were on the boat with them, did not resort to violence, nor did they really mistreat those travelling with them. He even describes the crew on the boat as 'nice people'.

The hardest part of the voyage, he says, was during a storm in the middle of the ocean. 'We spent a day just praying. People were saying goodbye to pictures of their family and the crew of five people was panicking,' Rami explains. Several days after the storm, the crew conceded that they were lost and were in danger of running out of fuel, so they transferred everyone save for two crew members from the metal fishing boat to a smaller dinghy that they had been dragging with them the entire journey. 'We had to carefully place our weight on the boat to balance it out. We didn't sleep for three days,' Rami explains. Eventually they reached Italian waters, and were rescued by an Italian ship.

Rami now lives in Amsterdam, having applied for asylum in the Netherlands and successfully completed a reunification process which enabled his wife to join him. They get by with government assistance, and describe their Dutch neighbours as 'so kind and neighbourly'. Rami couldn't be happier. His plan is to stay for five years and apply for citizenship. 'In Syria, as a Palestinian, you spend seventy years … you are born there, and nothing,' he explains. But in the Netherlands 'you can get citizenship, even though you are Arab'.

Rami's journey across the Mediterranean is one of the more common migrant-smuggling itineraries to emerge from Egypt since 2013. The finer details of migrant smuggling out of Egypt's north coast are constantly shifting in response to both local dynamics and to external events such as an uptick in violence in Libya and the emergence of the Aegean crossing, but even when accounting for these changes, a basic schematic of the migrant-smuggling networks in Egypt can be sketched out.

The Long Trip to Italy

As with smuggling networks operating out of Turkey and Libya, recruiters and interlocutors working for smuggling networks in Egypt tend to work according to nationalistic lines. Brokers based in Cairo and Alexandria offer an array of payment options. Several Syrians interviewed in Cairo and in Alexandria said brokers offered them a free trip in exchange for recruiting six to ten other Syrians to make the journey with them. Others arranged a payment plan that saw them paying half up front and half upon arrival, with a third-party broker in either city acting as the intermediary. Some migrants do pay up front, but they do so with few guarantees.

Despite being one of the rare Syrians who has successfully found employment in Egypt, *Hassan, a thirty-four-year-old IT specialist working for a computer company in Cairo, has looked into hiring a smuggler to go to Europe. 'Life has gotten worse for Syrians after rumours about Syrians being Islamists and supporting Morsi,' Hassan says. 'I get harassed. The police seize any opportunity to bother me.'

When Hassan first started looking into travelling to Europe, the going rate was around $3,200. But now, in mid-2015, he says, the price is closer to $2,000 or as low as $1,800—evidence, he says, of the fact that Syrians who have money can fly to Turkey from Egypt, and cross the Aegean. With reduced demand, smugglers are reducing their prices, Hassan posits. For Hassan, leaving from Egypt is still more appealing than going to Turkey. He knows that crossing from Turkey into Greece is safer than crossing from Egypt all the way to Italy, but he fears the twenty-day journey through the Balkans, and believes that if he can find the right smuggler with the right reputation, the maritime voyage from Egypt can be safe.

'Usually, you leave the money with a third party whose house the smugglers know and they take the money from them. They don't rob them because if they do, they would lose all their customers,' Hassan explains, when asked to describe the payment plans he has been offered. 'Believe it or not, they have a reputation to maintain and they need the people to at least trust them a little,' he continues. 'If you think they might go and kill your family, or extort them, less people would go.'

Hassan says that if he finds the right smuggler who can guarantee a better ship and a safer experience, he would be willing to leave, using a third-party guarantor. 'Some people choose the smuggler based on their prices, but I will base my decision on their track records. I will ask around about them.'

According to *Tarek, a Syrian man in Alexandria who paid smugglers to take two of his sons to Italy, Syrians normally do not pay up front, because they know how the system works and smugglers would lose a key part of their business if they abused Syrians. 'The money was held with a third party at a Syrian restaurant here in Alexandria,' Tarek explains. 'We went to the restaurant, me and the smuggler, so that he could witness me giving the money [$2,000 for each of his sons] to the Syrian restaurant owner and then when my sons arrived in Italy, I called the owner and told him he could deliver the money to the smuggler.'

*Sayid, another Syrian living in Egypt, decided to send his wife and daughter to Europe after his daughter had been kidnapped, along with another Syrian girl in Alexandria. 'Some Egyptian gang took them by force from our street to an unknown place but the UNHCR along with the police rescued them,' Sayid recounts. 'But both the girls broke down and were not able to leave their rooms, living in fear inside their own homes until they both left with a boat.'

Sayid's son went to a smuggler along with some friends and colleagues who he knew from back home who were living in Alexandria. They were thirty in total, and his son negotiated free passage for himself, the two girls who had been kidnapped and Sayid's wife in exchange for having brought so much business to him. 'I was so afraid when my wife and daughters went, I stayed on the beach looking at the sea for three days,' Sayid recalls.

Sayid's family has successfully made it to Germany, and he hopes that the family reunification process will spare him from making the journey himself. Until then, he has been acting as a liaison between smugglers and people who wish to make the journey. 'After my wife went, the Syrians in the neighbourhood started asking me how I had organised the trip for her and with which smuggler, so I made some kind of reputation in the Syrian community,' Sayid explains. 'The smugglers kept calling me asking to help them get more people. One of them offered me $300 per each passenger I get for his trip. I always refuse this money but I help people to get to the right smuggler who takes care of them and treats them as humans.'

Once the matter of payment has been settled, the next order of business for migrant-smuggling networks is moving migrants from Cairo and Alexandria to launch points along the north coast, either avoiding authorities or, in other cases, coordinating with them.

Twenty-eight-year-old *Sami fled to Egypt with four friends in hopes of finding employment. Back home in Syria he had sold cotton fabrics at a shop, but, with little education and few marketable skills, he found it tough to find anyone willing to hire him. Thankfully, Sami came to Egypt with several thousand dollars of savings and, since he did not have a wife or children, he was able to get by with small odd jobs here and there. With time, however, he and his friends concluded that there were few opportunities for them in Egypt, and it was time to risk everything to reach Europe.

After asking around, Sami contacted a broker in Cairo who was well known amongst Syrians. He knew the broker typically charged $2,200, but he was able to negotiate a flat fee of $10,000 for all five of them. The broker told them they would be leaving in three days, and would be transported to Alexandria. When they arrived in Alexandria, they spent one night in a hotel and then were put in a bus and driven to a farm outside the city, where they stayed in an abandoned building for several days.

Sami realised that this house was a consolidation point where smugglers house people until they have sufficient numbers to warrant a trip, or while the final logistics of a launch are being arranged. In fact, he ran into a Syrian he had known back in Cairo. Neither of them had any idea that the other was planning to cross the sea, and both were surprised when they learned that despite the fact they used different brokers, there they were, using the same smuggler.

The whole operation, according to Sami, was very well organised. After several days in the abandoned farmhouse, the smugglers—all of whom were armed from that point forward—began loading migrants into buses every few hours. Sami's bus travelled for hours in the desert, and at one point they were stopped by what he described as an armed gang. The armed handlers on board disembarked and, after a few tense minutes, negotiated their continued passage.

The bus eventually stopped in the middle of nowhere, at which point they walked through the desert for an hour until they reached several abandoned houses. After an hour of waiting, another vehicle arrived and took them to the coast, where a small boat was waiting for them.

For *Sara, a twenty-three-year-old Syrian woman who fled Syria during her second year of university, her interactions with her smuggler went quite smoothly at first. She paid him only $1,100 through a third-party broker based in the back of a restaurant in Cairo and says she was given a discount because she and her friends came to him in a group of ten. When they arrived in Alexandria, a smuggler met them at the street and took them to a hotel. They waited there for a few hours, but were then picked up by a bus and taken to another location in the city. It was evening by then and, after waiting again, another bus arrived. 'It was so dark because they covered the windows with some kind of curtains.'

After driving for several hours they were dropped off at an isolated farm near the sea. 'There, the Egyptian guys, the bus driver and his friends started harassing the girls in the group. Touching us in all our bodies, cursing us in a very bad way and talking in a very aggressive sexual way,' Sara says. 'Then they told us we should give them our phones because we won't be able to use them. They were able to collect like sixteen or seventeen phones without giving them back,' she continued. 'After, they brought another bus and a big pickup which they put us in and covered us with some kind of fabric.'

According to Sara, around 3 a.m. the smugglers heard that police were monitoring the beach, so the truck turned around and returned to the farm, where they spent the night 'under the trees'. The next night the smugglers stacked the passengers into a lorry and covered it with a curtain. The smugglers told them it would be a thirty-minute trip. It took three hours.

'Finally we arrived at a place where we were not able to see the sea but we smelled it. Someone asked us to start running towards the beach and to leave our bags and we would find them on the boat,' Sara recounts. 'We started running to find the three small boats waiting for us way inside the water,' she continues. 'We were struggling to reach the boat amid the big waves and the cold.'

The majority of boats leaving the north coast of Egypt are small fishing boats that can take between fifty and eighty people. One local analyst in the port city of Alexandria, who has interviewed brokers and recruiters working on behalf of smugglers, reported that smugglers prefer to limit the number of migrants placed on fishing boats because, from their perspective, the launch is the riskiest step in the process. Loading migrants onto the boat takes time, and thus the risk of being caught by Egyptian authorities is greater the longer it takes. It is easier, they tell him, to arrange for several boats of fifty people to be loaded and consolidated offshore.

It was during this phase of the journey, for example, that Egyptian authorities caught Sami and his friends. They were escorted by smugglers to a remote location outside Alexandria, but police arrived just as their small boat was preparing to launch. He and his friends jumped off the boat, and tried to run away, but they were detained.

Though there are no set routes or itineraries, most analysts and observers interviewed in Egypt, as well as migrants who successfully made the trip to Europe, confirm that fishing boats are taken about 3 or 4 kilometres out to sea, where they link up with a bigger ship. In some cases there may be yet another step in which several boats are consolidated into yet another vessel once they reach international waters.

From there, the 'mother ship', which typically carries up to 300 people, travels for several days until it gets close to the territorial waters of Italy or Greece, at which point migrants are put in vessels they consider disposable, such as dinghies, rafts or smaller wooden ships.

'This is where it gets dangerous,' one migrant explained. 'Because these boats are a lot smaller, if anyone falls, the whole thing could capsize. The good boat must leave because they [the smugglers] don't want it to get caught. They don't care about the small [boat] or the people on it.' In some cases 'surplus' migrants, whom smugglers cannot fit into the disposable ships they either towed or transported to Italian waters, are thrown overboard, leaving them with only their life vests to rely on for survival.

During this final transfer, smugglers or designated migrants shoot up a flare or call in an SOS for local coastguards to find them. Before Italy's Mare Nostrum mission was shut down and replaced by the more restricted, EU-led naval mission Triton in the Mediterranean, it was not uncommon for smugglers to abandon the large ship altogether, and return home on a smaller vessel.

According to a sixteen-year-old Syrian boy who successfully made the journey from Egypt, he was on the mother ship for three days in the middle of the ocean, waiting to receive people from other boats. They were already 200 people on the boat when another ship, which was coming from Libya, arrived and the smugglers began loading them onto the mother ship. 'The passengers refused, as there was already 200 persons, but the smugglers didn't obey them and they stuffed the boat with people.'

Sara's first boat capsized shortly after launch, but she was luckily rescued by another smuggling boat, and transferred to what she described as a faster, 24-metre boat. That boat, piloted by 'three young Egyptians between the ages of seventeen and twenty-three', eventually linked up with a large ship with 200 people already on board. When she boarded, the passengers told Sara that the ship had not moved for two days, and the smugglers had said they were waiting for sufficient numbers before continuing to Italy.

The same methodology was used in April 2016: one boat was put to sea from the Egyptian coast with around 300 people aboard. In the mean time, a smaller boat carrying around 200 people left from Tobruk in eastern Libya. After many hours the two vessels met at sea in the dead of night, and the smugglers attempted to transfer everyone onto the bigger boat, at which point it started taking in water. The boat sank a few hours later, killing as many as 500 people on board.[2]

According to several interviews with local analysts and migrants who made the journey between 2013 and 2015, the price of crossing the Mediterranean has steadily declined. In 2013, for example, the going rate for a Syrian to buy a place on a boat leaving from Egypt's north coast was believed to be $3,000 to $4,000. In 2014 the price fell to somewhere between $2,500 and $3,500. By 2015 prices had fallen as low as $2,000. Prices are at their lowest just before October, when the calm waters of 'sea-crossing season' give way to rougher seas, and smugglers are looking to move migrants before the season ends.

It is not entirely clear why prices in Egypt have declined with each year, but interviews with migrants suggest that it has a lot to do with the rapid expansion of the Aegean route. Even after Egypt ostensibly closed its doors to Syrians, there were still Syrians trying to find their way in, either to seek asylum or to use Egypt as a transit country. No longer able to enter Egypt without visas, many Syrians who initially fled to Turkey or Lebanon flew to Sudan, where they do not need visas to enter. From Sudan they would cross into Egypt irregularly, using the same networks that facilitate the movement of Sudanese, Eritreans and Ethiopians into Egypt. Once in Egypt these Syrians would quickly link up with smugglers who could take them to the north coast.

According to those familiar with these schemes, Syrians pursuing this route could be in Egypt for as little as five days, especially if they made arrangements from their departure country and were picked up in the Sudanese capital, Khartoum, by someone who could facilitate their passage all the way to the north coast. A more expensive variant of this route has Syrians departing from Lebanon and Turkey, paying $2,000 to obtain an Egyptian visa through the black market, and, after arriving in Egypt, quickly seeking out smuggler services.

With the emergence of the Aegean route, fewer Syrians in Turkey or Lebanon feel compelled to fly all the way to Sudan only to risk a journey that is more expensive and more dangerous than the crossing from Turkey to Greece. Instead they fly in the opposite direction, travelling back to Turkey in hopes of joining the hundreds of thousands of Syrian migrants washing ashore in Greece.

Having twice paid smugglers only to see his trip foiled by Egyptian authorities, Sami has decided to save money and fly to Turkey, then cross the Aegean. One Syrian woman interviewed in Alexandria said that her family's original plan was to save up enough money for her, her husband and their two young boys to pay a smuggler to take them to Italy. Having watched videos of the Syrians crossing into Greece from Turkey, and having read online about the relative straightforwardness of the Aegean crossing, they decided on a new plan. Her husband would fly to Turkey, take a boat to Greece, and continue on to Germany, from where he would seek asylum and apply for family reunification. In the mean time, she and her boys would live off their savings in Egypt.

Despite a diminished Syrian market for their services, migrant-smuggling networks in Egypt are still thriving. Demand still exists within the Syrian community in Egypt, in part because some still prefer to leave from Egypt in an attempt to reach Italy directly rather than embark upon the Aegean route, which, even after arriving in Greece, requires an arduous overland journey through the Balkans and Eastern Europe before one reaches preferred destinations in Western Europe. Furthermore, in the wake of the EU–Turkey deal approved in March 2016, the Aegean route is no longer a sure thing, even for Syrians who have little trouble claiming refugee status.

The decreasing demand for smuggler services among Syrians has been replaced by a growing market of non-Syrians living in Egypt or travelling to Egypt with hopes of reaching Europe, as well as Egyptians themselves who wish to migrate to Europe. In 2014 the majority of people leaving from the north coast, per local monitoring organisations, were Syrian nationals. In 2015 the demographics shifted, and the majority of those leaving from Egypt were believed to be Sudanese, along with other Sub-Saharan African nationalities. Smugglers, in turn, lowered their prices to reflect the purchasing power of their new client base.

Cooperation and Complicity

Egypt's migrant-smuggling infrastructure is primed and ready to accept new clients. It may have been built on Syrian demand, but it now caters to an array of nationalities, and, taken together, the profits to be made from human smuggling in Egypt are considerable. The size of the people-smuggling economy is easily in the tens of millions. Local fisherman who would normally struggle to earn a living, are paid as much as $30,000 per trip to crew the boats to Italy, which, as one observer noted, 'is enough to give up fishing altogether'. And because there is so much money to be made, particularly for those at the top of this still nascent criminal economy, there are a number of indications that the smuggling industry is not only expanding, but professionalising and taking on the characteristics of major organised crime syndicates seen in other parts of the world.

One such indicator of increased professionalisation is the extent to which smugglers appear to be coordinating their efforts with local security authorities. 'They are in league with the Egyptian police,' says one migrant who claims to have witnessed such collusion. 'They [smugglers] speak freely on the phone and often make you wait, not just until the seas calm, but until they get the green light from the police.'

While smugglers have been using the method of loading several small ships in different locations simultaneously in order to mitigate risk, local observers, as well as migrants who have been detained, suggest that smugglers will also intentionally sacrifice one boat to the authorities to ensure that the others successfully reach international waters. Sudanese, Ethiopians, Somalis and Eritreans, who are less likely to have the kinds of networks or influence to pay in instalments or via escrow systems, are particularly susceptible to these schemes. In those cases, where money has been paid up front without any assurances or guarantees, the smuggler gets to pocket the money, and the security forces can claim success in the phony war against smuggling networks.

A thirty-five-year old Syrian in Alexandria, for example, said that when it came time for smugglers to transfer him to the beach, they did not move him and the forty other migrants with him into a bus. Instead, they walked them to an area not far outside Alexandria. He

141

believes that he and his fellow travellers, almost all of whom were sub-Saharan Africans, were deliberately given up to the police by his smugglers. 'We passed under two bridges and all the people and cars saw us before going to the sea,' he explained. 'We were obvious to everyone. That was at 9 p.m. Also the drivers were talking in a weird way and at some point one of them told the others that [police] were on their way. I think they meant the coastguards and they knew they were going to arrest us because they just came one hour after.'

In addition to increased collusion between smugglers and security authorities, the emergence of several key characters at the top of the smuggling economy further indicates increased professionalism and organisation within the smuggling trade in Egypt. One of the biggest smugglers in Egypt, for example, is known as 'the Doctor'. His moniker was used in interviews with smugglers, migrants and law enforcement in Egypt, as well as in interviews with migrants in Europe who said that they had been smuggled via his network. 'The Doctor' is believed to have connections to move migrants past established checkpoints and to coordinate with contacts within the Egyptian security apparatus. Most people believe he is an Egyptian national with specialised connections in Lebanon, Syria and Jordan. Some others suggested that 'the Doctor' is a composite title affixed to one powerful network.

Other such characters include 'the General' and 'the Captain', both of whom were mentioned across a wide array of interviews in Alexandria and Cairo. 'The General' is rumoured to be a former general in the Egyptian military with considerable connections in Sudan and Libya. 'The Captain' is rumoured to move migrants via the inner workings of his large shipping companies. One person interviewed in Alexandria, for example, says he paid $5,000 to have his son sent on one of 'the Captain's' boats. The boat, he says, left from a heavily guarded industrial seaport, which further suggests that 'the Captain' has high-level connections.

It may very well be that these are mere caricatures that provide a convenient and cogent representation of what are very complex, impenetrable networks. Yet the type of people described, and the type of contacts they have, are consistent with the typologies that experts, analysts and local activists all described both in Egypt and outside. With professional criminal networks of this kind, complex protection economies are required to protect the trade, and these have serious implications for the security and integrity of the state.

Compared to those operating in Libya and Turkey, migrant-smuggling networks operating out of Egypt have garnered relatively little international attention. And, as previously mentioned, officials in Europe are hesitant to pressure the Egyptian government on the issue. In a world of limited resources and finite diplomatic capital, maintaining the delicate relationship with the Egyptian government over a range of security issues means that pressing the Egyptian government on migrant smuggling is unlikely. As with Libya and Turkey, however, EU officials are concerned that the Islamic State group, which has a presence in Egypt's Sinai region, may try to use these smuggling networks to send its own operatives to Europe.

'Our major concern is that among smugglers and migrants there may also be militants from the Sinai, affiliated to al-Qaeda or the Islamic State,' an EU official told Reuters news agency in late February. Yet, just as the EU has other priorities, so too does the Egyptian government. 'The authorities are too busy with other issues to deal with this.'[3]

7

DESERT HIGHWAY

AGADEZ AND THE SAHEL

Alghabass* agreed to meet me after being introduced by a friend of a friend. In true Tuareg fashion he wore a turban that obscured all but his eyes. He spoke in hushed, barely audible tones, and was reluctant to talk to a stranger. Yet two cigarettes into our third meeting, six months after our first, whatever reservations he had once held about talking to a stranger had dissipated. It turns out that Alghabass is a natural story-teller, and on this night in November 2014 he is eager to talk about his most notorious score to date.

Alghabass has never heard of the character Omar from the TV series *The Wire*, but he smiles at the idea of a 'stick-up boy' in urban America whose primary occupation is robbing drug dealers. Alghabass, after all, is a part-time 'interceptor', which is to say that he occasionally assembles a crew and hijacks convoys trafficking high-value contraband, usually narcotics, through the Sahara.

'I can tell you for a fact that *Aziz is a narco-trafficker,' Alghabass says in reference to an Arab man who at the time was among the most well-known and powerful drug traffickers in northern Niger. 'You know how I know Aziz is a narco?' he asks rhetorically. 'I know he is a narco because I intercepted one of his convoys.'

This particular score, as Alghabass explains it, took place 60 kilometres outside a town in northern Niger, which in part explains how he was able to catch Aziz's convoy off-guard. 'We knew when they were leaving and where they would be,' Alghabass says. According to Alghabass, 80 per cent of successful interceptions take place because an insider sold out the convoy, as was the case here. A fellow Tuareg who fought alongside Alghabass in an ill-fated rebellion against the government in 2007 had been working under Aziz. He contacted Alghabass and offered him information in exchange for a cut of whatever Alghabass was able to pry out of the convoy.

Alghabass got in touch with people he trusted and, within thirty-six hours, they were able to assemble a team of competent former rebels and ex-military men, equipped with several Toyota pickup trucks. 'We had M-80s, 12.7s, and 14.5s,' he recounts, referencing some of the heavy weaponry at their disposal, in addition to the Kalashnikov assault rifles that are ubiquitous throughout the Sahara.

Alghabass and his team moved in on the convoy just after nightfall. The convoy's leader immediately realised that they were outgunned and out-manoeuvred, and waved turban fabric out of the side of his car to signal Alghabass over.

'He told me that his boss wanted to talk to me, and handed over a telephone,' Alghabass says. On the other end of the satellite phone was Aziz. 'He asked me how much it would cost for me to let the convoy go.'

According to Alghabass, the trucks were carrying *passeport marocain*, a slang term for cannabis resin, more commonly known as *kif*, or hashish. Grown on an industrial scale in the Rif Mountains of Morocco, *kif* is widely smuggled throughout the region, and for traffickers, Niger's northern desert, wide open and impossible to police, makes an ideal corridor for reaching regional markets in Libya, Egypt, and even larger ones in Europe and the Middle East.

Alghabass made an initial offer of roughly $200,000 but, as with everything in Niger, the price was negotiable. After a few rounds of haggling, they arrived at $150,000. Alghabass and his crew kept their guns fixed on the convoy while a rendezvous between associates of both parties took place back in Agadez. A few hours later, after a member of Aziz's crew handed the cash over to Alghabass's representative, Alghabass let the convoy continue into the desert night.

The story of Alghabass ripping off Aziz is not an uncommon one. These types of standoffs in the desert happen from time to time, and only a fraction of them are ever reported or recounted outside the circles of smugglers and traffickers. But within those circles, these are the tales that fill conversations over beers in dingy bars and pots of tea in nondescript courtyards across countless backwater towns that dot the Sahel and Sahara. In this part of the world, trafficking and smuggling of licit and illicit goods forms the economic basis of entire communities, which in turn means that trafficking and smuggling also forms the basis of politics for entire communities.

The most remarkable part of this particular story, however, is not the nature of the score, but that Alghabass is willing to talk so openly about Aziz to an outsider with a pen and notebook. When I ask around, there are two prevailing theories as to why Alghabass can afford to talk to me. The first is that because he comes from a prominent family in northern Niger, his family name and political connections afford him protection that even powerful barons such as Aziz are reluctant to challenge. That is the theory that many people here in Agadez want to believe, in part because it appeals to a widely held nostalgia for days when traditional conceptions of power, based on notions of nobility, lineage, ethnicity and race, provided stability under the guise of a natural order.

The second theory is much less romantic and, given the nature of drug trafficking, more realistic. It posits that Alghabass's family name alone was not enough to protect him from Aziz, and that after Aziz pinned the heist on him, Alghabass made amends several months later. He lent his services to Aziz and 'smoothed over' a dispute in which a different Tuareg interceptor tried to steal an entire stash of drug cargo rather than take a cut or hold it for ransom.

With rare exceptions, these stories are unverifiable and, like any good tale, the details tend to be embellished with each retelling. When I ask a local journalist about the story of Alghabass and Aziz, he reacts as if I am the last person privy to outdated gossip.

'Everybody knows that story. But no one would ever report it,' he says. 'When it comes to reporting on Aziz, the problem is not only what you can prove, it is the consequences.'

When I ask a local military intelligence official whose job is ostensibly to keep tabs—to the extent that anyone can—on flows of activity near Niger's border with Libya, he refuses to say whether or not he had even heard of the story, let alone comment on its veracity. He did, however, offer one bit of folksy wisdom that all but confirmed that at least some parts of the story of Alghabass and Aziz are true: 'The desert is mysterious, but it's bad at keeping secrets.'

The desert may be bad at keeping secrets, but that does not mean that any single person can really claim to know the full story of what is going on here, especially when it comes to the local smuggling and trafficking networks in this part of the world. These days, the most lucrative and therefore most important thing to be smuggling is not narcotics or weapons, but people, to the tune of hundreds of millions of dollars. In fact, Alghabass himself has given up intercepting altogether, and has invested some of his criminal proceeds into migrant-smuggling networks that guarantee him a steady stream of income, and the rest into artisanal gold-mining.

To make sense of how Agadez in Niger, an ancient city in the middle of a desperately poor, landlocked African country on the wrong side of the Sahara, has become a gateway to Europe, one must view it through a lens with local, regional, and global focal lengths. And even when viewed at just the right angle and from just the right distance, all that Agadez brings into focus are more disquieting questions about the volatility of our world.

To understand what is going on today in Agadez and its global implications, you need to understand Niger. And to understand Niger, you need to understand the Sahel. And to understand the Sahel, you need to understand the Sahelian cosmos that former Libyan dictator Muammar Gaddafi created, and the geo-political black hole left by his absence.

* * *

Understanding the Sahel

Libya shares a total of 4,339 kilometres of land borders with six countries: Algeria, Chad, Egypt, Niger, Sudan and Tunisia. For the vast majority of migrants from sub-Saharan Africa attempting to use Libya as a gateway to Europe, the most viable path is to enter through its southern borders by transiting through either Niger, Chad, Algeria or Sudan.

For a combination of political, geographical and security reasons, crossing into southern Libya from these countries, which requires traversing the Sahara and a vast strip of land below the Sahara known as the Sahel, is virtually impossible without the assistance and permission of the populations who inhabit the area. Separating the Sahara from the savannah, the Sahel stretches across the African continent, bisecting parts of Mauritania and Senegal on the West African coast, and continuing across parts of Mali, Algeria, Burkina Faso, Niger, Nigeria, Chad, Sudan, South Sudan and Eritrea.

The zone is characterised by dramatic variations in rainfall and is prone to cyclical drought, the effects of which are further exacerbated by the tide of desertification that makes the Sahel less hospitable with each passing year. These climatic challenges severely affect the sustainability and livelihoods of the predominantly pastoral economies of the region, placing stress on its populations, which are some of the most vulnerable on earth.

In 2015, for example, Niger sat squarely at the very bottom of UNDP's Human Development Index, with Chad and Mali also jockeying for positions near the bottom.[1] Furthermore, because the Sahelian band cuts across several countries but does not encompass any of them completely, populations living within the Sahel and Sahara are often disproportionately economically disadvantaged within their own countries. With central governments failing to meet the most basic needs of communities living in the Sahel and Sahara, economic marginalisation has often translated into political turmoil and, in many cases, armed rebellion against the state.

As a long-standing survival strategy, the populations of the Sahel and Sahara, which includes an amalgam of black African, Berber and Arab tribes, have thus become highly dispersed and mobile, migrating between communities scattered across the region in response to environmental factors. The free movement of people and goods has long served as a resilience strategy, creating a web of economic, political and cultural networks dispersed across the Sahara and the Sahel in which ethnicity and kinship remain an important organising principle. In fact, within the context of the Sahel and Sahara, these conceptions of connectivity are just as important as—perhaps more important than—geographical proximity. As Judith Scheele writes in one study of Saharan connectivity, people's relationships and identity 'are inherently flexible and developed through sustained communication. They can at

149

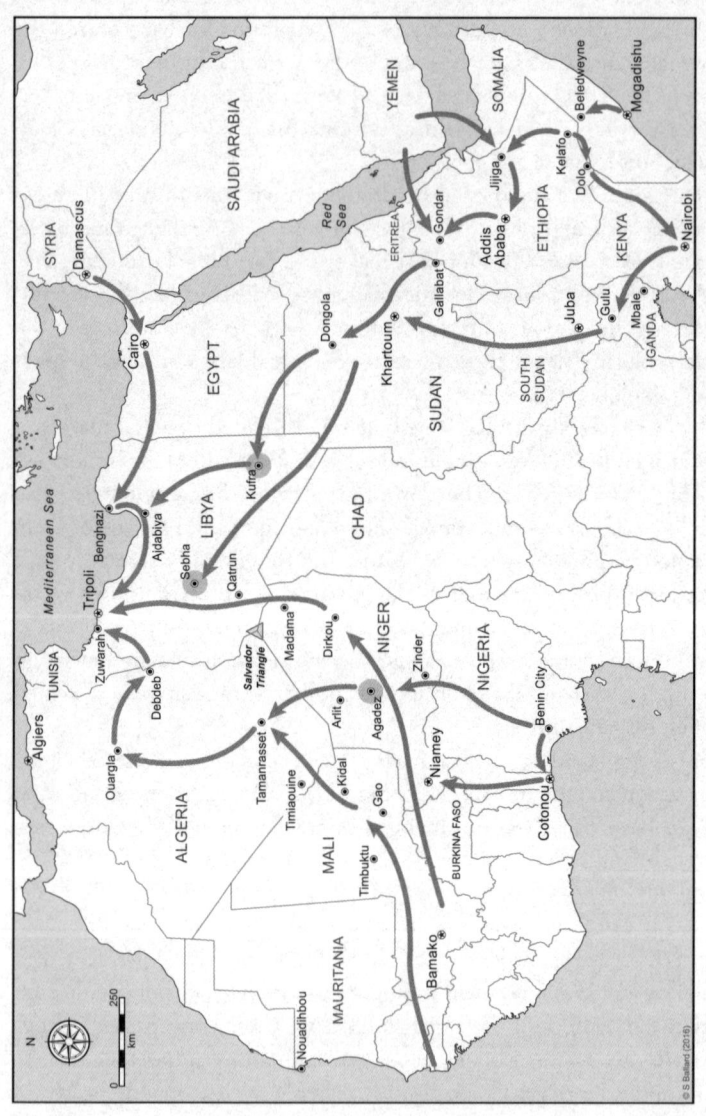

Map 5: Migrants passing through Sahel zones of control

times include places situated at considerable distance, while excluding areas close by.'[2]

Over the past half-century since the end of colonial rule, most Sahelian states have failed to provide even a minimum of social and economic development, particularly for their nomadic populations in the Sahara, and policy decisions partially sponsored by the international development community have eroded traditional pastoralist livelihoods. Famines were frequently used as a means to weaken marginal populations, while border controls increased, and control over common assets (such as grazing reserves) were turned over to state control, often to the personal enrichment of state officials. Consequently, pastoralism, once the main livelihood for the vast majority of the people of the Sahel, receded as a viable means of survival and these communities became increasingly dependent on cross-border smuggling. The bulk of this activity came in the form of subsidised goods from North Africa, but also included a range of illicit commodities: fake cigarettes, counterfeit goods, hashish, small arms and weaponry, and occasionally harder drugs such as cocaine or heroin, but also involved the movement of people.

Two groups in particular, the Tuareg and the Toubou, have enjoyed a long-standing dominance over the trade in the movement of people, with a recorded history dating back to the sixth century, working first as slave transporters, then as smugglers.[3] Partly due to ethnography, but also by negotiation, the Toubou and the Tuareg historically worked different routes. According to an old political agreement signed between the two groups in 1875, Tuaregs are in charge of territory to the west of the Salvador Triangle (which is situated where the borders of Algeria, Libya and Niger intersect, and is considered one of the most important corridors for all trans-Saharan trafficking) and the Toubou to the east of it. As the map below shows, both populations span several borders, though they represent extreme minorities in all of them.

Many migrants coming from East Africa and the Horn travel through the landlocked territory of Chad, a country that has been at war with itself or its neighbours for the bulk of its post-colonial history. The country is a melting pot of ethnicities and peoples, welded into the Sahel and greater Sahara through networks with little use for modern borders. In addition, like many landlocked states, Chad is a crossroads across which all manner of licit and illicit goods flow.

Thanks to the country's highly clientelistic governance structure, control over these flows are operated by small groups of economic entrepreneurs deeply embedded into and controlled by parts of the state, who enjoy near-perfect immunity due to connections to the president's inner circle. As one international official based in the Chadian capital of N'Djamena explained, 'There aren't any real crime lords in Chad—all the big criminals are all in the Government.'[4]

Political power being so closely linked to access to resources has led to an 'armed factionalism' where armed rebellion has become central to securing influence.[5] This competition has provoked a political volatility, with repeated defections from the government, including by members of the president's family (many of whom hold strategic or cabinet positions), resolved only when defectors are offered a greater share of power and resources. Rebel leaders who lay down their arms have been rewarded with ministerial posts or high military ranks, and former rebel troops are regularly integrated into an increasingly bloated army. This practice has given birth to an officer corps where many have received their commissions only as a means to neutralise them as political opponents, and where some of these high-ranking officers, with questionable merits, are alleged to be involved in crime and trafficking.

Regarding transnational crime and trafficking, Chad is very well positioned, both geographically and socio-economically. It stands as a bridge between East and West Africa, as well as between North Africa and sub-Saharan Africa. Chad is one of the most heavily trafficked transit countries for thousands of migrants a month. Those from northern Nigeria seeking refuge from Boko Haram, those displaced by conflict in Sudan and South Sudan, migrants from Ghana, Cameroon and a limited number of other Central African countries may find Chad a more convenient thoroughfare than Niger to the west. But for all migrants Chad is a dangerous and difficult country to cross, not just due to the four decades of its own high levels of militarisation, but also because it is a hub for the sale of arms to its continually conflict-prone neighbours. Across the country, the importance of being armed is central to survival, political influence and profit. Or, as one international security liaison told us, 'in Chad you're not a man if you don't have an AK-47.'[6]

Chad's immense desert to the north bordering Libya is Toubou territory. The Toubou are a semi-nomadic, pastoralist tribe of African descent, whose population of approximately 250,000 is concentrated predominantly in Chad, but also in southern Libya and northern Niger.[7] Northern communities rely heavily on exchanges with southern Libya, with which most have commercial and personal ties. In the words of one Chadian journalist, 'Northern Chad lives entirely from traffic to and from Libya.' The first of Chad's many rebellions started in the north, and the area remained a war zone for decades, with rebel factions fighting both the government and each other.

A Libyan claim to the Aouzou-band, an area rich with oilfields, led to the presence of Libyan forces fighting at times alongside and at other times against various rebel groups for more than twenty years, with Gaddafi's meddling hand always at work to tip the balance of strategic battles and influence the outcomes. Only recently has relative peace come to the region, but Chad remains a place awash with weapons, littered with landmines, and the presence of the central state remains limited throughout much of the country. Despite hailing from the north himself, the regime of the current president, Idriss Déby Itno, continues to rely on the military and alliances with the Toubou to control the desert and its borders, giving them unprecedented influence over politics in Chad and the north.[8]

This was not a privilege that they enjoyed in Libya, however, as the Toubou had a highly complex relationship with the Gaddafi regime. Initially, in the 1970s, Libya's mercurial leader preferred the Toubou, but his preference for Arab and Berber tribes eventually soured into a campaign to marginalise the Toubou in favour of the Arab Zwaye. Not only did Gaddafi finance the Zwaye to move in on what were historically Toubou trafficking routes,[9] he systematically persecuted and oppressed the Toubou in a campaign of discrimination that the UN retroactively described as being tantamount to ethnic cleansing.[10]

Gaddafi denied the Toubou social support, including access to education and land rights, and in 2007 proceeded to strip Toubou residents in Libya of their citizenship. However, when the Gaddafi regime began to crumble under popular resistance, he appealed to the highly armed Toubou for military support, promising to return citizenship in exchange. The Toubou initially bought into the deal, but turned on Gaddafi midway through the revolution, playing a key role in his downfall.

Having abandoned Gaddafi, the Toubou have consistently stayed largely aloof from post-revolutionary militia politics, instead using the chaos of conflict and the paralysis of political transition as an opportunity not only to reassert their authority over their traditional networks and turf, but to expand their zone of influence all along Libya's southern border, from Kufra to the Salvador Triangle (and in the process securing some key oil fields in the east), as well as southwards into Niger. In early 2012 the Toubou began a prosperous clandestine alcohol-trafficking operation from Niger to Libya. State officials demanded a cut from the contraband trade to supplement their incomes, as salary payments by the struggling central state became increasingly infrequent. The system of payment and complicity laid the foundation for the Toubou to traffic a far wider range of goods, from looted construction equipment to stolen cars, to weapons that would proliferate throughout the region and find themselves used in the conflicts in northern Mali and northern Nigeria.[11]

This expanded zone of control and the trafficking routes from southern Libya deep into Africa's heartland aligned the Toubou perfectly to facilitate the movement of migrants from East Africa and the Horn into Libya. Coordinating loosely with tribes operating smuggling networks throughout the Horn and in Sudan, the Toubou picked up migrant convoys and facilitated their passage through Chad and parts of Sudan, across Libya's southern border, and either up to Kufra or across towards Sebha. South of Sebha, towards the Libyan border with Niger and West toward Algeria, the Toubou's expanded influence would bring them into direct competition with ethnic Tuareg smugglers who have long dominated certain routes in southern Libya.

Niger, Agadez and the West

Chad's neighbour to the west is Niger, a weak state by almost any measure, whose ability to overcome state weakness is inhibited by the mutually reinforcing challenges of limited resources and limited state capacity. Though the country is rich in uranium and recently became an oil producer, neither of these natural endowments has translated into economic prosperity for the people who live there. Niger finishes at the very bottom of a range of development indicators, and the vast majority of the 17 million people who call Niger home remain some of the poorest in the world.

As with the other countries in the Sahel, the livelihoods of the different populations within Niger are predicated on how they orient themselves with concomitant communities in neighbouring states to engage in trade. The Toubou, concentrated primarily in Niger's north and east, control specific commercial exchanges with Toubou communities in Libya and Chad, while ethnic Songhai and Djerma communities in Niger's south-west trade with similar communities in Mali, Burkina Faso and Benin. Hausa merchants in the south—specifically those concentrated in the urban centres of Maradi and Zinder—and Kanuri traders in the south-east rely on trade with equivalent populations in northern Nigeria. In the north, Nigérien Tuaregs link with Tuareg communities in Mali, Libya and Algeria, as do Niger's Arabs, who share commercial and cultural ties with ethno-linguistic kin in Mali, Libya and Algeria.

In contrast to the Toubou, the Berber Arab Tuareg enjoyed periods of great favour during Gaddafi's four-decade rule. He welcomed Tuaregs displaced by 'black' governments in Mali and Niger, encouraging them to settle in Libya and depicting them as a bulwark against black Africa. He publicly referred to them as the 'Arabs of the South', 'Lions and Eagles of the Desert' and 'Defenders of the Sahara'.[12] Having long fostered the goal of a unified cross-border Saharan region, Gaddafi sought to take advantage of the marginalisation of the Tuareg in Mali and Niger by stoking their nationalism abroad and supporting Tuareg separatist movements. In 1979 he created the 'Islamic Legion', an approximately 8,000-strong auxiliary armed militia group comprised mainly of Tuaregs, which was to serve under his personal direction.[13] Many of these young recruits would later form the core of the 1990–5 Tuareg rebellion in northern Niger.

In addition to cross-border trade, Niger has long depended on neighbouring economies as a source of employment, and all of its neighbours house significant populations from the Nigérien diaspora. The resultant socio-economic connectivity leaves Niger particularly vulnerable to external shocks emanating from its volatile neighbours. In the last five years alone, Niger's government has scrambled to maintain stability, first amid the collapse of the Gaddafi regime and the ensuing civil war in Libya; then the collapse, Islamist takeover and subsequent French-led intervention in neighbouring Mali; and the ongoing violence in northern Nigeria due to the Islamic State in West Africa (formerly Boko Haram). All of these pressures, both internal and external, have had a profound impact on the way in which Niger is governed and the relationship between the government and its citizens.

As with other fabled desert towns in the Sahara such as Timbuktu in Mali, Agadez has served as a crossroads for centuries. These were places where ideas, people and goods from sub-Saharan Africa, North Africa, the Middle East and Europe were exchanged. But as the legendary caravans of the Sahara have long ceased being profitable and cities such as Agadez are no longer centres of global scholarship and commerce.

These days, those who travel to places such as Timbuktu and Agadez could be forgiven for feeling as though these storied cities are now simply desert way stations a few hundred years past their prime. In reality, however, they remain inextricably linked to regional economies and the broader global economy. They might constitute the rough, outer edges of our globalised world, not yet sufficiently sanded by the emery board of free trade and neoliberalism, but what goes on in places like Agadez can nonetheless be of global import.

* * *

The contemporary smuggling economy in northern Niger can be traced back to the 1970s, when networks emerged to facilitate the illegal flow of subsidised goods such as fuel and foodstuffs from Libya and Algeria into Niger and neighbouring Mali. Livestock and labour flowed in the opposite direction, almost always evading official channels, and forming the basis for informal trade for the entire region. During the late 1980s and early 1990s networks developed throughout the region around the mass smuggling of cigarettes from West African ports across the Sahel and Sahara into North Africa. The maturation of these markets, in which Niger emerged as a major transit zone, coincided with a boom in migration across the Sahel to North Africa.

Like many of the towns that had served as strategic consolidation points and pivots for the trans-Saharan caravan trade, as legitimate trade began to move predominantly by sea, Agadez began to emerge as a multidirectional hub for the smuggling of licit and illicit goods of all sorts. Arms, vehicles, construction equipment, subsidised fuel and foodstuffs were all smuggled from Libya down to Niger, usually for onward travel. Hashish grown in Morocco was smuggled east to west. Cocaine shipped from South America to the West African coast followed a similar route, arriving west from Mali and south from Nigeria and Benin. Alcohol, pharmaceuticals, cigarettes and an array of licit goods were smuggled south to north, or north to south, depending on the product and market.[14]

While analysts often prefer to dwell on the illegal or criminal aspects of these activities, all of these commodities and trades, despite being illicit, represent an income-generating opportunity not only for local populations but also for government officials. In some cases government officials profit from levying informal taxes on these goods. In others they make fortunes offering official registration for licit goods that have entered the country illegally (cars, equipment, subsidised goods, etc.).

As these networks were developing in the 1980s and 1990s, the Nigérien government, based in the capital city, Niamey, in the south and consisting mostly of elites from southern Niger, struggled to deal with on-again, off-again rebellions originating from the country's north. In 1990, for example, several Tuareg, Arab and Toubou rebel groups took up arms in response to what they perceived as years of political and economic marginalisation as well as violent repression by the Nigérien state.[15] Their goal at the time was to carve out an independent state in the Sahara, though this was later recalibrated to aspirations of political and economic autonomy within Niger. Years of violence between Niger's armed forces and a jumble of rebel factions finally subsided in 1995 with the signing of the Ouagadougou Accords, which succeeded in ending the majority of the fighting.

As part of the accords, state power was decentralised to cities, departments and regions. Rebel combatants were integrated into the civil service and security forces, and, in a gesture that implicitly gave them a mandate to regulate politics in the north of the country, rebel leaders were appointed to senior public offices and given a share of central government power.[16]

In 2007 a new group, the Niger Movement for Justice, known by its French acronym, MNJ, claimed responsibility for a series of attacks on military outposts in northern Niger, marking the start of a new rebellion that lasted from 2007 to 2009. The MNJ's rebellion did not last nearly as long as its antecedents, in part because it was not as well organised or equipped, but also because the government of then President Mamadou Tandja chose a heavy-handed military response.

President Tandja, as well as Tuaregs from the previous rebellion, who were by then members of Niger's political and military elite, successfully portrayed the MNJ and its allies as a front for trafficking interests, particularly those of MNJ leader Aghali Alambo. Regardless of whether or not these allegations were true, it is clear that the MNJ did not initially enjoy the same levels of local support as those who had led the rebellion in the 1990s, and that protecting trafficking routes was certainly part of the equation. Trans-Saharan trafficking had reached an unprecedented level of profitability around this time, due to the recent introduction of cocaine to the region. Cocaine was entering the continent through the littoral nations along the West African coast, brought by South American cartels seeking a new route to Europe. Small states with weak post-colonial governments, of which Guinea Bissau is the most notorious but by no means the only example, had become an entrepôt for an estimated 20–40 per cent of Europe's cocaine consumption, some $2.1 billion annually. While only a fraction of this total was estimated to have travelled by land across the Sahara, it nonetheless had a significant impact, enriching those who trafficked it and further eroding Sahelian states with corruption.[17]

Over the course of the rebellion, enriched by the illicit flows of trafficking, the MNJ not only emerged as a serious political and military opponent to the government, but also became a vehicle for young Tuaregs and members of the Tuareg diaspora who felt betrayed by an older generation of Tuareg leaders.[18] As the rebellion progressed, the MNJ fractured into several factions, with certain members of the Tuareg 'old guard' joining the fray, and thus lending it more perceived legitimacy.

The rebellion eventually subsided thanks to talks mediated by the Gaddafi regime, whose personal interventions in northern Mali and northern Niger had, for better or worse, often acted as a force for stability as much as they had undermined the governability of those areas. The circumstances in which both rebellions came to an end still have a tremendous impact on the way Niger is governed and how stability is maintained. As previously mentioned, the first rebellion ended with promises of decentralisation that were haphazardly implemented and had ostensibly codified the status of former rebel leaders as northern Niger's political elite.

The circumstances under which the second rebellion dissipated are much less clear, as are its legacies. 'Some rebel leaders and ex-combatants still disagree with the government on the basics of that agreement,' an official for an international organisation tasked with developing and implementing peace initiatives in northern Niger told me in the spring of 2014. 'Gaddafi called all the parties involved, listened to them, and then tried to use money to keep their mouths shut,' he continued. 'There was no real political agenda. So they never went through planned, organised, DDR [disarmament, demobilisation and reintegration].' Instead, as had been the case after the previous rebellion, trafficking interests were interwoven into the central state and into politics in the capital.

Thus, when Niger's current president, Mohamadou Issoufou, was elected in 2011, he inherited a country that lacked many of the most basic trappings of a state. A veteran politician who had spent close to twenty-five years either holding senior positions in government or as a key figure within the opposition, Issoufou came to office during a time of relative stability and on the promise of lifting Niger out of poverty through various development programmes. But, only a few months into his presidency, external shocks from neighbouring states fundamentally altered the economic and security environment within Niger's borders, and burgeoning threats both foreign and domestic meant that security imperatives quickly came to dominate Issoufou's presidency.

The civil war in Libya in 2011 drove as many as between 150,000–260,000 Nigériens—many of whom were economic migrants working in Libya—back to Niger, depriving entire communities that were reliant on remittances from Libya of their source of income and placing extreme socio-economic pressure on an already vulnerable population.[19] Issoufou's government began sounding the alarm early on, advocating for a negotiated solution to the crisis in Libya and voicing opposition to Western airstrikes.

Among those returning to Niger were Gaddafi's 'Lions of the Desert', armed Tuareg rebels who had been recruited and trained by him in Libya to fight on his behalf. The flood of unemployed, battle-hardened young men equipped with heavy weaponry threatened to destabilise northern Niger, and, as it turned out, neighbouring Mali.

While Issoufou showed remarkable prescience in his response to the threat, combining a set of security and socio-political measures to integrate the returning fighters,[20] Mali's president at the time, Amadou Toumani Touré, did not handle the influx of Tuareg fighters and guns with the same aplomb. Mali, long misdiagnosed as a model of African democracy, descended into chaos after low-ranking soldiers ousted Touré just six weeks before scheduled elections.

Prior to the coup, frustrations with the civilian government had been growing as an assortment of rebel groups attacked military installations in northern Mali. The initial insurgency was led by a group called the MNLA, a primarily ethnic Tuareg movement with the stated goal of establishing an independent state in the north called Azawad. Emboldened by the arrival of experienced ethnic Tuareg fighters from Libya, the MNLA launched a series of attacks on towns in Mali's remote north.

When rebels captured the northern garrison town of Aghelhok, local reports claimed that the Malian soldiers defending the outpost had surrendered after running out of ammunition and provisions. When pictures emerged suggesting that the soldiers had been summarily executed by their captors, hundreds of Malians protested in the streets of the capital city, Bamako.

The coup itself was triggered weeks later when the defence minister, Sadio Gassama, met with disgruntled soldiers at a military base in the city of Kati. By all accounts the meeting did not go well. A cadre of low-ranking officers chased Gassama from the site and proceeded to Bamako, where they occupied the national TV station and took over the presidential palace.

Rebel groups in the north were quick to capitalise on the chaos in Bamako. Less than two weeks after the coup, the Malian military conceded the north in its entirety, leaving weapons, equipment and vehicles behind in a 'tactical retreat'. The secular MNLA and its allies of convenience, a Tuareg-led Islamist group called Ansar Dine, swept across the Sahara to seize the three major northern cities of Kidal, Gao and Timbuktu in an astonishing three-day offensive between 30 March and 1 April 2012. By 6 April, a mere week after the offensive began, the MNLA declared its objectives achieved and proclaimed the independence of northern Mali as Azawad.

Soon after declaring themselves rulers of an independent state, however, MNLA fighters were outmanoeuvred by their one-time allies, Ansar Dine. Led by Iyad Ag Ghali, a Tuareg leader whose bid to lead the MNLA was rejected months earlier, Ansar Dine established working relationships with al-Qaeda in the Islamic Maghreb (AQIM) and the Movement for Unity and Jihad in West Africa (MUJAO). This fractious coalition of Islamist groups in northern Mali consolidated their control over the territory, sustaining themselves with self-enriching criminal enterprises—most notably kidnap-for-ransom and smuggling of contraband—while governing the territory according to their own extremist interpretation of sharia law.

Meanwhile, paralysis in Bamako laid bare the full extent to which corruption had seeped into every level of Malian politics. While the northern two-thirds of the country were under a brutal Islamist occupation and hundreds of thousands of Malians were in dire need of humanitarian assistance, Mali's insouciant political class in the south was preoccupied with pickings over the carcass of the Malian state.[21] The intransigence was the apotheosis of not just a corrupt political system, but an entire political culture in which corruption, fuelled by an influx of illicit cash from criminal networks and systematic theft of international aid, had become the norm.

Few thought that the Islamist gunmen who ruled northern Mali could make it to Bamako, but after the Malian army failed to stop an audacious rebel push southward in January 2013, there was little indication the Malian government had either the will or capacity to stop them. Amid fears that Mali could become 'Africa's Afghanistan', the international community intervened to prevent the rebels' final move towards the capital. France launched Opération Serval, an expansive air and ground campaign consisting of over 2,000 French troops, further reinforced by thousands more soldiers from Mali and neighbouring African countries.

For its part, Niger sent 600 troops to help French and Chadian forces secure cities and towns in northern Mali, from which the

Islamist forces retreated days into the French air campaign. In tandem with troops from Chad, French Special Forces continued into Mali's mountainous north-east to kill and capture hundreds of jihadists and uproot a vast network of weapons caches, fuel depots and food hidden among the countless caves and grottoes that dot northern Mali.

Yet even the operation's most ardent cheerleaders concede that the result of the French offensive was to cause many of the jihadists who occupied northern Mali to melt into the landscape or retreat into northern Niger and southern Libya.

To counter this, Western powers such as the USA and France have significantly increased their military and intelligence footprints in the region, now viewing the Sahel and Sahara as places where terrorist plots against them can incubate and emerge.

Until recently, the majority of international attention paid to Niger stemmed from its vast uranium deposits and newly discovered oil reserves. But in light of the collapse of Mali and the ongoing terror threats thought to be germinating in southern Libya, Niger has gradually become a more integral part of France's security strategies for the region. In the wake of a string of abductions of French citizens in the Sahel in 2010, France consolidated its forces to improve its capacity to respond to abductions and strengthen the security of the uranium mines operated by French nuclear giant AREVA. With Special Forces located throughout the country, France is also flying surveillance aircraft, including drones purchased from the United States, out of airfields in Niger.

Determined to keep the jihadist groups operating in the Sahara and Sahel on the run, France launched a new counterterrorism initiative in the Sahel, dubbed Opération Barkhane, consisting of 3,000 troops spread across five countries and supported by supply helicopters, transport aircraft, fighter planes, drones and armoured vehicles. Operating from a constellation of military installations and forward operating bases in Mali, Chad, Mauritania, Burkina Faso and Niger, Opération Barkhane is an attempt to build upon the success of the French Serval campaign in Mali by actively hunting jihadists. So far this has manifested itself in French airstrikes and raids on convoys passing through northern Niger and southern Libya. As the conduit between northern Mali and southern Libya, as well as home to vital French economic and energy interests, northern Niger is at the heart of France's counter-terror policy in the region. In fact, France keeps 200 troops and attack helicopters at a remote base in Madama, in northern Niger, a mere 96 kilometres from the Libyan border.

The United States also considers Niger a key security partner and ally in the region. Since 2002 it has sought to strengthen its military cooperation with governments in the Sahel and Sahara as part of the Trans-Saharan Counter-Terrorism Initiative, later renamed the Trans-Saharan Counter-Terrorism Partnership (TSCTP). In 2014 Niger hosted an annual military exercise sponsored by the United States, called Flintlock, which was carried out in Niamey and forward operating bases in and around the urban centres of Agadez, Tahoua and Diffa, in conjunction with Special Forces from the USA, Canada and a range of European countries and several countries within what the USA calls the 'Pan-Sahel'. In January 2013 the US Central Intelligence Agency set up a drone base out of the airport in Niamey, and began flying MQ-9 Reaper drones from there.

Meanwhile, terrorist attacks are proliferating throughout the region. On the ground, people talk of a 'new normal', one in which dealing with terrorist attacks and mitigating risk from groups such as AQIM, the Islamic State in West Africa, and smaller offshoots within, is now a part of life.

Governments of the Sahel and Sahara, Western powers and China, eager to extract resources from the region and tap into its emerging markets, are struggling to adapt to this 'new normal'. As the region is increasingly viewed through the militarised lens of counter-terrorism and security, focusing on military solutions to a complicated problem-set encompassing issues of economics, politics, climate change and culture, an equally transformative phenomenon is taking place outside the purview defined by governments and the international community: migrant smuggling.

With migrant smuggling now a billion-dollar industry, and with payouts going to an array of actors with their own political and military ambitions, the future of the Sahel and Sahara might not be shaped by young men with guns so much as by young men with trucks.

New Masters

Decent Italian cuisine is hard to come by in the Sahara, but Le Pilier, a restaurant run by a half-Tuareg, half-Italian man named Ernesto, used to offer everything from gnocchi to polenta. There was a time when tourists from all over the world would stay a few nights in Agadez before setting out on Saharan adventures under the care of Tuareg tour guides. But after a spate of kidnappings in the broader region and a string of terrorist attacks closer to home, the US State Department and French government warned their nationals to steer clear of northern Niger. The tourism sector in Agadez died overnight. Some tourists still pass through, but not enough to sustain an entire industry.

Ernesto's father runs a separate Le Pilier in the southern capital, Niamey, where expats and wealthy Nigériens fill the tables for lunch and dinner, and multi-course Italian cuisine is on offer. In the evenings the franchise in Agadez is equally busy, but with an entirely different crowd, and the menu has been streamlined to meet the preferences of its new clientele. The white tablecloths and red wine in Niamey are nowhere to be found in these parts, and the only entrées on the menu are pizza and a few local dishes, all of which can be paired with cheap beer or hard alcohol.

'There are no tourists,' says Ernesto. 'Our clients are some old Tuaregs who would come with their white friends. But now it is young transporters who come from Libya.'

'Toubous', he clarifies, 'lots of Toubous.'

That young, hard-drinking Toubou now comprise the majority of the clientele at a place like Le Pilier is a sign of the times. And if you ask Ernesto, he'll tell you why there are so many young Toubou men flashing money around town. 'They are transporters of people,' he explains. 'And some other things.'

Ernesto is not the only one who has noticed the shift in demographics.

'Don't they know this is a Tuareg town?' asks Alhousseini, loud enough for the nearby table of young Toubou to hear him. 'Don't worry, these animals don't speak French. Even if they do, I don't care,' he continues.

The boisterous foursome of twenty-something Toubou in question, it turns out, do speak some French, but they are too busy guzzling

Johnny Walker Red by the bottle and enjoying the company of young Nigérien women to care what Alhousseini, an older Tuareg who is inebriated in his own right, has to say.

The friction at Le Pilier spills out into the nocturnal streets, where dive bars and nightclubs that once catered to tourists, NGOs and locals now entertain those making a killing off of migrant smuggling. Some are young men just back from a trip to Libya, flush with cash and looking to unwind after a stressful trip through the desert. Others are people who have come from throughout West Africa and North Africa, testing the waters to see if they can make some money as a back-end facilitator in the new smuggling economy.

Though Agadez has always been a smuggling hub, the city is buzzing with a new energy. The markets are stocked with fresh produce. Banks are open and ATMs actually work. Mansions are sprouting up and new neighbourhoods on the outskirts of town are sprawling beyond the traditional limits of the city. Things have changed. The tempo is faster. The stakes seem higher. And, for better or worse, anything seems possible.

Few would have predicted the economic boom a few years ago. But this is the post-Gaddafi Sahel. Old networks are being reimagined, fresh alliances are being forged, and new masters are emerging.

Quite early in the post-revolution period, the Tuareg and Toubou managed to negotiate an agreement over border control along the 1,400 kilometres of Libya's southern border: the Tuareg administered the western region from Sebha, via Ubari, to Ghat, exerting military control through their own militias and parts of the emerging national army, whereas the Toubou were left to manage the region eastward from Sebha to Kufra on the eastern border with Egypt. They agreed on a buffer zone between the Tumu border post run by Toubou and the Anai Pass, which was under Tuareg control.[22]

This agreement did not last very long, however. With several factions within Tuareg smuggling networks preoccupied with and divided by the machinations around the establishment of Azawad in northern Mali, and with attention, funds, weapons and fighters being funnelled south towards the Azawad project, Tuareg capacity to control certain territory in Libya was being challenged on two fronts: by the Zintani forces to the north-west, and by the Toubou to the east. At the same time, some of the more lucrative trafficking routes controlled by the

Tuareg, particularly those that facilitated the flow of narcotics, had been interrupted by instability and the subsequent French intervention in northern Mali.

The post-intervention period in northern Mali has placed great attention on the Tuareg, as the international community seeks to paper over the cracks of Mali's fractured governance and restore the country to a constitutional democracy. With yet another round of political pacification measures on the table within the frameworks of past agreements and accords between the central government and communities from northern Mali, the Tuaregs are as splintered as ever amidst competing political, economic and ideological priorities, underpinned by a desire to defend territory and certain trafficking interests.[23]

The Toubou, meanwhile, have quietly consolidated and expanded their zone of control by trafficking primarily in goods of little interest to international security officials. They have translated their financial profits into military strength, which has in turn allowed them to position themselves vis-à-vis the international community as a credible interlocutor and provider of security along Libya's southern border.

This new posture began with a strategic manoeuvre to control the business of 'protecting' the many oil facilities that are scattered across the desert, which produce an estimated 75 per cent of the country's oil. As with many protection rackets, the Toubou's move into the oil industry quickly morphed into extortion. In 2012, for example, Toubou guards at the Elephant oil field, one of Libya's largest sites, blocked production and access to demand higher salaries for a greater number of local community guards. With schisms in the central government causing a deadlock, foreign oil companies were forced to deal directly with the militia groups to settle disputes.[24]

In parallel, the Toubou leveraged themselves with the international community as potential partners in countering the emerging threat from the Islamist 'terrorists'[25]—and at the same time highlighting a clear distinction between themselves and the Tuareg, some of whom were tainted by their alliances to or membership in jihadist groups in Mali. They argued that only an indigenous force could ever hope to chart a path through the ever-morphing smuggling networks and terrorist groups active in the Sahara, and that they were best placed to play that role.[26]

DESERT HIGHWAY: AGADEZ AND THE SAHEL

Given the neurotic preoccupation of the international community around the threat of violent extremism and terror, there is much that Western policymakers are prepared to overlook for security cooperation at this level. The Toubou's burgeoning involvement in the migrant-smuggling trade, which is an issue of negligible importance in the eyes of Western security officials anyway, was certainly not going to raise any concerns on the part of the international community, when matters of energy security and terrorism were at stake.

These core assumptions could not have proved more short-sighted, as it took only a few months before a network of brokers and recruiters was unspooling from the Libyan coast back to sub-Saharan Africa, telling people throughout the region that 'the time to go to Europe is now'.

In 2013, when the smuggling industry was still developing according to the new realities of the region, large groups of migrants from all over Africa would congregate outside banks and money-transfer houses in Agadez before boarding trucks to begin their journey to Libya. Operating with almost complete impunity, smugglers in Agadez were moving as many as 5,000 West Africans every month between March and August in 2013. According to the International Organisation for Migration (IOM), more than half of the estimated 80,000 migrants who had reached Lampedusa in Italy in 2014 passed through Agadez.

In the wake of a heart-wrenching discovery in October 2013 in which the bodies of ninety-two migrants, mostly children, were found in the desert, Nigérien authorities vowed to crack down on migrant-smuggling networks. Yet, as recently as spring 2016, the industry is anything but underground.

On a calm Monday morning, just as the city is starting to come to life, dozens of migrants have gathered outside a bank thirty minutes before it opens. As they wait outside, making phone calls home and listening to music, you can hear just about every major language spoken in the region. *Djibril, from Burkina Faso, says he wants to go to a country where he can study computer science. In his home town of Bobo Dioulasso he used to work at a cyber-café, which is where he developed his fascination with computers. He graduated from high school two years ago, but says that there aren't many opportunities in Burkina for those who want to 'study computers'. Djibril says his ultimate goal is to make it to Europe, but he is willing to see if there are any opportunities in Tripoli first. 'I've heard it is okay in Tripoli,' he says.

Travelling alone, Djibril is financing his trip with personal savings from working at the cyber-café and with money his father reluctantly provided. 'He doesn't want me to go, but he understands my dream,' Djibril tells me.

For Boubacar and Sidiki, two seventeen-year-old boys from the Louga region of Senegal, garnering parental support was no challenge. They say they are following in the footsteps of many boys from their area, whose families and communities pooled resources to 'send' them to Europe with the hope they would find work and send money back home. According to Sidiki, men and women used to go abroad via Mauritania and Morocco, but now everyone is going through Niger.

Also waiting outside the bank is Aliou, a twenty-three-year old Malian from the region of Kayes who wants to link up with people he knows in Italy. 'They are farmers in Italy and they make a lot of money,' he tells me, alluding to the West African farmhands working in southern Italy.

The young men tell me getting to Agadez was relatively easy and there is no real need for them to hide from authorities. For the vast majority of West Africans, reaching Agadez is a matter of taking several long, gruelling bus trips. As explained in Part 1, those who hold passports belonging to the Economic Community of West African States (ECOWAS), which includes fifteen states of West Africa, but excludes Mauritania, are free to enter and travel through any other ECOWAS state without a visa for ninety days.

Once they reach Agadez, however, West Africa ostensibly ends, and the ocean of sand that separates it from North Africa begins. To cross the Sahara, the services of a smuggler are required. The perilous journey includes the challenge of navigating the ever-shifting sands of the desert and to weave a safe path through competing militias. And that is where people like Ibrahim, a young Toubou from southern Libya, and his cohort, referenced at the introduction of this book, come in.

When I met Ibrahim and his colleagues in their grubby, smoke-filled room on an April morning in 2014, migrant smuggling out of Agadez was no longer an iterative process. It had reached an efficiency borne out of repetition. Informal agreements, repeated thousands of times, can produce an order akin to formal codification.

Every Monday, dozens of convoys would leave locations on the outskirts of Agadez and its environs, in tacit coordination with elements of the Nigérien military that are unofficially part of the enterprise. Each vehicle in the convoy—usually a Toyota four-wheel-drive pickup—is filled with twenty-eight to thirty migrants, sometimes as many as thirty-five. They avoid falling off by clinging onto wooden poles fixed to the sides.

According to Ibrahim, passengers were paying between $200 and $300 at that time, depending on their final destination in Libya: $200 would get you to Qatrun, $250 to Marzuq, and $300 would get you all the way to Sebha. From there, passengers pay between $400 and $600 to continue to Tripoli and Libya's north coast. But to do so they would have to enlist the services of different smuggling networks, controlled by Arabs from Libya. These figures, Ibrahim says, are the bare minimum that one can expect to pay and are predicated on the unlikely scenario that everything will go to plan.

All three towns are situated on the fault-lines of the ongoing civil war in southern Libya, where ethnic Toubou clash with Arab tribesman, Tuaregs, and each other, for control of economic turf that has been up for grabs since the fall of Gaddafi. While Ibrahim and his cohort are making good money as smugglers, approximately $750 per trip, most of the payout goes to powerful actors on both sides of the border—government officials, quasi-state officials, drug kingpins, militia leaders, Islamist gunmen linked to al-Qaeda—who are organised along a dizzying array of shifting alliances born out of economic interests, tribal affiliations, political ambitions, ethnic ties, ideological persuasions and even personal animosities.

Ibrahim tells me that once they reach Libya, the lines between human smuggling and human trafficking can blur. When his migrants disembark from his truck, he has no idea what fate awaits them. Many will be abused and robbed. Some, especially those who do not have enough money for the next leg of their journey, will find themselves coerced into indefinite, unpaid labour, which for women can mean forced prostitution and sexual slavery. Ibrahim also describes heavily armed bandits who prey on migrant-smuggling convoys, extorting migrants and sometimes taking everything, including the vehicles carrying them. 'They have no morals and they will leave you to die in the desert,' he says.

During an hour of frantic conversation, fuelled by a constant stream of nicotine and mint tea, Ibrahim repeatedly changes the subject away from migrant smuggling. At a certain point it is clear that he is growing impatient. He is happy to talk to me, but rather than describe the schematics of the smuggling industry, he would rather I appreciate his own tribulations, how difficult his life has become and how much he has lost since the collapse of Libya.

The others eventually join in, describing southern Libya as a place of sleepless nights, bloody street battles, and friends being rounded up and executed. Together, the group describes Sebha as an unmitigated war zone. 'Mogadishu! Mogadishu!' Ibrahim yells as he snaps his fingers, knowing that referencing the conflict-ridden city in Somalia as a means of comparison won't require translation. 'Big problems! Big problems!' he continues in broken English.

Ibrahim has incipient wrinkles near his eyes that seem like an anachronism on his otherwise boyish face. He speaks rapidly in Arabic, but occasionally switches to Toubou when he says something that he wants my translator to understand, but not his non-Toubou colleagues. When we get to the touchy subject of southern Libya and what is going on there, not everyone in his posse shares the same loyalties, and at one point the conversation gets so heated that the young Arab among them storms out. My translator later explains that he was upset because the others were describing his tribe as terrorists.

After he leaves, an incredulous Ibrahim points at his shirt. He is wearing a Chinese knock-off of FC Barcelona, one of the most famous football clubs in the world. The club's official badge has a red cross on its top right corner. 'The Arabs … the bearded ones who are with al-Qaeda, they started harassing me and asking me if I was Christian, pointing to my shirt,' Ibrahim says. 'I thought these imbeciles were going to kill me!'

When I ask my translator if most people in southern Libya are armed, the group gasps and laughs before he can even finish translating the question. 'Everyone is armed to the teeth,' says Ahmed Hamdi, a young Tuareg in the group who is aghast at the stupidity of my question. 'Even the women!'

Eventually, it becomes painfully clear that these young men, like the desperate migrants they pack into the back of their trucks, see themselves on the raw end of a deal that they never agreed to. Powerful global forces made it on their behalf. Ibrahim, under the impression that I am an incredibly influential American reporter, repeatedly asks me to convey to the American people 'that there are no human rights in Libya'. On several occasions he breaks silences by pestering my translator, 'Did you tell him there are no human rights in Libya?' while glaring at my notebook to make sure I am writing something down.

'Does Obama know how bad it is?' Ahmed Hamdi asks.

Part of me wants to tell them that Africa is the lowest priority at the highest levels of American government. That most US lawmakers would not know how to pronounce Niger, let alone be able to pick it out on a map; that most Americans probably think Libya is in the Middle East, and that many of the people in Washington and Paris who were so eager to bomb Gaddafi out of power have never heard of the Toubou or Tuareg, let alone considered their fate when deciding to press the thumb on the scales in favour of the rebel forces. But looking at Ibrahim and Ahmed Hamdi at that moment, the idea of speaking with such honesty seems needlessly cruel. Sometimes you just have to listen. Or lie.

Eventually, they tell me they need to move to a different location within the city. On my way out of the door, out of the darkness and into the oppressively bright morning sunlight, Ibrahim calls me back in.

'Tell the Americans there are no human rights in Libya,' he pleads. The others, perhaps less naïve or just less hopeful, laugh at his insistence.

'Don't worry, I will,' I say back, before waving and giving a thumbs-up.

* * *

Ibrahim and his crew might cut a pathetic figure, but the unprecedented profits that they and thousands like them are generating has injected hundreds of millions of dollars into the local economies. Their activities are reshaping the balance of power in northern Niger and southern Libya, and not just in socio-economic terms.

With the majority of these networks now controlled by ethnic Toubou, they are increasingly asserting their newfound economic power to expand not only their areas of operation, but also the types of smuggling in which they are involved. And it is from this vantage point that the political and security implications of the current migrant boom are only starting to come into focus.

*Barka spends most of his time between Niger and Libya, rarely staying in either for more than a few weeks at a time. He is Chadian by birth, and used to have a Chadian passport, but he was living in Niger when it expired and he decided it was easier to buy a Nigérien passport on the black market than to bother with the Chadian embassy in Niamey. 'They don't like Chadians here anyway,' he tells me. 'We have a bad reputation.'

Skinny, with bulbous eyes and a long, narrow nose that gives him the appearance of a raccoon, Barka is quick with a smile and doesn't seem to have a threatening bone in his body. He walks with a swagger, sports a fake gold Rolex, and is almost always wearing aviator sunglasses.

He shows me the building where the migrants he drives are housed. Behind a metal gate a handful of men sit on plastic chairs and mats, watching local TV and drinking tea in the courtyard. There is nothing conspicuous or out of place about the building, which like most of the structures in the neighbourhood, is a mix of mud-brick, cheap concrete and exposed rebar.

The house is owned by a Nigérien Arab from the northern commune of Ingall and staffed by Nigériens, mostly ethnic Hausa and Tuaregs, who are from Agadez. They watch over the migrants, unlock the gate that allows them to leave and enter, and bring food, water and other provisions to them. All of these men were brought to the house by a recruiter who receives a commission for each person he brings. In many cases the recruiter scoops up his clients at the bus station when they arrive in Agadez.

Barka is completely removed from the day-to-day operations of the house and is not involved in recruiting either. Whenever he is in town, usually back from a trip to Libya, he notifies the person who runs the house, who contacts Barka when they have reached sufficient numbers for him to load migrants into his Toyota and transport them to Tourayat, from where they will again wait until either the following Monday or Tuesday, depending on the circumstances, to drive in a convoy of dozens of cars towards Libya. Tourayat is full of similar houses, some of which were recently built for the express purpose of housing migrants.

Like the boat trip from the Libyan coast, the smuggling industry in this part of the world is built on economies of scale. A driver like Barka wouldn't dream of interacting with migrants: the value of his vehicle keeps him above all that dirty work. It is the recruiters and brokers who need to hustle and gather enough migrants to fill a car.[27] The magic number is usually twenty-five, but a few more or a few less might also work.

'It's all coordinated,' Barka tells me. 'Even with the military. There are no problems, until after Dirkou.'

Though Barka has never fought in a war, nor has he ever been part of an army or militia, war and conflict have been the backdrop to his entire life. He grew up in Faya, a desert oasis town in the middle of neighbouring Chad. In Niger he identifies as Toubou, but in Chad he prefers to go by Daza, the subset of Toubou to which he and Chad's former president, Hissene Habre, both belong. He grew up in a family with connections to the Habre regime, which did not make him wealthy, but meant that they lived a comfortable life. His father was a mid-ranking official in the Chadian military, but was killed when Barka was only two years old, when Chad was at war with Libya in what became known as the Toyota wars due to the central role of weaponised Toyota 4x4s in the conflict.

A few years later, President Habre was overthrown by Idriss Déby, a man for whom Barka harbours deep animosities. The same dislike is extended to Déby's ethnic group, the Zaghawa. The trickle-down clientelism that Barka and his fellow Toubou enjoyed under Habre dissipated, and his community in Faya stopped benefiting from some of the privileges that came with being linked to the regime. In fact, they bore the brunt of a backlash against the Toubou.

Driving cars and trucks is really the only thing Barka has ever done, and he been doing it since he was fourteen, when he started joining his cousins on smuggling runs, moving everything from petrol to canned goods and cigarettes between Libya, Chad and Sudan.

Family and friends of his participated in various conflicts in all three countries, but Barka says he was never a combatant. His claim to having led an exclusively civilian life catches me off guard. I assumed that he had some military training or combat experience based on his skill-set and his apparent comfort around guns. On his phone, he shows me picture after picture of him posing with all sorts of weapons, but the two that feature the most are his trusted pistol and his Belgian-made FNC assault rifle, which he calls 'his little Belgian'.

Barka shrugs when I ask how he knows how to handle weapons. 'We all know how to handle weapons,' he laughs. 'It's like that with Toubou. We are combatants by nature. That is the reality.'

In talking with Barka over several months, at times in person, other times over the phone or via social media, it becomes clear that he is drawn to smuggling by more than just economic imperatives. He posts pictures of himself drinking tea with friends against scenic desert backdrops, or posing with his car. In one photo he is talking on a satellite phone with his 'little Belgian' slung over his shoulder and a car full of migrants in the background. The photo is clearly staged, but if *Forbes* magazine ever does a profile on the 'top 40 Toubou smugglers under 40', they won't need to send a photographer.

These are the aspects of the smuggling lifestyle that draw many young men to the industry. It is full of adventure. It gives them a sense of purpose and economic empowerment. And more than anything, it is better than the alternatives. If you ask Barka, he will tell you that his current lifestyle is the best he has ever lived. It is dangerous and fun. And most of all, it is lucrative. The alternatives, to the extent that there are any, are boring and unrewarding.

Barka says that if he earns enough money, he might drive less and start financing his own fleet of cars, but there is too much uncertainty at the moment to make such investments. He would rather keep his money stashed with people he trusts on both sides of the Niger–Libya border. The ground keeps shifting in Niger, he tells me, and it is never clear if the government is going to actually crack down on smuggling and smugglers. 'I'm still little,' Barka tells me. If the government chooses to make an example of smugglers, even for show, he does not have the connections to make sure he is not sacrificed in the name of keeping up appearances.

Barka has had plenty of close calls in the desert and has lost migrants along the way. Once, a migrant passed out in the back of the truck and died of what he thinks was dehydration. A family member wanted to keep his body in the truck, but the others forced him to leave it behind. Barka said he was indifferent, but he insisted that they had to keep moving, as other convoys were passing them, and he didn't want word to get out that they were just sitting there, a potential target for bandits.

In another instance, Barka says his convoy was fired upon by heavily armed bandits in an area that is out of the reach of the Nigerien government, but not close enough to Madama to warrant the attention of the French forces stationed there. He was able to escape them, but two men he was transporting had been wounded and bled out before they had a chance to stop. The bandits, he says, held up another car in their convoy, and Ibrahim had no choice but to leave them behind.

'It is very sad, but it is the reality. You have to be selfish because if you stop to help others, you will find problems for yourself,' he tells me with convincing nonchalance. The desert, he says, is littered with the bodies of those who died along the way, and the carcasses of vehicles that either broke down or were shot up.

On more than one occasion he has found small groups of people stranded in the desert, the result of a vehicle mishap or an agreement gone wrong. Once they encountered thirty people left in the middle of the desert with an unserviceable truck. They told him that their pickup had broken down and that the driver had left with another vehicle in their convoy and told them he would be back with a new car or spare part to fix the broken one. They had been there for nine hours and the driver had not yet returned.

'I looked at their car, and it was truly broken. There was nothing I could do for them,' Barka explains. 'They begged us to take some of them, but we did not have any places for them. We gave them some water and continued. Their destiny was up to God.'

Barka seems more at ease with his profession than Ibrahim, Ahmed Hamdi and the jittery nicotine fiends who spoke of nothing but horror stories in southern Libya. Whereas they claimed to be smugglers by necessity who yearn for the way things used to be, Barka has been tacking to the local economic and political winds all his life, and seems to like the direction they are taking him these days.

In fact, Barka believes that whatever greater process is at work is a good thing, not only for the people who want to go to Libya and Europe, but for the Toubou in general. He knows that the powerful Toubou warlords in southern Libya are, first and foremost, seeking profits, but he also believes that their ascendancy will be good for the Toubou in the long run.

'Things are much better for the Toubou now,' he says. 'Under Gaddafi we were completely oppressed,' he continues. 'Gaddafi preferred the Tuareg to us because they were more useful. They were

175

happy to fight for him. Now, every community in Libya is searching for their true territory.'

Barka believes that consolidating power in southern Libya is the first step to achieving broader political ambitions for the Toubou, who he says have been systemically marginalised by Niger and Chad as well. 'All three states try to keep us down,' he claims, citing lack of educational and employment opportunities for Toubou in all the states where they are present. He even draws comparisons to the Kurds in the Middle East.

'All the other ethnic groups have advocates who protect their interests, but never the Toubou. Now, all three governments are afraid of us, and this is good thing because when they are afraid, one can win power,' Barka explains. 'Look at the Tuareg and Arabs in Mali and Niger. They have power because the government is afraid of them,' he continues, referencing how in both countries Arabs and Tuaregs have at times parlayed military success on the ground into concessions from the central government dominated by other ethnic groups.

Barka, it seems, believes that creative destruction is at work; that something better than the entrenched status quo will emerge out of this hyper-capitalist landscape of death and opportunity.

'The Toubou are always fighting in wars that serve other people's interests,' he says. 'Now, there is opportunity for us.' He pauses. 'That is just my view.'

Amidst the optimism that runs through Barka's quasi ethno-nationalist rhetoric, it is easy to forget that we are talking about the smuggling of human beings. But it brings home the fact that with this much money involved, we are talking about more than just a group of trucks in the sand.

A single convoy in the desert creates an ephemeral path that enriches a few. Repeated a few thousand times, it creates a new order of things.

Everybody is Eating

In the summer of 2014, Nigérien government authorities claimed to have intercepted 500 migrants trying to cross the Sahara into neighbouring Algeria, and to have destroyed and uprooted networks of migrant safe houses, over a four-month period. Yet these half-hearted measures did nothing to curb demand, and while migrant networks might not be operating as brazenly as they were before the government vowed to crack down on smuggling, the industry in Agadez continues to grow.

In 2015, for example, after the government passed an anti-trafficking law under heavy pressure from the international community, the number of migrants leaving Agadez ballooned to 2,000 each week, sometimes reaching as many as 10,000 per month. Smugglers say that recent crackdowns, in the form of sporadic arrests and repatriations, are simply for show, and only smugglers who have failed to sufficiently pay off the government, or who upset the wrong officials, need actually fear being arrested.

The practical effect of 'cracking down' on smuggling networks in Niger is that they have been pushed only slightly to the margins. Traffickers say that the authorities they need to bribe, both in Agadez and along the route to Libya, can hold the threat of arrest over them, which in turn has led to a slight increase in prices.

A retired customs officer who is familiar with how these networks work, in part because they are what allowed him to retire early, told me that before the crackdown it was only $150 to go to Libya, but the price soon went up after the international community started pressuring the Nigérien government to 'do something'.

Military officials knew they could use the crackdown as an excuse to raise prices on the smugglers. The price of maintaining the veneer of respectability, in other words, had been passed on to the consumer. According to one customs official who has worked at several outposts on the Algerian border, the going rate smuggling convoys pay for passage increased again in early 2015.

Similarly, the 2015 'crackdown' meant that smuggling networks had to invest in some minimal infrastructure in order to make their activities less blatant. Some networks began providing safe houses, and in some cases arranged for food and water to be provided until the next convoy left for the north. Some have also taken to using other towns outside Agadez, where there is little to no government presence, to consolidate migrants before leaving for Libya. Wealthy entrepreneurs have financed new buildings in these towns, technically billed as hotels and guest houses, but built to warehouse migrants.

Whereas migrants used to arrive in Agadez and simply ask for smugglers, the thin veil of 'illegality' now means that smugglers have enlisted local recruiters, often aspiring migrants themselves, to gather migrants at a price of $25 to $50 per head. In other cases smugglers offer these recruitment brokers free passage in exchange for recruiting enough migrants to fill an entire truck.

One of the reasons it is so hard to crack down on migrant smuggling, however, is that the vast majority of people who come to Agadez for onward passage to Libya are in Agadez legally. As previously mentioned, those who hold ECOWAS passports or identification documents do not need visas to travel through Niger. Similarly, there is nothing technically illegal about driving a truck full of people in the desert. In fact, the migrant-smuggling convoys often follow routes that are commonly travelled in northern Niger. Whether heading to Algeria via the town of Arlit, or to Libya via the town of Dirkou, there is nothing inherently suspicious or out of the ordinary about a truck full of young men heading north from Agadez.

But even if the Nigérien government could crack down on migrant smuggling, they have little incentive to do so. The smuggling economy has injected millions of dollars into Niger's restive north, providing income and livelihoods, and spurring local investment during a time of security concerns and volatility. In 2014, when I spoke with government officials about the migrant-smuggling industry, it was only months after twin suicide attacks carried out by Islamist militants had rocked northern Niger. There was a growing concern that migrant 'ghettos' full of both foreign nationals and Nigériens seeking employment and opportunity in cities like Agadez could provide fertile recruiting grounds for extremist groups.

'The conflict in Libya is on our doorstep,' said Ahmed Koussa, an assistant to the mayor of Agadez. 'Southern Libya is full of terrorists. If we don't have projects that reach out to our young people, they will join the terrorists. We have to create jobs for them,' he told me. 'Everyone converges on Arlit and Agadez, because the rural communities think all the opportunities are here,' he explained. 'Those who left Libya. The West Africans who want to go to Libya. The people in the south who are pushed north by Boko Haram … Everyone comes to Agadez.'

These demographic pressures, Koussa said, are part of what keeps him awake at night, worrying about the next terrorist attack. 'Agadez has 100,000 official residents but [there are] 150,000 people in Agadez at any given time,' he told me. 'All of these factors make it so that if these young people don't find work, they will fall into the hands of the terrorists. We are afraid that the terrorists fully understand this dynamic. They will come and recruit from urban centres,' he continued. 'We have moderate Islam here, but with urban poverty, fundamentalists can infiltrate.'

In fact, religious conservatism—which can be a gateway to as well as a bulwark against violent extremism—has been growing across Niger, north and south, as citizens find themselves struggling to cope with the poverty, instability and impunity provided by their secular elites. For many in Niger, the rapid growth of extremism in Mali, under similar conditions, remains a cautionary tale.

As Koussa outlined these concerns, he flipped through documents and development plans drafted with these challenges in mind. Smuggling networks were the least of his concerns. 'We know what is going on with organised crime. We know who is here and what they do, so we can control it,' he said. 'But terrorism, we don't have the same intelligence. That is why we are more worried.'

Rhissa Feltou, Agadez's ex-rebel mayor, who has a reputation as a deal-cutter, echoed Koussa's sentiments. While he said that banditry still existed in the north, and that narco-trafficking and people smuggling were obviously prevalent, he told me that the north had by and large been stabilised since the chaos that ensued after the fall of Gaddafi.

'It's complicated. The presence of foreign troops and Nigérien troops in the north has changed the dynamic,' Feltou told me during a March 2014 interview in his office. Both Feltou and Koussa were hesitant to admit it openly, but they tentatively acknowledged that the influx of money associated with migrant smuggling was actually a good thing for Agadez, providing jobs and new opportunities—two things in short supply.

By the summer of 2015, however, when the migrant-smuggling industry had fully blossomed, Nigérien officials, including Koussa, were openly discussing the extent to which migrant smuggling was a boon for the local economy and an important contributing factor in keeping northern Niger stable.

'Many are eating off these migrants,' Koussa told the *New York Times*. 'The drivers, the fixers, the landlords.' Koussa even acknowledged that

179

government officials, via payoffs, were benefiting from the system. 'Police are eating, too.' he conceded.[28] In fact, a report by HALCIA, Niger's anti-corruption agency, found that bribes paid by migrants were essential to keeping state security forces functioning. 'The security forces recognise that they take money but they have no choice. That is money they use to do their jobs,' the deputy head of HALCIA told Reuters news agency. Without these bribes, HALCIA concluded, security forces would not be able to buy diesel or spare parts for vehicles, or even food.[29]

Abdourahamane Moussa, deputy secretary-general for the regional government in Agadez, went even further, telling the *Wall Street Journal* that migrant money was 'bringing our city life'. Moussa's comments made it clear that the priorities of European policymakers and those of officials in Agadez clearly diverge when it comes to the migrant issue. 'Migrants are buying things, consuming our goods, animating our economy', he said. 'People here are benefiting … how can we stop it?'[30]

It's an important question, and one that pertains to the Nigérien government as well as to the international community. With the realisation that the economics of migrant smuggling is one of the few things holding northern Niger together, European governments find themselves facing a tricky security paradox, in which their stated desire to stem the flow of migrants through the Sahel and into Libya may run counter to their interest in maintaining stability in northern Niger and the broader Sahel.

The international community, namely the EU, is pressuring Niger to crack down on the trade, and is slated to pour $680 million in aid into Niger between 2016 and 2020.[31] But unless that money addresses the needs of those who are actively partaking in migrant smuggling and the communities benefiting from it, it is unclear how basic development aid and assistance in anti-trafficking measures is likely to work, especially if demand for smuggler services remains at an all-time high. More recently, and clearly inspired by the billions of dollars Europe plans on paying Turkey to outsource dealing with migration, the Nigérien government has said that it would need €1 billion to have an impact in countering irregular migration.[32] Yet it is hard to see how even that sum could have a measurable impact when the majority of smuggling in the region is in fact merely legal transportation within the ECOWAS zone.[33]

Furthermore, it is worth asking to what extent such anti-smuggling measures might make the problem worse for all parties involved. In lieu of doing anything to curb demand, such efforts are likely to make migrants less safe by forcing smugglers to use more dangerous routes and drive up prices, in turn enriching the very actors that Europe is desperate to stop.

Furthermore, anti-smuggling programmes could have the wider effect of upsetting the delicate security equilibrium that Niger's government is desperate to maintain. How, for example, might members of Niger's coup-prone army stationed in the restive north react if one of their key revenue streams is cut off? What might the smugglers, many of whom are former combatants with a skill-set that makes them useful to all manner of armed groups operating in the Sahel and Sahara, do if they cannot make money smuggling migrants?

The desert may soon let us know.

8

TURKEY

THE CROSSROADS

Turkey knowingly stands at the epicentre of Europe's refugee crisis. It has been the largest source of Syrian refugees making their way to Europe, and the gateway for migrants from Central Asia and the Middle East who are following the trail blazed by Syrians. It is also the home of arguably the most active and far-reaching smuggling networks bringing people to Europe by air, sea and land. If Europe has any hope of controlling the flow of migrants into Europe, it will need the cooperation and commitment of the Turkish government.

Human smuggling through Turkey is not a new phenomenon. For decades, smuggling networks based in Turkey, Europe and Asia played a central role in the irregular movement of people from Asia and Africa to Europe. Many of the routes and networks operating today were established over the last three decades, and some of them were used not only to smuggle people into Europe, but various types of illicit substances and contraband, namely weapons and drugs.[1]

The war in neighbouring Syria brought nearly 3 million refugees to Turkey, and since 2012 the country has borne the spiralling cost of accommodating them, an endeavour that at the start of 2016 the government estimated was costing $500 million a month.[2] In addition, Turkey has become the convergence point for irregular migrants who

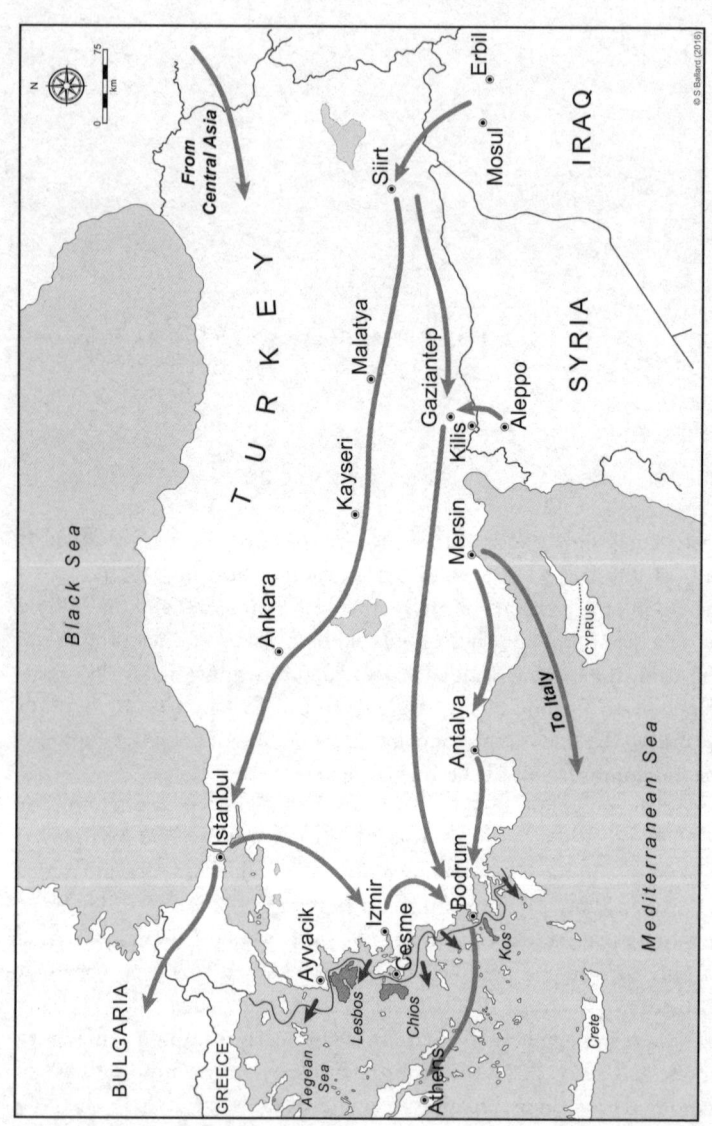

Map 6: Routes through Turkey

have come to Turkey from places such as Iraq, Afghanistan, Iran, Bangladesh and the continent of Africa. Thus, the pool of prospective clients for migrant-smuggling networks operating in Turkey has swelled to unprecedented levels. In 2015 the dam of Turkey's borders broke wide open, sending hundreds of thousands of people rushing towards Europe over the course of only a few months.

Whereas between 2008 and 2014 the number of people recorded along what Frontex refers to as the 'eastern Mediterranean route' hovered in the region of 50,000 a year, in 2015 Frontex recorded nearly 900,000 people crossing into Greece from Turkey. Some migrants during this period used Turkey's land borders with Greece and Bulgaria, but by far the majority came from Turkey into Europe by sea. The causes of this sudden and extraordinary spike in arrivals are widely debated, as is the credibility of solutions being proposed to stem this flow to manageable levels, but what is absolutely true is that in the age of migration, the fates of Turkey and Europe are inextricably linked, and both sides of the equation are seeking to leverage the fears and anxieties of one against the other.

Izmir

In the summer of 2015 it wasn't hard to find a smuggler in the coastal city of Izmir in Turkey. Recruiters linger at public parks, railway stations and bus terminals. They populate well-known cafés and bistros. They loiter outside certain hotels, shops and travel agencies. If you haven't made an arrangement with a smuggler before arriving in Izmir, you can find one within minutes of arriving in the neighbourhood of Basmane.

1367 Street is a narrow, cobblestone isthmus that links two of Basmane's main thoroughfares, Fevzi Paşa Boulevard and Gazi Boulevard. Recruiters do their work here in a mix of Turkish, Arabic, English, Kurdish and Dari. The street is packed with boutique hotels, cafés and eateries where the daily hustle is the business of migrant smuggling. The next street over feels like a carbon copy, as does the one after that.

On this early afternoon, one recruiter named Hassan holds court near the corner of 1367 Street and Fevsi Paşa Boulevard. He is wearing Merrell hiking boots, tactical cargo pants, a grey t-shirt that reads

'Cleveland Varsity' and a black baseball cap. Equipped with his native Arabic and intermediate English, Hassan fields a constant stream of calls with a Bluetooth earpiece. He has an external battery to charge his phone tucked into his trouser pocket, and over the course of two hours I count twenty-two people, sometimes in small groups, who approach him. Phone numbers and pieces of paper are exchanged, followed by handshakes and head nods. Just like that, it's over. Migrants have found a smuggler. The recruiter has done his job.

On the opposite side of the street a group of men who also look the part—mobile phones powered by external battery packs tucked into the front pouches of hoodies or trouser pockets—are in the midst of a heated conversation that, judging by the finger-pointing and gesticulating, seems to be escalating quickly. The disagreement, overheard by my waiter, centres on whether one of them was undercutting the others by quoting migrants a lower price than the going rate.

At the table next to mine four young men from Syria peer at a smartphone, trying to figure out where exactly Çeşme is. That's the city to which the 'collector' to whom they each paid $100 up front told them they would be taken in advance of their sea crossing to Greece. Based on the map, they conclude that their boat is destined for the Greek island of Chios. A debate ensues regarding whether Kos, the island they've read about online, and Chios, the one nearest to Çeşme, are the same island.

A baby-faced twenty-something man wearing a fake leather jacket, acid-washed jeans, and sporting slicked-back hair stands on the same block, glued to his iPhone and occasionally speaking into the microphone of his ear-bud headphones. A young man approaches, they have a brief conversation, and he diligently goes back to staring at his iPhone, his thumbs constantly toggling against the screen.

'He took my number, and he said he will call me,' says *Barat, an ethnic Hazara who has reached Izmir from Herat in Afghanistan and just had an exchange with him. Barat knows little about the person with whom he has just interacted aside from the fact that they share a common language and the common facial features that often distinguish Hazara from other ethnic groups in Afghanistan. Barat assumes he is Afghan, based on his appearance and the fact that he speaks Hazara. 'My friends gave me his number,' Barat explains, referring to someone he knows who has already reached Europe.

A short walk down the street from where Barat and I were chatting, in the lounge of the Omerim Hotel, under painfully tacky blue fluorescent lights, a Turkish staff member who speaks English pleads with a Syrian refugee who also speaks English to help him write a sign in Arabic that outlines the nightly rate. Most of the hotel signage, normally in Turkish and English, now has a corresponding piece of paper with a handwritten translation in Arabic. Translating the 'no smoking' sign into Arabic has proved an exercise in futility, as has just about any rule the hotel had hoped to impose. One person can stay there for 70 Turkish lira, roughly the equivalent of $22. It seems a badly kept secret that a half dozen people are staying in each room for the price of one. The hotel is overbooked and the lobby is full of families, many of which have no intention of staying there or paying to stay there. They are simply waiting until they get the call from their smuggler telling them it is time to move. 'It's difficult, but it's good business,' the young lady behind the desk tells me.

The same language barriers that are frustrating everyone in the hotel spill out into the street, where an elderly hawker in ragged clothes has arrived, trying to sell t-shirts and socks to the migrants passing their day on the roadside. He speaks in pidgin Arabic and, when it comes time to bargain, a third person is brought in to help translate. You can travel for years and wonder whether a hawker like this man ever actually makes a sale. But on this day he seems to have a client every few minutes.

A few blocks from what one local Turk derisively calls 'little Syria' are two hotels that, through word of mouth and social media, cater almost exclusively to Iraqis. One of the young men I meet in this neighbourhood is *Mahaman, who came to Izmir from Basra and is travelling with four close friends. All in their mid-twenties, they have left their families behind, including wives and young children.

'I want to go to Finland. There are jobs there,' Mahaman tells me, further elaborating that he had heard as much from an Iraqi he knows in Germany. Mahaman and his fellow travellers arrived in Izmir the day before, having flown directly from Basra. Within hours they had met and paid an Iraqi interlocutor, who told them where to meet him in Izmir. Having already purchased life jackets, they are enjoying a meal and smoking some shisha before it is time to move.

They find it unremarkable that within thirty-six hours of boarding a plane in Basra they will be floating in the Aegean Sea and on their way to Greece. They are also unfazed by the fact that they don't know how they will get to Finland. They know their next two steps after Greece, are Macedonia and Serbia, and are comfortable improvising from there. 'We learn along the way,' Mahaman says. 'So far, it has been easy. You just need money. If you have money, people will help you.'

On Fevzi Paşa Boulevard, leading down to the coast, a clothing shop has taped a sign to its front window. It reads, in incorrect English:

Discount
The original vest sell
Reliable
Budget
Made in Norway
Made in Turkey
Life Vest
IMPRTANT FOR OUR LIFE

The shop purports to sell clothing by global brands such as Lee and Wrangler, as well as popular local labels such as Ruba, Rabin and Sabri Özel, but, upon entering, it is clear that despite the fact that the mannequins in the window are wearing blazers and jeans, the usual stock has been moved to the basement.

Seconds after I enter the shop, *Ghaith has crept up behind me and begins draping an orange life vest over my shoulders. Like any good salesman, he has you wearing your jacket and looking at yourself in the mirror before you can even get around to discussing the price.

Ghaith is from Aleppo in Syria, and came to Istanbul in 2013 with the intentions of paying a smuggler to take him overland to Europe, via Bulgaria. After being ripped off by a Turk in Istanbul who claimed to work for a smuggler, he used what little money he had left to come to Izmir, where he was told he could put his Arabic and English skills to use working with smugglers. Instead, he ended up working for the Turkish man who owns the clothing shop that now sells only life jackets. With business at an all-time high, Ghaith says he does not have an incentive to risk his life crossing the sea to Greece. He is making enough money here to rent a small apartment, which he shares with a few Syrian friends, and he even sends money back to his parents, who are now living in Lebanon.

Ghaith tightens the straps around my waist, and explains why this particular jacket, bright orange and with an attached emergency whistle, is the best quality and the 'right one' for me. Even after I tell him I'm not a migrant, he is happy to walk me through the different kinds of vests on offer and lists the pros and cons of each one. For approximately $25 I can purchase the one I am wearing or a similar one, made by the same company in Turkey, that has reflectors but no whistle. For a few dollars less I can get a black one made by Yamaha, which does not have reflectors or a whistle.

But the real distinction, Ghaith tells me, is the difference in performance once you are in the water. The orange vest is thicker, and is good for ten hours. The slightly cheaper Yamaha only floats for 'six to seven hours, maybe', Ghaith explains as he wobbles a flattened, outstretched hand to give the universal sign for 'more or less'. He seems to take pride in the quality of the product he sells. When I ask them if they are real or fake, he insists they are real. Other merchants were found selling life vests filled with sponge that would absorb water and be more likely to cause a migrant to sink than float.[3] He then puts a hand to the side of his mouth and whispers to me that the ones being sold next door—in the kiosk that is not nearly as tidy as the boutique where he works—are fake. 'These are my people,' Ghaith says, referring to the Syrians who make up the bulk of his clients. 'I would not be able to sleep at night if I were selling them bad vests.'

Ghaith then walks me over to life jackets for children, and shows me the small, doughnut-shaped tubes that people buy for babies. If it were not for the fact that the customers for these little contraptions are the parents of children fleeing war and grinding poverty, you could be forgiven for thinking the small flotation kit adorable. But in reality, the market forces at work are shaped by the grim truth that tens of thousands of parents have decided that in order for their children to have any chance at a real future, they'll have to risk drowning in the sea.

In fact, there is something surreal about the extent to which our conversation is so matter of fact. Ghaith wears a pink polo shirt and has his hair gelled into a fauxhawk. The shop we are walking through blares techno music and smells like an adolescent who has just discovered cologne. A flat-screen TV is set to a channel showing music videos that do not correspond to the thumping beats being piped in over the loudspeakers. If you closed your eyes, you could trick yourself into thinking you are at a retail outlet anywhere in the world. But then you open your eyes, and see desperate Afghan teens trying to haggle over the price of life vests despite the fact that the shop owner has told them, a dozen times or more, that the prices are fixed and that he will not give them a discount. You see a Syrian mother holding her baby boy up in the air, as a father holds a small inner tube next to the infant, determined to find one small enough to keep him afloat without him falling through.

As the sun sets the city calms down, at least for a few hours, and down by a stretch of seaside walkways and parks it is not difficult to differentiate the migrants from the residents. Amid the young lovers, troublesome teens and elderly couples strolling the banks of the sea, there are young men with overstuffed backpacks and their family members lugging cumbersome blocks of flotation devices in black plastic bags. Looking out to sea, they settle in for what they hope are their last few hours in Izmir. These are the proud, terrified owners of tickets for places on a rubber dinghy and cheap life jackets, which taken together, might be enough to get them to Greek shores alive.

Back near the main roundabout in Basmane, the early evening lull gradually changes into something more urgent. Outside one hotel, taxi drivers jam people, their bags and their life jackets into their vehicles. In other places, it is a private car or an unmarked van. In every case, there are more passengers than seats.

At the main roundabout about two hundred migrants—men, women, children and infants—wait with their bags alongside a dozen taxis and half a dozen buses. A father's phone rings and his family knows what to do. They pile into a taxi and take off for the rendezvous point that their smugglers have chosen for them. Two facilitators, both Syrian and evidently employed by the travel companies whose offices face the roundabout, regulate who gets on which bus, organising their human cargo along familial lines and finding solo travellers to fill leftover seats. With rare exceptions, these people have no idea where they are actually going. The cars, vans and buses take them to various undisclosed locations on the coast, and many of them will be drifting towards Greece in the dark, choppy seas of the Aegean within hours.

Two young African women wearing converse trainers, jeans and tank tops, each carrying an inconspicuous camping backpack, wait in the same area. Even after a few minutes of observing them, it is hard to tell if they are migrants or tourists. A tall, skinny black man wearing a Manchester United jersey and his stout accomplice, in jeans and a t-shirt, approach them. He asks a question, they nod their heads, and he pivots and gives the universal sign for 'follow me' with his right hand.

The four of them meander through alleyways and side streets, past cafés and life-jacket vendors, past a fast-moving flock of Syrians and a group of snoozing Afghans. They continue past a brothel that calls itself a bar, and continue past barbers' shops and fruit stalls. Finally, they arrive at Paşa Konaği Hotel located just off Hatuniye Park. After ascending the stairwell that leads to the lobby, it becomes obvious that the place has become a staging ground for sub-Saharan Africans seeking to enter Europe via Turkey. Conversations are being held in a patchwork of languages: French from Cameroon; English from Nigeria; local languages from everywhere between Senegal and Eritrea.

The small park across the street is nestled between a mosque and a hill, surrounded by cafés and small shops. Some migrants are preparing for the call to prayer; others, for the call from their smuggler. The anxiety-inducing sounds of packaging tape rips through the hum and chatter of migrants and cuts through the American hip-hop coming from a nearby café. Men and women are diligently wrapping their valuables in plastic bags and balloons, then meticulously sealing them with rolls of packaging tape to waterproof their life's possessions. Hawkers, peddling everything from underwear to knock-off life jackets, begin packing up their wares for the night. It is an odd symmetry, watching those about to make the journey and those who are not, kneeling next to each other as they pack their livelihoods into overstuffed bags.

Twenty minutes later, the two African women from the roundabout emerge from the hotel, having changed into looser clothing and now carrying life vests in addition to their backpacks. They scurry across the street, ignoring African men whistling and hissing at them, and enter a stream of migrants that is slowly making its way through the guts of the city, back towards the roundabout. At 3 a.m. they board a van filled with other African migrants. The tall, skinny man in the Manchester United jersey slides the door shut and taps it twice to signal to the driver that the cargo is loaded. The nondescript van reverses and enters the flow of traffic.

MIGRANT, REFUGEE, SMUGGLER, SAVIOUR

This is downtown Izmir in the summer of 2015. A place where those who work for smuggling networks discuss their business within earshot of a bustling café on a major boulevard, even as police officers patrol the streets. Where in certain parts of town it is assumed that you are a migrant until you present overwhelming evidence to the contrary. Where everyone from the politically connected industrialist to the desperately poor street vendor is making a buck, and where legitimate enterprises have recalibrated their business models to cater to the needs of migrants. Here, in Izmir, the inner workings of an entire city have been retrofitted to meet the demands of a new multi-billion-dollar industry premised on smuggling people from Turkey to Greece.

* * *

Though Izmir is the hub of the migrant-smuggling industry on the Turkish coast, two other Turkish towns, Çeşme and Bodrum, which are close to a group of Greek islands in the Aegean, have also become key assembling points for migrants destined for Greece. Given the comparative ease of the sea crossing, Turkey's migrant-smuggling industry first developed as a relatively uncontrolled market with low barriers to entry for enterprising entrepreneurs. Yet a sharp spike in demand in 2015 and the corresponding profits to be made spurred the development of established networks. It also fostered the emergence of best practices and drove market consolidation via organised criminal groups who were well positioned to take over the market. By mid-2015 the migrant industry had matured to a point where one could sketch out a nascent typology of operators in the Turkish market, and interviews with migrants and smugglers on the ground indicate that there are a number of high-level operators making profits in the tens of millions of dollars.

For those making the journey to Europe, the first person they will interact with at the street level are 'recruiters' and 'collectors'. These are the front men of the operation, who tend to be based in key migrant centres on the coast, such as Izmir, Bodrum, and Çeşme, but also other major cities like Istanbul. They are often migrants themselves, and speak the languages of their prospective clients. They identify migrants or are approached by them through word of mouth or social media. Migrants communicate directly with these individuals, and often pay the full fee to them through an 'insurance agency'.

Collectors liaise with Turkish smugglers, and pay them the money they receive from the migrants. They tend to work on commission and, based on interviews with several collectors in Izmir and Bodrum, they make between $50 and $100 per migrant. Usually, this amount also constitutes the non-refundable fee that migrants must pay in order to secure a money-back guarantee from a smuggling network. Some collectors, such as Hassan described earlier, may receive a monthly salary, but the vast majority are operating on a model based on commission.

Insurance offices and third-party guarantors are another key piece of the migrant-smuggling industry in Turkey, overseeing what amounts to 'refugee escrow' schemes that provide a modicum of consumer protection for migrants. In order for migrants to have any assurances that they are not being taken advantage of by the recruiter or collector with whom they are dealing, money is often paid through a third party, who holds the money until a migrant successfully makes the journey to Greece. The third party will give the migrant a code, which he or she can use at any point to reclaim the full amount. If the migrant is not heard from after an agreed number of days (usually due to successful transit or as a result of drowning), the money is released to the smuggler, minus an agreed cut taken by the third party.

Operating above recruiters, collectors and third-party guarantors are the smugglers themselves. Due to the nature of the business and the diversity of actors involved, it is hard to construct neat categories for smugglers in Turkey. Different networks have different structures but, broadly speaking, actors accurately referred to as smugglers in Turkey operate on three different levels.

At the very top are high-level smugglers, individuals unlikely to be implicated in the smuggling operation, as they maintain their distance from day-to-day activity. They tend to have strong, financially beneficial links to law enforcement, security officials and members of government to ensure that their operations are allowed to continue unabated. These smugglers almost always operate in cooperation with long-established criminal organisations and are almost always engaged in other business activities, which enables them to launder their profits through legitimate enterprises. Though the vast majority of smugglers at this level oversee the networks that are facilitating the flow of migrants to Greece via the use of thousands of small boats headed for the Greek islands, there are others whose business model is predicated on the use of large container ships.

The *Financial Times*, for example, interviewed a man they dubbed 'the Doctor' (not to be confused with the smuggler in Egypt who purportedly goes by the same name). Reportedly wanted by Europol, according to two Western diplomats interviewed for the story, 'the Doctor' not only runs boatloads of refugees across the Aegean, he also allegedly has plans to start moving migrants 400 at a time from Mersin, on Turkey's Mediterranean coast, on a four- or five-day voyage to a point off Italy, from where fishermen will take the refugees the final few kilometres. According to the *Financial Times*, 'the Doctor', a surgeon from Syria who failed to cross the Aegean as a refugee and has since become a smuggler, has already made a $1.5 million cash payment for the container ship.[4]

In 2015 two journalists writing for the *New Republic* interviewed an alleged smuggling kingpin from Syria, referred to as 'al-Khal', who made similar claims of having used a boat leaving from Mersin to go directly to Italy. Charging $10,000 per person, al-Khal said he and his cousin made nine trips from Mersin to Italy, transporting 150 people each time. Al-Khal says he left Mersin after his cousin left for Germany and the government started to clamp down on human smuggling.[5]

*Murad, a seventeen-year-old ethnic Yazidi from Sinjar in northern Iraq, reached Europe via a large ship like the one that al-Khal described to the *New Republic*. According to Murad, after his father paid an Iraqi middleman $5,500 via a *hawala* transfer in Iraqi Kurdistan, a smuggler in Mersin took him to a hotel. Five days later the smuggler moved Murad to an apartment where some other Yazidi and Kurdish migrants were waiting. After midnight they were all moved to a remote village, where they stayed at a farm under the supervision of armed guards for two weeks. Murad says his guards told them their trip had been delayed because the Turkish authorities had started a security operation on the coast. 'During these two weeks, more and more people from different nationalities kept arriving, there were more than forty Yazidi families,' Murad recalls. 'Then the trucks took us to the coast and we slept in the mountains for two days. During that time, the Iraqi middleman was coming and taking between twenty and thirty persons each time.'

When it was Murad's turn, he walked for three hours with thirty other people under the supervision of three armed Turkish smugglers.

When they arrived at a rocky beach, they were quickly loaded onto a speedboat piloted by a Turk. The boat travelled for thirty minutes, without lights and in complete darkness, until they reached a large ship in the middle of the sea.

After boarding the ship via a ladder, Murad was immediately pushed inside the hold, where he found himself with at least 250 other people. 'Everybody was in very bad conditions, vomiting. There were many small children and old women. I recognised many Yazidi families, so I kept with them. After four hours they brought the last thirty persons and the ship started to move,' he recounts.

Below high-level smugglers such as 'the Doctor' and al-Khal are the mid-level smugglers who oversee operations on the ground. A key responsibility at this level is organising the bulk of migrant transport, from the bus and van pick-ups of migrants to drop-off points on the coast. They also organise the purchase of boats and motors, as well as their delivery to the remote beaches. These mid-level smugglers liaise with those operating below them and with the high-level smugglers several steps removed from the process on the ground. They usually earn a monthly salary.

The low-level smugglers operating in Turkey, beneath the mid-level smugglers, work primarily at the local beaches. They receive and pre-pare the boats, equip them with motors, and manage migrants at the beachfront, often with the help of translators. They pay out locals who might provide services such as towing a boat with a tractor, or spotters and informants whom they pay to keep tabs on the Turkish coastguard or security personnel on land. If launches from the coast are delayed, these low-level smugglers are tasked with providing food and lodging for the migrants, and managing the local relationships necessary to carry out their activities.

Low-level smugglers in Turkey reportedly earn a fixed rate per head, so it is in their interest to get as many people on board each dinghy as possible, which often leads to heated disputes with migrants who were promised a different type of boat by the collector, or a boat with fewer people. At other times, migrants, many of whom have never seen the sea before, get cold feet and need to be forced onto the boat. Recent interviews carried out with migrants in Greece confirm that low-level smugglers at the Turkish coast are almost always armed, and often coerce migrants into compliance with the threat of violence.

Once a migrant has made the necessary arrangements with a smuggler in Izmir, he or she is usually transported to an undisclosed location with other migrants, often under the supervision of armed guards. As such, migrants rarely have any say in, let alone any knowledge of, where exactly they are going once they have left Izmir. Many of the migrants arriving in Greece, therefore, have no idea exactly where they are once they have arrived.

Networks that specialise in dealing with Syrians, which are largely staffed and operated by Syrians, are the most lucrative. As explained in Part 1, Syrians not only comprise the largest nationality seeking to cross, they are also the ones with the most money. As a result, smugglers want to smuggle Syrians not only because of their numbers, but because they are the most capable of making payments. Yet the Syrians' relative purchasing power and ability to pool resources also makes them the most 'demanding' segment of the migrant-smuggling consumer base. Because Syrians are the most lucrative and therefore the most 'competitive' commodity in the eyes of smugglers, networks need to cater to their needs and demands, which in part explains why schemes such as 'refugee escrow' have developed and matured beyond levels previously seen within migrant-smuggling networks. Providing what are perceived to be honest and transparent services is important, because reputation is everything, and if a smuggler's name is besmirched, there are plenty of other networks eager to cater to Syrian clientele.

In Izmir, the vast majority of collectors and recruiters prowling the streets of Basmane are Arab Syrians who seek out Arab clients from Syria. Yet the collectors and recruiters from other backgrounds, who specialise in finding clients of their own ethnic or linguistic kin, tend to work for the same networks as their Syrian counterparts. These Afghan, Pakistani, Iraqi and Kurd collectors feed clients into pipelines that were built upon Syrian demand. As a result, many of the people working at the lower levels also have no idea who they actually work for, or that they might be working for the same high-level smugglers.

Interviews with both low-level smugglers and migrants indicate a smuggling economy in which Turkish nationals are at the very top as well as at the ground level. Syrian nationals who have emerged as mid- and high-level smugglers cannot function without Turkish collaborators. Their operations require partnerships with Turkish nationals who have access to the highest levels of the Turkish security apparatus, but also individuals who can facilitate the day-to-day operations on the ground. Thus, even the Syrian 'kingpins' who have been interviewed by several Western media outlets are almost certainly operating under the protection of powerful Turkish actors, and are reliant on their ability to function within criminal structures at the local, regional, and even national level.

Binding all of these people with a range of backgrounds and skill-sets together are the windfall profits to be made from smuggling people from Turkey to Greece. Because the industry operates in the shadows, exact figures cannot be obtained, but estimates based on interviews with migrants and smugglers, combined with numbers collected by international organisations such as IOM, suggest an average of at least $2 million in revenue per day in 2015.

Migrants interviewed over the course of several months at the end of 2015 say they paid as little as $800 or as much as $1,300 for a place on a rubber dinghy that was typically loaded with between forty and fifty people, depending on its size. Some said their dinghy had as many as sixty people on it. Either way, a dinghy loaded with only forty people each paying $800 will generate $32,000 in revenue, while a dinghy maxed out at sixty people paying $1,300 each will gross $78,000. The majority of migrants paid between $1,000 and $1,200, meaning that every dinghy of forty-five people generated revenues of $45,000 to $54,000. This in turn means that during the peak periods in the summer of 2015 that saw 5,000 migrant arrivals in Greece from Turkey per day, smuggling networks were generating $5 million in revenue every day.

Calculating the revenues generated by smuggling networks by multiplying the number arriving in Greece against the fees migrants paid to smugglers in Turkey, however, does not even begin to capture the breadth of the migrant-smuggling economy and its trickle-down impact. As previously noted, everyone from the high-level smuggler to the street hawker is profiting from the migrant-smuggling industry.

The business of people smuggling requires a range of fixed and recurring overhead expenses. To start, smugglers need to buy a new boat for every trip they arrange to Greece. Most people interviewed on the Turkish coast put the cost of a rubber dinghy, depending on the size and the quality, in the range of $6,000 to $8,000, with motors ranging in price between $1,000 and $4,000, again depending on the quality. Analysis by the EU border monitoring agency, Frontex, said that the serial numbers found on the boats left punctured on the beach showed serial numbers registered in series, indicating that these were ordered in bulk and purchased for the purpose of migrant smuggling.[6]

Smugglers must also pay the landowners who rent their private beach-front property from where the dinghies launch. In some cases, smuggling networks pay a flat monthly fee to landowners for access to their beaches, but the most common arrangement, according to smuggling sources on the Turkish coast, is one in which property owners calculate their fees on a per-launch basis, or even on a per-migrant basis. Though estimates vary, the figures most commonly cited in interviews and local reporting are in the range of $5,000 to $8,000 per launch, depending on the size of the boat and how exactly the fee is calculated.

As one Syrian smuggler named Mohamad told Patrick Kingsley of *The Guardian*, smuggling networks will rent beaches from several different landlords in order to ensure that they have various choices of launching points, depending on the activities of the Turkish authorities. 'We keep an eye on the points, and once we see one is clear, we use it,' he told Kingsley. 'Nothing is haphazard and everything is planned.'[7]

Beyond purchasing the boats and renting land from which to launch them, those at the top of smuggling networks have to pay the middle-men described above, as well as the costs associated with procuring and maintaining vehicles to transport migrants to the coast, the wages of handlers who escort and monitor the migrants, and whatever local officials they need to bribe. For smuggling networks that prefer to have the requisite numbers for an entire boat already gathered before leaving Izmir for another coastal location, some networks rent entire blocs of rooms in hotels.

The costs of doing business fluctuates depending on a range of market forces, and though the basics of the business model are the same across various smuggling networks in Turkey, certain networks might have access to better deals at various points in the supply chain. It is also important to note that the majority of expenses that smuggling networks incur are paid out locally, injecting millions of dollars into local economies in the process. In certain communities, entrepreneurs are investing migrant-smuggling proceeds into infrastructure such as restaurants, apartments and hotels. In places like Bodrum, for example, these investments are not only an effective means of money laundering, they constitute low-risk investments that can cater to both the tourist economy and the migrant-smuggling economy, depending on which is more lucrative at the time.

The Mob: Criminal Market Consolidation

In bustling hubs such as Istanbul, Izmir, Bodrum and Çeşme the gears of the migrant-smuggling machine are hidden in plain sight. From the vantage point of smuggling boom towns, where even street hawkers are getting a piece of the action, one could be forgiven for mischaracterising the migrant-smuggling industry as a libertarian free-for-all, where anyone who is a willing buyer can find a willing seller. But in actuality, the freelancers and entrepreneurs who have come to embody the hustle at the micro level are operating within a strict set of parameters set by organised crime syndicates at the macro level. As one moves further away from the urban centres along Turkey's coast, the blurriness of organised chaos comes into focus as organised crime.

The laws of smuggling nature dictate that if the profits around a given activity are large enough, either already-established crime syndicates will move in or new organised criminal networks will develop around it. If outside pressures are placed on smuggling networks while demand remains, then it is all but certain that organised crime will flourish. In the case of Turkey, Turkish crime syndicates, already well established, were perfectly positioned to exploit the profit-making opportunities presented by the flow of migrants.

Organised crime in Turkey is a structured, social phenomenon that in many ways resembles the Italian mafia, both in genesis and evolution. Local strongmen and fragmented vigilante groups have existed since the transition from the Ottoman Empire to the Turkish Republic.[8] Organised crime remains broadly divided into two factions which follow the ethnic divide of Turkey itself—Kurds and ethnic Turks—with the Kurds geographically controlling the areas to the east and south, on the borders with Syria, Iraq and Iran, and the Turkish 'Black Sea Mafia' controlling the north.[9] Locally, these groups are engaged in protectionism and extortion. But for transnational trafficking, geography necessitated that they collaborate and overcome any ethnic divisions, as Kurds essentially controlled the routes into the country from the east and the Turks oversaw routes into Europe.

Organised crime in Turkey has its foundation as the primary supplier of heroin from Afghanistan into Europe. From there, Turkish crime syndicates diversified into a range of associated activities, from extortion and money laundering, to the trafficking of other drugs, including methamphetamines, cannabis and cocaine. According to Mark Galleoti, diversification and professionalisation prompted the erosion of the traditions and familial structures that had characterised Turkish crime, transforming it into a 'business-minded criminal elite willing and able to forge alliances across ethnic and national divides'.[10] Data from the Turkish drug-enforcement agency suggests that the organised criminal groups in Turkey have alliances that developed around heroin trafficking as the primary foundation with counterparts in sixty-four countries, including in South America, Western Europe, Africa, the Caucases, Central Asia, the Middle East and the Balkans. These connections are further expanded to distribution networks within the Turkish diaspora and local criminal networks in all of Europe's major capitals.[11]

This same infrastructure and arrangement was perfectly placed to facilitate the trafficking in human beings. As with the trans-Saharan route through Agadez, in which the ancient and state-sanctioned trade routes coincide with the newer drug-trafficking routes, in the case of Turkey, trafficking routes track with the ancient Silk Road, across Central Asia to Istanbul and beyond.[12] Trafficking in Turkey emerged as a low-risk enterprise that exploited the poverty, inequality and instability of the post-Soviet period. Profiting from a strong collaborative relationship with Albanian criminal networks already in place, the Turks established an active trade, exploiting the poverty of the Balkan states to traffic women into the sex industry and men into unpaid labour arrangements in Western Europe, a phenomenon that raised few eyebrows anywhere along the chain, even as it escalated in volume and profit over time.[13] In the eyes of security officials, human trafficking and migrant smuggling was, and remained, a low-priority crime compared to that of the drug trade.

* * *

It was not until images of the lifeless body of three-year-old Alan Kurdi, washed up on a beach near Bodrum, were shown worldwide that international outrage and ensuing pressure to 'do something' prompted Turkish authorities to arrest several purported human smugglers.[14] Yet the symbolic crackdown did little but drive some smugglers and migrants back to Izmir, where their activities continued in plain view of local authorities. Other insincere attempts to stem the flow of migrants, such as encouraging bus companies not to sell tickets to migrants and prohibiting taxi drivers from delivering them to drop-off points, proved inconsequential. Black markets for these services emerged quickly, and an inability to actually enforce such policies meant that many operators were willing to risk the fines and sanctions that would come with being caught against the rewarding profits to be made.

In August 2015, just after one 'crackdown' on the Turkish coast, interviewees who had only just arrived in Greece were already using terms like 'mafia' and 'mob' to describe the people they dealt with. One Syrian, *Wael, said that everyone he dealt with was Turkish and carrying a weapon. 'From Istanbul until the boat, they had guns,' he told me, visibly upset. 'It's a mob, man. It's a mob,' he explained, referring to what he considered a mafia. Wael was referred to his smuggler via a friend who had made the journey to Europe months before. Upon his arrival in Bodrum the smuggler told him that 'new people were in charge of the area' and, for a fee of $50, he offered to introduce him to the right people. Bodrum, it appeared, had acquired new criminal overlords by the time Wael made his journey.

The *Financial Times* interviewed a Syrian national who had been shipping 'at least a single boatload of people across to Greece each night', until 'a man with a small handgun visited him and asked that he pay the mafia $40,000 a month to keep operating'. According to the *Financial Times*, the smuggler paid the fee to the mafia, but the price was raised five months later by an additional $1,000 per person on each boat. At that point, the entrepreneurial smuggler quit. The same smuggler told the *Financial Times* that 'at least 20 other small-time operators had been squeezed out of the business as well'.

A range of sources confirmed that the Turkish mafia is not only charging for protection, but is also emerging as a boat supplier as well. The *Financial Times*, for example, interviewed a boat importer in

Istanbul whose import licence allowed him to import Chinese-made boats and sell them for as much as $10,000 each, until 'two well-dressed Turkish men in a black luxury car' threatened him with a hand-gun and told him to stop his business. 'He and others say those groups that pay the mafia can buy boats from a small factory outside Ankara for about $400 while those who do not are paying as much as $6,000 for smaller vessels,' the *Financial Times* reported.[15]

One person I interviewed in Lesbos in September 2015 told me that he had worked as a recruiter for a smuggler until what he described as the 'Turkish mafia' pushed his superior out of the business. At that point the recruiter, who initially came to Turkey from Iraq with plans to migrate to Europe until he found employment working for smug-glers, decided it was time to make the journey himself.

*Yasser came to appreciate the full extent to which migrant smug-gling was a well-organised criminal enterprise when he found himself standing on a Turkish beach, seemingly in the middle of nowhere, peer-ing out into the sea. As he tried to discern the Greek island just over the horizon, he marvelled at the fact that only hours before he had been in Aksaray, a neighbourhood in Istanbul that has become a Syrian ghetto of sorts. His original plan was to enter Greece via its overland crossing with Turkey, near the Greek town of Evros. Yet he changed plans after reading on social media that masked men who were believed to be Greek police were arresting people at the border, beating them, and forcing them back to the other side of the fenced-off border.

Yasser decided to contact a smuggler on Facebook, who provided him with three different phone numbers. A Syrian smuggler came to his hotel and they agreed to a price of $1,300, to be paid via a *hawala* deposit. A few days later the smuggler came to the hotel and told him to be ready to leave in three hours. The smuggler put him in a normal taxi to move him to another location in Istanbul, where an Afghan smuggler guided him to a back street. There, a large lorry was waiting for them and, over the next thirty minutes the Afghan smuggler met and loaded sixty people from a range of nationalities into the back of the truck. An armed Turkish smuggler was put inside with them, who instructed them to turn off their mobile phones and threatened to beat anyone who was caught using one. According to Yasser, the truck drove overnight for nine hours. Finally, it stopped and someone opened the container. Having spent hours in darkness, it took time for Yasser's eyes to adjust to the morning sunlight. Once they did, he realised they were on the Turkish coast, where an armed smuggler was waiting for the group of sixty with a rubber dinghy.

For *Sahin, a fifty-two-year-old Kurdish man from Syria, the complicated logistics that moved him from Izmir to the Turkish coast clarified the extent to which his fate was in the hands of a sophisticated network of well-connected criminals. After paying a smuggler $1,200 for each of his four family members, they were provided lodging in an apartment. The next day the smuggler told them to go to the bus station, where someone was waiting for them with bus tickets to the town of Ayvalık. When they arrived in Ayvalık, a person waiting for them moved them to a farm on the outskirts of town, where five armed guards, two Syrians and therr Turks, were overseeing 120 migrants.

After several days waiting at the farm, the 120 people were put into two covered trucks and taken to a village on the coast. From there, two armed guards led the entire group through hills for forty minutes and told them to hide in bushes next to the sea. As soon as a boat belonging to the Turkish coastguard had passed they were brought down to the beachfront and crammed onto two dinghies.

Dozens of people interviewed on the Greek islands of Kos and Lesbos, as well as in Athens, described a similar process. After departing from major smuggling cities and towns on transport provided by smugglers, they were moved to remote locations where they were monitored by armed guards—usually Turkish nationals, but often Syrians and Iraqis, particularly Kurds. After days, sometimes weeks, of assembling a large number of migrants, smugglers then put them in trucks and moved them closer to the beachfront from where they would launch. Armed escorts often led them by foot through hills and mountains until they reached a predetermined launching point.

Most of the time boats would be waiting for the migrants, and they would leave as soon as they arrived. Yet unforeseen circumstances, from weather, to unexpected police or coastguard patrols, to logistical hiccups meant that migrants could find themselves camping outside for a few days until arrangements could be made.

One migrant, an information technology specialist from Damascus who found his smuggler in Izmir, told me that he spent a night sleeping in the bushes with ten boatloads of migrants as his smugglers watched the Turkish coastguard pass several times. Then, when there was a lull in the action, all ten boats were loaded. Several minutes after the lights of the last Turkish coastguard ship were no longer visible, one of the smugglers fired a gun into the air, and all ten boats launched. 'It's a mafia. They all work together. Very organised,' he said, bringing his two index fingers together to imply that smugglers and elements within the Turkish security forces are working in tandem.

When it comes time to board the boat, according to interviews with dozens of migrants who crossed from Turkey to Greece, final arrangements are made and instructions are given. In some cases, one of the migrants has been pre-selected to pilot the boat. In others, one of the migrants is given a crash course in how to operate the motor. The pilot is also given a long knife and instructed to destroy the vessel upon arrival.

Smugglers tell those tasked with piloting the boat that if the Turkish coastguard approaches them, they should not, under any circumstances, comply with their orders. If the boat stops and the passengers are forced to board the coastguard boat, they can be brought back to Turkey. Conversely, migrants are told that if they are approached by the Greek coastguard, then they are in Greek territory, and they should immediately drop the engine into the sea, giving the Greek authorities no choice but to rescue them and bring them safely to Greece.

Rasha, who fled Syria after her husband joined ISIS, saw this exact scenario play out, with terrifying consequences. 'After ten minutes of leaving the [Turkish] shore, we saw another three boats that were leaving at that moment. The Turkish coastguard was surrounding them, going in circles around them to force them to stop. They almost killed them. Two of them stopped and surrendered to the coastguards, but the last one rejected to stop and continued,' Rasha explains. 'After ten minutes another small boat from the Turkish coastguard was attacking that boat, causing a lot of waves, going in circles around it. We saw how some people fell into the water. We heard the noise of shooting.'

According to Rasha, a coastguard ship started rushing in the direction of her boat as well, but gave up pursuit. Rasha thinks they must have already reached Greek waters, because just after the Turkish boat stopped chasing them, the Greek coastguard appeared. The young men in the back of the boat immediately dropped the engine into the sea, as they had been instructed to do.

'The coastguards threw a rope to us, shouting that they would rescue us. They pulled us next to their boat. Everybody stood up, trying to reach the boat. The coastguards became nervous and started to shout for everybody to sit down. Then they took my daughters first and the other three small children.'

The vast majority of boats, however, reach the coast undetected by the Greek authorities. And before the autumn of 2015, when hundreds of volunteers flocked to the Greek islands to assist migrant arrivals, most migrants arrived to empty beaches. As a safety measure against being 'pushed back' to Turkey by Greek authorities, a practice that is illegal under international law yet believed to have been taking place sporadically throughout the crisis, smugglers gave someone on each boat a large knife with which to slash the boat upon arrival, thus making 'push back' impossible. The boat engines, worth anywhere from $4,000 to $10,000 depending on the model, were almost always quickly snapped up by Greeks, some of whom made small businesses out of spotting boats at sea and helping them reach the mainland in order to have the first chance at grabbing the engine.

Those who crossed the sea via dinghies tell heartbreaking stories of failed engines, sinking boats, people falling overboard, and smugglers threatening to shoot them if they turn around. One Syrian told me that several women on his boat, after being intercepted by the Turkish coastguard, threatened to jump into the sea with their babies unless the Turkish coastguard allowed them to continue to Greece. After an hour of deliberation amongst the Turkish crewmembers, they decided not to call the Syrians' bluff and let them continue.

Another Syrian, a young Christian man named *Michel, said that the pilot of his boat, who volunteered because he had been a fisherman back home in Latakia, confided to his fellow passengers an hour into their journey that he didn't think they could make it. The winds had picked up and the sea had become too choppy. They were at risk of capsizing. Those on board decided that they would rather die at sea than 'return to the streets of Aksaray', so they rearranged themselves to increase their chances of survival. Those who could swim were put around the edge, with small children and the elderly packed into the middle. After three hours of trying to keep the dinghy on course, the engine died and everyone on board began 'preparing himself for death' as water began to fill the boat. Miraculously, the Greek coastguard found them, but just as the last three men, including the pilot, were due to board the coastguard's ship, a large wave swept them away.

'He was a very good pilot. For three hours he saved us, he told us that we had lost our way, without lying to us,' Michel says, recalling the experience that has left him emotionally scarred. 'To be stuck in a war for almost two years left me without any feelings, I was not afraid,' he continued. 'When I saw the children in the sea in the middle of that horrible storm, I felt all the fear I was denying to myself during the war. After that storm, I crashed down psychologically.'

For those who seek a less harrowing trip and can afford to pay premium prices, an alternative to joining the armada of dinghies crossing the Aegean is to find a smuggler who has access to a yacht or speedboat. Whereas using dinghies is appealing to smugglers because they are disposable and do not require a hired pilot on board, smugglers who use yachts or speedboats have to be willing to risk losing the boat and the pilot being arrested.

*Souzan, a twenty-seven-year-old Christian from Syria, was willing to make the journey on a rubber dinghy, but her fiancé, who had access to money, insisted on sending her with a smuggling ring that used safer boats. Souzan's uncle, who had been working in Turkey as a recruiter for a smuggling network, knew someone who provided such services and escorted her personally from Izmir to Bodrum to introduce her to the smuggler. After Souzan paid $3,500 via a third party, the smuggler took her to a flat by the sea where other refugees, all Syrian, were waiting. The day of the trip, the smuggler asked everyone to be well dressed. A Turkish man came to the flat and began ushering them to the seaside in groups of three to the seaport, where they were issued tickets before boarding a yacht.

'During the first hour, the captain was driving parallel to the coast, very slowly. At one point he changed direction and started driving faster. Then two men came out of the cabin, holding weapons. They told us to go inside the cabin and that, whatever happened, we should not make any noise,' Souzan explains. 'We didn't know what was going on, but the yacht stopped for almost one hour. The waves were rocking it, so we all were dizzy and vomiting. When the yacht started to move again, one of the armed men told us to clean ourselves and come out of the cabin.' The captain told Souzan and another man to pretend they were a couple. When they landed at the seaport, cars were waiting for them, which dropped them off in downtown Kos.

Thirty-two-year-old *Khalil, a Yazidi from Mosul in Iraq, was living in the shadows in the Aksaray neighbourhood of Istanbul when a smuggler offered him two options for getting to Greece. He could pay $800 for a dinghy, or $1,600 for a speedboat. Khalil opted for the speedboat, and his smuggler took him from Istanbul to Bodrum, where they arrived at a luxurious villa close to the sea. Fourteen other Iraqis were staying there, hidden in plain sight at the height of tourist season. The plan had been to leave from a waterfront property close to the villa, but the smugglers said that the Turkish police had bolstered their surveillance of the beaches in tourist areas.

The smugglers moved them to a flat in the centre of the city, where they stayed until one day they boarded a truck and drove for thirty minutes outside the city. They were dropped off at a beach, and half an hour later a pick-up truck towing a speedboat arrived. One of their handlers, a Syrian from Latakia, tried the engine and was unsatisfied with its condition. He made a phone call and not long afterwards another truck arrived with a new one. After they replaced the engine, the dozen or so passengers climbed in the boat and they sped towards Kos. The trip only took twenty-five minutes, and upon arriving they simply walked onto the island and acted as if they were tourists.

* * *

As previously noted, at the end of 2015 Turkey hosted an estimated 2.2 million refugees from Syria, which did not include the influx of irregular migrants who came from the broader region fleeing violence and seeking employment opportunities. Taken together, estimates suggested that refugees and irregular migrants constituted a workforce of between 500,000 and 1,000,000, living and working in the shadows. Their existence is one of substandard wages without protections or access to legal recourse, which combine to make them vulnerable to abuse. For smugglers, the pool of potential clients had reached unprecedented levels.

In Izmir there are not only former migrants who became key players in the smuggling trade, but also people who came from source countries with the explicit goal of working in the migrant-smuggling indus-try. One Syrian recruiter told me about Nigerians who have set up operations in Izmir, recruiting sub-Saharan Africans to come to Turkey via falsified documents and overstayed visas. Other recruiters described Pakistanis and Afghans associated with smuggling networks that pre-date the Syrian crisis who have come to work on the 'front end' of these networks, which start as far back as regional capitals in both countries. Rather than recruit clients on the ground, these agents are in charge of facilitating the last leg of the journey to Greece, linking migrants with local networks for onward transport to the coast.

When the Aegean route from Turkey to Greece reached its apex in the summer months of 2015, most experts and analysts at the time predicted that the flow of migrants would ebb with the onset of colder weather and rougher seas in the winter. In fact, many smugglers were operating under the same assumption, offering discount prices towards the end of 'smuggling season' in advance of the winter. Writing for *Politico*, Slovenian journalist Boštjan Videmšek interviewed a Pakistani smuggler in the summer of 2015 who had come to Turkey 'without papers or any other sort of formal identification' in order to become a smuggler. He told Videmšek that he is 'mostly in charge of the Afghan and Pakistani refugees'. Like many smugglers, the unnamed Pakistani told *Politico* that his greatest concern was not the authorities, but 'that the entire business will grind to a halt in the winter'.[16]

Yet three interlinking factors proved these predictions wrong. To start, the fear that Europe would close its borders and that Turkey might eventually clamp down on the flow of migrants caused a 'refugee rush'. That is, people who might have waited out the winter until it was safer to attempt the arduous sea and land journey began factoring European policies into their decisions on whether to cross. There was a 'now or never' mentality, especially as prospective migrants saw the rhetoric coming out of Europe as increasingly hostile to refugees.

In addition, many of those who are only now fleeing Syria, rather than those who have been living outside it in camps, increasingly see Europe as their only option for refuge, since the international refugee system has failed so comprehensively. Many of the people who are fleeing new onsets of violence, and increased aerial bombardment from Russia, the USA and a range of actors who are increasing their involvement in Syria, have friends and family who were living in camps and have since left. Those fleeing Syria are making the calculation that seeking refuge in camps in Lebanon or Turkey is a temporary and untenable solution. It makes more sense to bypass the years in limbo by going straight to Europe.

Lastly, smuggling networks have become so sophisticated in their recruitment and advertising that they are able to overcome whatever reservations many people once held about crossing to Europe. Though Western media are quick to highlight the perils of the Aegean crossing, statistically, the chances of surviving the trip are very high. As M. Sophia Newman notes in an article for *Vice*, for every 10,000 people who crossed, only 37 died. Not only is this number quite small, it is significantly smaller as a percentage compared to the year before, when people were dying at a rate of 117 per 10,000 successful crossings.[17] Due in part to better routes, more effective smuggling networks, a modicum of professionalism born out of Syrian demand, and a proliferation of volunteer organisations patrolling the sea to rescue tens of thousands of refugees who might have otherwise perished, crossing the Aegean sea became a less risky endeavour than the chance of losing that window of opportunity altogether.

While in Western media the images from the migrant crisis are human-interest stories that highlight tales of suffering and hardship, by contrast, many of the pictures and posts that populate social media within migrant and refugee communities are those of people joyously posing together, having successfully reached Europe. With migrants and refugees growing more desperate, the dangers of crossing are just one part of the calculation, but they are being weighed against the alternative of living in a war zone or languishing for years in a refugee camp. These considerations are also being weighed against the fear that the open door to Europe will finally, after three years, clang shut.

The fact that millions of dollars are being distributed along the chain of actors described earlier in this chapter in part explains why Turkish authorities failed to stem the flow of migrants into Europe. With so much money being made, there were plenty of people who had a vested interest in allowing it to continue. But corruption and complicity are only one, and by no means the most salient, reason why migrant smuggling in Turkey continued in unprecedented numbers throughout the summer and autumn of 2015.

The €6 Billion Question

For a variety of reasons, the Turkish government had little incentive to stop the flow of migrants who were treating Turkey as a transit country. As a country hosting 2.2 million refugees, at a cost of €7.5 billion and counting,[18] Turkish authorities had little sympathy for European countries, which, on receiving a mere fraction of the number of refugees received by Turkey, proceeded to treat their arrival as an existential crisis. Turkey, after all, had been dealing with both a larger influx of refugees and all the other complications resulting from instability in neighbouring Syria and Iraq. Most of all, the people leaving Turkey for Europe *wanted* to go to Europe, which meant that Turkey had little incentive to spend time, energy and resources acting as Europe's external border while an intransigent international community failed to bring about any sort of meaningful resolution to the ongoing conflicts in Syria and Iraq.

For his part, Turkey's president, Recep Tayyip Erdoğan, was keen to use European hysteria to get concessions out of Europe. Erdoğan saw an opportunity to reset what had become strained relations between Ankara and leaders in Brussels, both over the international community's handling of the crisis and over Erdoğan's own increasingly authoritarian tendencies at the domestic level.

Erdoğan had long argued that the real solution to the migrant crisis is ending the war in Syria, and that, short of ameliorating the situation in Syria, the international community ought to carve out a 'safe zone' in northern Syria for displaced people so that they do not have to go abroad in search of safety. By the late summer of 2015 European concerns over the influx of refugees crossing into the EU from Turkey had reached levels of panic, and various European leaders were happy to overlook Erdoğan's authoritarian streak, his treatment of the Kurds, and his stance on Syria in exchange for his cooperation on the migrant issue.

At an EU–Turkey summit convened hurriedly in November 2015, European leaders struck a controversial deal with Turkey that promised more than €3 billion in aid and an array of political concessions to Turkey in exchange for increased border controls. The deal included money to improve the conditions for the 2.2 million Syrian refugees living in Turkey at the time, the possibility of more liberal visa policies for Turkish citizens, and a reopening of talks regarding Turkish accession into the EU, in exchange for tighter border controls and a crackdown on migrant-smuggling networks.[19] In later remarks to the press, EU president Donald Tusk stated that this was not a 'simple trade—money for refugees. It's impossible, it's immoral';[20] but a mere six months later, this position was to be revised substantially.

In the weeks following the agreement with the EU, Turkish authorities launched several operations targeting migrant smugglers and migrants on its western shores. In late November, in what local authorities called the largest single operation to date, a force of some 250 security officials swept along the Turkish coast, detaining five smugglers and stopping an estimated 1,300 migrants trying to board boats to Greece. Days later, Turkish forces followed up with what, according to *The Guardian*, was thought to be the largest mass arrest of migrants and refugees since the beginning of the crisis. Police reportedly rounded up 3,000 migrants, mainly from Syria and Iraq, in the area around the north-western town of Ayvacık, from where migrants often leave for the Greek island of Lesbos. Police told local media that they had also detained thirty-five suspected smugglers and confiscated hundreds of rubber dinghies.[21] Given, however, the size of both the migrant and smuggler populations, these sweeping arrests barely impacted the market.

One of the prevailing truisms of migratory flows is that transit countries have every incentive to remain transit countries. But even in the case of those countries that do try to stem the flow of migrants passing through their territory, there is a persistent problem of figuring out what to do with those that they detain. Holding centres in places such as Egypt, Libya and Turkey, for example, are often overflowing with detained migrants in prison-like conditions, and international law affords these detainees certain rights and protections before deportation. More often than not, the solution for overwhelmed local authorities is to release migrants, rather than funnel them into domestic processes that are either underdeveloped or underfunded, if they exist at all. In most cases, migrants also prefer these 'catch-and-release' policies as it gives them the chance to plan another journey, rather than languish in bureaucratic limbo or seek asylum in a country where they do not want to live.

When the EU made the November 2015 deal with Turkey, as many as 70,000 people were officially registered as refugees in Izmir alone, with local government officials telling journalists that they were not sure what to do with those stranded on the coast. The vast majority of those who registered were believed to be people who came to Izmir hoping to reach Greece, only to run aground financially. Others suggested that many of these migrants registered as a formality in order to hedge against the possibility of Europe somehow managing to stem the flow of migrants from Turkey.

It is also worth considering that Turkey's inability to deal with the flood of migrants might not just be a question of will or capacity, but one of inexperience. 'Even for us, it's a learning process—we have never had to deal with anything like before,' Himmet Uygun, head of migration policies for the province of Izmir, told the *Financial Times*. 'Now we are taking strict measures, and they know—if they get into this business, they will be caught,' he continued. Even so, Uygun also told the *Financial Times* that 800 people had been arrested and 450 convicted for smuggling, which raises the question of whether mass arrests have had any tangible impact on migratory flows.[22]

One area where such crackdowns on smuggling did have a noticeable, if temporary, impact was in Çeşme, a posh resort town that, before it became a gateway for boats headed to the Greek island of Chios, had been a tourist hub for beachgoers and nightlife revellers. In the days following the sweeping arrests of alleged migrant smugglers and migrants, locals reported a lull in migrant-smuggling activity, only to see it completely re-emerge in less than two weeks, further evidence that the networks involved are highly responsive to the dynamics on the ground.

Yet despite arrest claims by Turkish authorities and reports of certain hot-spots along the coast going cold, if only for a few days or weeks at a time, the numbers suggest that actions by Turkish authorities did little during this time to stem the flow of migrants at a macro level. In December 2015 the UNHCR reported 108,742 arrivals into Greece, meaning that 250 per cent more people crossed in December 2015 than all of 2014.[23]

In response to the continued influx of refugees despite the initial EU–Turkey deal, several European officials questioned whether Turkey had any intention of keeping its end of the bargain. Turkish authorities might claim that it is a question of capacity and resources, yet European officials remained sceptical.

'I have serious concerns that Turkish human traffickers get support from authorities,' Greek President Prokopios Pavlopoulos told the German newspaper *Süddeutsche Zeitung*. Pavlopoulos accused Turkey of not doing enough to prevent migrants from boarding boats to Europe, and of deliberately not living up to its end of the agreement despite the fact that the European Commission had already transferred approximately €500 million as part of the deal. He went so far as to say that Greece would only uphold its part of the deal to provide funds after Ankara delivered on its promise to halt migrant crossings into Europe. 'Turkey has so far not delivered,' he said.[24]

Frans Timmermans, the European Commission's first vice president, struck a less accusatory tone. 'We are all committed as part of the joint action plan to bring the figures substantially down. It's quite clear that over the last couple of weeks the figures have remained relatively high,' he said at a news conference in Amsterdam with Dutch and EU leaders. 'So there's still a lot of work to do there.'

'We are a long way from being satisfied and we will continue our efforts to make sure we deliver the results we agreed with Turkey,' Timmermans continued, according to the *Financial Times*.[25]

Ahmet Davutoğlu, Turkey's prime minister, however, told the *Financial Times* that when Turkey signed the deal with the EU it offered 'no guarantees', and that the flow of refugees would depend on events in Syria, not at the Turkish coast. 'Turkish officials say the funding promised by the EU was to sustain migrants within Turkey and is not contingent on stemming numbers,' the *Financial Times* reported.[26]

Not only did the plan—either through ineffective implementation or just flaws in its design—fail to stem the flow of migrants, it also came under heavy criticism from advocacy groups that accused Europe of outsourcing border security to its neighbours rather than addressing any of the root causes of mass migration.

'Asylum seekers fleeing most countries today cannot obtain effective refugee protection in Turkey. Syrians are given only temporary protection, and Afghans and Iraqis don't receive even that,' said Human Rights Watch, in a statement following the EU deal with Turkey. 'Preventing people from travelling to the EU will deny protection to many people who need it,' the report continued. 'Without such greatly expanded safe and legal routes to reach Europe, people are likely to throw themselves on the mercy of unscrupulous boat smugglers to reach the EU.'[27]

After the initial deal did little to stem the flow of migrants arriving in Greece, the EU went back to the negotiating table, finally prepared to make a major concession. Once a new deal was struck in March 2016—a further €3 billion[28] plus acceleration of the extension of visa-free travel for Turks to the Schengen zone[29]—there was a sudden dip in the number of arrivals. Prior to the deal, in January and February 2016, the numbers had slowed, but not conclusively: 67,000 people arrived in Greece from Turkey in January, 57,000 in February. But by April the number had plunged to only 3,400, despite the better weather conditions.

Though it is too early to tell what exactly is behind the drop in arrivals, there are early indications that stemming the tide of migrants from Turkey into Greece was less a question of capacity or resources than of giving Turkey the right incentives. The deal allows Greece to send back 'all new irregular migrants' in exchange for Europe agreeing to accept one refugee residing in Turkey for every migrant sent back to Turkey. The arrangement is of questionable legality according to international human rights law and is already being challenged by rights groups, as well as refugees themselves, in the European Court of Justice.

Having played the long game, Erdoğan has forced Europe to strike a Faustian pact. It is now for Europe to live with the uncomfortable consequences. Although the first act of the EU engagement with Turkey on the issue of migration has concluded, it would be foolish to think of this as anything but a recurring drama with subsequent acts to follow. As long as more than 2 million Syrians reside within Turkey's borders, their entry and exit is a tap that can be switched on and off as Turkey sees fit. When the relaxation of surveillance begins—perhaps as Erdoğan identifies another priority—there is nothing to stop the human-smuggling trade from exploding once again.

Smugglers we spoke to in May 2016 all stood ready and waiting to resume this most profitable of local enterprises as soon as the opportunity should present itself.[30] Turkey, after all, has been a candidate for EU accession since 1999, and has been negotiating hard to formally begin the process since 2005. The Turkish government once thought the benefits of economic integration and a belief in shared democratic values was the path to Turkish membership in the EU, but it now seems more likely that European panic over 'swarms' of migrants has a greater likelihood of delivering that long-sought-after prize.

9

SCHENGEN AND BEYOND

When you sit on the shores of the Greek islands of Kos or Lesbos watching hundreds—sometimes thousands—of people wash ashore every day, there are certain moments during every arrival that catch your eye. You watch from afar as an unintelligible mass appears over the horizon. The people inside are struggling to stay afloat, surrounded by an unsentimental sea waiting to consume them. As the vessels draw closer, you can discern the commotion on board and, in some cases, hear their screams. All but the most callous among us would demand that we rescue them.

When they arrive, your attention is drawn to the families, who collectively express an array of emotions as they reconfigure themselves on the rocky shores. There are crying mothers and terrified children. Some fathers are stoic. Others are jubilant. Tears of terror blend with tears of joy. These are the scenes that have come to define the crisis in newspapers and magazines the world over. But the vast majority of those who arrive do not immediately drop to their knees to kiss the ground, nor do they embrace loved ones. Rather, they ditch their life jackets, check to make sure they have all their belongings, and start moving.

Most of those arriving are young men for whom reaching Greece only highlights the incompleteness of their quest for a better life, and seeing others travelling with loved ones only reaffirms what is at stake. Their goal is not just to cross into Europe, but to penetrate deep into the

Schengen zone and start building a new life as quickly as possible so they can send money home. Their escape is only the first step in liberating their wives, children, parents and extended families from the daily terror of Syria, the soul-crushing indignity of life in a refugee camp, or the vulnerability of getting by in the shadows of Istanbul or Beirut.

To achieve their end goal, whether it be the UK, Germany, Sweden, the Netherlands, France or any other of the preferred rich states of Western Europe with prosperous economies and generous benefits, there is still a long and complex course to chart: off the islands, out of Greece and, eventually, back into the Schengen zone. As explained in Part 1, although Greece is a member of the Schengen zone, it shares no land borders with any other Schengen members, which means for all but a few migrants who do decide to seek asylum in Greece, their arrival on the Greek islands is just one leg of an unfinished odyssey.

Cracks in the Fortress

The Greek islands represent one of the few junctures of the migrant journey to Western Europe where demand for smuggling services is near non-existent. New arrivals do not need smugglers to move around the islands, nor do they need to hire smugglers to move onward to the Greek mainland.

When I find *Beja, on the Greek island of Kos, he has been there for twelve hours. He seeks not food, or water or shelter, but bureaucratic efficiency. On this particular day in August 2015, he and about 300 other Syrian men are losing their patience. They have been waiting for hours to check in with the Greek authorities in order to receive their transit papers, a simple administrative process that should take only a few minutes and is the key to getting off the island and out of Greece for good.

Without this paper none of the hundreds of thousands who have washed ashore on the tiny islands of Greece can continue their journey to the mainland and onward into the heart of Europe. Just as crucially, the paperwork they seek does not constitute official registration or an official asylum claim, which means that should any of the countries they enter after Greece see fit to detain and or deport them under the auspices of the Dublin Regulation, they will not be able to prove that they should be returned to Greece for processing.

'We have been waiting here all day for nothing,' Beja says, in exasperated, broken English. 'I don't want to be here, but they keep me here,' he continues, pointing to the handful of Greek police dressed in riot gear who guard the door of the local football stadium, which has become an impromptu registration centre. 'Future life', he continues, pointing out into the distance, 'life is not here, life is out there,' he repeats, maintaining eye contact with me. He says the phrase again, this time looking downward and nodding, as if to reassure himself, 'Life is out there.'

Soft spoken and visibly exhausted, Beja tells me how he left his family behind in Aleppo. Unsure of what exactly the journey to Europe would entail, and afraid to expose his wife and two daughters to whatever dangers might lie ahead, Beja decided to come to Europe first. Once he reaches his final destination, he says, he will send instructions to his wife on how to get to Europe.

Beja says his goal is to get to Belgium, where he has family. His second choice is the Netherlands, where a friend lives. Like so many of the men and women arriving in Kos, he knows exactly where he wants to go and exactly how to get there, courtesy of modern communications technology. Vibrant social media networks give updates on border crossings, shifting European policies, and smuggling info in real time. 'I will go to Athens,' he explains. 'Then I go to Macedonia, Serbia, Hungary [sic], Austria, Germany, Belgium.'

Beja never aspired to live in Europe. He liked his life in Aleppo, where he found his work as a graphic designer both intellectually rewarding and sufficiently lucrative to support his growing family. Talking to him, you realise, as you often do when speaking to those who have come to Europe, that his journey is not a story of finding hope, but of losing it altogether. 'I finally gave up,' he says. 'It's like an infinity war. It will never end.'

Beja didn't have any trouble finding people who claimed to be smugglers in Turkey, but he did struggle to find an honest one. He dealt with several people, both Turkish and Syrian, who seemed like decent men and whose presentation suggested a veneer of professionalism, but all of them strung him along for weeks. He spent three weeks haemorrhaging money in cheap hotels, waiting for phone calls that never came and making down-payments that never moved the process along. His

219

luck changed when a Syrian family he befriended at his hotel in Izmir texted him the number of a smuggler who had helped them reach Greece. Beja had actually heard of this smuggler before, who apparently had a good reputation among Syrians in Izmir. News of honest, reliable smugglers spreads quickly in migrant circles.

'People call him Ali,' Beja explains. 'When my friend gave me [Ali's] number, I was so happy.' After only a few texts, Beja was handing $1,200 dollars to one of Ali's brokers in the back room of a café where Arabs hang out. The broker told him to be at a particular street corner in the heart of the city at 8 p.m.

After just a few minutes of talking to Beja I could tell that he was urbane and educated, yet anything but street-savvy, which in part explains why he was burned by unscrupulous smugglers and strung along for weeks by opportunists in Izmir. Paying a broker in advance was also a huge mistake, but luckily Beja escaped disaster. An associate of the broker met him at the assigned corner, and walked him to a hotel. By the early morning Beja was in a van with other Syrians, on his way to a remote location on the Turkish coast.

For those who had made it to Kos in August 2015, their first experience with 'Fortress Europa' was, almost literally, a fortress. Greek authorities had chosen the local football stadium as the processing centre for incoming migrants, and every day newly arrived migrants gathered by the hundreds on a small patch of asphalt at the gates of the stadium. Wedged between a restaurant and a private home, these new arrivals would wait for days as a phalanx of Greek police officers in full riot gear guarded the entrance.

On one of the days that I visited in mid-August 2015, the queue was particularly long after a spell of good weather had facilitated unprecedented arrivals onto the island. I spoke with dozens of people from Syria, Iraq, Afghanistan and elsewhere, desperate to get inside the stadium, frustrated that only a dozen or so people were being processed every hour.

Ironically, it was only two days earlier that many of these people had been desperate to get out of the stadium after local authorities, in an effort to clear migrants off the tourist beaches and esplanades where thousands of them had set up a tent city, conducted a sweeping operation to round up migrants and lock them into the stadium. In theory, the Greek government was providing them with a place to stay. In practice, some 1,000 men, women and children were confined to what can only be described as an open-air prison. According to representatives from Médecins Sans Frontières (MSF), who were able to access the facility, the dire conditions lacked basic amenities, including food and drinking water. Only two toilets were available for over a thousand people. The only authorities on the inside were police in riot gear, while NGOs trying to provide basic medical services found themselves on the outside looking in.

Having been locked into the stadium for one and a half days, the migrants inside launched an ostensible revolt as dozens suffered from heat exhaustion, dehydration and panic attacks. At least four people required hospitalisation. Police responded with what MSF described as 'excessive use of force' on the inside of the stadium, while tear gas was fired into crowds that gathered outside the building. The incident was sufficiently ugly to garner international media attention,[1] and even in the days that followed, after the literal smoke had cleared, the details behind the motives of the local authorities, and what exactly transpired inside the stadium, remained unclear.

Julia Kourafa, a spokeswoman for MSF, told me days later that the stadium debacle was really the culmination of years of mishandling of irregular migrant arrivals on Kos and growing local pressure on the government to be more proactive. 'MSF has been working on the island of Kos for many months now. Since April, we have been trying to provide medical assistance and humanitarian help to the refugees who are arriving,' said Kourafa. 'There is no official reception system in place, so there are no official reception conditions for the people arriving.'

According to Ms Kourafa and other officials working in Kos, irregular migrants had been living in the Captain Elias, an abandoned hotel that became infamous for its squalid conditions. In lieu of an actual refugee reception centre, hundreds of people lived in the hotel without running water and electricity, until MSF installed showers and latrines, and provided basic medical services.

But with the unprecedented and unforeseen surge in arrivals in the summer of 2015, the ramshackle system, in which local authorities issued transit papers and left migrants to fend for themselves, reached breaking point. With no space left in the dilapidated hotel, new arrivals moved to the streets and public spaces, creating a tent city of over a thousand people living and lingering on a thin lawn that stretches along the coast. In the absence of any response from the national or local government, MSF began distributing tents, handing out water, and providing mobile medical facilities out of a van.

Images of tourists cycling past piles of young men sleeping on scraps of cardboard appeared on popular news sites, as did pictures of corpulent, sunburned holidaymakers sunbathing near desperate Syrian families and the detritus of their sea crossing. The striking images, combined with the real urgency of an unfolding humanitarian crisis, prompted authorities on Kos to take action.

When the local authorities did develop a response, it was the ill-conceived attempt to 'house' the migrants by locking them into a stadium without necessary provisions, and supervised by riot police. 'I don't think they actually thought a lot about this decision,' says Kourafa. 'It was not a logical decision to lock a thousand people inside a stadium.'

While criticism of the authorities in Kos is certainly well deserved, Kourafa, like many others working in the humanitarian sector, was careful not to blame the shortcomings on specific individuals. The problems, she explained, were multi-faceted and systemic.

Once known for its large-scale emigration, Greece became a country of destination for Central and Eastern European immigrants after the fall of the Soviet Union and other communist regimes in the region. More recently the country has become one of entry and transit for hundreds of thousands of unauthorised immigrants from Africa, Asia and the Middle East.

As a result, Greece is now grappling with a multitude of issues directly and indirectly related to the migrant crisis. The challenges of controlling its borders, processing asylum applications, dealing with a faltering immigrant detention system, and allegations of human rights violations come at a time when the country is struggling under the weight of the worst economic recession in recent memory. Huge public debt and the government's decision to borrow from the International Monetary Fund (IMF) and the EU have entirely changed the economic, political and social environment of immigration and social policy in Greece. Employment and income have shrunk for both the native-born and immigrant populations, while competition within and between the two has increased. This stagnation has resulted in lower wages, a contracting labour market, and fewer regularised immigrants, which has exacerbated tensions around the migrant question, as well as the overall cohesion of modern Greek society.

'There is not a lot of [human resource] capacity, financial capacity, and coordination capacity. There are so many different actors in Greece dealing with refugees, and it is not easy, especially with the financial crisis, to actually be able to respond to this emergency situation,' Kourafa explained. 'On the other hand, Greece has been receiving refugees for many years now, and there has not been an official reception system put in place. So it is a lack of political willingness to do it. I think the authorities need to take responsibility because now they are going to have to deal with a refugee crisis.' Most importantly, Kourafa warned, there was a simmering tension on the island, which was not only inspiring rash decisions and poor policies, but had the potential to turn violent.

* * *

On the day that I meet Beja, only two days after the stadium disaster, emotions are running high. None of the thousands of irregular migrants wants to be in Kos, and most of them have the means to continue on, but they are at the mercy of Greek bureaucracy. Inefficient at the best of times, Greek administrative processes were further stultified by a lack of resources, political paralysis in Athens, and a succession of ever-changing ad hoc polices being implemented by local authorities who had little choice but to improvise their way through the crisis.

Outside the stadium, hostility among migrants is forming along ethnic and national lines, and minor quarrels begin to erupt between Syrians and everyone else. Afghans resent the Syrians for their passports and the fact that Greek authorities are giving them preferential treatment. Syrians resent the Afghans and Iraqis, who they believe are clogging up a process meant for them.

Some of the Syrians concede that the Iraqis and Afghans might also be in need of asylum, but they resent the fact that many Iraqis, well aware of the preferential treatment given to Syrians, are pretending to be Syrians who have lost their passports. Some of those in the queue had purchased stolen or counterfeit Syrian passports on the black market in Turkey, which draws the ire of some of the Syrians, suspicious of those who, despite their paperwork, do not look or sound Syrian. At one point, three Syrian men begin interrogating two young Sudanese men whom they accuse of trying to hoodwink the overwhelmed and utterly confused Greek registration authorities. The Sudanese men speak Arabic, but their skin colour and dialect, the Syrians allege, are not those of Syrians. Just as it appears as if the altercation might turn physical, others intervene and cooler heads prevail, but not before the Sudanese men are forced to give up their place in the queue.

The Syrians, Iraqis and Afghans all turn their frustrations towards the Pakistanis, Bangladeshis, Iranians and the handful of Africans in the queue, who they believe are not 'real' refugees. The vast majority of those there, however, are not trying to work the system. These are people from places such as Eritrea, Somalia, Bangladesh, Pakistan and Iran, who, with varying individual circumstances, are fleeing persecution and violence. All they want is for Greece to give them a transit permit so they can continue to a place they think will offer them a life with dignity. Almost to a person, they are confident that, if given the opportunity to tell their story, they will be granted asylum, and even in the likelihood that they are denied, many believe that living and working on the margins of European society offers greater security and opportunity than the lives they have left behind.

The hostilities between different migrant communities at the gates of the stadium become physical. Some Syrians start forcibly removing non-Syrians from the queue in an effort to help the hapless local authorities sort people according to nationality. After what feels like hours of jostling and heated conversations, the Pakistanis, Iranians and Bangladeshis finally agree to form their own queue, at which point the authorities march them over to the police station. The crowd of Syrians cheers and claps, relieved that the registration process might actually start moving. Some go so far as to taunt their 'fake' refugee counterparts.

Removing the non-Syrians from the overcrowded gates of the stadium, it turns out, does not reduce the chaos, it merely displaces it. Down the street at the police station, the non-Syrians have been placed in an ostensible holding pen, and it would be an understatement to say that language barriers abound. The Greek police officers tasked with implementing Greek policy—or at least their best guess as to what Greek policy might be—are struggling to communicate with the crowd of young, brown men who have been extricated from the registration process at the stadium.

'I speak English, please, listen to me, I speak English,' exclaims a Pakistani man who moves to the front of the crowd to plead their collective case. The self-appointed spokesperson tells the guards that he and his compatriots have been on the island for days, without food or water, and they just want to understand why they cannot get transit papers. The officer tells him, in broken English, that they must register at the stadium, not at the police station. The incredulous Pakistani man relays the information to the crowd, at which point all hell breaks loose. They try in vain to tell the officers that they just came from there, but the moment is quickly subsumed by the mass confusion.

Some of the Pakistanis and Bangladeshis stay at the police station. Others meander back over to the stadium, where the process of sorting and pre-screening migrants that just took hours to negotiate begins anew as non-Syrians try to re-enter the queues.

Throughout the island, the underlying tension is not just between migrants and the authorities, nor is it only among the migrants themselves. Part of the reason why the authorities in Kos were scrambling to find a way to move migrants out of public spaces was due to pressure from locals, who were growing increasingly intolerant of both the migrant arrivals and the inadequate government response.

'If I am being honest, I am the dog. I am here to guard the restaurant,' says a man named Korstos, who is paid to sit at the side entrance of a restaurant adjacent to the patch of asphalt where migrants must wait for hours to enter the stadium. Korstos is in his sixties and has lived in Kos his whole life. He says that between the economic crisis and the migrant influx, things have never been more difficult for the people of Kos.

'It's more and more every day, 400 to 800,' Korstos says. 'Our island used to be known for Hippocrates, now we are known of this,' he laments, pointing towards the lines of downtrodden migrants baking in the sun without food or water. 'I feel sorry for them and I feel sorry for us, too.'

Down the street, a manager at the restaurant near the police station is sympathetic to the plight of those arriving, but with reservations. 'We don't mind the Syrians. They are fleeing war,' he tells me. 'But what the hell are people from Bangladesh doing here?' Visibly frustrated, yet trying to remain politically correct, the manager tells me that the migrant crisis has crippled his business, because tourists do not spend time on this part of the island.

'In 2014, this view was the sea, cruise ships and yachts. Now it is garbage, diapers and laundry,' he says, pointing to the stone walkway directly ahead, where a handful of migrants are setting down clothes that they have just washed in the sea. 'This patch of grass is their lavatory, which means my restaurant smells like a lavatory.'

When I press him for some theories as to why non-Syrians are coming to Greece, he refrains from answering and calls over to a man named Iannis. 'If you want to know what is really going on, ask Iannis.'

Iannis, who would give only his first name upon learning I was a journalist, claimed to have served as an intelligence officer in the Greek army in Cyprus. He too struck a sympathetic tone when it came to the Syrians. 'I have no problem with them. I am with them,' he said. 'But look at the others,' he explains, beginning to lay out his conspiracy theory. 'Afghanistan, Pakistan … all young men,' he pauses. 'All of them … All of them are young men. Where do they get the money? Who is funding their trip?' he asks rhetorically. 'I know from experience. I recognise these types of people. These are fighters,' he asserts, referencing once more his time in Cyprus. 'You will see. In two years, the bombs will be going off every day.'

* * *

Greek islands like Kos became gateways to Europe because of political geography. Their proximity to Turkey, in some cases only a few kilometres from the Turkish mainland, made them a logical destination for irregular migrants from the Middle East, Asia and Africa who had managed to reach Turkey. The fact that the Greek islands became a chokepoint in the migrant crisis, however, is a result of policy. As previously mentioned, rather than set up any sort of formal registration process, the Greek government pursued a policy in which irregular migrants were given a transit permit that allowed them to continue their journey to the Greek mainland. The system, predicated on the understanding that getting off the islands was a mutual priority shared by both the migrants and the local officials, worked for a time.

It was only after the explosion of the Aegean route and the unprecedented influx in the summer of 2015 that the situation in places such as Kos, Lesbos and Chios went from inadequate to completely untenable. Having backtracked from locking migrants into a football stadium, the Greek government decided to charter a cruise ship, the *Eleftherios Venizelos*, that, with a capacity of 2,500, would serve as a floating registration centre and temporary shelter that could move asylum seekers off the island, and onward to the Greek mainland. It was the latest in a string of ad hoc ideas, and news of the ship's pending arrival had every migrant on the island scrambling to prepare for the next phase of their trip.

As previously mentioned, islands such as Kos are one of the few parts of the migrant odyssey where demand for smugglers is non-existent. Migrants wait to register so they can take one of the several ferries that leave daily for the Greek mainland. And since the Greek government was determined to move the tens of thousands of migrants off the overwhelmed islands, many of these boats were provided by the government, free of charge for those who could not afford to pay.

Nonetheless, the process of migrant smuggling is everywhere, even if smugglers are absent. Migrants waiting for the next boat off the island plan what they will do once they reach Athens. After sending an SMS or posting a selfie on Facebook to let friends and family know they made it alive, most migrants take to social media and messaging apps in search of the latest news, as well as to trade gossip regarding what routes to Western Europe are open, how to get there, and how much it will cost.

Street-side cafés, where new arrivals can fill up on caffeine and take advantage of free WiFi, take on the energy of a stock exchange. Some establishments refuse to cater to migrants, only allowing 'tourists'—a crass euphemism—as patrons. Those that do accept migrants are packed and messy. Bathrooms, much to the chagrin of the staff, become places to change, bathe and wash clothes. Seats next to electrical outlets are effectively commoditised. When someone relinquishes a spot near an outlet, there is a mad rush to be the first to the socket. Aside from transit papers, there is nothing more important at this point than a charged mobile phone, for that is what allows people to liaise with smugglers in Athens.

For many on the island, the first step in planning their future journey is figuring out where they are in the first place. Some had no idea they were even on an island, hundreds of kilometres from the Greek mainland. One migrant I spoke with, a twenty-something from Iraq, began to cry when I told him that he needed to get onto another boat. His harrowing journey across the Aegean was the first time he had ever seen the sea, and he had hoped it would be his last.

An unaccompanied sixteen-year-old from Syria named *Saif came over to me with his phone and started typing in Arabic. He popped it into a translation app on his phone and asked, 'How long from Lesbos to Athens?' I tell Saif that he is in Kos, not Lesbos. He seems confused and calls over some of his fellow travellers, one of whom brings a map. On the map they point to Lesbos. Eventually, I'm able to communicate that they are in Kos. With that matter settled, Saif moves on to the next question, using a mix of his own English and that which the translation app can provide.

'Is it right [meaning true or correct] that they closed the line [meaning border] between Serbia and Hungary?' he asks. It had been an on-again, off-again rumour for days that Hungary was going to seal its border with Serbia in an attempt to stem the tide of migrants passing through Hungarian territory. Should the rumour prove true, it would have far-ranging repercussions with those whose goal was to reach a country within the Schengen zone, allowing onward travel to countries such as Germany and Sweden. If the border between Serbia and Hungary was closed, new routes would have to be discovered, or created.

I told Saif that as of that day, the border was open and people were still passing through, but that things were constantly changing. This was before the emergence of an alternative 'Balkan route' that bypassed the border with Serbia and Hungary—and, in some cases, Hungary altogether—by passing through Slovenia. Looking at the map, one might conclude that the best route was to enter Hungary through Bulgaria, but Bulgaria, in the eyes of many of the migrants I talked to on Kos and later in Lesbos, is a non-starter.

'Bulgaria is no good,' Saif tells me, alluding to stories, since corroborated by an array of human rights groups, of asylum seekers being arrested, abused, tortured and extorted by both Bulgarian police officers and organised crime syndicates. They even say they have seen videos of such incidents, which quickly go viral on migrant message boards and online communities. Even those who do not speak any English manage to say, 'No Bulgaria. No Bulgaria.'

As the *Eleftherios Venizelos* pulled into the harbour, a pack of reporters descended on Major-General Zacharoula Tsirigoti, head of the Aliens and Border-Brotection Branch of the Hellenic Police, who had the unfortunate job of trying to portray the vessel as something other than the floating manifestation of a half-baked idea. As the journalists press her for details regarding who is paying for the ship, how long it will stay, what will happen to the migrants once they arrive in Athens, Tsirigoti struggles to give concrete answers, not because she does not have a mastery of the details, but rather because the ad hoc plan doesn't have any details. In front of a dozen cameras and two dozen journalists, not having answers is a bad look and Tsirigoti senses it. She quickly pivots to the broader issues at work. 'This is not Greek problem, this is a Europe problem,' she tells the crowd. When one reporter asks if the Greek government is expecting more migrants, Tsirigoti demurred. 'Because of the weather, it is very easy to come to the island, after that, we will see.'

Six weeks later, when I visit Lesbos, it is clear that the worst possible scenario has come to fruition. Not only has the rate of arrivals swelled to unprecedented numbers, but the Greek government, the EU and the broader international community have failed to make any significant progress on diagnosing the problem, let alone responding to it.

At the port in Lesbos, a tent city has emerged in the shadows of the *Ariadne*, a ship that will ferry only a fraction of the migrants stuck on Lesbos to the Greek mainland. A reporter next to me notes the significance of the name. In Greek mythology, he explains, it was Ariadne who helped a traveller escape from a labyrinth on a Greek island.

The makeshift camp at the port spills onto the streets and into the cafés and bars normally occupied by holidaymakers and local college students. Syrians with sufficient cash search for hotels that are willing to accept them, but just about everyone else on the island is sleeping on the street, or in the remote reception areas that are only just being established. Large crowds have emerged outside every travel agency.

Those who have obtained their transit papers are anxious to get onto the first boat or plane off the island.

On the other side of the island, near the town of Skala Sikamineas, hundreds of migrants are coming ashore every day, with only a few dozen volunteers there to receive them. The volunteers, some of them Greek but many from Sweden and Denmark and the children of immigrants themselves, offer new arrivals solar blankets, water and biscuits. Those arriving on the rocky beach quickly disembark and shed their life jackets and soaked clothes. Some immediately contact their Turkish smuggler to confirm that they made the trip. Others take it upon themselves, per the instructions of their smuggler, to slash the rubber boat. Many require urgent medical care for themselves or a family member, and look around frantically for someone to help.

Despite the fact that the vast majority of boats arrive near Skala Sikamineas, the reception centres for refugees are on the other side of the island. Local volunteers say that they have been trying to establish a small centre on the outskirts of town to provide some assistance, even if it is barely better than first aid, but that the local community, while welcoming of their efforts, fear that the town will lose its appeal to tourists if it is turned into a de facto refugee camp. The majority of those who arrive must hike between 8 and 15 kilometres on winding, mountainous roads until they reach areas from where transport is provided. In lieu of any official support from the local government or international organisations, migrants and refugees have to rely on the charity of NGOs and volunteers to find transport to these reception centres. The small cadre of volunteers is able to offer bus rides for women, children, the elderly and the injured, but many pass up these opportunities for fear of being separated from their loved ones. Upon surviving abuse from smugglers and the perils of the Aegean Sea crossing, refugees arriving in Kos face a gruelling 40–60-kilometre hike across the island.

In late September, despite the fact that the crisis had been going on for months, a formal reception system was only just getting off the ground, with two separate registration centres, both across the island from where most asylum seekers were washing ashore, established. The better staffed and equipped of the two centres, in the town of Kara Tepe, is designated exclusively for Syrians. There, Syrians can register and obtain the six-month permit that allows them to move freely within Greece. All other nationals have to go to a separate centre in Moria, where meagre facilities mean that new arrivals wait in squalid conditions until they receive their one-month transit permit.

As with Kos, the dynamics of migrant smuggling are everywhere in Lesbos, even if there are few, if any, smugglers on the island. Agents working for transport companies based in Athens pass out flyers written in Arabic that advertise all-inclusive packages from Athens to the border with Macedonia. According to one of them, the deal includes one night's accommodation and all meals. The advertisement specifies that the enterprise is legal. And while it is technically true that these companies are engaged in legitimate enterprise, it is equally true that they are in the business of moving migrants to the next phase of their illegal journey.

Not all of those who facilitate the flow of migrants are partaking in organised crime, therefore, even if the practical effect is helping them evade border controls and continue on a journey that is technically illegal. As with migrant-smuggling operations along other parts of the eastern Mediterranean route, some of these less uniform schemes are run by opportunists, entering the criminal market for the first time by seizing an illegal entrepreneurial opportunity. Others are part of migrant-smuggling rings that have operated in Greece for decades, providing fake documents, paying off relevant authorities, and offering safer forms of illegal transport at premium prices.

Greek Tragedy

In Athens, the rush to Western Europe begins where it left off in Turkey, and the idle business of waiting for days on the Greek islands for paperwork gives way to the critical work of executing plans hatched from cafés, hotel rooms and transit terminals along the way. A falafel joint just off Acharnon Street in downtown Athens is just one of many gathering points for migrants from Syria and Iraq. The food is inexpensive, tasty and quickly prepared, but the main draw is the business that goes on in the courtyard, where the tables are completely occupied, some by patrons, others by loiterers, but mostly by smugglers and fixers meeting with prospective clients.

Two elderly men have set up a plastic table from where they sell bus tickets that will take you north. The two-man operation is humming. One man meticulously fills out the relevant passenger information in Arabic in his ledger, tearing each ticket from its underlying carbon copy. The other counts the money being handed over in fistfuls. It is the worst-kept secret in Athens that these tickets are for buses headed directly to Greece's border with neighbouring Macedonia. Their legal status is unclear.

The next morning, at a small public park in central Athens, a group of twenty Syrian refugees waits for their interlocutor who works for a travel agency adjacent to the park. When he gives the signal, the Syrians move with the purposed frenzy of a spooked herd. Everyone, including children, are wearing backpacks, and most adults are carrying plastic bags filled with additional supplies. They cross the street oblivious to the flow of afternoon traffic, unfazed by the blaring horns of frustrated Athenians at rush hour.

Their interlocutor waves two hands in the air and signals them to a convenience store, where an unmarked bus is parked. One of the people waiting to board the bus is Tony, who features in the introduction of this book, who left his wife and children in Syria in hopes of making the journey and then sending for them. Tony, who communicates with me in the English he learned from watching American films, tells me that many in this group of travellers are Christian, which he thinks will help them during the asylum process. Only days before, Slovakia had said they would be willing to take in Syrian refugees, but only Christians. Rumblings on social media had suggested that other countries might do the same, and Tony says he read on Facebook that anti-migrant gangs and vigilantes along the Balkan route are less likely to harm you if you are Christian.

Courtesy of updates on Facebook, Tony is well aware of the chaos and confusion at the Macedonian and Hungarian borders, but he is undeterred. 'I have no choice,' he tells me, referencing his wife and children, who are counting on him. 'I want to go to Sweden, but my choice is anywhere but Syria.' Next to Tony, an adolescent in desperate need of chemotherapy is leaning on his father. 'There is no treatment for him in Syria. But in Sweden, maybe they can help him,' Tony says, with a palpable sense of existential dread.

As the Syrians wait to board, passers-by hand them biscuits, bananas and water. One elderly Greek woman shakes her head in pity as she walks by, and decides to turn around and enter the convenience store facing the bus. She walks out of the shop with a bag full of drinks and snacks. She hands them out until they are gone, and then realises that her act of charity has reached only a fraction of those waiting. She re-enters the shop. After three more trips, having handed out dozens of bananas, bottles of water and packets of biscuits, she clasps her hands and raises them just over her head, as if to say, 'goodbye and good luck'.

So as to not be accused of trafficking or doing anything illegal, employees of the travel company operating the bus check everyone's paperwork before they board. As the men wait in line to present their papers issued by the Greek authorities, women groom their children or sneak in one last nappy change. They have been told that the bus is not stopping until it reaches the Macedonian border, and that the trip will probably take six to nine hours.

No one seems sure to what extent this bus operation is technically legal. It certainly isn't clandestine, but it doesn't feel entirely transparent either. The bus operators and their Arabic-speaking interlocutors seem perturbed by my presence, and they aren't all that forthcoming when I ask if I can buy a ticket for one of these buses.

'Where are you trying to go?' the agent asks me.

'I'm trying to go wherever they are going,' I tell him. 'Where exactly are they going?' I ask.

'These people are going north. Go to our office down the street. You can buy tickets there,' he concludes, ending the conversation by ushering me away from the bus and pointing me down the street. At the office, the sole employee lists the cities for which they sell bus tickets, none of which are the destination of the bus that has just departed. Even though they are technically legal, it is clear that they have reservations about openly advertising the fact they are in the business of moving migrants to the border.

A month later I went to the same travel agency to find windows covered with pieces of paper written in Greek, English and Arabic, offering deals for those seeking to go to Macedonia. Taped between the advertisements were detailed explanations regarding the paperwork required for crossing the border. A professionally dressed Greek woman sitting behind a computer quoted me prices in fluent English. 'And unlike some of the other companies, it is one hundred percent legal,' she added, as she counted a wad of euros that one of her Arabic-speaking employees had just collected for her. After marking each one with a pen to check for counterfeit bills, she gives her co-worker, an Iraqi who has been in Greece for months, a nod of approval and prints several tickets.

Bus companies such as these are very much a part of the networks that facilitate the flow of migrants to their various destinations across Europe. They are not illegal, and it would not be fair to label those who work for them with the pejorative moniker of 'smuggler', but their business models and techniques do, in many ways, mimic those of their non-legal counterparts in the migrant-smuggling chain. And while these types of services can exist legally within the murky, ad hoc laws and policies being put in place as a result of the influx of refugees, demand for smuggler services is necessary to fill in the gaps between the quasi-legal and the completely illegal.

Bus companies of this type employ people with the requisite language skills—often migrants themselves—to recruit and round up migrants who want their services. You can find many of these recruiters at the restaurants, parks and hotels where migrants congregate, handing out flyers that advertise their services in Arabic and English. They hang out at the ports of Piraeus and Kavala where migrants coming to the mainland arrive from the islands, and some employ people on the islands, advertising package deals that include hotels, meals and bus tickets upon arrival on the mainland.

Though Syrians are the most coveted clients because they are the easiest to transport from a legal perspective—their paperwork allowing them to stay in Greece is good for six months and can be renewed—certain networks cater to different nationalities, and employ different interlocutors to find prospective clients. Some of the men who work as recruiters for these legal transport companies also work for higher-level smugglers.

*Karzan, an ethnic Kurd who fled Syria because his family's political activism meant that they were constantly targeted by both the Assad regime and rival militias, is just one of the many refugees in Athens working for these new transportation companies. The company he works for organises buses to transport migrants from Athens to the village of Idomeni, close to the Macedonian border. For his services, Karzan earns €1,800 a month, which is more than enough to pay for the flat he shares with ten other Syrians, all of whom also work in the transport industry. In addition to paying rent, each of the ten men living in the apartment pays €100 a month to the Greek front man whose name is on the lease. According to Karzan, this arrangement is a common one in the neighbourhood, organised and overseen by a Syrian smuggler in Athens who specialises in acquiring fake documents that allow refugees to pass through the airport.

For his part, Karzan has used his steady income to send both of his sons to Sweden via the second type of model. He knew, thanks to his employers, that getting as far as the Hungarian border was not an issue, but feared that his sons might get stuck in Hungary, where the government seemed determined to stop the influx of refugees.

So Karzan identified a smuggler who had the requisite criminal connections to smuggle his sons from Macedonia all the way to Sweden, for €750 each. Both sons have since reached Sweden, and Karzan's nephew, using the same smuggling network, has managed to get most of their extended family to Sweden. His sons, who are both under the age of eighteen and therefore minors who can apply for family reunification, have started the process that will enable Karzan to join them. Until then, he plans on living and working in Athens.

At the port of Piraeus and at certain parks in Athens, *Omer, an Iraqi who has been in Greece for over a year, is tasked with triage. Omer tells me that when he meets someone who wants to join the flow of migrants going from Athens to the border with Macedonia, he ushers them towards a bus company. When he meets someone who seeks a more sophisticated service—one that might require fake documents, for example—he gives them the necessary contact information to initiate the process. 'I'm helping these people,' says Omer, who winces at the idea of being called a smuggler, even though he receives a salary from one. 'They are lost. Someone needs to help them,' he says.

Omer tells me he will probably use one of the latter services when the time comes, obtaining falsified documents that will allow him to join his relatives in Western Europe.

Balkan Odyssey

Throughout much of the summer and autumn of 2015, but especially after Germany ostensibly tore up the Dublin Regulation in August, demand for smuggling services out of Greece was minimal, in part because smugglers were unnecessary. Well aware that they were mere transit countries, the governments of Greece, Macedonia and Serbia implemented an informal policy of ushering migrants through their territory, which meant that anyone who could acquire the requisite paperwork stating that they were a potential asylum seeker could migrate through the Balkans for the cost of public transport and a few meals. The goal, from the perspective of migrants, was to reach Austria, another transit state, but one which, as a contiguous member of the Schengen zone, was tantamount to reaching the rest of Europe because it meant unfettered travel across the borders of Western Europe.

With the migrant highway connecting Greece to Austria wide open, hundreds of thousands of migrants flowed through the Balkans in the span of only a few months. In July 2015 38,000 people crossed into Hungary, the last country before Schengen Austria. That number rose to 58,000 in August, and swelled to 138,000 in September. The openness of the Balkan corridor met its first real challenge in the form of Viktor Orbán, Hungary's right-wing prime minister.

Even though Hungary was almost exclusively a transit country, the last of those separating Schengen members Greece and Austria, Orbán took it upon himself to stem the flow of migrants out of principle. Orbán believed that Europe was committing suicide by opening its borders to an indefinite number of migrants and asylum seekers. He went on record, stating that 'one does not have a fundamental right to a higher standard of living, only a right to safety and human dignity', and that migrants had no right to cross Europe at will.[2] Under the auspices of protecting Europe from Angela Merkel's 'refugees welcome' policies, Hungary began building a 175-kilometre fence along its border with Serbia.

At what became a heavily policed Serbian–Hungarian border, migrants found themselves stuck for days—sometimes weeks—at a time, waiting to cross into Hungary. Those who did so found themselves blocked at railway stations and transit hubs, without access to food, water or adequate living conditions.

Hungarian police dressed in riot gear beat back the tide of migrants that would occasionally try to storm the border crossing. On several occasions tear gas was fired into crowds that included women and children. Some migrants tried to cross on foot through portions of the border that were not yet fenced off in the hope that if they were caught Hungarian authorities would funnel them towards the Austrian border rather than push them back into Serbia. A few succeeded, but most joined the swollen ranks in Hungary's migrant detention centres.

As migrants began pooling at the Serbia–Hungary border, smuggling networks quickly seized the opportunity to redirect migrant flows towards Croatia, from where migrants could enter Hungary and continue on to Austria, or reach Austria via Slovenia.

* * *

On a miserable rainy day in the Serbian capital, Belgrade, the park adjacent to a four-star hotel oddly named Design Mr President Hotel is buzzing with migrants debating the best course of action. They are a short walk from a main transit terminal, but it's not clear which border they'll be allowed to cross, and by which means of transport. In recent days both Hungary and Croatia have closed their borders, only to open them and then close them again within the span of a few days. Should any of these people decide to use a taxi or a private car, rather than public transport, there are plenty of Serbian drivers and smugglers waiting to be the supply to their demand.

One Syrian family has been in Belgrade for two weeks, living under a tent in an increasingly chilly and muddy park. They are getting by courtesy of some volunteer organisations that bring food and blankets to supplement the UNHCR mats the family brought with them all the way from Turkey. They had made it to the Hungarian border, but, after one of their children fell sick, chose to retreat to Belgrade, where they knew there were more aid organisations potentially able to help them.

A Serbian man named Dejan*, who, with a tracksuit, shaved head and dark rings around his eyes is the embodiment of shady, sits at the edge of the park, leaning against his taxi, saying 'Taxi … Border … Taxi … Border …' in heavily accented English to everyone who walks by. When I ask him how much, he tells me €100. Then I ask which border; he says, Croatia. I tell him I'll consider it.

Map 7: Alternative routes through the Balkans[3]

At the café outside the Design Mr President Hotel a Serbian man, also dressed for the part with Adidas trainers, a windcheater and receding hair tied back into a ponytail, is discussing business with some young Iraqi men I had met earlier in the morning. They talk furtively and he keeps looking over at my table, suspecting that I might be paying attention to their discussion.

After a few more minutes one of the Iraqi men turns to a group of two women, three children and one elderly woman and says, 'Let's go,' in Arabic. The pony-tailed man escorts them over to a mini-van. The family gets in, and the mini-van takes off immediately. It could be that this was just a simple discussion about going to the Hungarian or Croatian border, or it could be that they were negotiating a more complex deal that would smuggle them further afield. But the fact that it was all happening in Belgrade is indicative of the fact that at this time and place Belgrade had become, via political geography, a key launching point for those wishing to get to Western Europe or Scandinavia.

With the Hungarian border sealed off, Belgrade became the place to which some people retreated as they planned a way around, or through, Hungary. One reason to come all the way back to Belgrade, the theory went, was to tap into the expertise of the more sophisticated networks one could find in the city, as opposed to the criminal entrepreneurs operating in small border towns.

After spending some time in the park I decide to revisit Dejan and see if he is willing to drive me to the border. He quotes me €100, the same price as before. When I tell him it is too much he lowers it a bit and, after a few volleys back and forth, we arrive at the 'friend price' of $80, not euros.

Dejan throws my bag into the back of his taxi, and removes the taxi sign from the top of his car in case we try to cross the border. At this point he is under the impression that I am Syrian, and that what he is doing is not, technically speaking, legal. He tells me that once we get to the border, if it is closed, he can find a way to get me across, for a price to be negotiated once we are there.

As we leave Belgrade for the town of Sid, on the Serbia–Croatia border, where migrants re-routed from the Hungarian border are crossing into Croatia, there is almost no traffic, save for a few cars. That morning, Croatia had decided to close its border with Serbia, meaning that Dejan has the entire road to himself, zooming down an impeccable two-lane highway that runs through a green, flat landscape dotted with cornfields and apple orchards.

As we get closer to the border, hundreds of trucks are parked, single-file, at the side of the road, stretching for miles, waiting for the border to open. It's a sight that brings out Dejan's nationalistic ire, which he can only barely articulate in English. 'Croatia, no good. Big problem, Croatia. Serbish [sic] people, good. Croatian people, yuck.' Over the course of what would become a four-hour trip, Dejan repeats those four, declarative statements consecutively, without deviation, no fewer than ten times before I stop counting.

The border is officially closed, but migrants on the messaging service WhatsApp, as well as Dejan's contacts, insist that people are still crossing. We go to the official border crossing and are blocked. Dejan parks the car about 50 metres from a police checkpoint and walks over to get some information. He then tells me we need to go to Morovic, a village not far from Sid. We drive along the border, through small towns and side roads buttressed by cornfields, forests and streams. The view is stunning, and I wonder why people do not just attempt to cross on foot.

Those musings subside when I see the signs along the border warning of landmines, a remnant of the brutal internecine conflict that precipitated the break-up of Yugoslavia, and the last time Europe had to deal with a 'refugee crisis'. Volunteers in Croatia and Serbia, after catching wind of the fact that migrants would be attempting to reach Hungary via Croatia, began creating and distributing maps highlighting areas with landmines via social media.

As we keep driving, I start to question Dejan's smuggling bona fides and wonder if his contacts who insist that people are crossing are correct. The newswires are still claiming that the border with Croatia is closed, and faced with the real possibility of not being able to cross the border legally or illegally,[4] we start to consider whether the best option is to drive to Bosnia and enter Croatia from the Bosnian border. Just as we agree to head for Bosnia, we see three parked buses at the side of the road, with migrants emptying out.

Two plain-clothes Serbian police officers are ushering them towards a path in the woods, which leads to Croatia. As Dejan and I watch, more buses arrive. As I weigh the option of crossing with them, Dejan makes the mistake of telling them I am an American who wants to cross with them, at which point our presence is no longer welcome. The Serbian officer walks to my side of the car and says, in perfect English, 'Please, you have an American passport ... please cross the border legally.' I tell him I would like to but the border is officially closed, and I need to get to Croatia by tomorrow morning. 'You really shouldn't be here,' he says, 'Please go.'

Dejan and I continue towards Bosnia, having concluded that it is the only way I can get into Croatia by nightfall. When we reach the border, Dejan receives a call from one of his contacts that the Serbia–Croatia border will be opening soon. It's not on the newswires, nor is it on social media, and by this point I've lost what little faith I had in Dejan. He insists that his source has good information, but I tell him I would like to continue on to Bosnia regardless, just to play it safe. Thirty minutes later the local news services confirm that the border is opening. Dejan and I cross back into Serbia, and continue all the way to Sid, from where we enter Croatia and part ways in the small town of Tovarnik. At the railway station, hundreds of migrants, who reached Croatia courtesy of smugglers, criminal entrepreneurs and enterprising Serbian officials, are waiting to see where the train will take them.

* * *

When it became clear that Hungary's fence along its border with Serbia did little but divert the flow of refugees to Croatia, from where they could still cross into Hungarian territory, Hungary extended the fence to include its border with Croatia. The end result was 523 kilometres of 4-metre-high razor wire sealing Hungary off from neighbouring Serbia and Croatia.[5]

Regardless of what one thinks of Orbán's policies, the fence proved ruthlessly effective. In September 2015 10,000 people were crossing into Hungary every day. By November that number had dropped to only 315. Viktor Orbán had effectively redrawn Central and Western Europe's border with the outside world.[6]

These shifts in policy, where facts are in short supply and governments provide contradictory information, make smuggler services appealing to even those who wish to reach the Schengen zone legally, or without paying criminals. Smugglers can offer migrants a path to their destination that is impervious to fickle European policy-makers and the whims of local officials who are implementing policy on the fly. With so much at stake, many migrants who had the misfortune of arriving in Greece after the Balkan corridor closed sought smugglers who could offer bespoke packages that bypassed the Balkans altogether.

The criminal machinations that facilitate these types of schemes operate in the shadows, but the initial rendezvous that sets them in motion often takes place out in the open. I watched several such gatherings between associates for high-level smugglers and prospective clients take place on the patio of a charming Middle Eastern restaurant at the edge of one of the grimier parks in central Athens. With colourful sofas and rows of shisha pipes at its entrance, there was nothing to suggest that illegal activity might be taking place among the steady stream of customers from all walks of life. Yet a local journalist with good access to the migrant community in Athens told me that this particular patio was a preferred meeting spot for smugglers who offer all-inclusive packages to places such as Germany and Sweden.

When I arrived, my acquaintance nodded his head in the direction of a table with three people. A young couple, both elegantly dressed, sat facing their prospective smuggler. From a few tables over, the furtive conversation looked serious. Yet according to the journalist I was sitting with, it is not uncommon to hear smugglers talking business over the phone, discussing prices and quantities in barely coded language that anyone who speaks Arabic or Kurdish can overhear and understand. Over the next two hours I counted three such meetings, in which the same smuggling interlocutor left, only to come back later to meet with a new group of prospective clients.

The smugglers who operate at this level, broadly speaking, tend to offer two types of packages out of Greece. The goal in both scenarios, at a minimum, is to get their clients from Greece to another Schengen country, from where the migrant can travel to their country of choice and claim asylum. The first type of package offers travel to the Schengen zone by plane, which requires using either authentic documents that are bought, borrowed or stolen, or fake documents that are sufficiently convincing to withstand scrutiny at customs and border controls. The second option is to go by land, most often by car or train, either using fraudulent documents or trying to evade border controls through sleight of hand and deception, disguising migrants within the regular traffic of European citizens.

*Miriam, who travelled to Greece with her disabled daughter from Syria via Turkey, had such a bad experience in Turkey that she decided she did not want to undertake the uncertain journey through the Balkans, putting herself and her daughter in the hands of men she did not know and could not trust. Via connections her husband made on the internet, Miriam arranged to leave Athens by plane. For a fee of €4,500 her smuggler arranged to have someone with a Belgian passport fly to Greece carrying two more passports that could credibly pass for Miriam and her daughter. Once he arrives, Miriam says, the three of them will fly back to Belgium together. Until then, the smuggler is allowing Miriam and her daughter to live with him free of charge.

He is her smuggler. He is her saviour.

Dead Ends of Europe

Even for those migrants who do reach Schengen Europe, challenges to movement abound. In the early phases of the crisis, in 2012 and 2013, migrants were arriving primarily by boat in Italy and transiting northwards. Getting to their country of choice could come in the form of an overpriced taxi, a lift from an acquaintance or the cost of a ticket on public transport. Back then, there was little evidence of smugglers within the Schengen zone, in part because they were unnecessary. But as the crisis prolonged and intensified, with growing attention from law enforcement and a proliferation of once-unthinkable border closings, the laws of smuggling nature came into effect.

As Austria, Hungary, Croatia, Serbia, Macedonia, Sweden, Denmark and Norway began closing their borders—sometimes only for certain nationalities, but in other instances for all irregular migrants—new smuggling networks quickly emerged. Where borders were porous and uncomplicated, low-level criminal entrepreneurs, opportunists or even good Samaritans emerged to facilitate passage. The former charged relatively little for their services, the latter offered them for free. Yet in cases where borders were well policed and hard to penetrate, more sophisticated, professional crime syndicates were uniquely positioned to prosper. Sometimes these groups took over operations completely, wresting control from the amateurs who first conceived of the schemes. At other times they co-opted them, demanding a cut of the profits in exchange for protection, expertise and the right to continue with their activities.

Europe's new internal borders breathed life into well-established criminal groups whose roots can be traced to the Balkans, spawned and nurtured during the collapse of the Soviet Union and the break-up of Yugoslavia. Unlike their counterparts in national law enforcement, these organised crime syndicates are multi-ethnic, cross-border, and tap into diasporas that span all of Europe. Their connections and distribution networks stretch from Afghanistan to the United Kingdom, having cut their teeth in the Afghan heroin trade, the smuggling of stolen licit goods such as cars and cigarettes, human trafficking, and arms dealing.[7]

With the Balkans closed, the €6 billion EU–Turkey agreement in place, and tens of thousands of migrants stuck in Greece, demand for smuggling services has skyrocketed, especially for the all-inclusive packages described above.[8] These bespoke packages, which rely heavily on the use of fake or falsified documents, high-level bribes and criminal connections across multiple borders, are exactly what established organised crime syndicates can offer. In other words, European policy-makers have made migrant smuggling more profitable, and steered these profits directly into the hands of organised crime syndicates.

'Every time we pick someone up [for migrant smuggling], we already know them', a member of the British National Crime Agency (NCA) told me in October 2015, 'it's the same drug trafficking, human trafficking, gun running groups that were there before, just with a new clientele.'

Within the EU, a number of places serve as 'criminal hot-spots' according to the European police agency, Europol. Cities high on its watch lists include Athens, Berlin, Budapest, Calais, Copenhagen, Frankfurt, Hamburg, Hoek van Holland, London, Madrid, Milan, Munich, Paris, Passau, Rome, Stockholm, Tornio, Thessaloniki, Vienna, Warsaw and Zeebrugge. Transport infrastructure hubs such as railway stations, airports and bus stations are seen as primary recruitment points for organised crime syndicates that, until recently, could not be bothered with the business of migrant smuggling.[9]

* * *

On a cold, dreary October day, at a railway station a few stops before Calais in France, a dozen migrants are milling about on the platform. They are Kurds from Iraq, Hazara boys from Afghanistan who have been living in Iran, and a young, married Ethiopian couple. The Iraqis have arranged to meet their smuggler upon arriving at the station. They have spent last night sleeping at a guest house at a nearby town, where they met with an intermediary who put them in touch with the smuggler who will meet them at the station. Equipped with fresh haircuts and winter coats, they have packed very light, as they expect to be in the United Kingdom in a matter of days, if not hours.

'My cousin lives in London, and I'll meet him there,' one of the Iraqis tells me in English, in an accent that could pass for American. 'Me, I know someone in Birmingham,' says another. Upon arriving in Calais, they immediately liaise with a pot-bellied Iraqi man with slicked-back hair and pockmarked skin. He is wearing a leather jacket and a white turtleneck. They all shake hands and kiss on the cheek, but once the formalities are over, they quickly start moving.

Those who have not made arrangements to meet a smuggler in Calais start meandering towards 'the Jungle', a tent city on the outskirts of town. 'The Jungle' is not an official refugee camp, overseen by international organisations and operating with the blessing of a host government. Rather, it is an unsanctioned colony where 6,000 people from all over Africa, Asia and the Middle East dwell in a shanty town built from cardboard, rubbish and tarpaulin. Everyone in the Jungle wants to get to the United Kingdom.

'Welcome to Suzan Restaurant,' says Amadine, a thirty-something Ethiopian who, along with his business partner Suzan, has opened a restaurant in the heart of the Jungle. 'Suzan Restaurant … Jungle 5 Star!' he continues, urging people to come in and enjoy a cup of Lipton tea or a meal of bread and fried eggs. Clients walk in and say hello as if they are catching up with old friends. They greet and make small talk, sitting on rows of cushioned benches. The restaurant even has two guitars on offer, which several people take for a spin, some even trying to play along with the Ethiopian music being piped in by a jerry-rigged sound system the owners have set up.

Amadine operates his business in an array of languages, but the lingua franca of the Jungle is English. When an Eritrean man walks in with a gash on his knee, the product of a botched attempt to sneak into the Channel Tunnel that links Calais to Dover in the United Kingdom, Amadine reaches for a medical kit under the cot next to the stove where Suzan prepares the meals. He makes some Lipton for his friend and dutifully cleans, treats and dresses the wound.

'Okay, my patient,' Amadine says, letting out a giggle and wagging his finger. 'Three days, no drink, no smoke,' he jokes. The entire restaurant, full of young men in damp, muddy clothes, laughs.

Some of the patrons at Suzan Restaurant have been living in the Jungle or its antecedents for months, waiting for a wire transfer from abroad to come through, or the right opportunity to enter into the UK to present itself. While they aren't exactly putting down roots, the entrepreneurs among them, like Amadine and Suzan, are building more permanent structures for their fledgling businesses.

Across from Suzan Restaurant is a barber's shop, advertising an array of hairstyles and shaves. The clippers are run via a generator, and there is a range of shaving creams, balms and hair products on offer. Around the corner, a row of restaurants and tea houses have emerged. Afghan and Iraqi cuisine is easily available, and a few more businesses are being constructed. An Iraqi man walks past with a saw he borrowed from an Ethiopian woman who no longer needs it. The wooden frame she has erected is ready to be adorned with tarpaulin and whatever other material she can find.

Competing Afghan restaurants face each other. The one that cooks chicken more thoroughly is preferred by the local volunteers who spend their days in the Jungle offering basic medical services out of the back of a trailer. One of these aid workers, who would not give his name for fear of putting his own organisation at risk, warns me to be careful.

'It's fine to walk around, but don't ask too many questions,' he advises. 'The mafia has descended on this place.'

With thousands amassed at Europe's dead end in Calais, organised, multi-ethnic criminal groups based in nearby cities such as Dunkirk have moved in, sensing an opportunity to exploit the desperation of those living in the squalid conditions. In addition to using their unique skill-set, born out of decades of trafficking drugs, guns and people from France into the UK, the Dunkirk mafia also trawls the camp for potential recruits who can help not only in finding prospective clients, but also help funnel women and children into their trafficking rings that specialise in prostitution, forced child labour and extortion. In fact, Europol estimates that at least 10,000 unaccompanied migrant children disappeared after arriving in Europe, with intelligence officials worried that a significant number of them have fallen into the hands of organised trafficking syndicates that specialise in child exploitation.[10]

Amid fears that the Jungle had become a den of organised crime, the French government began regular patrols throughout the camp searching for weapons and suspicious persons. The patrols, in which heavily armed police cautiously move their way through the Jungle, look more like an occupying power trying to send a message to natives than a local force trying to police its own territory.

To the extent that there was an enemy to be found, he was hiding in plain sight, among the squalor of the Jungle. In response to increased scrutiny by local authorities, smuggling networks operating in Calais began adapting. Organised crime syndicates on both sides of the channel began arranging for migrants to move further afield, out of the watchful eye of authorities, from where transport to the UK could be arranged. The complex nature of moving people across (or under) the heavily regulated English Channel meant that aside from the overly ambitious freelancer, organised criminal groups with transnational connections were the only actors positioned to capitalise on demand for smuggler services.

'There is always someone in Britain, a UK national or otherwise, who receives either money or migrants or has links with transport companies to arrange for drivers to smuggle people through,' Amélie Le Sant, the public prosecutor in Dunkirk, told *The Telegraph*. 'There are links in every case. The British nationals tend to come over every now and again to deliver cars bought in the UK—usually flashy Mercedes or BMWs—as well as money or to carry out a "guaranteed" service in which they deliver migrants to a willing lorry driver paid to stow them away. Then they usually go back alone on the train.'[11]

In police investigations, European citizens have been found to act as bankers and guarantors for migrants, paying their smugglers either directly in the countries of origin or along the route via Western Union and other money services. They also wire money to local smugglers to rent hotel rooms or pay drivers before making the crossing. In the case on which Ms Le Sant was commenting, two Kurdish smugglers who had worked with three local French accomplices had received €318,000 over the past year, in cash sent mainly from the UK.[12] This is by no means just a British phenomenon. Europol, for example, claims to be tracking 40,000 suspects of more than 100 different nationalities, and have 1,551 open investigations on networks active in the EU, 56 per cent of which include EU nationals.[13]

With demand for their unique skill-sets reaching unprecedented levels, and low-level criminal entrepreneurs pushed out of the market, organised crime groups now have carte blanche to abuse and extort their clients. Migrants in turn find themselves caught between crime syndicates and European policies that have, in effect, criminalised the act of migration.

Through reinforced borders and ever-shifting policies that no migrant can hope to navigate alone, European policy has provided the perfect environment for these types of networks to flourish. Inside Fortress Europa, the criminals are king.

CONCLUSION

The World We Live In

Generosity is a virtue for individuals, not governments. When governments are generous it is with other people's money, other people's safety, other people's future.

P. D. James, *Children of Men*

P. D. James's dystopian novel, *Children of Men*, describes a future world in which a sterile human race has descended into anarchy. A deluge of asylum seekers desperately attempts to penetrate the few remaining stable states, which, in an effort not to be overrun, have become heavily militarised to the point of inhumanity. Electrified fences, menacing concrete watchtowers manned by armed guards, barbed-wire holding pens and vicious prison guards ring the British Isles in order to preserve the last remaining vestiges of 'civilisation' and humanity by using means that are neither civilised nor humane. The book, a shocking read when it was first published, and later made into a powerful film, resonates even further these days because many of the fictions designed to appeal as a thought-provoking work of art are in fact already a reality of modern-day immigration control in various parts of the globe.

As we conclude this book in mid-2016, the much-vaunted Schengen zone is fragmenting into closed, contested borders. European states are struggling to find consensus on a proactive approach to managing the ongoing influx of migrants, engaging instead in a race to the bottom of incoherent policies that are of questionable legitimacy under international law. Many of the policies being entertained and implemented are in obvious defiance of human rights conventions. Others, owing to their underlying cruelty, shock us on a more visceral level. Over the course of Europe's 'migration crisis', urgency and a sense of panic have led to policies that range from the cynical to the unconscionable.

Switzerland, a financial sanctuary for the planet's super-rich and one of the world's wealthiest and most stable countries, seizes jewellery and other assets from refugees in order to cover their legal fees and resettlement costs. Denmark and Germany have implemented similar measures.[1]

In January 2016 hitherto amicable neighbours Sweden and Denmark imposed photo ID requirements along borders for the first time in fifty years, and suspended free passage along the historic Øresund Bridge, which has long stood as a proud monument to integration.[2] By June the bridge was adorned with fences, heat sensors and guards to prevent the smattering of refugees attempting to walk along the railway tracks across the bridge.[3] Austria has built a fence on its borders with Slovenia and Italy.[4] These are actions that few would have thought necessary, let alone politically palatable, not long ago.

Overwhelmed German municipalities, attempting to accommodate 1.5 million new migrants, took the controversial step of housing refugees in the notorious former concentration camps of Dachau and Buchenwald.[5] As previously discussed, in August 2015 local administrators on the Greek island of Kos caged approximately 2,500 people into a football stadium, with neither food nor water for more than twenty-four hours, in an attempt to get migrants off the streets and offer the illusion of normality to tourists and residents.

The debacle in Kos foreshadowed the misery that was to come at the Idomeni camp established in the winter of 2015/16 on the Greek border with Macedonia. In the six months before borders began to close across the Balkans, this tiny town, whose population is officially registered at 154 people, saw over 500,000 pass through in a two-month period. After the border closure, 12,000 people were stuck, living in a makeshift camp where access to sanitation was non-existent, cases of Hepatitis A were detected, and a photograph of a newly born infant being washed with bottled water outside a mud-soaked tent prompted fleeting moral indignation on social media.[6] Smugglers circled the camp like vultures, but doctors reported that those who tried to cross the border often returned badly beaten by the police on the Macedonian side.

Countries in the Balkans, whose democracies consider themselves too new and fragile to deal with an influx of newcomers, have militantly refused to permit migrants to linger. Refugee families, including young children, have been shot with rubber bullets and showered with pepper spray and tear gas in an effort to maintain public order.[7]

But these stories barely shock any more. Europeans have become desensitised to the bloated cadavers of men, women and children washing up on their shores or being hauled from rough seas within European territorial waters by volunteer rescue crews. Citizens of rich and prosperous nations became immune to the stock pictures of anonymous families huddled on beaches, at borders and railway stations, sleeping rough on the streets and walking for days on end to find the smallest bit of sanctuary.

There have been sporadic fits of moral outrage surrounding the plight of Syrian refugees, but these episodes have done little more than inspire opinion columns and editorials, only to dissipate from the public consciousness days later. Images of three-year-old Alan Kurdi (initially reported as 'Aylan'), dead on the shores of Turkey after drowning in an attempt to reach Europe, spawned a Twitter hashtag #AylanKurdi that captured the world's attention. Alan was briefly a cause célèbre, but after a string of overtures and appeals from celebrities, as well as a series of evocative graphics, the crisis faded into the background. Searches for the word 'refugee' or 'migrant' declined by half less than a month after Alan's tragic death.[8]

As Europe follows the examples of other countries and regions that have engaged in long-term struggles against illicit migration, border controls are rising, lengthening and thickening. Despite the assurances of UNTOC, the UN Refugee Convention and other international human rights legislation, there is a worrying trend towards the criminalisation of migration and of the migrant himself, rather than of the smuggler, and the popular rhetoric around migration is becoming worryingly nationalistic and intolerant. Far-right parties are gaining traction across the continent, and attacks against migrants as well as against charities providing services to them are becoming more common.

After a protracted period of economic downturn, as a result of which many European countries are struggling with high levels of unemployment and widespread cuts in government budgets and social support, the public are being sold the threat of 'predatory' economic migrants by segments of the political class. Attitudes among polities that initially welcomed refugees have turned sour as legitimate but exaggerated fears of terrorism have trumped Europe's humanitarian impulse and commitment to human rights norms. Not only has tension over migration caused EU member states to reconsider some of the core tenets of integration, in the case of the United Kingdom it played an outsized role in the decision to leave the EU altogether.

Protests by migrants at key European borders, and instances of criminality and violence, including gender-based assault perpetrated by members of migrant communities across Europe, have led to hostility towards the predominately male, Muslim newcomers. In Finland, vigilante militia groups are patrolling small towns housing asylum seekers in the name of protecting Finnish women from migrant 'predators'.[9] One-third of the mosques in the Netherlands have experienced threats and at least one incident of vandalism, attempted arson and other acts of aggression such as the placement of pigs' heads at their doors. In early 2016 an anti-immigration regional government in Lombardy in Italy approved a new law that would make it difficult to construct new mosques as Muslim refugees settled in the area. The wealthy province, of which Milan is the capital, also joined a number of other European states in banning the wearing of *burqas* and *niqabs* in public.[10] In one terrifying incident in January 2016 in Sweden, in an unprecedented alliance between two Swedish far-right football-hooligan groups, 200 masked men stormed Stockholm's railway station and indiscriminately beat anyone who didn't appear to be Swedish, including refugee children.[11]

Meanwhile, in addition to the thousands of kilometres of barbed wire that have been laid down throughout the Schengen zone, NATO warships now patrol the Aegean and Mediterranean to deter migrants. Armed guards monitor the migrant settlements and informal camps that dot the continent, and Europe has approved the creation of a common border and coastguard that will enter the sovereign littoral states to defend the Bloc's increasingly embattled shores and borders. Under its Faustian pact with Turkey, Europe will return those deemed economic migrants, and even those who have 'legitimate' asylum claims but used smugglers in order to reach safety. The cost of outsourcing the dirty work to Turkey: €6 billion and the contentious prospect for visa-free travel for Turks.

At no time in history have so many people attempted to cross international borders without authorisation, and at no time has a collection of democratic governments purportedly committed to human rights and international law gone to such inhumane lengths to stop them. But these types of policies are not without precedent, however, and experience elsewhere shows that there is a predictable trajectory, one that inevitably leads to negative outcomes on both sides of the borders involved. Before deciding if this is the path it wants to pursue, Europe would do well to learn from a number of macabre cautionary tales in other parts of the world.

Postcards from the Front

Since 11 September 2001 the United States has spent well over $100 billion on immigration and border controls in an effort to prevent the smuggling of migrants, drugs and weapons across its borders. Its Customs and Border Protection agency (CBP) is the largest federal law-enforcement agency in the entire country. With more than 60,000 employees, CBP is bigger than the FBI, DEA, Secret Service, US Marshals and the NYPD combined. In addition to its staggering manpower, the CBP operates a fleet of over 250 aircraft, consisting of planes, helicopters and unmanned aerial equipment—including MQ-9 drones most often associated with Iraq, Afghanistan and combat missions abroad. Taken together, the CBP's aerial capacity is greater than that of the entire national air force of Brazil.

Yet despite this impressive paramilitary strength, victory is proving elusive, and managing the US border increasingly resembles a counter-insurgency in which state institutions are on the losing side. Retaining quality agents and maintaining integrity has been an enormous challenge. As reported in *Politico* in 2014, between 2005 and 2012 an average of nearly one CBP agent was arrested every day on charges of abuse and misconduct, a statistic that almost defies belief. The CBP also holds the national record for the highest number of fatal shootings per year by any such agency. Despite the fact that 1,700 complaints of abuse and brutality were lodged against the agency between 2007 and 2012, not one single agent had been subject to criminal trial, or disciplined for excessive use of force as of 2014.[12] For many, the CBP represents a travesty of modern-day policing, operating with a complete lack of transparency or accountability.[13]

The CBP also suffers from chronic corruption at the southern border, the extent of which is so widespread as to be almost unmeasurable. A 2015 report by the American Department of Homeland Security concluded that the CBP needed to double its internal investigation capacity to target corruption and the use of excessive and unnecessary force against migrants.[14] CBP officers have been found not only to have taken bribes to allow all manner of contraband to cross the border, but have been caught selling information regarding locations of surveillance equipment and timing of border patrols, as well as abusing and trafficking migrants (including for sexual exploitation) and actively engaging in the trafficking and the sale of narcotics.

Yet, regardless of all the supposed deterrents the USA places on its southern border, hundreds of thousands of irregular migrants cross the militarised area every year. They are facilitated by smugglers, known informally as 'coyotes', whose complex networks reach across Mexico and deep into the three violence-plagued countries of the Northern Triangle: Guatemala, El Salvador and Honduras. Since 2006 at least thirteen sophisticated drug tunnels have been found between Mexico and the state of California alone. Countless others, some of which are barely more than 'gopher holes', are believed to exist along the rest of the US–Mexico border. The most impressive among them are hundreds of metres long, equipped with electricity, ventilation and even rail systems. While most of these are created to service the drug-trafficking industry, the drug cartels 'rent' the tunnels to human smugglers for a fee that is passed directly on to the migrant. The drug cartels have been reported to demand as much as $5,000 per head from the smugglers, with unquestionably credible death threats used to ensure payment.

With hundreds of thousands of migrants crossing the border every year, migrant smuggling into the USA is a billion-dollar business, profits are generated as much in the USA as in source countries. A 2015 investigation by the *Pittsburgh Tribune-Review* found that migrants from Mexico and Central America pay an average of $3,095 to travel from the Mexican border to Houston, Texas, a journey of about 565 kilometres or $5.48 per kilometre. But for the even shorter journey between Houston and Phoenix, the rate is almost double, $11.63 per kilometre, due to the risk of detection.[15]

With this kind of money in play, border communities themselves have become invested in the migrant-smuggling trade, recruited by vicious smuggling gangs. The *Pittsburgh Tribune-Review* investigation revealed that of the 3,254 people convicted of smuggling migrants from Mexico into the United States in 2013 and 2014, 60 percent were American citizens. Americans are the predominant nationality among those who drive migrants across the border, report on CBP movements, bring migrants from the border to safe houses inside the USA and oversee the safe houses as migrants await the next phase of their journeys.

The only activity more likely to be performed by a Mexican citizen rather than an American or a dual citizen is the guiding of migrants across the border on foot, rather than in a vehicle. In 2015, the governor of Texas, incredulous at the inability of the federal government to control either its agents or the border, ordered the indefinite deployment of 1,000 troops from the Texas National Guard, allotting $815 million of the state budget for border control and turning some border areas and communities into de facto war zones.

The situation is even worse on the other side of the border. In 2011 the Mexican police were accused of actively working for the brutal Zetas drug cartel, which sought to gain the upper hand over their rival Gulf cartel in a war for control of cross-border migrant smuggling and human trafficking. In San Fernando the police not only worked as lookouts, but participated in mass kidnapping and executions of migrant workers. More than three hundred bodies were found after a three-year investigation in which the involvement of state officials and law enforcement was confirmed.[16]

The US example also suggests that it would be foolish to expect deportations to solve the problem. The United States' enforcement-only posture fails to fully address the complex factors behind migrants' decisions to move, the consequences of which are increasingly punitive and often deadly.[17] In fact, deportation schemes may have the adverse effect of exacerbating the root causes of irregular migration and migrant smuggling in the first place.

In recent years the USA has overseen deportations at a rate that is unprecedented in the country's history. Data from the Department of

Homeland Security shows that the Obama administration has removed or returned in excess of 4 million people.[18] As a result of the 2014–15 'child immigration crisis', in which some 250,000 women and children crossed the border irregularly, overwhelming immigration and justice services in the process, the government reformed migration laws in order to accelerate the deportation process for minors. Much like the EU has sought to do in its 2016 deal with Turkey, the intent was to send a clear message that irregular immigrants would be detained and deported rather than rewarded with status and citizenship.

Journalist Michael Carr found a direct correlation between the prevention and deterrence strategy used by the US Border Agency and migrant deaths. While estimates of the total differ from between 3,861 to 5,607, these figures rose in parallel to the growing numbers of CBP officers.[19] An article in *The Economist* described the speed at which the USA is preventing and expelling Central American migrants as 'bordering on cruelty', with not only enormous consequences for the migrants, but also serious implications for the stability of the region as a whole.[20]

The overzealous deportation policy also raises significant questions about the integrity of the justice system, and the US government's commitment to ensuring human rights and due process. In interviews with children held in detention centres, the UNHCR found that 58 per cent of the children crossing the border described situations that would make them eligible for protection under international law. These children had been personally affected by the ever-increasing violence in their home regions perpetrated by organised criminal groups, including drug cartels and gangs. A striking 38 per cent of the Mexican children had been recruited by smuggling organisations and cartels to work as guides. In addition to their smaller size and greater tolerance for risk, it is widely understood that if these children are caught, they would simply be returned to Mexico or Central America without criminal penalty, which makes them particularly useful to criminal groups.[21]

Instead of receiving protection, migrant men, women and children from Mexico and Central America are summarily rounded up, put on planes and buses and returned to their country of origin, which are woefully underprepared to receive or reintegrate them. This vicious cycle further exacerbates the problems of displacement which, if left unattended, could result in serious consequences for the Americas as a whole, both North and South.

As Jorge Chabat, an expert on drug trafficking and national security at the Centro de Investigación y Docencia Económicas (Economic research and academic centre) in Mexico, cautioned, 'We are witnessing now a fragmentation of the territory where we can still see some trace of security, peace and prosperity among the violence associated with organised crime. This demographic phenomenon is pressurising the safest areas, threatening livelihoods, education and employment. If we do not take action, we will face a permanent state of social decomposition that will affect the communities to which they emigrate, exacerbating insecurity.'[22]

Some of those who have returned to the south-western state of Michoacán, for example, have taken up arms, joining the controversial vigilante groups that are attempting to combat the drug gangs. These informal yet heavily armed groups are now present in thirteen of Mexico's thirty-two states, challenging the government's ability to provide security and exercise a monopoly on the legitimate use of force.

As the EU considers its border control and immigration strategies, Europe has to ask itself whether or not it is prepared to emulate this model and deal with the corresponding fallout. Is Europe prepared to criminalise non-violent offenders, and put children and babies behind barbed wire, in the name of immigration control? How does this practice align with its human rights values, or even the principles of contemporary policing, justice, and the rule of law that have taken generations to cultivate? And what might be the impact to Europe's social fabric in this scenario? How far down this slippery slope is Europe prepared to slide in its efforts to 'break the business model' of the smuggling industry? Is this the world that Europeans want to live in?

While the US example of border policing is full of discomforts, it is by no means the most troubling cautionary tale. The draconian policies that the Australian government has pursued in order to deter illicit and irregular migration have proven ruthlessly effective yet morally repugnant. While Australia offers generous relocation packages for the limited number of refugees who are processed at source countries and resettled in Australia, for those seeking to reach Australia irregularly, the consequences are severe.

To deter arrivals by boat on Australian territory, the Australian government holds asylum seekers on what are in effect prison ships for weeks pending the processing of their asylum claims. In addition to funding detention centres on Nauru and in Papua New Guinea, where migrants can linger for years, the government introduced a policy of 'excision' that declared the over 5,000 Australian islands as being 'offshore excised places' in which people entering illegally would be considered unlawful and subject to mandatory detention without access to the asylum procedures available on the mainland.

More recently, as part of the country's Operation Sovereign Borders, the government has come under fire for allegedly paying smugglers to turn back migrant boats. According to various reports, border-control officers paid six crew members AU$32,000 to divert sixty-five asylum seekers, going so far as to provide them with a map detailing where on Indonesia's shores to land.[23] In May 2015 this strategy of 'pushing them back' left a small convoy of 6,000 refugees and migrants stranded at sea between Thailand, Malaysia and Indonesia for more than three weeks before they were grudgingly allowed to land.[24] By that time hundreds had died of thirst or hunger, despite the fact that the fiasco was widely covered by the international press as it unfolded.

Wider Ramifications

European hysteria over 'swarms' of migrants has also critically damaged its credibility in international affairs. It is hard for Europe to preach the doctrine of the 'responsibility to protect' while at the same time wilfully refusing protection to asylum seekers. Furthermore, the countries bearing sizeable refugee populations, many of which have done so for prolonged periods of time, look askance at Europe's reaction to comparatively minuscule refugee arrivals. Some governments are even following the example of Turkey and taking advantage of Europe's panic as an opportunity to re-evaluate their own responsibilities. Why, asked Kenyan officials in May 2016, should they continue to house 330,000 Somalis in the world's largest refugee camp if the EU cannot handle a far smaller migrant population?[25] What incentives do countries such as Lebanon and Jordan have for continuing to shoulder the heaviest burdens of displacement from the war in Syria? Where are their billion-euro incentives to make sure the 'crisis' does not reach European borders?

The problem is that the task of addressing irregular immigration, and developing coherent migration policies in general, is too often subsumed by broader questions of border security and terrorism. Largely unfounded fears that terrorists are populating migrant flows, or that migrants serve as drug couriers and mules, result in an over-securitisation of borders, while altogether ignoring the root causes of irregular migration.

Regrettably, policies predicated on deterrence—building higher walls, criminalising migration through overzealous returns, cracking down on smugglers, increasing maximum fines and sentences—not only tend to cause more problems than they solve, but they often exacerbate the very problems that they are meant to ameliorate.

Absent any measures that curb demand for smugglers, these militarised policies serve only to enrich and empower smugglers, allowing them to raise prices for their services. These swollen profit margins in turn attract more hardened and professional organised crime groups, who combine human smuggling with other forms of illicit trade and trafficking to create an even more pernicious and violent smuggling ecosystem in which migrants are vulnerable and therefore subject to greater abuse.

The end result is an increase in people who are forcibly recruited into drug trafficking, prostitution, indentured servitude, or are held captive for a second payday in the form of kidnap-for-ransom and extortion. Even worse, those who find themselves in these situations are much less likely to go to the police, because the victim in these cases is also considered a criminal and often treated as such.

The Zetas cartel, for example, decided to exploit the vulnerability of migrants by using industrial-scale kidnapping to generate additional revenue. The territory under their control in eastern Mexico is one of the busiest corridors for migrants from the Northern Triangle moving towards the United States. In an effort to diversify their business portfolio, the Zetas began policing these routes and abducting huge groups of migrants from buses and trains. A 2009 report by the Mexican National Human Rights Commission estimated that 10,000 people were kidnapped in a six-month period. These hostages were then taken to ranches, brutally beaten, and starved until their families paid ransoms for their release. On average, $2,000 was paid per migrant, which, if estimates are correct, equates to $20 million in revenue in only half a year. This practice continues to this day with minimal interference, as the drug cartels intimidate and kill both journalists and prosecutors brave enough to investigate.[26]

The kidnapping for ransom phenomenon is by no means exclusive to Mexico and the Americas. A similar narrative played out in the Sinai in the period between 2009 and 2013, when those fleeing the Horn of Africa through Egypt had little choice but to hire smugglers, who turned out to be traffickers. Described in chilling detail in the Human Rights Watch report entitled 'I Wanted to Lie Down and Die', smugglers from the Bedouin and Rashaida tribes systematically engaged in what might be the most hideous exploitation of migrants on record.[27]

Migrants from the Horn of Africa, most often Eritreans, were kidnapped and held for ransom in 'torture camps' where they were subject to physical and psychological torture, including beatings, rape and being forced to sleep in open graves containing dead bodies. Kidnappers used their suffering to extort families and diaspora communities for enormous ransoms of up to $50,000 per person. The practice, which is estimated to have claimed between 25,000 and 35,000 victims, of whom more than 40 per cent were under eighteen, is said to have earned $600 million over a four-year period, bankrupting entire villages and perpetuating cycles of poverty, vulnerability and despair.[28] Those for whom ransoms went unpaid were forced into debt bondage, sexual slavery, or trafficked for their organs and murdered.

Sixty per cent of those recorded had passed through one torture camp controlled by a Bedouin trafficker of the Hedara tribe, an ethnic group with a large population in Saudi Arabia. Despite his name and location being known to the Egyptian authorities, and the majority of the ransoms being paid via Western Union or MoneyGram to Saudi Arabia or Israel, the case was never investigated. Instead, the practice ended when the Egyptian military launched an aerial bombing campaign against the villages where the practice was most concentrated— not to free the migrants, but to crack down on possible terrorist groups in the region. Once the traffickers fled, the migrants were not rescued, but left to find their own way to safety and support.[29]

Practices such as these are already visible on and within Europe's borders. Since the signing of the EU–Turkey deal and the closing of borders across the Balkans there has been a marked increase in the brutality of the smuggling groups. The director of a Serbian NGO providing frontline support to migrants crossing the Balkans told me she receives migrants covered in cuts and bruises, having been beaten by police and smugglers alike. Worse yet, she reported that every woman[30] she saw who had come with a smuggler had been raped, including girls as young as twelve. In some cases the violation was filmed so that it could be sold on the internet as pornography, another illicit business in which the groups are actively involved. The NGO documented cases of sexual extortion in which smugglers would send nude photos of children to family members back in the country of origin and demand more money before taking the children, as originally promised, over the border.[31]

Not only do these acts of violence exponentially compound the misery of the migrants during their journey, it forces them into impossible choices. The abuse and suffering they have experienced, like all traumas, has long-term consequences for which the EU's short-term policies rarely account. Those who have been raped, beaten and tortured on their way to Europe arrive with significant mental health problems, for which countries offering them asylum will have to devote adequate resources.

In essence, European policy has created a vicious cycle: fear of security threats and migrant deaths lead to calls for border controls and intensified action against people smugglers; which leads to more militarised anti-smuggling measures and tougher borders, which leads to smuggling under more dangerous conditions, which in turn leads to even more migrant deaths and even more profound security challenges within EU borders. Violence and abuse is not a necessary part of the migrant-smuggling industry, but militant approaches by states mean that that smuggling is pushed into the hands of organised crime or that groups become more organised, sophisticated and violent themselves. A longitudinal study of Haitian and Cuban migrants showed clearly how the level of violence inflicted onto migrants, and between smuggling groups, correlated exactly with the extent to which national government policies favoured securitised approaches.[32]

Faced with enormous prevailing demand, and in the absence of safe and legal alternatives, these militarised border strategies and rigid immigration controls do little other than enrich and empower migrant smugglers. Instead of taking a long-term view, the European Commission and its national leaders have largely sought instruments for migrant control rather than measures for migrant integration. Many policymakers have begrudgingly arrived at these policies in order to protect the idea of the Schengen zone against the current tide of nationalism. But this short-sightedness in the name of political expediency may well backfire when it comes to national security. Hypocritically, the EU and UN have often warned refugee-hosting nations that insufficient support for refugee populations and self-interested deployment of resources can lead to issues of chronic non-integration and insecurity.[33]

Realistically, the €6 billion EU–Turkey deal is a stop-gap measure. It may stem the tide of migrants temporarily, but it cannot do so forever. Should it survive the myriad of legal challenges it is currently facing, the deal will eventually be exposed for what it is: a political pay-off. Support for the 2.2 million refugees displaced within Turkey's borders will continue to fall well short of the amounts deemed necessary by international humanitarian organisations. Meanwhile, none of the underlying security, political or economic motivations underpinning the mass movement of people into Europe are any closer to being resolved.

As smugglers become increasingly necessary, both for refugees seeking safety and economic migrants seeking opportunity, the power dynamics between migrants and smugglers shifts further in favour of the smuggler, all but guaranteeing that the industry becomes more exploitative and abusive. In order to save migrants from exploitation, prevent their own citizens from turning to criminality and deny existing criminal networks from tapping into a new, unprecedented revenue stream, European countries should learn from the failed efforts at immigration control in other parts of the globe. Perhaps the biggest lesson, and one that many are unwilling to acknowledge even in the face of overwhelming evidence, is that a completely different set of policy responses is needed.

The first step towards solving the problem is diagnosing the problem, and in order to do so policymakers must recognise that there is a new global paradigm when it comes to migration. In this new world, a world we created, existing strategies of border control do more harm than good.

Closing an Industry: Supply and Demand

In the introduction to this book we promised neither a call to action nor an expression of moral outrage. We set out to explain, through a blend of policy analysis and reporting from the field, how migrant-smuggling networks are facilitating an unprecedented flow of people from Africa, Asia and the Middle East into Europe. We hope that those who have reached this far in our narrative have a better understanding of how these networks are structured, how they operate, and how they adapt.

By now, we hope readers recognise that within the context of the mass movement of people to Europe, there is no one single smuggling industry. Instead, there are several local markets, serviced by a vast network of actors, that combine to enable transnational movement. In each of the key migration 'hubs' along the myriad of routes to Europe, smuggling markets have evolved—and continue to evolve—in response to demand for smuggling services. Their forms and structure are shaped by interlocking sets of local conditions, which are often very specific to the socio-political or economic realities of the people living and working in that environment. At the same time, such is the nature of globalisation that systemic shocks reverberate from the centres of global power all the way to far-flung smuggling hubs on the edges of the international system, and vice versa. Smuggling networks, therefore, are at once hyperlocal and global.

This analysis comes at a time when European policymakers and powerful actors within the international community are desperately searching for solutions to the current 'migration crisis'. Yet, as we have argued in Part 1, many of the underlying drivers of this recent mass migration into Europe represent not a confluence of extreme circumstances, but an irreversible paradigm shift that is challenging the very norms and institutions that govern our international system.

In this last section, rather than evade some of the policy questions presented by this new reality, we conclude by identifying some of the possible means by which the international community can manage refugee flows and irregular migration without empowering professional criminal networks that are detrimental to all concerned.

As we have demonstrated, migrant-smuggling economies develop primarily in response to demand—a need or desire by people to move illegally across borders. Therefore, like many contemporary transnational threats, the problems of migrant smuggling and irregular migration are not ones that states can expect to police their way out of. In fact, security-first and security-exclusive strategies, whether they manifest themselves in the form of warships, border patrols or criminal investigations, are benign symbolic gestures at best, and counterproductive measures with far-reaching negative repercussions at worst.

Herein lies the challenge of responding to human smuggling: the current tendency is to view it first and foremost as a crime. Its place within UNTOC, the UN's convention on organised crime, reinforces this proclivity. Accordingly, the inclination among policymakers and law-enforcement officials is to respond to human smuggling with the full weight of the criminal justice arsenal: policing, prosecutions, border control and barriers. As the case studies outlined in this book have illustrated, demand for smuggler services increases whenever barriers to migration become greater. As smugglers become more necessary, the amounts that they can charge for their services and the extent to which they can exploit their clients increase. Thus, a purely criminal justice response to human smuggling only serves to strengthen the very industry it is trying to undermine, enhancing the criminality of networks and increasing the vulnerability of its victims.

Instead, policymakers must acknowledge that human smuggling is a business that operates in a market, and requires a comprehensive response. Such responses need to pragmatically bring to bear a range of economic and political incentives that address both sides of the equation: demand (the migrant) and supply (the smuggler).

Messaging to the Market

While we are broadly critical of the EU–Turkey deal and its implications for human rights, the deal did succeed in sending a clear signal to the smuggling networks that they could not continue with business as usual. Even those critical of the arrangement acknowledge that a message needed to be delivered, given that 885,000 people used the Aegean route in 2015, and the number of Afghan migrants arriving in

Greece was exceeding Syrians by January 2016. The willingness of European states to accept refugees notwithstanding, the flow of irregular migrants into Greece from Turkey had become unmanageable, with nationalities from all over the world joining the rush to Europe.

Legality and morality aside, the effectiveness of the EU–Turkey deal rests in its emulation of the Australian model. Both schemes make a clear distinction between what protections and procedures will be afforded to those arriving illegally (rapid deportation) versus those who follow the 'proper' channels for seeking asylum. Where the deal is weak, however, is in its execution. The EU was neither able to establish a rapid and robust means for assessing the legitimacy of asylum claims closer to source countries, nor was it able to create a safe return option for those arriving illegally.

The principle of non-refoulement means that no asylum seeker should be returned to a place where their safety and human rights cannot be guaranteed—and in several cases, Turkey has been deemed unable to guarantee those rights.

By May 2016, two months after the deal came into effect, Greece had yet to return a single person, and Greek authorities had only rejected 30 per cent of the asylum claims they had processed, falling far short of policymakers' expectations.[34] When a Greek court of appeal declared, as it did in late May 2016, that a deportation order for a LGBT Syrian man was unlawful, the credibility of the EU's capacity to see through its threat was substantially undermined.[35] Subsequently, several other legal challenges have further called into question the durability of the agreement. Therefore, the EU's inability to actually implement its own policy has reduced even the symbolic value of its actions. Even if the EU were to reach an agreement with source and transit countries that is legally and morally sound, smuggling networks now operate under the assumption that Europe is unable or unwilling to actually implement its own policies.

Another means of signalling to the smuggling industry that they cannot operate with impunity is through symbolic prosecutions. We emphasise, however, that the value of these prosecutions in most of these cases is in their symbolism, not their ability to actually hinder the operations of smuggling networks. As we have noted a number of times throughout this narrative, in the key smuggling hubs throughout the globe the industry that surrounds the illicit movement of people towards Europe is vast, consisting of tens of thousands of migrants. Arresting everyone implicated in the industry would be impossible, and the majority of those that law enforcement will be able to arrest and prosecute—such as recruiters and transporters—are operating at the lowest levels. These actors are the least skilled and are easily replaceable. Much as in the fight against drug trafficking, a criminal-justice-driven response will result only in overburdening the justice and penitentiary systems, with little impact on the market as a whole.

Prosecutions can be used as an effective strategy within a broader set of responses, however, when they signal to the rest of the smugglers in the industry that law enforcement is capable of prosecuting them and that being caught leads to serious penalties. Where possible, a limited number of arrests of mid-level and controlling members of smuggling groups, coupled with the impounding of boats or cars, asset seizures of profits and the competent dismantling of their crew can send a strong message and increase the costs of doing business. Finding ways to amplify that message across multiple hubs in combination with other actions could take the wind out of the sails of many operators, and would certainly knock the most opportunistic players out of the market.

But such measures cannot be the only strategy, as the shock effect of prosecutions diminishes over time, and criminal groups tend to be very effective at transferring risk to the most expendable members of their networks, while the more competent actors maintain a lofty distance. Furthermore, as we have reiterated on several occasions throughout this book, if law-enforcement measures make the smuggling environment more challenging, established and more violent criminal organisations are likely to move in, filling in gaps in the market once occupied by opportunists and criminal entrepreneurs. These scenarios not only place migrants in greater danger, they help create a criminal infrastructure within source, transit and destination countries that can be even more challenging to eradicate in the long term.

A further word of caution is that while successful prosecutions can be used to great effect to signal serious intent, unsuccessful criminal justice responses can send the opposite message. One of the challenges in addressing transnational crime effectively, particularly in more frag-ile states with weak institutions, is the extent to which corruption at all levels is often a central component of illicit economies. If enough boats or trucks continue to get through, the border will always appear porous. If enough arrests are waived without prosecution, enough cases dismissed for nebulous reasons, or enough convictions made but with penalties that are a mere slap on the wrist, then criminal justice institutions and the rule of law are actually undermined rather than reinforced, and an atmosphere of impunity results.

Worse yet is the prospect of high-profile embarrassment, such as the unfortunate case in June 2016 of Medhanie Tesfamariam Kidane, an Eritrean accused of being a 'smuggling kingpin' in an Italian investigation dubbed Glauco. Kidane was reportedly the organiser of a fateful crossing from Libya to Lampedusa in October 2013, which led to the loss of over 300 lives. He stood accused of heading a network that moved mainly Eritrean nationals from Sudan through Libya to Italy. The Italian investigation was expanded to other European police agencies over the next two years, from 2014 to 2016, with thousands of wire-taps, intelligence operations and cooperation with law-enforcement authorities in Sudan and Ethiopia. It finally culminated in the highly celebrated arrest and extradition of Kidane from Khartoum to Italy in May 2016.

Self-satisfied press releases were issued, loudly trumpeting the success. This victorious moment, however, was to be short-lived. Within twenty-four hours, through Meron Estefanos, an NGO interlocutor and advocate from the Eritrean diaspora, it became apparent that the authorities had arrested the wrong man. Instead of taking Medhanie Tesfamarian Kidane, the European police, under the guidance of Sudanese authorities, had apparently extradited a young Eritrean refugee named Medhanie Yehdego Mered, who bore the same first name. Photographs of 'Kidane' disembarking the plane under police escort quickly showed that the man they had arrested bore little resemblance to the supposed kingpin, and was at least ten years his junior.[36]

As a result of this error, the smuggling networks we had been monitoring and engaging with quickly closed ranks. Previously amenable interlocutors refused to take our calls, suspicious that we might also be intelligence officers. Yet at the same time smuggling went on unabated, and a record number of people were put to sea from Libya in June 2016. The botched investigation sent a message to the smuggling community that the European authorities are not only ineffective and out of their depth, but that interlocutors in general are not to be trusted. Networks have receded further into the shadows, but the migrant flows continue just the same.

Militarisation

One of the primary European responses to the recent influx of migrants is the use of military assets. A succession of naval forces has been deployed under various bodies of command, but all have had the same basic objective: to 'destroy the business model of smugglers', as stated by Frederica Mogherini, the EU's foreign policy chief.[37]

To a certain extent, deploying warships has become the default response to public outcry regarding illicit migration or migrant deaths at sea, especially when they occur too close to European shores. In the spring of 2016, following a weekend with a particularly high number of fatalities in the central Mediterranean, then UK prime minister David Cameron immediately pledged to add additional warships to ongoing EU patrols.[38]

Yet judging the effectiveness of these types of operations is by no means straightforward. Operation Sophia, an EU Common Security and Defence Policy (CSDP) mission which started on 22 June 2015, for example, was lauded by its commanders. Lieutenant-General Wolfgang Wosolsobe, director-general of the European Union Military Staff, cited lives saved and the destruction of boats as indicators of success in combating migrant movement.[39]

Yet the IOM figures suggest that such operations have had little if any impact on the flow of migrants crossing the Mediterranean. It may be that the numbers would have been higher were it not for Operation Sophia, but these counterfactuals are impossible to prove. Furthermore, there is strong evidence to suggest that changes in the numbers of migrant crossings and deaths at sea are more attributable to the seasons than to any European interdiction efforts.[40] A report to the British Parliamentary Select Committee in May 2016, literally entitled 'Operation Sophia: Impossible Challenge', summarised the shortcomings of the operation in frank terms:

> The mission does not, however, in any meaningful way deter the flow of migrants, disrupt the smugglers' networks, or impede the business of people

smuggling on the central Mediterranean route. The arrests that Operation Sophia has made to date have been of low-level targets, while the destruction of vessels has simply caused the smugglers to shift from using wooden boats to rubber dinghies, which are even more unsafe. There are also significant limits to the intelligence that can be collected about onshore smuggling networks from the high seas. There is therefore little prospect of Operation Sophia overturning the business model of people smuggling.[41]

Fundamentally therefore, while the deployment of naval patrols has served as a visible intervention that governments can show to their electorates, it has done little to disrupt human-smuggling networks, and is a sub-optimal solution to saving lives. Furthermore, such operations are an expensive and limited solution given the ability of smuggling networks to change their routes. A naval blockade of the entire 1,770 kilometre Libyan coast is a fantastical suggestion;[42] accounting for departures from across the entire North African coast even more so.

Deployment of military assets along land borders may be marginally more effective, but as the 'postcard' from the United States indicated earlier, it often comes with devastating consequences. Encouraging heavy military deployment to borders may also risk fanning the flames of simmering conflicts and long-standing animosities. Military exercises by the Greek army over the Idomeni camp escalated tensions between Greece and Macedonia, while Turkish patrols over the Aegean island of Oinousses, in Greek airspace, similarly strained diplomatic relations between the two governments.[43] In June 2016 Eritrea and Ethiopia clashed along their shared border, the first major fighting between the two countries in sixteen years, further highlighting the risks of a militarised approach in a region where borders themselves are often contested.[44]

Militarised approaches to border security also have a tendency to go hand in hand with human rights violations. The Turkish, Greek, Hungarian and Macedonian armies, when deployed to their borders, have all been accused of using excessive force against migrants. According to the Syrian Observatory for Human Rights, sixty civilians were killed by the Turkish army in the first half of 2016 trying to cross the border, and in June 2016 eleven refugees including three children were confirmed killed trying to escape Syria and enter Turkey.[45] Human Rights Watch reported that refugees are regularly beaten and shot by the Turkish army as it patrols the now heavily militarised border.[46]

The negative long-term implications of a militarised border-control strategy, therefore, whether on land or sea, often outweigh the ephemeral benefits of reducing migration flows in the short term.

Diplomatic Solutions

Many of the discussions surrounding irregular migration during the most recent 'crisis' have come in the form of bilateral negotiations between states, with more and more governments choosing to assert their sovereign right to decide who is allowed entry into their country.

The challenges associated with managing migration flows are by no means new, yet many long-existing cooperation agreements between pairs of states or sub-regions to allow or restrict the movement of people across national borders have been overwhelmed by the contemporary migration 'crisis'. As EU member states attempt to negotiate with source and transit countries, the policy focus has increasingly boiled down to this single issue of asserting sovereignty in the narrowest terms, with broader development, governance and stability goals being thrown by the wayside.

In a June 2016 communiqué the EU launched a hastily developed New Migration Partnership Framework, which stated: 'The message that migration issues are now at the top of the EU's external relations priorities has not yet been fully communicated to and appreciated by partners.'[47]

Under this Framework, the EU will spend €8 billion over five years on aid to more than a dozen countries in Africa and the Middle East, which, in return, are expected to cooperate in accepting the return of more irregular migrants, to crack down on smugglers, and to improve their migration-management systems more generally.[48] This initiative comes in addition to the €1.8 billion promised under the EU Emergency Trust Fund for Africa, which was launched at the EU–Africa Valletta Summit in November 2015. In the same June 2016 communiqué the EU says it will use its trade, aid and visa policies to reward countries that cooperate, and that 'there must be consequences for those who do not cooperate on readmission and return'.[49]

Maintaining the policymaking dialogue at state level presents a number of challenges, however. Firstly, as our narrative has shown, many of the states where the migrants and refugees originate, and where the major smuggling hubs exist, are either mired in conflict and crisis or are critically weak with minimal institutional capacity. While Niger, for example, may claim that with €1 billion it would be able to control the flow of people through its vast desert north, it is highly questionable whether it could in fact do so.[50] The nation has received far greater sums over more than a decade to counter terrorism and build up state institutions, but the results have been negligible.[51]

Negotiating such agreements with stronger states may prove more effective, but pose different problems. As the EU–Turkey deal has highlighted, making migration control conditional on the promise of funding and development assistance effectively leaves the EU open to blackmail. In the six months following the signing of the agreement, Turkish president Recep Erdoğan has repeatedly threatened to withdraw from the agreement if the EU's promised commitments on visa liberalisation are not expedited, despite the country's refusal to meet the EU's requirements on pivotal issues such as its anti-terror laws.[52]

The negotiations around the Horn of Africa's Khartoum Process have taken a similar turn. Established in 2014 under the EU–Africa partnership, the initiative brings together the EU's twenty-eight member states with six Horn of Africa states plus Egypt and Tunisia to address human trafficking, smuggling and irregular migration.[53] The negotiation process reveals that the nature of this dialogue consists of lengthy 'train and equip' shopping lists for state security institutions, with no agreement on monitoring its implementation or measuring its impact. Experts and human rights advocates have described the agreement as 'foxes guarding the henhouse'.[54]

The repressive policies of authoritarian regimes of several parties to the Khartoum Process, such as Sudan and Eritrea, are significant drivers of irregular migration and asylum seeking in the first place. Building their capacity to police their borders at any cost is likely only to exacerbate the root causes of migration, the human rights implications notwithstanding. Furthermore, such measures provide the wrong incentives, making it more advantageous for states to keep their displaced populations in highly visible camps than to find productive long-term integration options within the region.[55] The Kidane affair also called into question the extent to which European authorities can expect reliable cooperation from states such as Sudan, and reinforced the need to consider the vested interests of states, migrants and the smugglers themselves in crafting appropriate policy responses to migrant smuggling.

Finally, as we have demonstrated in previous chapters, the smuggling industry is deeply interwoven with ethnic and political groups that live on the margins of their states and societies. In some cases these are groups also engaged in long-term separatist struggles against a central state, such as the Tuareg in Mali or the Kurds in Turkey. In others, smuggling is facilitated by the marginalised and oppressed, such as the Toubou in Chad, Libya and Niger, or the Amazigh in Libya, whose exclusion from political expression and resource sharing have led them to depend on illicit trades as an income and resilience strategy. In both cases, if the governments in question had the ability or the inclination to address the underlying issues prompting these groups to form a symbiotic relationship with the smuggling industry, would they not have done so already? In cases where the politics of identity and marginalisation is a dominant force, exclusive engagement with the central state and funnelling additional resources into state institutions is beyond counter-productive.

Vested Interests

As we noted in the introduction, it is easy to lose sight, amid the heated rhetoric and polemics of the current migration debate, of the fact that migration is almost universally a positive phenomenon. For refugees it is a lifeline, but for almost all migrants it is a chance to find opportunities that do not exist at home. Source countries benefit from remittances sent back to local communities. Towns serving as hubs in transit countries benefit from being situated along major migration routes. The smugglers themselves often have profiles not dissimilar to their clients, and the livelihood earned from facilitating illicit movement often builds resilience for themselves and their families. Despite being vilified in the European media, migrants are a net positive for destination countries, playing a crucial role in supporting and invigorating economies with ageing populations and deficits in the labour force.

CONCLUSION

The goal, therefore, should not be to limit migration, but to untangle the aspirations of people who wish to migrate from the worst elements of the smuggling industry, which facilitates and encourages their movement illegally, and often puts migrants at risk. There is no silver bullet or a one-size-fits-all solution. Quite the contrary; responding effectively requires several sets of creative and nuanced engagements with various different actors.

In each hub, and along each major route, the smuggling market needs to be analysed for its unique political economy in order to understand the motivations of those moving through the route, those engaged in the trade, those who protect it, and those who are profiting. These types of analysis are critical in understanding the vested interests of different actors. They are the key to engaging the industry effectively.

Political economy analyses also highlight why states may not be the ideal counterpart for stemming migration. For many of the major source countries, especially those in sub-Saharan Africa and the Middle East, migration contributes to economic growth and stability through the remittances sent home. In West Africa, for example, after foreign direct investment (FDI), remittances from migrants are often the region's largest source of foreign inflows and a powerful driver of development linked to reductions in poverty, improved health and education outcomes, and increases in business investments.[56] In Nigeria, whose citizens consistently rank in the top five nationalities arriving in Europe, remittances were worth $21 billion in 2015—a level of resources that no European government can hope to match. Furthermore, with the levels of corruption greasing the wheels of the smuggling industry, individual officials are unlikely to enable or encourage anti-migration policies that will harm their own payoffs.

Instead, a more granular level of analysis that examines the interests and incentives of sub-national groups would allow policymakers to identify leverage points that are focused on local political and economic dynamics. For example, rather than providing generic development assistance to be allocated by national governments, interventions could target specific groups involved in facilitating smuggling. Development resources would then be allocated according to their priorities, rather than those of central governments.

A financial flows analysis would help to identify the priorities of each group. For example, for groups engaged in smuggling in the Sahel, the majority of profits are invested in their own communities and livelihoods: livestock, housing, cars, dowries, medicines for family members and education for children. Here, well-crafted, sustainable development investments could provide an alternative to those groups. Many of the smugglers we interviewed in Turkey were former refugees, and the funds they earned went to supporting and sustaining wives and children because they received nothing from the state and the international community.

By contrast, some smuggling groups in Libya have reinvested their profits to build up militias in order to capture a greater share of the political market and amplify their voices in negotiations. Within this context, investing sufficient time and resources into internationally sponsored political dialogue, calibrated to the local economic and political realities, would be a more strategic investment than the untold millions spent deploying warships in the Mediterranean to minimal effect.

This kind of analysis also suggests what will happen when and if the demand for smugglers is successfully closed down, as it has been, for example and at least temporarily, by the EU–Turkey deal. A smuggler we interviewed in Turkey in May 2016 predicted darkly: 'It has a very negative impact on the smugglers, and on the people in Turkey. These people don't have money any more. And as a result, the number of robberies will increase, the number of homicides will also increase, we will have more mafia groups appearing because there is no other way of earning money.' When in June 2016 we asked a Toubou smuggler in Agadez what he would do if the flow of migrants was to stop, he cheerfully responded: 'We would go back to war, and to kidnapping white people.' The many positives migration can bring, and the potential negatives that can result from supressing the market, must also be built into policy choices about how to address the industry.

Political economy analyses may ultimately result in the conclusion that there is no good intervention to be made, a finding that is valuable in itself. In certain contexts, if the drivers and vested interests are well understood by policymakers, then perhaps the best possible action is to monitor the situation, minimise the most negative outcomes, and wait until a change in the status quo presents an opportunity for nuanced interventions. A similar conclusion might be to pursue policies that engage other hubs along the same migration route and or target specific components of the smuggling value chain, while allowing others to continue.

On the Demand Side

In the long term, however, measuring the effectiveness of efforts to close down the smuggling industry, and mitigate the most negative dimensions of it, must be analysed within the context of the current scale of contemporary mobility. The only true way to eliminate the supply side of the smuggling industry is to drastically reduce demand.

The natural response from the refugee protection and human rights communities has been to argue that the only sustainable path to breaking the business model of human smuggling is to provide 'safe and legal routes', a phrase often repeated by the champions of the 1951 Refugee Convention.[57] While they are correct that more legal avenues would reduce the need for smugglers, and would probably enhance the safety of those seeking refuge, opening up safe and legal channels is by no means a panacea.

Safe and legal routes are, at best, a small and largely procedural response to refugee-producing situations such as the civil war in Syria. What is required in these contexts, however, is not just a safe path for those fleeing war and persecution, but opportunities for them to lead productive, fulfilling lives upon escape. Syrians seeking refuge in Europe are doing so in response to the international community's failure to provide them with any meaningful prospects of a better future after years of lingering in camps in Jordan and Lebanon and living in the shadows in Turkey and Egypt. The enormous wave of secondary movement is driven by a lack of dignity, rather than the absence of 'safe and legal' routes out of Syria.

In addition, the 'safe and legal routes' argument does not address the issue of predominantly economic migrants for whom the smuggling industry has served as a vector. The vocabulary used to describe Europe's recent experience with migration, consisting almost exclusively of terms such as 'migrant crisis' and 'refugee emergency', has steered policy discussions towards privileging short-term, politically expedient measures.

These flawed terminologies have obscured the extent to which Europe's 'migration crisis' is not a temporary condition, but actually an acute symptom of a larger phenomenon that is better understood as a new paradigm. Structural realities of global poverty, inequality and demography are challenging existing frameworks as well as commonly understood norms of trade and development in ways that should not be underestimated and cannot be ignored.[58]

A recent report by Oxfam entitled 'An Economy for the 1%' found that 1 per cent of the world's population have more wealth than the rest put together. The wealth of a mere sixty-two individuals is equal to that of the bottom half of the global population.[59] Despite global economic gains, global wealth is not equally realised.[60] Even among the more than a billion people who have been lifted out of extreme poverty since 1990 the desire to migrate is still strong, and recent research suggests that emigration actually rises with economic development, at least until countries reach upper-middle-income levels, which means that development assistance to low-income countries is unlikely to deter migration.[61]

Populations in North America, Europe and parts of East Asia are rapidly ageing, and experiencing labour shortages in their workforces. At the same time, the working-age populations of North Africa, sub-Saharan Africa, the Middle East and parts of Asia have been soaring and will continue to rise rapidly between now and 2050.[62] Countries in sub-Saharan Africa have the youngest populations in the world, with over 70 per cent of their populations below the age of thirty.[63] These demographic pressures come at a time when local economies are failing to provide viable livelihood opportunities for large numbers of their citizens, especially youth populations. In 2013 almost 75 million fifteen- to twenty-four-year-olds were unemployed, representing 38 per cent of the global unemployed.[64]

Beyond being likely candidates to migrate in search of opportunity, large pools of unemployed and underemployed youth have demonstrated a higher propensity towards both criminal behaviour and political violence, which in turn act as catalysts of forced displacement.[65] Migration, therefore, has inherently become one of the key 'solutions' to stability and global inequality in the twenty-first century.[66]

Around the globe, improvements in information and communication technology have highlighted inequalities more clearly. The have-nots are more aware than ever of how the more fortunate live, fuelling aspirations to enjoy the same lifestyles as those they interact with in other parts of the world. These technologies that connect us are the same tools that allow aspiring migrants to realise their ambitions. A self-reinforcing infrastructure of diaspora networks, frictionless remittance flows, and the ability to communicate with communities around the world at almost no cost have created and reinforced cultures of migration. They enable smugglers, but they also provide a means by which irregular migrants can better secure their own safety by making more informed decisions.[67]

For more than a decade migration experts have argued that the price of defending the European fortress from refugee and migrant arrivals is much higher than the costs of promoting prosperity and managing, rather than limiting, migrant flows.[68] Yet in response to the most recent influx of migrants, Europe and its allies have doubled-down on short-sighted policies that are more costly and less effective in the long term.

There is no escaping the fact that for an increasing number of people, livelihoods and economies are being organised according to trans-national paradigms that may involve dispersed families and multiple relocations over the course of a lifetime.[69] We have moved past the point as a global community where the desire to move in search of opportunities can be contained or reversed. All indications suggest that, if anything, the movement of peoples is set to increase. Therefore, the pragmatic next step is to see how migration can be managed, to the benefit of both migrants and host communities.

Proactive and open-minded strategies will require the unpacking of some long-standing attitudes around migration and the development of policies that may not be immediately popular with electorates in Europe. There is already a strong evidence basis that many of the core assumptions surrounding migration are no longer correct.

While it is still widely assumed that migration is predominantly a movement from the Global South to the developed North, for example, there is considerable evidence that the majority of migratory flows remain within the immediate region of source countries. Development investments, therefore, need to provide greater incentives for inter-regional migration. This support would address issues of security and development in the major cities of the Global South, but would also include addressing infrastructure requirements within regions, allowing equitable economic growth and regional trade, rather than maintaining a persistent focus on 'Western' markets.

A second assumption that needs to be jettisoned is the idea that migration is necessarily a one-way journey. Instead, there is mounting evidence that communities are adopting transnational lifestyles in which both labour and capital are constantly on the move. Future migration polices, which guarantee human rights protections and enforce labour standards, will have to be calibrated to this new reality of highly mobile, transnational communities. Failure to do so will drive migrants into the hands of smugglers.

For refugee movements triggered by violence, crisis and conflict, a more proactive and sustained commitment of support for neighbouring countries is essential. The drawdown of humanitarian assistance and the lack of long-term strategies for displaced populations has contributed to self-managed secondary migration and undermined the capacity of the international community to protect vulnerable populations.

Thankfully, a number of innovative dialogues concerning how to better manage refugee situations are currently taking place, and financial backing for experimentation should be encouraged. That said, support for displaced populations is likely to remain woefully inadequate for the foreseeable future, which means that demand for secondary movement, and corresponding demand for smuggler services, is likely to remain high.

A final assumption that needs to be abandoned, and one we have challenged throughout this book, is the concept of a smuggler as a nefarious character who must be stopped at all costs. While there are countless cases of smugglers who mistreat their clients, and traffickers whose only goal is to exploit their victims, our conversations with migrants and smugglers, further reinforced by what other researchers have found the world over, is that many of the men and women who facilitate the illicit movement of people are to be viewed on the spectrum between faceless service providers and heroes.

Many of the smugglers we spoke with were proud to be part of networks that save people from war and persecution. Who would not want to be part of an industry that reunites families and gives people hope, access to education and medical treatment? For some smugglers there is little else available that would offer the same financial returns, but the social returns—adventure, a sense of purpose, the thrill of risk-taking—are also rewarding. In many cases the idealism that drives them is identical to that of the young, ambitious aid and humanitarian workers one meets along the same smuggling trails.

In short, the time has come to recognise that when addressing irregular migration and migrant smuggling, simple dichotomies of good and bad, right and wrong, deserving and undeserving are a dangerous fallacy. The migrant crisis has only reinforced the fact that humans today live in a complex web of interdependencies, where long histories of interaction between peoples and nations have interwoven to bring us to our current state of global affairs.

Not everyone will welcome these new realities, nor should they be forced to, but nostalgia is not a policy, and it is no way to govern. Fighting for a return to an idealised status quo ante, a past that was never as good or as righteous as memory serves, is a blueprint for creating a world we do not want to live in. The time has come to open our minds and elevate the discourse so that we may find a pragmatic way forward; to create a world in which the most vulnerable can find their own place, and where, to find refuge and opportunity, one needs neither a smuggler nor a saviour.

NOTES

1. SMUGGLERS NEEDED

1. Matina Stevis and Joe Parkinson, 'Thousands Flee Isolated Eritrea to Escape Life of Conscription and Poverty', *Wall Street Journal*, 2 Feb. 2016: http://www.wsj.com/articles/eritreans-flee-conscription-and-poverty-adding-to-the-migrant-crisis-in-europe-1445391364

2. Regional Mixed Migration Secretariat, *Country Profile Eritrea*: http://www.regionalmms.org/index.php?id=14

3. In a survey undertaken with migrants from Ethiopia, a country far more open than neighbouring Eritrea, migrants were asked what behaviours they would tolerate from their smuggler without changing their migration plans: 44 per cent said degrading treatment and verbal abuse; 35 per cent said mild physical abuse; 33 per cent said extortion and robbery; 7 per cent said kidnapping for ransom; and 1 per cent said rape. Regional Mixed Migration Secretariat, *Blinded by Hope: Knowledge, Attitudes and Practices of Ethiopian Migrants*, Nairobi: RMMS, 2014.

4. For the clear explanation of refugee policy over the past few decades, we owe a debt of gratitude to Jeff Crisp, former Head of Policy and Evaluation at UNHCR. He patiently submitted to multiple discussions on the subject, whilst freely sharing his own prolific analysis.

5. Jeff Crisp, 'Local Integration and Local Settlement of Refugees: A Conceptual and Historical Analysis', *New Issues in Refugee Research*, no. 102, Geneva: UNHCR, April 2004.

6. UNHCR, *World at War: UNHCR Global Trends*, Geneva: UNHCR, January 2015.

7. Jeff Crisp, 'An End to Exile? Refugee Agency and the Search for Durable Solutions', *IDS Bulletin*, Brighton: Institute for Development Studies, 2016.

8. UNHCR, *Global Trends: Forced Displacement in 2015*, Geneva: UNHCR, June 2016.

9. Ibid.

10. Statement by François Crépeau, Special Rapporteur on the human rights of migrants at the 29th Session of the United Nations Human Rights Council, 15 June 2015: http://destination-unknown.org/wp-content/uploads/Statement_Francois_Crepeau.pdf

11. Ratifications as of 31 December 2015: https://treaties.un.org/pages/ViewDetailsII.aspx?src=TREATY&mtdsg_no=V-2&chapter=5&Temp=mtdsg2&lang=en

12. Asylum Access, *Global Refugee Work Rights Report*, Oakland, CA: Asylum Access, 2015: http://asylumaccess.org/wp-content/uploads/2014/09/FINAL_Global-Refugee-Work-Rights-Report-2014_Interactive.pdf

13. IOM, *World Migration Report 2015*, Geneva: IOM, 2015: http://publications.iom.int/system/files/wmr2015_en.pdf

14. The Migrants' Files, The money trails, June 2015: www.themigrantsfiles.com

15. Katy Long, 'Extending protection? Labour migration and durable solutions for refugees', *New Issues in Refugee Research*, no. 176, Geneva: UNHCR, 2009.

16. The fluid nature of Afghan identity, residence and legal status is neatly summarised in Daniel Kronenfeld, 'Afghan Refugees in Pakistan: Not All Refugees, Not Always in Pakistan, Not Necessarily Afghan', *Journal of Refugee Studies* 21, 1 (2008): 43–63: http://jrs.oxfordjournals.org/content/21/1/43.abstract.

17. The resilience strategies of the Sahel are well captured in Judith Scheele, 'Traders, Saints and Irrigation: Reflections on Saharan Connectivity', *Journal of African History* 51 (Cambridge University Press, 2010): 281–300, p. 282.

18. European Commission, *Study on the Smuggling of Migrants: Characteristics, Responses and Cooperation with Third Countries*, Brussels: European Commission, September 2015: http://ec.europa.eu/dgs/home-affairs/what-we-do/networks/european_migration_network/reports/docs/emn-studies/study_on_smuggling_of_migrants_final_report_master_091115_final_pdf.pdf

2. SMUGGLERS INC.

1. *Protocol against the Smuggling of Migrants by Land, Sea and Air*, supplementing the United Nations Convention against Transnational Organised Crime, art. 3(a).

2. *Protocol to Prevent, Suppress and Punish Trafficking in Persons, Especially Women and Children*, supplementing the United Nations Convention against Transnational Organised Crime, art. 3(a).

3. David Crouch, 'Danish Children's Rights Activist Fined for People Trafficking', *The Guardian*, 11 March 2016: http://www.theguardian.com/world/2016/mar/11/danish-childrens-rights-activist-lisbeth-zornig-people-trafficking

4. Imogen Brennan, 'Migrant Crisis: Man Faces Five Years in Jail for Attempting to Smuggle 4 Year Old from Calais "Jungle Camp" into the UK', ABC News, 7 January 2016: http://www.abc.net.au/news/2016–01–07/man-attempted-smuggling-4yo-refugee-into-uk-faces-jail-time/7073616

5. Khalid Khoser, 'The Economics of Migrant Smuggling', *Refugee Transitions (Summer 2009)*, Geneva: Geneva Centre for Security Policy, 2009.

6. John Salt and Jeremy Stein, 'Migration as a Business: The Case of Trafficking', *International Migration* 35:469 (1997): 467–94.

7. Ibid., p. 470.

8. UNODC, *Smuggling of Migrants: A Global Review*, Vienna: United Nations, 2010.

9. The full package has been described in a number of publications, including UNODC, *Smuggling of Migrants*, and Tuesday Reitano, 'Human Smuggling from West Africa to Europe', in *Illicit Financial Flows: Criminal Economies in West Africa*, OECD/AfDB, Paris: OECD Publishing, 2016, and has been well documented in studies in Asia, Latin America and Africa. It was confirmed as being relevant to smuggling networks bringing people to Europe in interviews conducted by the authors with European security and law-enforcement professionals in May and June 2015.

10. Khoser, 'The Economics of Migrant Smuggling'.

11. It is only 87 kilometres between Damascus and Beirut, and the same distance between the highly embattled city of Homs in Syria and Tripoli, Beirut's northernmost city.

12. Garret Barkley Clark, 'A New Mediterranean Mafia? An Examination of the Illicit Organizations Profiting from the European Migrant Crisis', MA thesis, Georgetown University, April 2016.

13. 'Group for Smuggling Routes by Land and Sea', September–November 2015: https://www.facebook.com/groups/866986486742355/

14. Interview with a migration analyst focusing on Afghanistan–Pakistan migration, February 2016.

15. Found on an Arabic-language Facebook page in July 2015: https://www.facebook.com/permalink.php?story_fbid=797738280340213&id=780020912111950

16. Frontex, *Annual Risk Assessment 2016*, Warsaw: Frontex, 2016.

17. European Commission, *Study on the Smuggling of Migrants*.

18. Stephen Ellis, *The Role of Organised Crime in the Smuggling of Migrants from West Africa to the European Union*, Vienna: United Nations Office on Drugs and Crime, 2011.

19. Christopher Horwood, *In Pursuit of the Southern Dream: Victims of Necessity, Assessment of the Irregular Movement of Men from East Africa and the Horn to South Africa*, Geneva: IOM, 2009.

20. Khoser, 'The Economies of Migrant Smuggling', p. 12.

21. Melanie Petros, *The Costs of Human Smuggling and Trafficking*, London: Migration Research Centre, University College London, 2005.

22. European Commission, *Study on the Smuggling of Migrants*.

23. Emma Herman, 'Migration as a Family Business: The Role of Personal Networks in the Mobility Phase of Migration', *International Migration* 44 (2006): 191–230, at p. 191.

24. Jeff Crisp, *Policy Challenges of the New Diasporas: Migrant Networks and their Impacts on Asylum Flows and Regimes*, Geneva: UNHCR, 1999; Jacob Townsend and Cristel Oomen, *Before the Boat: Understanding the Migrant Journey*, Brussels: Migration Policy Institute Europe, 2015.

25. Hein de Haas, *Migration System Formation and Decline: A Theoretical Inquiry into the Self-perpetuating and Self-Undermining Dynamics of Migration Processes*, IMI working paper 19, Oxford: International Migration Institute, University of Oxford, 2009.

26. David Kyle and Marc Scarcelli, 'Migrant Smuggling and the Violence Question: Evolving Illicit Migration Markets for Cuban and Haitian Refugees', *Crime, Law and Social Change* 52 (2009): 297–311.

27. UNODC, *Smuggling of Migrants*.

28. Khoser, 'The Economics of Migrant Smuggling'.

29. Since 2005 Nigerians have consistently been one of the nationalities entering illegally into Europe in the greatest numbers, thanks in part to their highly established human smuggling and trafficking networks. For more on how these developed as an integral part of the nation's criminal infrastructure see Stephen Ellis, *This Present Darkness: A History of Nigerian Organised Crime*, London: Hurst & Co., 2016, chapter 9 in particular.

30. World Bank, *Migration and Remittances Factbook 2015*, Washington DC: World Bank, 2015.

31. See, for example, Ronald Skeldon, 'Migration and Development (UN/POP/EGM-MIG/2008/4)', United Nations Expert Group on International Migration and Development in Asia and the Pacific, United Nations, 2008, first presented at the seminar 'People on the Move: International Migration and Development', Santander, Spain, 18–19 August 2008: http://www.un.org/esa/population/meetings/EGM_Ittmig_Asia/P04_Skeldon.pdf

3. STRUCTURE AND DESIGN

1. Rather than cite the myriad of specific case studies and literature that has described the human-smuggling industry, we suggest that you refer back to UNODC, *Smuggling of Migrants*, which provides a comprehensive literature review and further references for study.

2. Over the course of April–September 2015 we conducted 200 interviews with migrants of a variety of nationalities on their experiences being smuggled to Europe. The conclusions and findings of this research can be found in our policy-oriented publication: Tuesday Reitano and Peter Tinti, *Survive and Advance: The Economics of Smuggling Migrants and Refugees into Europe*, Pretoria: Institute for Security Studies, 2015.

3. Luke Harding, 'Police Fear as Many as 50 Migrants Dead Inside Lorry Left by Austrian Motorway', *The Guardian*, 28 August 2015: http://www.theguardian.com/world/2015/aug/27/migrants-found-dead-inside-lorry-in-austria

4. Presentation by the Hungarian prosecutor leading the case, May 2016.

5. This is genuinely a problem for the Swedish authorities, who have reported an exponential rise in Afghan men seeking asylum as minors, but who appear to be clearly over eighteen. It was reported to us in interviews with senior law-enforcement and immigration officials in September 2015, and in May 2016, as well as in their 2015 national police report (read in translation) and in the news, for example: Elisabeth Braw, 'When Underage Refugees Look Anything But', *Foreign Policy*, 13 January 2016: http://foreignpolicy.com/2016/01/13/when-underage-refugees-look-anything-but-age-tests-sweden/

6. Mark Shaw, 'WE PAY, YOU PAY: Protection Economies, Financial Flows and Violence', in Hilary Matfess and Michael Miklaucic (eds.), *Beyond Convergence: World without Order*, Washington DC: National Defense University, 2016.

7. Kyle and Scarcelli, 'Migrant Smuggling and the Violence Question'.

8. *Sahih Bukhari* (810–870 AD), Vol. 3, Book 41, No. 585.

9. Edwina A. Thompson, 'Misplaced Blame: Islam, Terrorism and the. Origins of Hawala', *Max Planck Yearbook of United Nations Law* 11 (2007): 279–305.

10. As estimated by Dr Roger Ballard, director of the University of Manchester's Centre for Applied South Asian Studies (CASAS).

11. FATF, *The Role of Hawala and Other Similar Service Providers in Money Laundering and Terrorist Financing*, Paris: FATF/OECD, 2013.

12. Frontex, *Annual Risk Analysis 2016*.

13. Malcolm Moore, 'Malaysia Airlines Jet: "A Fake Passport? Two Days

and £500, Please'", *The Telegraph*, 10 March 2014: http://www.tele-graph.co.uk/news/worldnews/asia/china/10687899/Malaysia-Airlines-jet-A-fake-passport-Two-days-and-500-please.html

14. Luigi Serenelli, 'EU, Interpol Fight Epidemic of Stolen, Fake Passports', *USA Today*, 21 May 2014: http://www.usatoday.com/story/news/world/2014/05/21/stolen-passports/9351329/

15. European Commission, *Study on the Smuggling of Migrants*.

16. Ibid.

17. Havoscope, 'Fake ID Cards, Drivers Licenses, and Stolen Passports': http://www.havocscope.com/fake-id/

18. Annual Police Report issued by the Swedish Police in 2015 (translated).

19. Serenelli, 'Epidemic of Stolen, Fake Passports'.

20. Agiza Hlongwane and Jeff Wicks, '"White Widow" Paid for SA Passport', IOL, 29 September 2013: http://www.iol.co.za/news/politics/white-widow-paid-for-sa-passport-1584186

21. Richard Greenberg, Adam Ciralsky and Stone Phillips, 'Enemies at the Gate', NBC News, 28 December 2007: http://www.nbcnews.com/id/22419963/ns/dateline_nbc-international/#.Ux4275SHw_k

22. UNODC, *The Role of Organised Crime in the Smuggling of Migrants from West Africa to the European Union*, Vienna: United Nations, 2011.

23. Jeff Goodell, 'How to Fake a Passport', *New York Times*, 10 February 2002: http://www.nytimes.com/2002/02/10/magazine/how-to-fake-a-passport.html

24. Interpol, 'AirAsia Becomes the First Airline to Pilot INTERPOL's I-Checkit System', 13 May 2014: http://www.interpol.int/News-and-media/News/2014/N2014–082

25. Goodell, 'How to Fake a Passport'.

26. 'Officers Seize "Fake" Passports', BBC, 4 July 2007: http://news.bbc.co.uk/2/hi/uk_news/england/london/6269210.stm

27. John Henley, 'How Thailand's Trade in Fake Passports Fuels Crime Gangs around the World', *The Guardian*, 10 March 2014: http://www.theguardian.com/world/2014/mar/10/thailand-trade-fake-passports-crime-gangs-world

28. http://www.theguardian.com/world/2015/sep/08/growing-concern-over-trade-in-fake-and-stolen-syrian-passports

29. Elahe Izadi, 'There's a Booming Black Market for Fake Syrian Passports', *Washington Post*, 21 November 2015: https://www.washingtonpost.com/news/worldviews/wp/2015/11/21/theres-a-booming-black-market-for-fake-syrian-passports/

30. Hurriyet, '1050 Foreign Passports Seized in Istanbul Raids', *Hurriyet Daily*, 3 February 2016: http://www.hurriyetdailynews.com/eight-

suspects-detained-for-migrant-smuggling-in-istanbul.aspx?pageID=238
&nID=94709&NewsCatID=509

31. Anthony Faiola and Souad Mekhennet, 'Nearly a Third of Migrants in Germany Claiming to be Syrians Aren't from Syria', *Washington Post*, 25 September 2015: https://www.washingtonpost.com/world/europe/ germany-calls-for-new-refugee-benefit-standards-in-europe/2015/ 09/25/bee704fe-616d-11e5–8475–781cc9851652_story.html

32. Vladi Vovcuk and Adi Cohen, 'Migrant Crisis Sparks Shopping Frenzy for Black Market Passports', Vocativ, 17 September 2015: http:// www.vocativ.com/231947/syrian-migrants-call-for-self-policing- to-weed-out-fake-ids/

33. From a confidential survey about attitudes towards migration with Afghans, conducted by a private-sector analyst in November 2015.

4. ROUTES

1. Frontex, *Annual Risk Assessment 2016*.

2. Interviews with Norwegian Police Directorate, October 2015, with the Norwegian Special Envoy on Migration in February 2016, and Andrew Higgins, 'Avoiding Risky Seas, Migrants Reach Europe with an Arctic Bike Ride', *New York Times*, 9 October 2015: http://www. nytimes.com/2015/10/10/world/europe/bypassing-the-risky-sea-ref- ugees-reach-europe-through-the-arctic.html

3. World Bulletin, 'Thailand: Transit Point for Smuggling Syrians to Europe', 7 February 2016: http://www.worldbulletin.net/news/169 180/thailand-transit-point-for-smuggling-syrians-to-europe

4. 'Hungary's Borders Trigger a Domino Effect', Reuters, 14 April 2016: http://www.reuters.com/investigates/special-report/migration/ #story/39

5. '15 Arrested in Spain for Smuggling Migrants from Morocco', the Local.es, 30 August 2015: http://www.thelocal.es/20150830/15-held- in-spain-for-smuggling-moroccan-migrants-on-jet-skis

6. IOM, Missing Migrants Project: http://missingmigrants.iom.int, with modifications by the authors.

7. UNODC, *Smuggling of Migrants*; Frontex, *Annual Risk Assessment 2016*.

8. Frontex, *Annual Risk Assessment 2016*; Frontex, *Annual Risk Assessment 2015*, Warsaw: Frontex, 2015; Frontex, *Annual Risk Analysis 2014*, Warsaw: Frontex, 2014.

9. 'Gaddafi Wants EU Cash to Stop African Migrants', BBC, 31 August 2010: http://www.bbc.com/news/world-europe-11139345

10. Frontex, *Annual Risk Assessment 2016*.

11. Tuesday Reitano, Laura Adal and Mark Shaw, *Smuggled Futures: The*

Dangerous Path of a Migrant from Africa to Europe, Geneva: Global Initiative against Transnational Organised Crime, 2014.

12. Reitano, 'Human Smuggling from West Africa to Europe'.

13. Regional Mixed Migration Secretariat, *Going West: Contemporary Mixed Migration Trends from the Horn of Africa to Libya and Europe*, Geneva: International Organization for Migration, 2014.

14. Sahan/IGAD (2016) 'Human Trafficking and Smuggling on the Horn of Africa–Central Mediterranean Route', Djibouti: Sahan Foundation and IGAD Security Sector Program (ISSP): http://igad.int/attachments/1284_ISSP%20Sahan%20HST%20Report%20%2018ii2016%20FINAL%20FINAL.pdf

15. Ibid.

16. RMMS, *Going West*.

17. Sahan/IGAD, 'Human Trafficking and Smuggling'.

18. UNODC, *Smuggling of Migrants*.

19. Frontex, *Annual Risk Assessment 2014*.

20. Frontex, *Annual Risk Assessment 2016*; Frontex, *Annual Risk Assessment 2015*; Frontex, *Annual Risk Assessment 2014*.

21. Reitano and Tinti, *Survive and Advance*.

22. IOM, Missing Migrants Project: https://missingmigrants.iom.int/mediterranean

23. 'Spreading across Europe, a Fortress of Fences', *The Migration Machine (special feature)*, Reuters, 4 April 2016: http://www.reuters.com/investigates/special-report/migration/#story/38

24. 'Migration Crisis: Italians Protest over Austria Border Fence Plan', *The Guardian*, 7 May 2016: http://www.theguardian.com/world/2016/may/07/migration-crisis-italians-austria-border-fence-germany-merkel

25. 'Migrant Crisis: NATO Deploys Aegean People Smuggling Patrols', BBC, 11 February 2016, http://www.bbc.com/news/world-europe-35549478

26. European Council, 'EU–Turkey Statement', press release, 18 March 2016: http://www.consilium.europa.eu/en/press/press-releases/2016/03/18-eu-turkey-statement/

5. LIBYA: OUT OF AFRICA

1. Frontex, *Annual Risk Assessment 2016*, p. 20.

2. John Davis, *Libyan Politics: Tribe and Revolution*, London: I. B. Tauris & Co. Ltd., 1987, p. 11. In January 2015 my father-in-law, Giorgio Reitano, died. He was one of twelve Permanent Ambassadors of Italy, serving as ambassador to Libya from 1984 to 1991, and I had the great

fortune to benefit not only from his accounts of the intricacies of dealing with the Gaddafi government, but also from inheriting his extensive library on the country.

3. Quoted in Alison Pargeter, *Libya: The Rise and Fall of Gaddafi*, New Haven, CT: Yale University Press, 2012, p. 151.
4. Mark Shaw and Fiona Mangan, *Illicit Trafficking and Libya's Transition: Profits and Losses*, Washington DC: United States Institute for Peace, 2014.
5. Yvan Guichaoua, *Transformations of Armed Violence in the Sahara*, Washington DC: World Bank, Saharan Knowledge Exchange, 2014.
6. Tuesday Reitano and Mark Shaw, 'Atlantic Currents and their Illicit Undertow: Fragile States and Transnational Security Implications', in GMF, *Atlantic Currents*, Washington DC: German Marshall Fund, 2015.
7. Shaw and Mangan, *Illicit Trafficking and Libya's Transition*.
8. Judith Scheele, *Smugglers and Saints of the Sahara: Regional Connectivity in the Twentieth Century*, New York: Cambridge University Press, 2012.
9. Vision Project, 'International Shipping: Globalization in Crisis', 2009: http://www.visionproject.org/images/img_magazine/pdfs/international_shipping.pdf
10. Mark Shaw and Tuesday Reitano, *The Political Economy of Trafficking and Trade in the Sahara: Instability and Opportunities*, Washington DC: World Bank, Saharan Knowledge Exchange, 2014.
11. Abdelkrim Araar, Nada Choueiri and Paolo Verme, *The Quest for Subsidy Reform in Libya*, Washington DC: World Bank, 2015.
12. Shaw and Mangan, *Illicit Trafficking and Libya's Transition*.
13. Ibid.
14. Estimates of how many people migrate within and outside regions in Africa remain hotly contested. While it differs from region to region, it is relatively safe to say, however, that it is only a small minority (under 10 per cent) that make their way to Europe, even with the heightened numbers of this present crisis. In West Africa, for example, the general rule of thumb is that 80 per cent of migrants stay within the ECOWAS zone or its immediately contiguous neighbours.
15. Reitano, 'Human Smuggling from West Africa to Europe'.
16. Patrick Kingsley, 'Libya's People Smugglers: Inside the Trade that Promises Refugees a Better Life', The Guardian, 24 April 2015: http://www.theguardian.com/world/2015/apr/24/libyas-people-smugglers-how-will-they-catch-us-theyll-soon-move-on
17. Patrick Kingsley, 'Libyan People Smuggler Derides EU Plan for Military Action', *The Guardian*, 21 April 2015: http://www.theguardian.com/world/2015/apr/21/libyan-people-smuggler-tells-eu-to-destroy-ships-and-help-coastguard

18. Ibid.
19. Interview with Frontex analyst, May 2015.
20. Interview with the chief prosecutor of Catania, June 2016.
21. Global Initiative and Rhipto, *Libya: A Growing Hub for Criminal Economies and Terrorist Financing in the Trans-Sahara*, Geneva: Global Initiative against Transnational Organised Crime, 2015.
22. Charles Heller and Lorenzo Pezzani, 'Death by Rescue: The Lethal Effects of the EU's Policies of Non-Assistance', report produced by Forensic Oceanography/Forensic Architecture, Goldsmiths, University of London, within the Economic and Social Research Council (ESRC)-supported 'Precarious Trajectories' research project: https://deathby-rescue.org
23. Human Rights Watch, 'Libya: Whipped, Beaten and Hung from Trees', 2014: https://www.hrw.org/news/2014/06/22/libya-whipped-beaten-and-hung-trees; Amnesty International, '"Libya is Full of Cruelty": Stories of Abduction, Sexual Violence and Abuse from Migrants and Refugees', London: Amnesty International, 2015: https://www.amnesty.org/en/documents/mde19/1578/2015/en/

6. EGYPT: THE NORTH COAST

1. UNHCR, 'Egypt: Country and Operations Profile 2015': http://www.unhcr.org/pages/49e486356.html
2. Lefteris Karagiannopoulos and Abdi Sheikh, 'A Knife-Wielding Human Trafficker Prevented Survivors of Migrant Disaster from Pulling Others to Safety', Reuters, 21 April 2016: http://www.businessinsider.com/human-trafficker-refugee-disaster-2016-4
3. Francesco Guarascio, 'Egypt Migrant Departures Stir New Concern in Europe', Reuters, 28 February 2016: http://www.reuters.com/article/us-europe-migrants-egypt-idUSKCN0W108K

7. DESERT HIGHWAY: AGADEZ AND THE SAHEL

1. UNDP, *Human Development Report 2015*, New York: United Nations Development Programme, 2015: http://hdr.undp.org/sites/default/files/2015_human_development_report.pdf.
2. Scheele, 'Traders, Saints and Irrigation', p. 282.
3. John Wright, *Libya, Chad and the Central Sahara*, London: Hurst & Co., 1989.
4. Interview with international official, N'Djamena, April 2014.
5. Marielle Debos, 'Les limites de l'accumulation par les armes: itinéraires d'ex-combattants au Tchad', *Politique africaine* 109 (2008): 167–81;

Roland Marchal and Victoria Bawtree, 'Chad/Darfur: How Two Crises Merge', *Review of African Political Economy* 33, 10 (2006): 467–82; Jérôme Tubiana, *The Chad–Sudan Proxy War and the 'Darfurization' of Chad: Myths and Reality*, Geneva: Small Arms Survey, 2008: http:// tamlyn-serpa.com/images/Chad_Sudan.pdf.

6. Interview with international official, N'Djamena, April 2014.

7. The size of the Toubou population is debated, with estimates ranging from 120,000 to several hundred thousand. See Laura Van Waas, 'The Stateless Tebu of Libya?' *Tilburg Law School Research Paper No. 010/2013*, May 2013.

8. International Crisis Group, *Le Nord-ouest du Tchad: la prochaine zone à haut risque?*, Africa Briefing No. 78, 2011.

9. As noted previously, Gaddafi used control over resources—including illicit ones—as ways to control the various tribes in Libya. For more on this see Shaw and Mangan, *Illicit Trafficking and Libya's Transition*.

10. OHCHR, *Summary Prepared by the Office of the High Commissioner for Human Rights in Accordance with Paragraph 15 (c) of the Annex to Human Rights Council Resolution 5/1: Libyan Arab Jamahiriya*, New York: United Nations General Assembly, 2010: http://www.univie.ac.at/bimtor/dateien/libya_upr_2010_summary.pdf.

11. Reitano and Shaw, 'Atlantic Currents'; Shaw and Mangan, *Illicit Trafficking and Libya's Transition*.

12. Ines Kohl, 'Libya's "Major Minorities": Berber, Tuareg and Tebu: Multiple Narratives of Citizenship, Language and Border Control', *Middle East Critique*, 23, 4, special issue (2014): 423–38.

13. Reitano and Shaw, 'Atlantic Currents'.

14. While tracking the routes of illicit flows and the networks that support them is always a challenge, the growth of illicit trade in the trans-Sahara/Sahel has been relatively well documented. See, for example, Tuesday Reitano and Mark Shaw, *Fixing a Fractured State: Breaking the Cycles of Crime, Corruption and Conflict in Mali and the Sahel*, Geneva: Global Initiative against Transnational Organised Crime, 2015; Peter Tinti, *Illicit Trafficking and Instability in Mali: Past, Present and Future*, Geneva: Global Initiative against Transnational Organised Crime, January 2014; and W. Lacher, 'Organised Crime and Conflict in the Sahel–Sahara Region', *Carnegie Papers (Middle East September 2012)*, Washington: Carnegie Endowment for International Peace, 2012.

15. In response to an attack by Tuareg gunmen on a police station, Nigérien forces arrested, tortured and killed hundreds of Tuareg civilians in what would become known as the Tchin Tabaraden massacre. The event sparked the creation of two armed Tuareg insurgent groups, and is widely cited as the official beginning of the Tuareg rebellion in 1990.

16. International Crisis Group, 'Niger: Another Weak Link in the Sahel?' *Africa Report* 208, 19 September 2013, p. 10; Yvan Guichaoua, *Circumstantial Alliances and Loose Loyalties in Rebellion Making: The Case of Tuareg Insurgency in Northern Niger (2007–2009)* MICROCON Research Working Paper 20, Brighton: MICROCON, 2009.

17. Mark Shaw, 'Illicit Narcotics Transiting West Africa', in *Illicit Financial Flows: Criminal Economies in West Africa*, OECD/AfDB, Paris: OECD Publishing, 2016.

18. Guichaoua, *Circumstantial Alliances and Loose Loyalties*.

19. Some estimates put this figure as low as 90,000, but there is wide agreement that the influx of people threatened to destabilise northern Niger.

20. International Crisis Group, 'Niger'.

21. Tinti, *Illicit Trafficking and Instability in Mali*.

22. Kohl, 'Libya's "Major Minorities"'.

23. Reitano and Shaw, *Fixing a Fractured State*.

24. Stratfor, 'Complexities of Future Energy Investment in Libya', 5 July 2012: https://www.stratfor.com/analysis/complexities-future-energy-investment-libya.

25. Guichaoua, *Transformations of Armed Violence in the Sahara*.

26. Alain Antil and Mansouria Mokhefi, *Managing the Sahara Periphery*, Washington DC: World Bank, 2014.

27. Reitano, 'Human Smuggling from West Africa to Europe'.

28. Adam Nossiter, 'Crackdown in Niger Fails to Deter Migrant Smugglers', *New York Times*, 20 August 2015: http://www.nytimes.com/2015/08/21/world/africa/migrant-smuggling-business-is-booming-in-niger-despite-crackdown.html

29. Daniel Flynn, 'Corruption Stymies Niger's Attempts to Stem Flow of Migrants to Europe', Reuters, 22 June 2015: http://www.theguardian.com/global-development/2015/jun/22/corruption-niger-attempt-stem-flow-migrants-europe-smugglers-sahara

30. Drew Hinshaw and Joe Parkinson, 'Agadez Traffickers Profit from Movement through Niger to Libya', *Wall Street Journal*, 19 July 2015: http://www.wsj.com/articles/agadez-traffickers-profit-from-movement-through-niger-to-libya-1437002559

31. Flynn, 'Corruption Stymies Niger's Attempts to Stem Flow of Migrants to Europe'.

32. Boureima Balima, 'Niger Tells Europe it Needs 1 Billion Euros to Fight Illegal Migration', Reuters, 3 May 2016: http://af.reuters.com/article/topNews/idAFKCN0XU1PG

33. Tuesday Reitano, 'What Incentives Does Niger Have for Cracking Down on Migrant Smuggling? Not Many', London: London School of

Economics—Africa at LSE, 13 January 2016: http://blogs.lse.ac.uk/africaatlse/2016/01/13/what-incentives-does-niger-have-for-cracking-down-on-migrant-smuggling-not-many/

8. TURKEY: THE CROSSROADS

1. UNODC, *The Role of Organised Crime in the Smuggling of Migrants*.
2. Mehmet Cetingulec, 'At a Cost of $500 Million Each Month, Turkey Staggers under Growing Refugee Burden', al-Monitor, 20 October 2015: http://www.al-monitor.com/pulse/originals/2015/10/turkey-syria-refugees-spent-billion-in-three-months.html
3. Sarah Kaplan, 'Does it Get Any Sicker? A Turkish Firm has been Selling Fake Life Vests—they Soak up Water—for Refugees at Sea', *Washington Post*, 7 January 2016: https://www.washingtonpost.com/news/morning-mix/wp/2016/01/07/does-it-get-any-sicker-a-turkish-firm-has-been-selling-fake-life-vests-they-soak-up-water-for-refugees-at-sea/
4. Mehul Srivastava, 'Organised Crime Moves in on Migrant Smuggling Trade in Turkey', *Financial Times*, 13 December 2015: http://www.ft.com/intl/cms/s/0/17cf4fc0-9ffa-11e5-8613-08e211ea5317.html#axzz483fVAewY
5. Loubna Mire and Miguel Winograd, 'The King of the Shores: An Interview with a Syrian Refugee Smuggler', *New Republic*, 2 November 2015: https://newrepublic.com/article/123247/king-shores-interview-syrian-refugee-smuggler
6. Frontex, *Annual Risk Assessment 2016*.
7. Patrick Kingsley, 'Hiding in Plain Sight: Inside the World of Turkey's People Smugglers', *The Guardian*, 29 November 2015: http://www.theguardian.com/world/2015/nov/29/hiding-in-plain-sight-inside-the-world-of-turkeys-people-smugglers
8. Ryan Gingeras, *Heroin, Organised Crime, and the Making of Modern Turkey*, Oxford: Oxford University Press, 2014.
9. Mahmut Cengiz, *The Globalization of Turkish Organised Crime and the Policy Response*, Washington DC: George Mason University, 2010.
10. Mark Galleoti, 'Turkish Organised Crime: From Tradition to Business', in D. Spiegel and H. van de Bunt (eds.), *Traditional Organized Crime in the Modern World*, Studies of Organized Crime 11, New York: Springer, 2012.
11. Cengiz, *The Globalization of Turkish Organized Crime*.
12. Louise I. Shelley, *Dirty Entanglements: Corruption, Crime and Terrorism*, New York: Cambridge University Press, 2014.
13. Cengiz, *The Globalization of Turkish Organized Crime*.
14. William Watkinson, 'Aylan Kurdi: Four Syrians Remanded in Turkey

over Drowning Death of Aylan Kurdi', *International Business Times*, 5 September 2015: http://www.ibtimes.co.uk/aylan-kurdi-four-syrians-remanded-turkey-over-drowning-death-aylan-kurdi-1518577.

15. Srivastava, 'Organised Crime Moves in on Migrant Smuggling Trade in Turkey'.

16. Boštjan Videmšek, 'In the Human Smugglers' Den', *Politico*, 22 October 2015: http://www.politico.eu/article/refugee-crisis-smugglers-syria-turkey-migrants-the-worlds-largest-human-bazaar-migration-refugees-smugglers-greece-turkey/

17. M. Sophia Newman, 'The People who Made 2015 a Safer Year for Migrants to Cross the Mediterranean', *Vice*, 19 January 2016: http://www.vice.com/read/the-people-who-made-2015-a-safer-year-for-migrants-to-cross-the-mediterranean?utm_source=vicetwitterus

18. Cetingulec, 'Turkey Staggers under Growing Refugee Burden'.

19. European Council, 'Meeting of Heads of State or Government with Turkey—EU–Turkey Statement', press release, 29 November 2015: http://www.consilium.europa.eu/en/press/press-releases/2015/11/29-eu-turkey-meeting-statement/

20. Georgi Gotev, 'EU and Turkey Agree on €3 Billion Refugee Deal', EurActiv.com, 30 November 2015: http://www.euractiv.com/section/justice-home-affairs/news/eu-and-turkey-agree-on-3-billion-refugee-deal/

21. Constanze Letsch, 'Turkish Crackdown Leaves Refugees in Limbo', *The Guardian*, 10 December 2015: http://www.theguardian.com/world/2015/dec/10/turkish-crackdown-leaves-refugees-limbo

22. Srivastava, 'Organised Crime Moves in on Migrant Smuggling Trade in Turkey'.

23. UNHCR, 'Refugees/Migrants Emergency Response—Mediterranean', 5 May 2016: http://data.unhcr.org/mediterranean/country.php?id=83

24. 'Greek President Slams Turkey for Facilitating Migrant Smuggling', PanArmenian.net, 18 January 2016: http://www.panarmenian.net/eng/news/203960/

25. Peter Spiegel, 'EU Deal with Turkey Failing to Stem Migration Flow', *Financial Times*, 7 January 2016: http://www.ft.com/intl/cms/s/0/d62b85ca-b539–11e5–8358–9a82b43f6b2f.html#axzz3y0BrmyJ8

26. Ibid.

27. Benjamin Ward, 'Dispatches: Risks of the EU–Turkey Migration Deal', Human Rights Watch, 1 December 2015: https://www.hrw.org/news/2015/12/01/dispatches-risks-eu-turkey-migration-deal

28. Matthew Holehouse, 'Refugees Sue EU over Turkey Deal', *The Telegraph*, 13 June 2016: http://www.telegraph.co.uk/news/2016/06/13/refugees-sue-eu-over-turkey-deal/

29. European Council, 'EU–Turkey Statement'.

30. A series of interviews with smugglers conducted by the Global Initiative and Migrant Report (www.migrantreport.org) in three locations in Turkey in May 2016, funded by the Hanns Siedl Foundation.

9. SCHENGEN AND BEYOND

1. Anemona Hartocollis, 'Greece Rounds up Migrants on Kos, Locking them in Stadium Overnight', *New York Times*, 12 August 2015: http://www.nytimes.com/2015/08/13/world/europe/greece-syria-iraq-migrants-locked-stadium-on-kos.html

2. Christopher Adam, 'Victor Orbán: Muslim Majority in Europe Coming Soon', *Hungarian Free Press*, 12 September 2015: http://hungarianfreepress.com/2015/09/12/viktor-orban-muslim-majority-in-europe-coming-soon/

3. Liz Alderman, 'Smugglers Prey on Migrants Desperate to Find Back Doors to Europe', *New York Times*, 12 March 2016: http://www.nytimes.com/2016/03/12/world/europe/european-union-migrant-crisis-smuggling.html

4. Dejan knows that I am not an asylum seeker by this point.

5. 'Hungary's Barrier Triggers a Domino Effect', Reuters, 14 April 2016: http://www.reuters.com/investigates/special-report/migration/#story/39

6. Margit Feher, 'Hungary Completes Croatia Border Fence to Keep Migrants Out', *Wall Street Journal*, 15 October 2015: http://www.wsj.com/articles/hungary-completes-croatia-border-fence-to-keep-migrants-out-1444927774

7. Dejan Anastasijevic, *Organised Crime in the Western Balkans*, Graz: HUMSEC, 2006.

8. Europol, *Migrant Smuggling in the EU*, The Hague: Europol, February 2016.

9. Ibid.

10. Mark Townsend, '10,000 Refugee Children are Missing, Says Europol', *The Guardian*, 30 January 2016: https://www.theguardian.com/world/2016/jan/30/fears-for-missing-child-refugees

11. Henry Samuel, 'Britons Deeply Involved in Cross-Channel Migrant Smuggling, Says Dunkirk Prosecutor', *The Telegraph*, 6 May 2016: http://www.telegraph.co.uk/news/2016/05/06/britons-deeply-involved-in-cross-channel-migrant-smuggling-says/

12. Colin Freeman and Henry Samuel, 'Belgian Police Fire at British Car after Fatal 125mph Chase with Smugglers Trying to Force Lorry Drivers to Take Migrants to UK', *The Telegraph*, 5 May 2016: http://

www.telegraph.co.uk/news/2016/05/05/belgian-police-rake-british-registered-car-with-bullets-during-h/

13. Europol, *Migrant Smuggling in the EU*.

CONCLUSION

1. Lizzie Dearden, 'Germany Follows Switzerland and Denmark to Seize Cash and Valuables from Arriving Refugees', *The Independent*, 23 January 2016: http://www.independent.co.uk/news/world/europe/germany-follows-switzerland-and-denmark-to-seize-cash-and-valuables-from-arriving-refugees-a6828821.html

2. David Crouch, 'Swedish Border Controls Hit Øresund Bridge Commuters as Well as Refugees', *The Guardian*, 4 January 2016: https://www.theguardian.com/world/2016/jan/04/swedish-border-controls-oresund-bridge-commuters-refugees

3. 'Fences to be Built to Prevent Refugees from Crossing Øresdund', *Copenhagen Post*, 6 June 2016: http://cphpost.dk/news/fences-to-be-built-to-prevent-refugees-from-crossing-oresund.html

4. 'Austria Steps Up Anti-Migrant Patrols at Italian Border', The Local. it, 25 May 2016: http://www.thelocal.it/20160525/austria-steps-up-anti-migrant-patrols-at-italian-border

5. Sophie Hardach, 'The Refugees Housed at Dachau: "Where Else Should I Live?"', *The Guardian*, 19 September 2015: https://www.theguardian.com/world/2015/sep/19/the-refugees-who-live-at-dachau

6. Jessica Elgot, 'Greece Promises Refugee Transfers as Camp Baby Photo Emerges', *The Guardian*, 12 March 2016: http://www.theguardian.com/world/2016/mar/12/refugee-camp-baby-photo-prompts-greece-transfer-promise

7. Stoyan Nenov, 'Greece Condemns Macedonia Tear Gas and Rubber Bullets against Migrants', Reuters, 10 April 2016: http://www.reuters.com/article/us-europe-migrants-greece-teargas-idUSKCN0X70CD

8. Kim Ghattas, 'The Sad Fading Away of the Refugee Crisis Story', *Foreign Policy*, 19 October 2015: http://foreignpolicy.com/2015/10/19/the-sad-fading-away-of-the-refugee-crisis-story/

9. Anthony Faiola, 'Soldiers of Odin: The Far-Right Groups in Finland "Protecting Women" from Asylum Seekers', *The Independent*, 1 February 2016: http://www.independent.co.uk/news/world/europe/soldiers-of-odin-the-far-right-groups-in-finland-protecting-women-from-asylum-seekers-a6846341.html

10. Barbie Latza Nadeau, 'Milan's New "Anti-Mosque" Law', *The Daily Beast*, 4 July 2015: http://www.thedailybeast.com/articles/2015/01/28/milan-s-new-anti-mosque-law.html

11. 'Sweden Masked Gang "Targeted Migrants" in Stockholm', BBC, 30 January 2016: http://www.bbc.com/news/world-europe-3545 1080

12. An outstanding account of the growth and challenges of the US CBP can be found in Garrett M. Graff, 'The Green Monster: How the Border Patrol Became America's Most Out of Control Law Enforcement Agency', *Politico Magazine*, November/December 2014: http://www. politico.com/magazine/story/2014/10/border-patrol-the-green-monster-112220?o=4

13. Brian Erickson, 'Death, Corruption and Abuse on the US–Mexico Border: How CBP Became the Largest Police Force in the World', in Tuesday Reitano and Sasha Jesperson (eds.), *The War on Crime: Militarised Responses to Organised Crime*, London: Palgrave Macmillan, 2017.

14. The full Homeland Security report can be accessed via the *LA Times* website: http://documents.latimes.com/homeland-security-advisory-council-interim-report/

15. Carl Prine and Justin Merriman, 'American Coyotes', *Pittsburgh Tribune-Review*, July 2015: http://triblive.com/AmericanCoyotes/

16. Associated Press, 'Mexican Police helped Cartel Massacre 193 Migrants, Documents Show', NPR, 22 December 2014: http://www.npr.org/2014/12/22/372579429/mexican-police-helped-cartel-massacre-193-migrants-documents-show

17. Erickson, 'Death, Corruption and Abuse on the US–Mexico Border'.

18. 'Deportation' is no longer the term legally used to describe the US policy of 'return and removal' of illegal migrants from the USA. For a useful overview of the distinctions see Anna O'Law, 'Lies, Damned Lies and Obama's Deportation Statistics', *Washington Post*, 21 April 2014: http://www.washingtonpost.com/blogs/monkey-cage/wp/2014/04/21/lies-damned-lies-and-obamas-deportation-statistics/. Data on irregular immigration is available at US Customs and Border Protection official website. Data is provided by fiscal year, from October to October. Data for 2014 concludes at 31 July 2014: http://www.cbp.gov/newsroom/stats/southwest-border-unaccompanied-children

19. Michael Carr, *Fortress Europe: Dispatches from a Gated Continent*, London: Hurst & Co., 2015.

20. Nuevo Laredo, 'United States Expulsion Policy towards Migrants Carries Big Human Cost, Bordering on Cruelty', *The Economist*, 8 February 2014: http://www.economist.com/news/briefing/21595891-united-states-expulsion-policy-toward-migrants-carries-big-human-cost-bordering-cruelty

21. UNHCR, *Children on the Run: Unaccompanied Children Leaving Central America and Mexico and the Need for International Protection*, July 2014:

http://www.unhcrwashington.org/sites/default/files/1_UAC_Children%20on%20the%20Run_Full%20Report.pdfacc08101

22. Interview with the Global Initiative against Transnational Organised Crime, September 2014.

23. Amnesty International, 'Australia: Damning Evidence of Officials' Involvement in Transnational Crime Uncovered', 28 October 2015: https://www.amnesty.org/en/latest/news/2015/10/australia-damning-evidence-of-officials-involvement-in-transnational-crime-uncovered/

24. Associated Press, 'Malaysia and Thailand Turn Away Hundreds on Migrant Boats', *The Guardian*, 14 May 2015: http://www.theguardian.com/world/2015/may/14/malaysia-turns-back-migrant-boat-with-more-than-500-aboard

25. Robyn Kriel, Brianna Duggan and Idris Muktar, 'Kenya to Close Refugee Camps, Displacing More than 600,000', CNN, 7 May 2016: http://edition.cnn.com/2016/05/06/africa/kenya-closing-refugee-camps/

26. For more information on migration in the Americas, Óscar Martínez's book *The Beast* (New York: Verso, 2013) is unparalleled. This was also documented in Ioan Grillo's account of the drug wars in Mexico: Ioan Grillo, *El Narco: The Bloody Rise of the Mexican Drug Cartels*, London: Bloomsbury Press, 2011.

27. Human Rights Watch, '"I Wanted to Lie Down and Die": Trafficking and Torture of Eritreans in Sudan and Egypt', 11 February 2014: https://www.hrw.org/report/2014/02/11/i-wanted-lie-down-and-die/trafficking-and-torture-eritreans-sudan-and-egypt

28. Mirjam van Reisen, M. Estefanos and C. R. J. J. Rijken, *Human Trafficking in the Sinai: Refugees between Life and Death*, European External Policy Advisors/Tilburg University, 2012: http://www.ehrea.org/report_Human_Trafficking_in_the_Sinai_20120927.pdf

29. Discussions with a UNHCR staff member who took hundreds of victim testimonials, January 2016.

30. For more information on the vulnerability of migrant women in transit in the Balkans see Nobel Women's Initiative, *Women Refugees at Risk in Europe*, March 2016: http://www.atina.org.rs/en/new-report-women-refugees-risk-europe

31. Discussion in March 2016 in Berlin.

32. Kyle and Scarcelli, 'Migrant Smuggling and the Violence Questions'.

33. Claire Hajaj and Tuesday Reitano, 'Caught in the Crossfire: United Nations Security and Policy Perspectives on the Refugee Crisis', Frederich Ebert Stiftung, June 2016: http://library.fes.de/pdf-files/id/ipa/12641.pdf

34. Nektaria Stamouli, 'Greece Struggles to Return Migrants under EU–

Turkey Deal', *Wall Street Journal*, 19 May 2016: http://www.wsj.com/articles/greece-struggles-to-return-migrants-under-eu-turkey-deal-1463653671

35. Apostolis Fotiadis, Helena Smith and Patrick Kingsley, 'Syrian Refugee Wins Appeal against Forced Return to Turkey', *The Guardian*, 20 May 2016: https://www.theguardian.com/world/2016/may/20/syrian-refugee-wins-appeal-against-forced-return-to-turkey

36. Crispian Balmer and Selam Gebrekiden, 'Whisked to Rome from Khartoum: People-Smuggling Kingpin or Wrong Man?' Reuters, 12 June 2016: http://www.reuters.com/article/us-europe-migrants-sudan-smuggler-insigh-idUSKCN0YY0W3

37. S. Peers, 'Analysis: The EU's Planned War on Smugglers', Statewatch No. 268, 2015: http://www.statewatch.org/analyses/no-268-eu-war-on-smugglers.pdf

38. R. Mason and P. Kingsley, 'David Cameron: Send More Patrol Ships to Turn Refugee Boats Back to Libya', *The Guardian*, 18 March 2016: http://www.theguardian.com/world/2016/mar/18/refugee-boats-david-cameron-early-intervention-libya-migrants-mediterranean-eu-leaders

39. Wolfgang Wosolsobe, oral evidence to the House of Lords EU External Affairs Subcommittee, London, 4 March 2016: http://www.parliament.uk/business/committees/committees-a-z/lords-select/eu-external-affairs-subcommittee/news-parliament-2015/european-union-military-staff-evidence-session/

40. Peter Roberts, 'The Militarisation of Migration: From Triton to Sofia: Assessing the Credibility of the EU's Naval Interventions against Migrant Smuggling in the Mediterranean', in Reitano and Jesperson (eds.) *The War on Crime: Militarised Response to Organised Crime*.

41. House of Lords European Union Select Committee, 'Operation Sophia, the EU's Mission in the Mediterranean: An Impossible Challenge', HL Paper 144, May 2016: http://www.publications.parliament.uk/pa/ld201516/ldselect/ldeucom/144/144.pdf

42. Roberts, 'The Militarisation of Migration'.

43. 'Greek Army Exercises Trigger Reaction from Turkey, FYROM', Ekathimerimi, 14 April 2016: http://www.ekathimerini.com/207937/article/ekathimerini/news/greek-army-exercises-trigger-reaction-from-turkey-fyrom

44. Salem Solomon, 'Heavy Fighting Reported on Ethiopia–Eritrea Border', Voice of America, 13 June 2016: http://www.voanews.com/content/ethiopia-eritrea-border-tensions/3373659.html

45. Ceylan Yeginsu and Karam Shoumali, '11 Syrian Refugees Reported Killed by Turkish Border Guards', *New York Times*, 19 June 2016:

http://www.nytimes.com/2016/06/20/world/middleeast/11-syrian-refugees-reported-killed-by-turkish-border-guards.html

46. Human Rights Watch, 'Turkey Border Guards Kill and Injure Asylum Seekers', 10 May 2016: https://www.hrw.org/news/2016/05/10/turkey-border-guards-kill-and-injure-asylum-seekers

47. European Commission, 'Communication from the Commission on Establishing a New Partnership Framework with Third Countries under the European Agenda on Migration (COM (2016) 385 Final)', 7 June 2016: http://eur-lex.europa.eu/legal-content/EN/TXT/?uri=COM:2016:385:FIN

48. European Commission, 'Commission Announces New Migration Partnership Framework: Reinforced Cooperation with Third Countries to Better Manage Migration', press release, 7 June 2016: http://europa.eu/rapid/press-release_IP-16–2072_en.htm

49. European Commission, 'New Partnership Framework'.

50. Reitano, 'What Incentives Does Niger Have for Cracking Down on Migrant Smuggling?'

51. Between 2012 and 2015 one of the authors was involved in the evaluation of an EU-funded technical assistance programme to Niger and the Sahel in counter-terrorism. This concluded that the massive investment by the EU through multiple channels had done little to increase the capacity of the country's security institutions. See Tuesday Reitano, Peter Knoope and Iris Oustinoff. *Final Review of the CT–Sahel Project*, Brussels: European Commission, 2015: http://ct-morse.eu/wp-content/uploads/2015/12/CT-Sahel-Final-review-EN-Dec-2015.pdf and Tuesday Reitano, Mark Shaw, Martin Ewi and Luke Gribbon, *Mid-Term Review of the CT–Sahel Project*, Brussels: European Commission, 2014: http://ec.europa.eu/europeaid/documents/mid-term-review-ct-sahel-2014-final-report_en.pdf

52. Mehul Srivastava, Peter Spiegel and Stefan Wagstyl, 'Recep Tayyip Erdogan Rejects EU Demands to Reform Terror Law', *Financial Times*, 6 May 2016: http://on.ft.com/23v3atz

53. 'Declaration of the Ministerial Conference of the Khartoum Process', Rome, 28 November 2014: http://italia2014.eu/media/3785/declaration-of-the-ministerial-conference-of-the-khartoum-process.pdf

54. Nick Grinstead, 'The Khartoum Process: Shifting the Burden', The Hague: Clingendael Institute, 22 February 2016: https://www.clingendael.nl/publication/khartoum-process-shifting-burden

55. Results of an expert seminar with negotiators of the Khartoum Process, held in Berlin, 22 June 2016 under the Chatham House rule.

56. OECD, *Development Cooperation Report 2014: Mobilizing Resources for Sustainable Development*, Paris: OECD Publishing, 2014.

57. Hajaj and Reitano, 'Caught in the Crossfire'.

58. Chris Horwood and Tuesday Reitano, *A Perfect Storm? Forces Shaping Modern Migration*, RMMS, May 2016: http://regionalmms.org/fileadmin/content/rmms_publications/A_Perfect_Storm.pdf

59. Oxfam, 'An Economy for the 1%', 18 January 2016: https://www.oxfam.org/sites/www.oxfam.org/files/file_attachments/bp210-economy-one-percent-tax-havens-180116-en_0.pdf

60. Michael Mandelbaum, *The Road to Global Prosperity*, New York: Simon & Schuster, 2014.

61. Michael Clemens, *Does Development Reduce Migration?* Working Paper 359, Center for Global Development, 2014: http://www.cgdev.org/publication/does-development-reduce-migration-working-paper-359

62. After 2020 there will be a decline for China. Predictions based on UN DESA, *World Population Prospects: The 2012 Revision*, New York: United Nations, 2012.

63. S. Boumphrey, 'Special Report: The World's Youngest Populations', Euromonitor International, 13 February 2012: http://blog.euromonitor.com/2012/02/special-report-the-worlds-youngest-populations.html.

64. UNDP, *MDG 2015*, New York: United Nations Development Programme, 2016.

65. Richard P. Cincotto, 'Half a Chance: Youth Bulges and Transitions to Liberal Democracy', Wilson Centre, Environmental Change and Security Programme (ECSP) Report no. 13, 2008–9; de Hoyos R., Rodgers H., and Székely M., 2015. *Out of School and Out of Work: Risk and Opportunity for Latin America's Ninis*, Washington DC: World Bank.

66. Branko Milanovic, 'Global Income Inequality by the Numbers: In History and Now—an Overview', World Bank Policy Research Working Papers, November 2012: http://elibrary.worldbank.org/action/showCitFormats?doi=10.1596%2F1813–9450–6259

67. Horwood and Reitano, *A Perfect Storm?*

68. Jaume Castan Pinos, *Building Fortress Europe? Schengen and the Cases of Cueta and Mellila*, Brussels: Centre for International Borders Research, 2008.

69. Crisp, 'An End to Exile?'.

BIBLIOGRAPHY

'15 Arrested in Spain for Smuggling Migrants from Morocco', The Local.es, 30 August 2015: http://www.thelocal.es/20150830/15-held-in-spain-for-smuggling-moroccan-migrants-on-jet-skis

Adam, Christopher, 'Victor Orbán: Muslim Majority in Europe Coming Soon', *Hungarian Free Press*, 12 September 2015: http://hungarianfreepress.com/2015/09/12/viktor-orban-muslim-majority-in-europe-coming-soon/

Alderman, Liz, 'Smugglers Prey on Migrants Desperate to Find Back Doors to Europe', *New York Times*, 12 March 2016: http://www.nytimes.com/2016/03/12/world/europe/european-union-migrant-crisis-smuggling.html

Amnesty International, 'Australia: Damning Evidence of Officials' Involvement in Transnational Crime Uncovered', 28 October 2015: https://www.amnesty.org/en/latest/news/2015/10/australia-damning-evidence-of-officials-involvement-in-transnational-crime-uncovered/

————, '"Libya is Full of Cruelty": Stories of Abduction, Sexual Violence and Abuse from Migrants and Refugees', London: Amnesty International, 2015: https://www.amnesty.org/en/documents/mde19/1578/2015/en/

Anastasijevic, Dejan, *Organised Crime in the Western Balkans*, Graz: HUMSEC, 2006

Antil, Alain, and Mansouria Mokhefi, *Managing the Sahara Periphery*, Washington DC: World Bank, 2014

Araar, Abdelkrim, Nada Choueiri and Paolo Verme, *The Quest for Subsidy Reform in Libya*, Washington DC: World Bank, 2015

Associated Press, 'Malaysia and Thailand Turn Away Hundreds on Migrant Boats', *The Guardian*, 14 May 2015: http://www.theguardian.com/world/2015/may/14/malaysia-turns-back-migrant-boat-with-more-than-500-aboard

BIBLIOGRAPHY

————, 'Mexican Police helped Cartel Massacre 193 Migrants, Documents Show', NPR, 22 December 2014: http://www.npr.org/2014/12/22/372579429/mexican-police-helped-cartel-massacre-193-migrants-document-show

Asylum Access, *Global Refugee Work Rights Report*, Oakland, CA: Asylum Access, 2015: http://asylumaccess.org/wp-content/uploads/2014/09/FINAL_Global-Refugee-Work-Rights-Report-2014_Interactive.pdf

'Austria Steps Up Anti-Migrant Patrols at Italian Border', The Local.it, 25 May 2016: http://www.thelocal.it/20160525/austria-steps-up-anti-migrant-patrols-at-italian-border

Balima, Boureima, 'Niger Tells Europe it Needs 1 Billion Euros to Fight Illegal Migration', Reuters, 3 May 2016: http://af.reuters.com/article/topNews/idAFKCN0XU1PG

Balmer, Crispian and Selam Gebrekiden, 'Whisked to Rome from Khartoum: People-Smuggling Kingpin or Wrong Man?' Reuters, 12 June 2016: http://www.reuters.com/article/us-europe-migrants-sudan-smuggler-insigh-idUSKCN0YY0W3

Boumphrey S., 'Special Report: The World's Youngest Populations', Euromonitor International, 13 February 2012: http://blog.euromonitor.com/2012/02/special-report-the-worlds-youngest-populations.html

Braw, Elisabeth, 'When Underage Refugees Look Anything But', *Foreign Policy*, 13 Jan. 2016: http://foreignpolicy.com/2016/01/13/when-underage-refugees-look-anything-but-age-tests-sweden/

Brennan, Imogen, 'Migrant Crisis: Man Faces Five Years in Jail for Attempting to Smuggle 4 Year Old from Calais "Jungle Camp" into the UK', ABC News, 7 January 2016: http://www.abc.net.au/news/2016–01–07/man-attempted-smuggling-4yo-refugee-into-uk-faces-jail-time/7073616

Carr, Michael, *Fortress Europe: Dispatches from a Gated Continent*, London: Hurst & Co., 2015

Cengiz, Mahmut, *The Globalization of Turkish Organised Crime and the Policy Response*, Washington DC: George Mason University, 2010

Cetingulec, Mehmet, 'At a Cost of $500 Million Each Month, Turkey Staggers under Growing Refugee Burden', al-Monitor, 20 October 2015: http://www.al-monitor.com/pulse/originals/2015/10/turkey-syria-refugees-spent-billion-in-three-months.html

Cincotto, Richard P., 'Half a Chance: Youth Bulges and Transitions to Liberal Democracy', Wilson Centre, Environmental Change and Security Programme (ECSP) Report no. 13, 2008–9

Clark, Garret Barkley, 'A New Mediterranean Mafia? An Examination of the Illicit Organizations Profiting from the European Migrant Crisis', MA thesis, Georgetown University, April 2016

Clemens, Michael, *Does Development Reduce Migration?* Working Paper 359,

Center for Global Development, 2014: http://www.cgdev.org/publication/does-development-reduce-migration-working-paper-359

Crisp, Jeff, 'An End to Exile? Refugee Agency and the Search for Durable Solutions', *IDS Bulletin*, Brighton: Institute for Development Studies, 2016

———, 'Local Integration and Local Settlement of Refugees: A Conceptual and Historical Analysis', *New Issues in Refugee Research*, no. 102, Geneva: UNHCR, April 2004

———, *Policy Challenges of the New Diasporas: Migrant Networks and their Impacts on Asylum Flows and Regimes*, Geneva: UNHCR, 1999

Crouch, David, 'Danish Children's Rights Activist Fined for People Trafficking', *The Guardian*, 11 March 2016: http://www.theguardian.com/world/2016/mar/11/danish-childrens-rights-activist-lisbeth-zornig-people-trafficking

———, 'Swedish Border Controls Hit Øresund Bridge Commuters as Well as Refugees', *The Guardian*, 4 January 2016: https://www.theguardian.com/world/2016/jan/04/swedish-border-controls-oresund-bridge-commuters-refugees

Davis, John, *Libyan Politics: Tribe and Revolution*, London: I. B. Tauris & Co. Ltd., 1987

Dearden, Lizzie, 'Germany Follows Switzerland and Denmark to Seize Cash and Valuables from Arriving Refugees', *The Independent*, 23 January 2016: http://www.independent.co.uk/news/world/europe/germany-follows-switzerland-and-denmark-to-seize-cash-and-valuables-from-arriving-refugees-a6828821.html

Debos, Marielle, 'Les limites de l'accumulation par les armes: itinéraires d'ex-combattants au Tchad', *Politique africaine* 109 (2008): 167–81

'Declaration of the Ministerial Conference of the Khartoum Process', Rome, 28 November 2014: http://italia2014.eu/media/3785/declaration-of-the-ministerial-conference-of-the-khartoum-process.pdf

de Haas, Hein, *Migration System Formation and Decline: A Theoretical Inquiry into the Self-perpetuating and Self-Undermining Dynamics of Migration Processes*, IMI working paper 19, Oxford: International Migration Institute, University of Oxford, 2009

Elgot, Jessica, 'Greece Promises Refugee Transfers as Camp Baby Photo Emerges', *The Guardian*, 12 March 2016: http://www.theguardian.com/world/2016/mar/12/refugee-camp-baby-photo-prompts-greece-transfer-promise

Ellis, Stephen, *The Role of Organised Crime in the Smuggling of Migrants from West Africa to the European Union*, Vienna: United Nations Office on Drugs and Crime, 2011

———, *This Present Darkness: A History of Nigerian Organised Crime*, London: Hurst & Co., 2016

Erickson, Brian, 'Death, Corruption and Abuse on the US–Mexico Border: How CBP Became the Largest Police Force in the World', in Tuesday Reitano and Sasha Jespersen (eds.), *The War on Crime: Militarised Responses to Organised Crime*, London: Palgrave Macmillan, 2017

European Commission, 'Commission Announces New Migration Partnership Framework: Reinforced Cooperation with Third Countries to Better Manage Migration', press release, 7 June 2016: http://europa.eu/rapid/press-release_IP-16-2072_en.htm

———, 'Communication from the Commission on Establishing a New Partnership Framework with Third Countries under the European Agenda on Migration (COM (2016) 385 Final)', 7 June 2016: http://eur-lex.europa.eu/legal-content/EN/TXT/?uri=COM:2016:385:FIN

———, *Study on the Smuggling of Migrants: Characteristics, Responses and Cooperation with Third Countries*, Brussels: European Commission, September 2015: http://ec.europa.eu/dgs/home-affairs/what-we-do/networks/european_migration_network/reports/docs/emn-studies/study_on_smuggling_of_migrants_final_report_master_091115_final_pdf.pdf

European Council, 'Meeting of Heads of State or Government with Turkey—EU–Turkey Statement', press release, 29 November 2015: http://www.consilium.europa.eu/en/press/press-releases/2015/11/29-eu-turkey-meeting-statement/

———, 'EU–Turkey Statement', press release, 18 March 2016: http://www.consilium.europa.eu/en/press/press-releases/2016/03/18-eu-turkey-statement/

Europol, *Migrant Smuggling in the EU*, The Hague: Europol, February 2016

Faiola, Anthony, 'Soldiers of Odin: The Far-Right Groups in Finland "Protecting Women" from Asylum Seekers', *The Independent*, 1 February 2016: http://www.independent.co.uk/news/world/europe/soldiers-of-odin-the-far-right-groups-in-finland-protecting-women-from-asylum-seekers-a6846341.html

Faiola, Anthony and Souad Mekhennet, 'Nearly a Third of Migrants in Germany Claiming to be Syrians Aren't from Syria', *Washington Post*, 25 September 2015: https://www.washingtonpost.com/world/europe/germany-calls-for-new-refugee-benefit-standards-in-europe/2015/09/25/bee704fe-616d-11e5-8475-781cc9851652_story.html

FATF, *The Role of Hawala and Other Similar Service Providers in Money Laundering and Terrorist Financing*, Paris: FATF/OECD, 2013

Feher, Margit, 'Hungary Completes Croatia Border Fence to Keep Migrants Out', *Wall Street Journal*, 15 October 2015: http://www.wsj.com/articles/hungary-completes-croatia-border-fence-to-keep-migrants-out-1444927774

'Fences to be Built to Prevent Refugees from Crossing Øresdund', *Copenhagen*

Post, 6 June 2016: http://cphpost.dk/news/fences-to-be-built-to-prevent-refugees-from-crossing-oresund.html

Flynn, Daniel, 'Corruption Stymies Niger's Attempts to Stem Flow of Migrants to Europe', Reuters, 22 June 2015: http://www.theguardian.com/global-development/2015/jun/22/corruption-niger-attempt-stem-flow-migrants-europe-smugglers-sahara

Fotiadis, Apostolis, Helena Smith and Patrick Kingsley, 'Syrian Refugee Wins Appeal against Forced Return to Turkey', *The Guardian*, 20 May 2016: https://www.theguardian.com/world/2016/may/20/syrian-refugee-wins-appeal-against-forced-return-to-turkey

Freeman, Colin and Henry Samuel, 'Belgian Police Fire at British Car after Fatal 125mph Chase with Smugglers Trying to Force Lorry Drivers to Take Migrants to UK', *The Telegraph*, 5 May 2016: http://www.telegraph.co.uk/news/2016/05/05/belgian-police-rake-british-registered-car-with-bullets-during-h/

————, *Annual Risk Assessment 2014*, Warsaw: Frontex, 2014

————, *Annual Risk Assessment 2015*, Warsaw: Frontex, 2015

————, *Annual Risk Assessment 2016*, Warsaw: Frontex, 2016

'Gaddafi Wants EU Cash to Stop African Migrants', BBC, 31 August 2010: http://www.bbc.com/news/world-europe-11139345

Galleoti, Mark, 'Turkish Organised Crime: From Tradition to Business', in D. Spiegel and H. van de Bunt (eds.), *Traditional Organized Crime in the Modern World*, Studies of Organized Crime 11, New York: Springer, 2012

Ghattas, Kim, 'The Sad Fading Away of the Refugee Crisis Story', *Foreign Policy*, 19 October 2015: http://foreignpolicy.com/2015/10/19/the-sad-fading-away-of-the-refugee-crisis-story/

Gingeras, Ryan, *Heroin, Organised Crime, and the Making of Modern Turkey*, Oxford: Oxford University Press, 2014

Global Initiative and Rhipto, *Libya: A Growing Hub for Criminal Economies and Terrorist Financing in the Trans-Sahara*, Geneva: Global Initiative against Transnational Organised Crime, 2015

Goodell, Jeff, 'How to Fake a Passport', *New York Times*, 10 February 2002: http://www.nytimes.com/2002/02/10/magazine/how-to-fake-a-passport.html

Gotev, Georgi, 'EU and Turkey Agree on €3 Billion Refugee Deal', EurActiv.com, 30 November 2015: http://www.euractiv.com/section/justice-home-affairs/news/eu-and-turkey-agree-on-3-billion-refugee-deal/

Graff, Garrett M., 'The Green Monster: How the Border Patrol Became America's Most Out of Control Law Enforcement Agency', *Politico Magazine*, November/December 2014: http://www.politico.com/magazine/story/2014/10/border-patrol-the-green-monster-112220?o=4

'Greek Army Exercises Trigger Reaction from Turkey, FYROM', Ekathimerimi, 14 April 2016: http://www.ekathimerini.com/207937/article/ekathimerini/news/greek-army-exercises-trigger-reaction-from-turkey-fyrom

'Greek President Slams Turkey for Facilitating Migrant Smuggling', PanArmenian.net, 18 January 2016: http://www.panarmenian.net/eng/news/203960/

Greenberg, Richard, Adam Ciralsky and Stone Phillips, 'Enemies at the Gate', NBC News, 28 December 2007: http://www.nbcnews.com/id/22419963/ns/dateline_nbc-international/#.Ux4275SHw_k

Grillo, Ioan, *El Narco: The Bloody Rise of the Mexican Drug Cartels*, London: Bloomsbury Press, 2011

Grinstead, Nick, 'The Khartoum Process: Shifting the Burden', The Hague: Clingendael Institute, 22 February 2016: https://www.clingendael.nl/publication/khartoum-process-shifting-burden

Guarascio, Francesco, 'Egypt Migrant Departures Stir New Concern in Europe', Reuters, 28 February 2016: http://www.reuters.com/article/us-europe-migrants-egypt-idUSKCN0W108K

Guichaoua, Yvan, *Circumstantial Alliances and Loose Loyalties in Rebellion Making: The Case of Tuareg Insurgency in Northern Niger (2007–2009)* MICROCON Research Working Paper 20, Brighton: MICROCON, 2009

————, *Transformations of Armed Violence in the Sahara*, Washington DC: World Bank, Saharan Knowledge Exchange, 2014

Hajaj, Claire and Tuesday Reitano, 'Caught in the Crossfire: United Nations Security and Policy Perspectives on the Refugee Crisis', Frederich Ebert Stiftung, June 2016: http://library.fes.de/pdf-files/id/ipa/12641.pdf

Hardach, Sophie, 'The Refugees Housed at Dachau: "Where Else Should I Live?"', *The Guardian*, 19 September 2015: https://www.theguardian.com/world/2015/sep/19/the-refugees-who-live-at-dachau

Harding, Luke, 'Police Fear as Many as 50 Migrants Dead Inside Lorry Left by Austrian Motorway', *The Guardian*, 28 August 2015: http://www.theguardian.com/world/2015/aug/27/migrants-found-dead-inside-lorry-in-austria

Hartocollis, Anemona, 'Greece Rounds up Migrants on Kos, Locking them in Stadium Overnight', *New York Times*, 12 August 2015: http://www.nytimes.com/2015/08/13/world/europe/greece-syria-iraq-migrants-locked-stadium-on-kos.html

Havoscope, 'Fake ID Cards, Drivers Licenses, and Stolen Passports': http://www.havocscope.com/fake-id/

Heller, Charles and Lorenzo Pezzani, 'Death by Rescue: The Lethal Effects of the EU's Policies of Non-Assistance', report produced by Forensic Oceanography/Forensic Architecture, Goldsmiths, University of London, within the Economic and Social Research Council (ESRC)-supported 'Precarious Trajectories' research project: https://deathbyrescue.org

Henley, John, 'How Thailand's Trade in Fake Passports Fuels Crime Gangs around the World', *The Guardian*, 10 March 2014: http://www.theguardian.com/world/2014/mar/10/thailand-trade-fake-passports-crime-gangs-world

Herman, Emma, 'Migration as a Family Business: The Role of Personal Networks in the Mobility Phase of Migration', *International Migration* 44 (2006): 191–230

Higgins, Andrew, 'Avoiding Risky Seas, Migrants Reach Europe with an Arctic Bike Ride', *New York Times*, 9 October 2015: http://www.nytimes.com/2015/10/10/world/europe/bypassing-the-risky-sea-refugees-reach-europe-through-the-arctic.html

Hinshaw, Drew and Joe Parkinson, 'Agadez Traffickers Profit from Movement through Niger to Libya', *Wall Street Journal*, 19 July 2015: http://www.wsj.com/articles/agadez-traffickers-profit-from-movement-through-niger-to-libya-1437002559

Hlongwane, Agiza and Jeff Wicks, '"White Widow" Paid for SA Passport', IOL, 29 September 2013: http://www.iol.co.za/news/politics/white-widow-paid-for-sa-passport-1584186

Holehouse, Matthew, 'Refugees Sue EU over Turkey Deal', *The Telegraph*, 13 June 2016: http://www.telegraph.co.uk/news/2016/06/13/refugees-sue-eu-over-turkey-deal/

Horwood, Christopher, *In Pursuit of the Southern Dream: Victims of Necessity, Assessment of the Irregular Movement of Men from East Africa and the Horn to South Africa*, Geneva: IOM, 2009

Horwood, Chris and Tuesday Reitano, *A Perfect Storm? Forces Shaping Modern Migration*, RMMS, May 2016: http://regionalmms.org/fileadmin/content/rmms_publications/A_Perfect_Storm.pdf

Human Rights Watch, '"I Wanted to Lie Down and Die": Trafficking and Torture of Eritreans in Sudan and Egypt', 11 February 2014: https://www.hrw.org/report/2014/02/11/i-wanted-lie-down-and-die/trafficking-and-torture-eritreans-sudan-and-egypt

———, 'Libya: Whipped, Beaten and Hung from Trees', 2014: https://www.hrw.org/news/2014/06/22/libya-whipped-beaten-and-hung-trees

———, 'Turkey Border Guards Kill and Injure Asylum Seekers', 10 May 2016: https://www.hrw.org/news/2016/05/10/turkey-border-guards-kill-and-injure-asylum-seekers

'Hungary's Barrier Triggers a Domino Effect', Reuters, 14 April 2016: http://www.reuters.com/investigates/special-report/migration/#story/39

'Hungary's Borders Trigger a Domino Effect', Reuters, 14 April 2016: http://www.reuters.com/investigates/special-report/migration/#story/39

309

BIBLIOGRAPHY

Hurriyet, '1050 Foreign Passports Seized in Istanbul Raids', *Hurriyet Daily*, 3 February 2016: http://www.hurriyetdailynews.com/eight-suspects-detained-for-migrant-smuggling-in-istanbul.aspx?pageID=238&nID=94709&NewsCatID=509

International Crisis Group, 'Niger: Another Weak Link in the Sahel'? Africa Report 208, 19 September 2013

————, *Le Nord-ouest du Tchad: la prochaine zone à haut risque?*, Africa Briefing No. 78, 2011

Interpol, 'AirAsia Becomes the First Airline to Pilot INTERPOL's I-Checkit System': 13 May 2014, http://www.interpol.int/News-and-media/News/2014/N2014-082

IOM, Missing Migrants Project: https://missingmigrants.iom.int/mediterranean

————, *World Migration Report 2015*, Geneva: IOM, 2015: http://publications.iom.int/system/files/wmr2015_en.pdf

Izadi, Elahe, 'There's a Booming Black Market for Fake Syrian Passports', *Washington Post*, 21 November 2015: https://www.washingtonpost.com/news/worldviews/wp/2015/11/21/theres-a-booming-black-market-for-fake-syrian-passports/

Kaplan, Sarah, 'Does it Get Any Sicker? A Turkish Firm has been Selling Fake Life Vests—they Soak up Water—for Refugees at Sea', *Washington Post*, 7 January 2016: https://www.washingtonpost.com/news/morning-mix/wp/2016/01/07/does-it-get-any-sicker-a-turkish-firm-has-been-selling-fake-life-vests-they-soak-up-water-for-refugees-at-sea/

Karagiannopoulos, Lefteris and Abdi Sheikh, 'A Knife-Wielding Human Trafficker Prevented Survivors of Migrant Disaster from Pulling Others to Safety', Reuters, 21 April 2016: http://www.businessinsider.com/human-trafficker-refugee-disaster-2016-4

Khoser, Khalid, 'The Economics of Migrant Smuggling', *Refugee Transitions (Summer 2009)*, Geneva: Geneva Centre for Security Policy, 2009

Kingsley, Patrick, 'Hiding in Plain Sight: Inside the World of Turkey's People Smugglers', *The Guardian*, 29 November 2015: http://www.theguardian.com/world/2015/nov/29/hiding-in-plain-sight-inside-the-world-of-turkeys-people-smugglers

————, 'Libyan People Smuggler Derides EU Plan for Military Action', *The Guardian*, 21 April 2015: http://www.theguardian.com/world/2015/apr/21/libyan-people-smuggler-tells-eu-to-destroy-ships-and-help-coastguard

————, 'Libya's People Smugglers: Inside the Trade that Promises Refugees a Better Life', *The Guardian*, 24 April 2015: http://www.theguardian.com/world/2015/apr/24/libyas-people-smugglers-how-will-they-catch-us-theyll-soon-move-on

BIBLIOGRAPHY

Kohl, Ines, 'Libya's "Major Minorities": Berber, Tuareg and Tebu: Multiple Narratives of Citizenship, Language and Border Control', *Middle East Critique*, 23, 4, special issue (2014): 423–38

Kriel, Robyn, Brianna Duggan and Idris Muktar, 'Kenya to Close Refugee Camps, Displacing More than 600,000', CNN, 7 May 2016: http://edition.cnn.com/2016/05/06/africa/kenya-closing-refugee-camps/

Kronenfeld, Daniel, 'Afghan refugees in Pakistan: not all refugees, not always in Pakistan, not necessarily Afghan', *Journal of Refugee Studies* 21, 1 (2008): 43–63: http://jrs.oxfordjournals.org/content/21/1/43.abstract

Kyle, David and Marc Scarcelli, 'Migrant Smuggling and the Violence Question: Evolving Illicit Migration Markets for Cuban and Haitian Refugees', *Crime, Law and Social Change* 52 (2009): 297–311

Lacher, W. 'Organised Crime and Conflict in the Sahel–Sahara Region', *Carnegie Papers (Middle East September 2012)*, Washington: Carnegie Endowment for International Peace, 2012

Laredo, Nuevo, 'United States Expulsion Policy towards Migrants Carries Big Human Cost, Bordering on Cruelty', *The Economist*, 8 February 2014: http://www.economist.com/news/briefing/21595891-united-states-expulsion-policy-toward-migrants-carries-big-human-cost-bordering-cruelty

Letsch, Constanze, 'Turkish Crackdown Leaves Refugees in Limbo', *The Guardian*, 10 December 2015: http://www.theguardian.com/world/2015/dec/10/turkish-crackdown-leaves-refugees-limbo

Long, Katy, 'Extending protection? Labour migration and durable solutions for refugees', *New Issues in Refugee Research*, no. 176, Geneva: UNHCR, 2009

Mandelbaum, Michael, *The Road to Global Prosperity*, New York: Simon & Schuster, 2014

Marchal, Roland and Victoria Bawtree, 'Chad/Darfur: How Two Crises Merge', *Review of African Political Economy* 33, 10 (2006): 467–82

Martínez, Óscar, *The Beast*, New York: Verso, 2013

Mason, R. and P. Kingsley, 'David Cameron: Send More Patrol Ships to Turn Refugee Boats Back to Libya', *The Guardian*, 18 March 2016: http://www.theguardian.com/world/2016/mar/18/refugee-boats-david-cameron-early-intervention-libya-migrants-mediterranean-eu-leaders

'Migrant Crisis: NATO Deploys Aegean People Smuggling Patrols', BBC, 11 February 2016, http://www.bbc.com/news/world-europe-35549478

'Migration Crisis: Italians Protest over Austria Border Fence Plan', *The Guardian*, 7 May 2016: http://www.theguardian.com/world/2016/may/07/migration-crisis-italians-austria-border-fence-germany-merkel

Milanovic, Branko, 'Global Income Inequality by the Numbers: In History and Now—an Overview', World Bank Policy Research Working Papers, November 2012: http://elibrary.worldbank.org/action/showCitFormats?doi=10.1596%2F1813-9450-6259

Mire, Loubna and Miguel Winograd, 'The King of the Shores: An Interview with a Syrian Refugee Smuggler', *New Republic*, 2 November 2015: https://newrepublic.com/article/123247/king-shores-interview-syrian-refugee-smuggler

Moore, Malcolm, 'Malaysia Airlines Jet: "A Fake Passport? Two Days and £500, Please"', *The Telegraph*, 10 March 2014: http://www.telegraph.co.uk/news/worldnews/asia/china/10687899/Malaysia-Airlines-jet-A-fake-passport-Two-days-and-500-please.html

Nadeau, Barbie Latza, 'Milan's New "Anti-Mosque" Law', *The Daily Beast*, 4 July 2015: http://www.thedailybeast.com/articles/2015/01/28/milan-s-new-anti-mosque-law.html

Nenov, Stoyan, 'Greece Condemns Macedonia Tear Gas and Rubber Bullets against Migrants', Reuters, 10 April 2016: http://www.reuters.com/article/us-europe-migrants-greece-teargas-idUSKCN0X70CD

Newman, M. Sophia, 'The People who Made 2015 a Safer Year for Migrants to Cross the Mediterranean', *Vice*, 19 January 2016: http://www.vice.com/read/the-people-who-made-2015-a-safer-year-for-migrants-to-cross-the-mediterranean?utm_source=vicetwitterus

Nobel Women's Initiative, *Women Refugees at Risk in Europe*, March 2016: http://www.atina.org.rs/en/new-report-women-refugees-risk-europe

Nossiter, Adam, 'Crackdown in Niger Fails to Deter Migrant Smugglers', *New York Times*, 20 August 2015: http://www.nytimes.com/2015/08/21/world/africa/migrant-smuggling-business-is-booming-in-niger-despite-crackdown.html

OECD, *Development Cooperation Report 2014: Mobilizing Resources for Sustainable Development*, Paris: OECD Publishing, 2014

'Officers Seize "Fake" Passports', BBC, 4 July 2007: http://news.bbc.co.uk/2/hi/uk_news/england/london/6269210.stm

OHCHR, *Summary Prepared by the Office of the High Commissioner for Human Rights in Accordance with Paragraph 15 (c) of the Annex to Human Rights Council Resolution 5/1: Libyan Arab Jamahiriya*, New York: United Nations General Assembly, 2010: http://www.univie.ac.at/bimtor/dateien/libya_upr_2010_summary.pdf

O'Law, Anna, 'Lies, Damned Lies and Obama's Deportation Statistics', *Washington Post*, 21 April 2014:. http://www.washingtonpost.com/blogs/monkey-cage/wp/2014/04/21/lies-damned-lies-and-obamas-deportation-statistics/

Oxfam, 'An Economy for the 1%', 18 January 2016: https://www.oxfam.org/sites/www.oxfam.org/files/file_attachments/bp210-economy-one-percent-tax-havens-180116-en_0.pdf

Pargeter, Alison, *Libya: The Rise and Fall of Gaddafi*, New Haven, CT: Yale University Press, 2012

Peers, S., 'Analysis: The EU's Planned War on Smugglers', Statewatch No. 268, 2015: http://www.statewatch.org/analyses/no-268-eu-war-on-smugglers.pdf

Petros, Melanie, *The Costs of Human Smuggling and Trafficking*, London: Migration Research Centre, University College London, 2005

Pinos, Jaume Castan, *Building Fortress Europe? Schengen and the Cases of Cueta and Mellila*, Brussels: Centre for International Borders Research, 2008

Prine, Carl and Justin Merriman, 'American Coyotes', *Pittsburgh Tribune*, July 2015: http://triblive.com/AmericanCoyotes/

Regional Mixed Migration Secretariat, *Blinded by Hope: Knowledge, Attitudes and Practices of Ethiopian Migrants*, Nairobi: RMMS, 2014

————, *Country Profile Eritrea*: http://www.regionalmms.org/index.php?id=14

————, *Going West: Contemporary Mixed Migration Trends from the Horn of Africa to Libya and Europe*, Geneva: International Organization for Migration, 2014

Reitano, Tuesday, 'Human Smuggling from West Africa to Europe', in *Illicit Financial Flows: Criminal Economies in West Africa*, OECD/AfDB, Paris: OECD Publishing, 2016

————, 'What Incentives Does Niger Have for Cracking Down on Migrant Smuggling? Not Many', London: London School of Economics—Africa at LSE, 13 January 2016: http://blogs.lse.ac.uk/africaatlse/2016/01/13/what-incentives-does-niger-have-for-cracking-down-on-migrant-smuggling-not-many/

Reitano, Tuesday, Laura Adal and Mark Shaw, *Smuggled Futures: The Dangerous Path of a Migrant from Africa to Europe*, Geneva: Global Initiative against Transnational Organised Crime, 2014

Reitano, Tuesday, Peter Knoope and Iris Oustinoff. *Final Review of the CT–Sahel Project*, Brussels: European Commission, 2015: http://ct-morse.eu/wp-content/uploads/2015/12/CT-Sahel-Final-review-EN-Dec-2015.pdf

Reitano, Tuesday and Mark Shaw, 'Atlantic Currents and their Illicit Undertow: Fragile States and Transnational Security Implications', in GMF, *Atlantic Currents*, Washington DC: German Marshall Fund, 2015

————, *Fixing a Fractured State: Breaking the Cycles of Crime, Corruption and Conflict in Mali and the Sahel*, Geneva: Global Initiative against Transnational Organised Crime, 2015

Reitano, Tuesday, Mark Shaw, Martin Ewi and Luke Gribbon., *Mid-Term Review of the CT–Sahel Project*, Brussels: European Commission, 2014: http://ec.europa.eu/europeaid/documents/mid-term-review-ct-sahel-2014-final-report_en.pdf

Reitano, Tuesday and Peter Tinti, *Survive and Advance: The Economics of Smuggling*

Migrants and Refugees into Europe, Pretoria: Institute for Security Studies, 2015

Roberts, Peter, 'The Militarisation of Migration: From Triton to Sofia: Assessing the Credibility of the EU's Naval Interventions against Migrant Smuggling in the Mediterranean', in Tuesday Reitano and Sasha Jespersen (eds.), *The War on Crime: Militarised Responses to Organised Crime*, London: Palgrave Macmillan, 2017

Sahan/IGAD (2016) 'Human Trafficking and Smuggling on the Horn of Africa–Central Mediterranean Route', Djibouti: Sahan Foundation and IGAD Security Sector Program (ISSP): http://igad.int/attach-ments/1284_ISSP%20Sahan%20HST%20Report%20%2018ii2016%20 FINAL%20FINAL.pdf

Salt, John and Jeremy Stein, 'Migration as a Business: The Case of Trafficking', *International Migration* 35:469 (1997): 467–94

Samuel, Henry, 'Britons Deeply Involved in Cross-Channel Migrant Smuggling, Says Dunkirk Prosecutor', *The Telegraph*, 6 May 2016: http:// www.telegraph.co.uk/news/2016/05/06/britons-deeply-involved-in-cross-channel-migrant-smuggling-says/

Scheele, Judith, *Smugglers and Saints of the Sahara: Regional Connectivity in the Twentieth Century*, New York: Cambridge University Press, 2012

————, 'Traders, Saints and Irrigation: Reflections on Saharan Connec-tivity', *Journal of African History* 51 (Cambridge University Press, 2010): 281–300

Serenelli, Luigi, 'EU, Interpol Fight Epidemic of Stolen, Fake Passports', *USA Today*, 21 May 2014: http://www.usatoday.com/story/news/world/ 2014/05/21/stolen-passports/9351329/

Shaw, Mark, 'Illicit Narcotics Transiting West Africa', in *Illicit Financial Flows: Criminal Economies in West Africa*, OECD/AfDB, Paris: OECD Publishing, 2016

————, 'WE PAY, YOU PAY: Protection Economies, Financial Flows and Violence', in Hilary Matfess and Michael Miklaucic (eds.), *Beyond Convergence: World without Order*, Washington DC: National Defense University, 2016

Shaw, Mark and Fiona Mangan, *Illicit Trafficking and Libya's Transition: Profits and Losses*, Washington DC: United States Institute for Peace, 2014

Shaw, Mark and Tuesday Reitano, *The Political Economy of Trafficking and Trade in the Sahara: Instability and Opportunities*, Washington DC: World Bank, Saharan Knowledge Exchange, 2014

Shelley, Louise I., *Dirty Entanglements: Corruption, Crime and Terrorism*, New York: Cambridge University Press, 2014

Skeldon, Ronald, 'Migration and Development (UN/POP/EGM-MIG/2008/4)', United Nations Expert Group on International Migration and Development in Asia and the Pacific, United Nations, 2008, first presented at the seminar 'People on the Move: International Migration and Development', Santander, Spain, 18–19 August 2008: http://www.un.org/esa/population/meetings/EGM_Ittmig_Asia/P04_Skeldon.pdf

Solomon, Salem, 'Heavy Fighting Reported on Ethiopia–Eritrea Border', Voice of America, 13 June 2016: http://www.voanews.com/content/ethiopia-eritrea-border-tensions/3373659.html

Spiegel, Peter, 'EU Deal with Turkey Failing to Stem Migration Flow', Financial Times, 7 January 2016: http://www.ft.com/intl/cms/s/0/d62b85ca-b539-11e5-8358-9a82b43f6b2f.html#axzz3y0BrmyJ8

'Spreading across Europe, a Fortress of Fences', The Migration Machine (special feature), Reuters, 4 April 2016: http://www.reuters.com/investigates/special-report/migration/#story/38

Srivastava, Mehul, 'Organised Crime Moves in on Migrant Smuggling Trade in Turkey', Financial Times, 13 December 2015: http://www.ft.com/intl/cms/s/0/17cf4fc0-9ffa-11e5-8613-08e211ea5317.html#axzz483f VAewY

Srivastava, Mehul, Peter Spiegel and Stefan Wagstyl, 'Recep Tayyip Erdogan Rejects EU Demands to Reform Terror Law', Financial Times, 6 May 2016: http://on.ft.com/23v3atz

Stamouli, Nektaria, 'Greece Struggles to Return Migrants under EU–Turkey Deal', Wall Street Journal, 19 May 2016: http://www.wsj.com/articles/greece-struggles-to-return-migrants-under-eu-turkey-deal-1463653671

Stevis, Matina and Joe Parkinson, 'Thousands Flee Isolated Eritrea to Escape Life of Conscription and Poverty', Wall Street Journal, 2 Feb. 2016: http://www.wsj.com/articles/eritreans-flee-conscription-and-poverty-adding-to-the-migrant-crisis-in-europe-1445391364

Stratfor, 'Complexities of Future Energy Investment in Libya', 5 July 2012: https://www.stratfor.com/analysis/complexities-future-energy-investment-libya

'Sweden Masked Gang "Targeted Migrants" in Stockholm', BBC, 30 January 2016: http://www.bbc.com/news/world-europe-35451080

Thompson, Edwina A., 'Misplaced Blame: Islam, Terrorism and the. Origins of Hawala', Max Planck Yearbook of United Nations Law 11 (2007): 279–305

Tinti, Peter, Illicit Trafficking and Instability in Mali: Past, Present and Future, Geneva: Global Initiative against Transnational Organised Crime, January 2014

Townsend, Jacob and Cristel Oomen, Before the Boat: Understanding the Migrant Journey, Brussels: Migration Policy Institute Europe, 2015

Townsend, Mark, '10,000 Refugee Children are Missing, Says Europol', The Guardian, 30 January 2016: https://www.theguardian.com/world/2016/jan/30/fears-for-missing-child-refugees

Tubiana, Jérôme, The Chad–Sudan Proxy War and the 'Darfurization' of Chad:

Myths and Reality, Geneva: Small Arms Survey, 2008: http://tamlyn-serpa. com/images/Chad_Sudan.pdf

UN DESA, *World Population Prospects: The 2012 Revision*, New York: United Nations, 2012

UNDP, *Human Development Report 2015*, New York: United Nations Development Programme, 2015: http://hdr.undp.org/sites/default/files/2015_human_development_report.pdf.

―――, *MDG 2015*, New York: United Nations Development Programme, 2016

UNHCR, *Children on the Run: Unaccompanied Children Leaving Central America and Mexico and the Need for International Protection*, July 2014: http://www.unhcrwashington.org/sites/default/files/1_UAC_Children%20on%20the%20Run_Full%20Report.pdf

―――, 'Egypt: Country and Operations Profile 2015': http://www.unhcr.org/pages/49e486356.html

―――, *Global Trends: Forced Displacement in 2015*, Geneva: UNHCR, June 2016

―――, 'Refugees/Migrants Emergency Response—Mediterranean', 5 May 2016: http://data.unhcr.org/mediterranean/country.php?id=83

―――, *World at War: UNHCR Global Trends*, Geneva: UNHCR, January 2015

―――, *The Role of Organised Crime in the Smuggling of Migrants from West Africa to the European Union*, Vienna: United Nations, 2011

―――, *Smuggling of Migrants: A Global Review*, Vienna: United Nations, 2010

van Reisen, Mirjam, M. Estefanos and C. R. J. J. Rijken, *Human Trafficking in the Sinai: Refugees between Life and Death*, European External Policy Advisors/Tilburg University, 2012: http://www.ehrea.org/report_Human_Trafficking_in_the_Sinai_20120927.pdf

Van Waas, Laura, 'The Stateless Tebu of Libya?' *Tilburg Law School Research Paper No. 010/2013*, May 2013

Videmšek, Boštjan, 'In the Human Smugglers' Den', *Politico*, 22 October 2015: http://www.politico.eu/article/refugee-crisis-smugglers-syria-turkey-migrants-the-worlds-largest-human-bazaar-migration-refugees-smugglers-greece-turkey/

Vision Project, 'International Shipping: Globalization in Crisis', 2009: http://www.visionproject.org/images/img_magazine/pdfs/international_shipping.pdf

Vovcuk, Vladi and Adi Cohen, 'Migrant Crisis Sparks Shopping Frenzy for Black Market Passports', Vocativ, 17 September 2015: http://www.vocativ.com/231947/syrian-migrants-call-for-self-policing-to-weed-out-fake-ids/

Ward, Benjamin, 'Dispatches: Risks of the EU–Turkey Migration Deal', Human Rights Watch, 1 December 2015: https://www.hrw.org/news/2015/12/01/dispatches-risks-eu-turkey-migration-deal

BIBLIOGRAPHY

Watkinson, William, 'Aylan Kurdi: Four Syrians Remanded in Turkey over Drowning Death of Aylan Kurdi', *International Business Times*, 5 September 2015: http://www.ibtimes.co.uk/aylan-kurdi-four-syrians-remanded-turkey-over-drowning-death-aylan-kurdi-1518577

World Bank, *Migration and Remittances Factbook 2015*, Washington DC: World Bank, 2015

World Bulletin, 'Thailand: Transit Point for Smuggling Syrians to Europe', 7 February 2016: http://www.worldbulletin.net/news/169180/thailand-transit-point-for-smuggling-syrians-to-europe

Wosolsobe, Wolfgang, oral evidence to the House of Lords EU External Affairs Subcommittee, London, 4 March 2016: http://www.parliament.uk/business/committees/committees-a-z/lords-select/eu-external-affairs-subcommittee/news-parliament-2015/european-union-military-staff-evidence-session/

Wright, John, *Libya, Chad and the Central Sahara*. London: Hurst & Co., 1989

Yeginsu, Ceylan and Karam Shoumali, '11 Syrian Refugees Reported Killed by Turkish Border Guards', *New York Times*, 19 June 2016: http://www.nytimes.com/2016/06/20/world/middleeast/11-syrian-refugees-reported-killed-by-turkish-border-guards.html

INDEX

detention centres, 91; exploitation of by criminal networks, 200, 259; flows of, 3, 5, 49, 52, 93, 96, 180, 183, 193, 199, 201, 208–14, 231, 237, 277; health issues faced by, 250; illicit, 257; irregular, 27, 32–3, 95, 183, 221–3, 226–7, 254, 257, 259, 263, 265, 270–1; LGBT, 265; mobility of, 30; potential role in tackling global inequality, 276; preferred, 27; protests at borders, 252; remittances from, 52–3, 273; 'safe and legal' routes concept, 275; settlements, 252; sexual exploitation/extortion/ trafficking of, 2, 40, 52, 104, 125, 130, 137, 169, 200, 254, 260–1

Mogherini, Frederica: EU Foreign Policy Chief, 268

money laundering: 40, 58, 66, 82, 200; efforts to counter, 71; methods of, 199

MoneyGram: use for ransom payments, 260; use for transferring money, 66

Morocco: 30, 86, 88, 90, 157, 168; Rif Mounains, 146

Morsi, Mohammad: anti-migrant rhetoric of, 130; removed from power (2013), 91, 132

Mother of All Snakeheads: 51

Moussa, Abdourahamane: 180

Movement for Unity and Jihad in West Africa (MUJAO): affiliates of, 161

Mozambique: refugee repatriation in, 22

Mubarak, Hosni: removed from power (2011), 130

Myanmar: refugee repatriation in, 22

Namibia: refugee repatriation in, 22

National Movement for the Liberation of Azawad (MNLA): establishment of, 165; insurgency activity of, 160–1

nationalism: 130, 239, 251

Nauru: asylum seeker detention centres in, 258

NBC News: 79

neoliberalism: 156

Netherlands: 45, 218; Amsterdam, 133; Hoek van Holland, 244; Islamophobic activity in, 252; Rotterdam, 39

New York Times: 179–80

Newman, M. Sophia: 209

Niger: 64, 145–9, 154–6, 163, 171, 174, 179, 181; Agadez, 1–2, 42, 92, 103, 106, 122, 124, 147, 156–7, 163–4, 167–9, 172, 177–9, 200, 274; Arab population of, 155; Arlit, 178; borders of, 147, 151; Diffa, 163; Djerma community of, 155; HALCIA, 180; Hausa population of, 172; Madama, 163; migrant smuggling networks in, 154, 169, 177–8, 274; military of, 161, 169; Niamey, 157, 163; smuggling economy of, 156; Songhai community of 155; Tahoua, 163; Toubou population of, 153, 164, 176, 272, 274; Tuareg population of, 170–2; Tuareg Rebellion (1990–5), 155, 157–9

Niger Movement for Justice (MNJ): members of, 158; rebellion of, 158

Nigeria: 20, 22, 52, 149, 157; Benin City, 19; Boko Haram Insurgency (2009–), 154; Edo

INDEX